JUMPERS
TO FOLLOW 2007-2008

EDITOR: MARK BLACKMAN
Deputy editor: David Dew

▶▶**Contributors** Steve Dennis
Daniel Hill
Ben Hutton
Paul Kealy
Andrew King
Rodney Masters
James Pyman
Laura Stephens
Alan Sweetman
Craig Thake
Matthew Williams

▶▶**Picture editor** David Cramphorn

Published by Racing Post, 1 Canada Square, Canary Wharf, London E14 5AP
2007 MGN Limited

Contents

Cover photograph: *Three mighty talents: Denman, My Way De Solzen and Kauto Star*
Inside photographs: *Edward Whitaker, Gerry Cranham, Martin Lynch and David Dew*

To believe or not to believe the hype – that is the question

With Kauto Star and Exotic Dancer in mind, editor **Mark Blackman** looks at names who could yet scale great heights

DON'T believe the hype: that's the mantra of all 'serious' punters. But hang on – does that apply to the Ten to Follow competition?

Take a look at two of last season's biggest scorers – Kauto Star and Exotic Dancer – and consider where they stood this time last year. Both had arrived from France with big reputations, but Kauto Star had ended his previous campaign with a crunching fall in the Champion Chase, while Exotic Dancer hadn't really hit the heights expected in his novice chase campaign. Should we fall in with the 'substance over hype' shrewdies and give them a swerve, or take a chance on these two justifying the lofty expectations of those close to them? A combined 341 points tells you all you need to know.

The Gold Cup one-two deserve to keep their places in the Hype Merchants' Ten to Follow, and here are a few names to complete the list:

Aran Concerto – the best Noel Meade has ever trained according to . . . Noel Meade. If that doesn't get the 'HMs' salivating, nothing will. Sure to win everything over fences.

Bewleys Berry – cost Graham Wylie an arm and a leg, but a real Aintree specialist now, and will surely recoup his price tag in the Grand National this time round.

Black Jack Ketchum – gave Blazing Bailey weight an easy beating before it all went wrong, but still the best thing since sliced bread. Might be a two-miler after all.

Crozan – just when you thought Nicky Henderson's superstar had gone, he goes and runs well before falling in the Ryanair Chase, and gets a reprieve.

Mad Fish – was favourite for the Champion Bumper before he'd even raced, and the best novice hurdler to come out of Ireland since Istabraq. Haven't you heard that too?

Racing Demon – the new Best Mate. Might yet win three Gold Cups himself if they decide to turn Cheltenham into a right-handed track.

Sweet Wake – a hype Hall of Famer, and devotees can still point to him finishing just a head behind Sublimity in the 2006 Supreme Novices'.

Zabenz – former Australian champion who is surely ready to win a big one now after his unlucky fifth in the Betfred Gold Cup.

One thing that needs no hype, of course, is the Ten to Follow competition itself, which continues to capture your imagination and comes with the promise of a huge windfall for one lucky punter when the curtain comes down on Grand National day. Regular players will be familiar by now with the mid-season transfer window, which is in place again to give hope to all who though they had dropped out of contention. What you won't know about are the three new bonus races at the Cheltenham Festival: the Arkle, Royal & SunAlliance Chase and Ryanair Chase.

Good luck, and I hope you enjoy this guide.
Mark Blackman, September 2007

Going for gold: the horses to follow all season long

Mark Blackman and David Dew select 20 horses who will be worth following throughout the season for a long-term profit

IF you followed our advice and backed the 20 horses in last year's jumps Gold List, you're probably busy compiling your Ten to Follow entry from the comfort of a sun lounger in Maui.

That's because the terrific 20 won 26 races from 65 starts – a colossal 40 per cent strike-rate – and returned a profit of £30.55 to £1 level stakes. Not bad for a sideline to the real business of the Ten to Follow competition.

Once again, for this year's Gold List, we've put together 20 that we think can make a decent profit if followed blindly for the remainder of the season. Whether you choose to include them on your Ten to Follow teamsheet as well is entirely up to you, but we certainly wouldn't put you off any of them.

▶▶**1004 Aces Four** (RPR 162+)
Ferdy Murphy

When the penny dropped in the spring of last year, Aces Four won three of his final four racing over hurdles, improving his Racing Post Rating with each of those victories. However, even the highest of those did not come anywhere near what he achieved when switched to fences last season. Although he ended up on the deck at the start and end of the campaign, he showed rapid progress in between, winning three times and recording a fine Racing Post Racing of 162+ when beating Faasel in the Grade 2 Mildmay Novices' Chase at Aintree. He'll be taking on the very best over

3m this season, but he's done everything asked of him so far and strikes as one who might have more to give. Finding the improvement to get the better of Kauto Star and co in the King George might be beyond him, but he'll be winning more races, that's for sure. *[DD]*

▶▶**1018 Amaretto Rose** (RPR 148+)
Nicky Henderson

Henderson certainly has the magic touch with mares. And he proved it again last season when this one won three of her four races over hurdles, failing only when finishing third in the Supreme Novices' at Cheltenham. She was beaten less than four lengths at the Festival, but returned a Racing Post Rating 7lb behind what she had achieved on her previous start. There's a fair chance that she will be switched to fences this term, and she could be just the type to rattle up a sequence. But if she stays hurdling, she will still be of major interest in the valuable 2m handicaps. *[DD]*

▶▶**1020 Amstecos** (RPR 135+)
Brian Hamilton

It's been three decades since Northern Ireland produced a real star of the jumping scene, but this son of Presenting has long threatened to do just that for his tiny yard, and this is the season when the long-held plan will hopefully come to fruition. Unbeaten in his last four starts, he completed his novice hurdle season with a battling neck defeat of the classy Ossmoses at Ayr, but it's been all about the

Blythe Knight has some way to go to reach the top, but is open to improvement

future over fences with this one, and he could prove a surprise package in the top 3m novice events. Bred and built for the job, he should do very well when the ground is soft. *[MB]*

▶▶1051 **Blazing Bailey** (RPR 163+)
Alan King

One of the top staying hurdlers last season, but Alan King insists he has strengthened up again during the summer, and that should come as no surprise, given that he is still very young. Five-year-olds have dismal recent record in the World Hurdle, so his third to Inglis Drever, beaten less than five lengths, goes down as a cracking effort. He had actually beaten Inglis Drever on softer ground the time before, and with normal improvement this term, he looks sure to be challenging for top honours. Few horses can find the extra gear that he does up the Cheltenham hill, and the softer the ground the better. *[MB]*

▶▶1055 **Blythe Knight** (RPR 151+)
John Quinn

Blythe Knight has a long way to go if he is to

prove up to Champion Hurdle class, but after just four hurdle starts there is plenty of scope for improvement, and he looked better than ever when winning a Group 3 on the Flat in the summer. He simply toyed with Grade 2 rivals at Aintree in April, racing on the bridle until the last, and while he still has to prove he will come up the hill at Cheltenham, there will be opportunities for him on easier tracks en route to the big one. Races like the Christmas and Kingwell Hurdle should be right up his street, and there are few better placers of horses in the game than John Quinn. *[MB]*

▶▶1077 **Celestial Gold** (RPR 171+)
David Pipe

This looks something of a forgotten horse. He did not race last season owing to a minor injury, but he looked pretty good in his box during the summer and will be back in action soon. That he has raced only 11 times in his whole career tells its own story about how fragile he is, but for one who has had more than his share of problems, he has done remarkably well. He notched a Racing Post

Rating of 171+ in the Betfair Bowl at Aintree when he was last seen in 2006, a performance that would see him in the shake-up of a typical Gold Cup. It might be that his chance of winning the big one has passed, but if he retains anything like his old ability, he will be back in the winner's enclosure this season. *[DD]*

▶▶1083 **Chief Dan George** (RPR 156)
James Moffatt

Moffatt can scarcely hide his enthusiasm for the horse who has quickly become his flag-bearer. The seven-year-old won five of seven races last season – his first with Moffatt – achieving most when beating Brit Insurance Hurdle winner Wichita Lineman by four lengths at Aintree. He had earlier finished only eighth to that rival at the Festival, but he reportedly came home slightly lame that day. In the ante-post market for the World Hurdle, Wichita Lineman is around 8-1 – although he is reportedly going chasing – while Chief Dan George is three times the price. I know which one I'd rather back, especially as the trainer is adamant he wouldn't change his star even for dual World Hurdle hero Inglis Drever. *[DD]*

▶▶1115 **Detroit City** (RPR 166+)
Philip Hobbs

It was a major disappointment when this five-year-old was being scrubbed along from an early stage in last season's Champion Hurdle. He finished only sixth, despite being sent off the 6-4 favourite, and it was no better at Aintree, where he was beaten further, again as the market leader. Before that, however, he had won three races back-to-back after reverting to the Flat to win the Cesarewitch. He recorded a Racing Post Rating of 166+ when landing the Greatwood Hurdle at Cheltenham last November, a performance that would have been good enough to finish second in the Champion itself. There are obvious question marks over him, but he has reportedly been treated for several problems, including a breathing difficulty. This may work, it may not. However, there are sure to be some decent prices about him this term, which makes the risk worth taking. *[DD]*

▶▶1136 **Exotic Dancer** (RPR 177+)
Jonjo O'Neill

When this seven-year-old made his return at Carlisle last November, it would have taken an optimist of extraordinary proportions to predict what he was to do during the rest of the campaign. He left that baffling performance well behind when going on to win Cheltenham's two autumn showpiece handicaps and the Cotswold Chase back at Prestbury Park in January before adding the Betfair Bowl. And just for good measure he finished second in the King George and the Gold Cup. His connections must be sick of the sight of Kauto Star because without Paul Nicholls' ace he would be the best staying chaser in the land. However, he was only a couple of lengths behind his old rival at Cheltenham in March and is open to further improvement. Of course, Kauto Star might also progress further this year, but it might just be that Exotic Dancer can really give the Nicholls camp something to think about during the next few months. *[DD]*

▶▶1155 **Gaspara** (RPR 146+)
David Pipe

This tremendous filly was just what Pipe jnr needed in his first season as a trainer. She went from strength to strength, winning four on the bounce, including the Fred Winter at Cheltenham, before an even better effort in defeat in the Grade 1 Aintree Hurdle when second to course specialist Al Eile. Connections are planning a crack at the new fillies' race at next year's Festival, in which she looks sure to go well. Before that, there will be plenty more races to be won, especially as she has already proved that she can hold her own against the boys. *[DD]*

▶▶1166 **Granit Jack** (RPR 146+)
Paul Nicholls

Stomach ulcers are not nice. And they stopped this French import from doing as well had been expected during the first half of last season. However, once his condition had been identified, he gave a glimpse of what he is capable of, hacking up in a little novice hurdle at Taunton before finishing second in the Supreme Novices' at Cheltenham. He's already won a clutch of races over fences in his homeland, and he looks sure to do well in that sphere in Britain this season. Connections reckon he might be good enough for championship honours come March. *[DD]*

▶▶1296 **Money Trix** (RPR 145)
Nicky Richards

He might not have raced since April 2006, but there are plenty of positive vibes knocking around that this imposing grey will be the real deal when finally sent over fences this term. He was last seen when chasing home Black Jack Ketchum in the Grade 1 Sefton Hurdle at Aintree, a performance that came on the back of three wins from three starts over hurdles. He will surely be placed to knock up a sequence in the north. *[DD]*

▶▶1307 **My Way De Solzen** (RPR 165+)
Alan King

This former World Hurdle winner looked an absolute powerhouse in novice chases at up to 2m5f last season, and his jumping was something to behold. Beaten only once in five starts over fences (by Fair Along over 2m at Sandown), he looks every inch a leading candidate for the Gold Cup, but would surely be favourite for the Ryanair Chase (now a Grade 1) if bookmakers were to price it up today. Whatever his Festival target, he has a bombproof look to him, and this seven-year-old should be one of the stars of the season. *[MB]*

▶▶1318 **Nickname** (RPR 170+)
Martin Brassil

A change to hold-up tactics proved the making of this French-bred chaser last year, and there is no doubt he is the dominant force among 2m chasers in Ireland. Nothing could get near him in soft ground last term, and the important consideration here is that connections simply won't run him when ground conditions are not in his favour. Given that, it's hard to see who will prevent him racking up another hatful of big wins. *[MB]*

▶▶1319 **Nine De Sivola** (RPR 143+)
Ferdy Murphy

There can't be many unluckier horses in training than Nine De Sivola, and he is certainly the highest-rated maiden over fences. A faller three out when travelling well in the four-miler at the Cheltenham Festival, he was also second in the Eider Chase, Irish National and Scottish National. Admittedly that hasn't done his handicap mark any good, but given

that he clearly comes good in the spring, it may be that he has dropped a few pounds by then, and he is included here in the hope that he can do a Hot Weld and go in at a big price on the big occasion. *[MB]*

▶▶1325 **Not Left Yet** (RPR 128+)
David Pipe

I remember being stunned at the Open meeting in 2005. The reason was because a novice hurdler with form figures 040 was sent off 15-8 favourite for a competitive handicap. I was even more stunned when it won. The horse in question was Not Left Yet, and there is a big suspicion among several pundits I have spoken to that he could be being prepared for another tilt at this meeting. This time, though, he will be sent to Prestbury Park for the showpiece Paddy Power Gold Cup. He has raced over fences only twice to date, but he won on his debut and then tipped up in the four-miler at the Festival, a race in which stablemate Celestial Gold finished second before winning the Paddy Power – and the Hennessy. Not Left Yet is lightly raced, thoroughly unexposed over fences and open to any amount of improvement. He will be winning plenty more races. *[DD]*

▶▶1361 **Patsy Hall** (RPR 151+)
Tony Martin

There would be lots to like about this son of Saddlers' Hall even if he hadn't moved to the yard of Tony Martin, but the fact that he is now with the County Meath maestro is the icing on the cake. Previously trained by Michael Cunningham, Patsy Hall showed some very smart novice chase form in the first half of last season, most notably slamming the classy Aces Four by 9l at Cheltenham last December, to earn his best RPR of 151+. Things didn't work out in the new year, when he was very highly tried, but as a result he starts the new campaign on a very handy official mark of 136, and there is no-one shrewder than Martin at exploiting it. With Leopardstown form figures of 2212U, expect the valuable Paddy Power Handicap Chase at the track's big Christmas meeting to be high on his agenda. *[MB]*

▶▶1376 **Predateur** (RPR 131+)
Paul Nicholls

This youngster looks the latest off the Ditcheat production line of classy young novice chasers,

James Moffatt has the highest hopes for Aintree winner Chief Dan George

and having shown good form over hurdles, there should be much more to come when he tackles the bigger obstacles. He was disappointing on his final start over timber, but showed bundles of promise when fourth to Katchit at Cheltenham the time before, and everything about his physique tells you he was never going to be at his best until given something substantial to jump. Expect him to do well en route to a crack at the Arkle. *[MB]*

▶▶**1462 Tidal Bay** (RPR 149+)
Howard Johnson

Has never finished out of the first two in eight career starts (two bumpers and six novice hurdles), but everything about this beautifully put-together gelding screams fences, and he looks sure to make a major impact on the novice chase scene this winter. Proven at up to 2m5f but expected to stay 3m without any problem, he has excellent Cheltenham Festival form (second to Massini's Maguire in March) and will take plenty of beating en route to a likely crack at the Royal & SunAlliance

Chase. Paddy Brennan could never hide the regard in which he holds this horse, and the son of Flemensfirth looks to have a huge future. *[MB]*

▶▶**1476 Twist Magic** (RPR 159+)
Paul Nicholls

Paul Nicholls has made no secret of the fact that he feels Twist Magic can make up into a serious Champion Chase contender this season, and with every viewing of the five-year-old's Aintree victory in April, his faith becomes more understandable. The most striking feature of his win was the speed with which he got away from his fences - in many ways, the hallmark of a quality chaser - and the form looks solid, with class act Fair Along swiftly put in his place from the last. It's anyone's guess how he would have fared up the hill at the Cheltenham Festival, but he was travelling very well when coming down two out, and to these eyes would have been the biggest danger to My Way De Solzen. His probable reappearance in the Haldon Gold Cup is something to really look forward to. *[MB]*

Is it thumbs up or thumbs down for the biggest names?

The Racing Post's betting desk experts on whether some of the season's leading lights should be followed or swerved

REGULAR readers of the Post's daily Trading Post tipping column will be familiar with their Bankers or Blowouts concept, where the betting desk experts turn their attentions to the day's shortest-priced favourites and decide whether they should be backed or laid.

So what about the Ten to Follow, in which the fate of a number of key horses can have a giant bearing on who scoops the prize? Should they be in your list, or should you be looking to jetison them?

We've picked out the ten jumpers we feel will prove the most popular in the competition, and asked our team of experts – Paul Kealy (betting editor), James Pyman (data editor), Craig Thake (big-race trends) and Matt Williams (Trading Post) – to decide whether they make each one a banker or a blowout. Here's what they had to say:

 ▶▶1112 Denman

Blowout Absolute tank of a horse, but if Kauto Star is being avoided, his races could be a lot more competitive than is usually the case. Has it to prove out of novice company anyway – he won't be allowed to bully the established rank. *[PK]*

Blowout Has the potential to notch a big score, as he will be kept apart from stablemate Kauto Star for most of the season, but he has plenty of questions to answer now stepping out

of novice company and I'm inclined to swerve him. *[JP]*

Blowout Generally, Royal & SunAlliance Chase winners have struggled to make an impact the following season. The rigours of the Cheltenham race seem to take their toll, and only two of the last ten winners have landed more than one win the next term. For every one Looks Like Trouble there are two One Knight and Lord Noelies. *[CT]*

Banker He's got to overcome the SunAlliance hoodoo, but you couldn't fail to be impressed with him at Cheltenham and if connections are going to keep him away from Kauto Star until the Gold Cup at Cheltenham, he could easily rack up a lot of easy points before the big day in March. *[MW]*

 ▶▶1136 Exotic Dancer

Banker But for Kauto Star we'd be hailing this one as a superstar after a phenomenal season. Travels and quickens and doesn't need to find much more to be a big threat to Kauto again – and will have McCoy in the plate. *[PK]*

Banker Too good to leave out. Improved with every start last season, could have more to offer and his affinity for Cheltenham should ensure he scores heavily. Ready to dethrone Kauto Star. *[JP]*

Blowout It is fairly common for horses to progress remarkably during their second

Inglis Drever: the dual World Hurdle hero is a unanimous 'blowout'

season over fences, and then struggle in the next campaign. This looks a classic case. With handicaps no longer an option, it's a question of whether he beat Kauto Star - and all evidence suggests he can't. *[CT]*

Blowout I want him in my list, but I just can't see him scoring anywhere near as heavily this time around and, because the constraints of this piece is forcing me into a 'banker or blowout' corner, I'm reluctantly going to give him a swerve, knowing the decision could easily come back and bite me on the arse! *[MW]*

 ▶▶1197 **Inglis Drever**

Blowout Can obviously win the World Hurdle again, but has had his problems and surely won't run enough to be included in the early part of the season. A possible for substitution if he proves he's fit and well. *[PK]*

Blowout Had more than his fair share of physical problems and what concerns me is that he has raced just seven times in two

seasons. I can't see him being one of the top points scorers - put one of the up-and-coming staying hurdlers in your lists instead. *[JP]*

Blowout Few staying hurdlers remain at the top of their game for more than a couple of seasons. This will be his fourth at the highest level, and as he always seems to have such a hard race, I have concerns about how enthusiastic he will be. No nine-year-old has won the World Hurdle since 1988. *[CT]*

Blowout He isn't the soundest horse these days and anyone putting him down as a banker is taking a big risk, in my opinion. Yes, he was outstanding on World Hurdle day at Cheltenham last season, but I can't see him repeating, and doubts about his ability to last the season prevent me from including him as a banker. *[MW]*

 ▶▶1220 **Katchit**

Blowout I've no problem with five-year-olds if I think they're good enough, but this one needs to find at least a stone to trouble

Our experts reckon Triumph Hurdle winner Katchit could struggle this term

the Champion Hurdle principals and given his size, I doubt he has the scope to do so. *[PK]*

Blowout Possesses a terrific attitude and a real money-spinner for connections, but it's hard to get away from the fact that he is only pocket-sized and it's possible that his industrious campaign last season will take its toll. I recommend you ditch him from your calculations. *[JP]*

Blowout The record of five-year-olds in the Champion Hurdle was well documented last year, and the long losing run continues. Very active juvenile hurdlers rarely train on, so this one will struggle given the Grade 1 penalty he will have. *[CT]*

Banker Detroit City put another nail in the five-year-olds' Champion Hurdle coffin last season, and you wouldn't say Katchit was any better than Philip Hobbs's horse was as a four-year-old. However, I'm keen to give him the benefit of the doubt, as he's always been an underdog, and I'm always keen to keep a fighter like him onside. *[MW]*

 ▶▶**1221 Kauto Star**

Banker Fed up with trying to find a reason to oppose him and being proved wrong.
Notwithstanding the overall poor record of Gold Cup winners in their next season, surely a class apart at any distance, and will frighten off a lot of opposition in pre-Festival races. *[PK]*

Banker and blowout Can you afford to leave him out? Not if we see the same horse who dominated the staying chase division last season, although his jumping remains a concern. He will be in most lists, so should he blow out and you do swerve him, it could be a master stroke. My advice: have two entries – put him in one and leave him out of the other. *[JP]*

Banker By far the best horse in training, and if he stays fit, who will beat him? Many Gold Cup winners have struggled the following season, but Best Mate notched plenty of points over a number of campaigns, as has top Irish chaser Beef Or Salmon. *[CT]*

My Way De Solzen: plenty of confidence behind a profitable campaign

Banker and blowout Unbeaten last season and, having read colleague James Pyman's comment on Paul Nicholls' chaser, I'm inclined to agree with everything he's got to say about the horse. *[MW]*

 ▶▶**1295 Monet's Garden**

Blowout High-class on his day, but has two ways of running and doesn't appear to like it down south. Turns ten in January and will be facing younger legs in the important races. I can't see too many points coming his way. *[PK]*

Banker Nicky Richards is going to keep the bold-jumping grey to his favoured flat tracks this season, and I can see him picking up three or four decent chases, so he is definitely worth a place on the teamsheet. *[JP]*

Banker Appears a specialist over 2m4f, a division that lacks depth. He will be hard to beat in the Ascot and Melling Chases again, so should bag decent points, but his best chances will come after the transfer window, so

may be just the job for mid-season substitution. *[CT]*

Blowout He'll always score points, because he wins a big race every season, but I think he's in competition with some absolute stars of the chasing division and, reluctantly, I'm going to leave him out this time. *[MW]*

 ▶▶**1307 My Way De Solzen**

Blowout May be the best Arkle winner we have seen for a while but is going to need to be if Kauto and Exotic Dancer are still the same forces. Exciting, but needs to be out of the ordinary to score very well. *[PK]*

Banker Tough, reliable, consistent, classy – he possesses all the qualities needed to make a weighty contribution. This horse is a winner, highlighted by the fact he has won ten of his 19 career starts, and, having looked a natural over fences last season, he has to be on your entry form. *[JP]*

Banker If any horse has the ability to take on Kauto Star, this is the one. To win the Gold

Sublimity: opinion is divided as to whether he should be followed this season

Cup these days, you need a horse who can travel and jump, and that is why so many of late had excellent form in 2m novice events at the Festival. Point scoring will depend on trainer's placement of the horse. *[CT]*

Banker Alan King made the right decision by running him in the Arkle, but don't be surprised if he is trained with the Gold Cup in mind this season. I'd love to see him line up against Kauto Star in the King George and could see him giving the champ a serious workout in that race, as well as in the Gold Cup come March. If it doesn't work out over the longer trip, there are other options. *[MW]*

 ▶▶**1445 Sublimity**

Blowout Shock Champion Hurdle winner last year and while there was no element of fluke, how many times is he going to run? Another possible for substitution but probably little point in having him in all season. *[PK]*

Banker Oozed class in the Champion Hurdle on only his sixth start over hurdles, and I can see him going in again at Cheltenham in March. Too good to leave out, although the

downside is that he is unlikely to be campaigned heavily. *[JP]*

Banker In recent years, the top Irish hurdlers have consistently been among the competition's highest scorers, and on that basis, he would be a banker. However, he doesn't take much racing and connections have indicated that he will be campaigned very lightly, in which case he is a blowout. There's also a possiblity he beat hurdlers in decline when successful at the Festival. *[CT]*

Banker He doesn't take a lot of racing and needs to win every time he steps on to the racecourse to justify inclusion. He is banker material, but only as a substitution after Christmas, which is when I think he'll do most or all of his scoring. Connections know the horse's needs inside out and he's got a huge chance of a repeat in the Champion Hurdle, as it's looking a weak division. *[MW]*

 ▶▶**1476 Twist Magic**

Banker Would have gone close in the Arkle but for falling, and bolted up at Aintree. Paul Nicholls loves him to bits and he has

Voy Por Ustedes: last season's Champion Chase hero looks one to take on

Champion Chase winner written all over him, although he may be better for a late sub, as he may not run too often before the spring. *[PK]*

Banker The 2m chase division lacks strength in depth, so it would be no surprise to see a progressive horse like Twist Magic emerge from the novice ranks and dominate. Paul Nicholls' slick chaser was awesome at Aintree and should pick up plenty of points. *[JP]*

Blowout There aren't many opportunities for 2m chasers to score points within the competition time-frame, and although he was so impressive at Aintree, winners of that race have only a modest record in their second season. *[CT]*

Banker Rather like Sublimity, he isn't one to include pre-Christmas, even though I think he'll take some beating on his reappearance, as all roads lead to the Champion Chase with this lad. I wouldn't be surprised to see him go to Cheltenham having had one, or a maximum of two, starts beforehand. *[MW]*

 ▶▶1484 **Voy Por Ustedes**

Blowout Won a poor Champion Chase last year and I'd be surprised if he had another in him. Will probably have to face Kauto Star in the Tingle Creek, so I can't see much scope for a big points haul. *[PK]*

Blowout Sets a fair standard in the 2m chase division, but his development may have plateaued, leaving him vulnerable to less exposed types. I reckon Twist Magic is the one to have on your side instead. *[JP]*

Blowout The same scenario regarding opportunities at home applies to last season's Champion Chase winner. It is a long time since we had back-to-back winners of the race (Viking Flagship in 1994 and 1995), and with Kauto Star being aimed at the Tingle Creek, Voy Por Ustedes may struggle to win. *[CT]*

Blowout Looked a star in the making in his novice season, but shown up as nothing more than an average winner of the Champion Chase last season and he'll need to improve again to defend his crown this time around. *[MW]*

Copsale Lad just one of a host of top names to consider

Rodney Masters with some likely contenders from Lambourn for the big races over fences and hurdles

▶▶Chasers

Stand by for a revival from **Copsale Lad**, whose season fizzled out like a damp firework when he ran below expectations at Cheltenham and Aintree, but who has subsequently undergone a breathing operation. That surgery is expected to resolve this flexible ten-year-old's inconsistency, and Cheltenham's Paddy Power Gold Cup will be an ideal launch pad; he was well fancied for the corresponding event last year, but lost all chance when brought to a standstill by a faller.

Copsale Lad is somewhat hamstrung in that he need left-handed courses, but nevertheless he should accrue plenty of points. Nicky Henderson has another possible candidate for the Paddy Power in **Oedipe**, though a conditions chase is a more likely objective for the five-year-old, whose one appearance last season resulted in a spectacular win at Kempton on Boxing Day. Although the handicapper punished him with a 20lb rise, there is no doubting the value of the performance, because the next four horses home were subsequent winners.

Many people will be deterred from including Oedipe because he was not seen again. However, I'm assure his problems were of a minor nature, and, at the time of writing, he is in particularly good form at Seven Barrows.

Although not such a reliable statistic in recent seasons, over the decades no end of stars like Drinny's Double, Skymas, Hilly Way, Badsworth Boy and Viking Flagship recorded

back-to-back wins in the Queen Mother Champion Chase, and for that reason few lists will omit the six-year-old **Voy Por Ustedes**.

On the way to the Festival, he is likely to mop up bucket loads of points in other races such as the Desert Orchid and Game Spirit.

In terms of trip, few chasers are blessed with the versatility of **My Way De Solzen**. He was placed most expertly by Alan King last season, topped off by the Arkle Trophy, after many outsiders suggested the former World Hurdle winner would be tapped for toe. In the first half of the season, the King George will be the target, but after that all options are open because he is such an admirably flexible performer.

▶▶Staying chasers

Possibly because he does not court publicity like some colleagues in the same profession, even many of those who follow racing closely have overlooked Andy Turnell's achievements in training winners of major chases such as the Grand National, Queen Mother Champion Chase, Hennessy and Whitbread Gold Cups, but now he again has a horse blessed with the ability to propel him back to that league.

Currently rated 131, the strapping **Bible Lord** will need to secure a win or two to guarantee a place in Newbury's Hennessy Cognac Gold Cup, but that looks a realistic objective for the former point-to-pointer from Ireland. He has been given what is most

To include or not to include: former SunAlliance Chase winner Trabolgan

accurately described as an old-fashioned preparation. Accordingly, he has raced just five times under Rules, and he has progressed most impressively, winning his two most recent starts at Kempton and Lingfield. As far as the Lambourn region is concerned, Bible Lord is the must-include in our list.

The old adage that 'they never come back as good' usually rings true when it comes to chasers returning from more than a year on the sidelines due to injury, but can we afford to omit **Trabolgan** from the list? The answer is probably no. By the time he returns to the racecourse, he will have been off for two years, but it is difficult to erase memories of his wins in the Royal & SunAlliance Chase and Hennessy. At the moment the tendon he damaged is A1, and if it remains that way, he may still be a serious contender for the King George and Cheltenham Gold Cup.

▶▶Hurdlers

As, for some reason, so many top-class juveniles fail to deliver in their second season, we are faced with a dilemma of whether or not to include the brilliant **Katchit**. He displayed such enthusiasm, it may be unwise to overlook him.

Without him, our region may be found wanting for representatives at the highest level, though we've several who may eventually impact on that grade, including Charlie Mann's

currently 147-rated **Mobaasher**, who was third in the Triumph Hurdle and may have finished a place closer but for meeting with interference at the final flight.

A winner for Sir Michael Stoute, he was having only his second race over hurdles at Cheltenham and always looked as if he would achieve more in his second season. He will be campaigned with the Champion Hurdle in mind, and while that may prove beyond him, he should win decent races.

Mann's 143-rated **My Turn Now**, who made the headlines last winter after surviving a horror fall at Sandown, has been mentioned as a potential novice chaser, but don't be surprised if he is competing over hurdles. He won half a dozen races last season, and gave indisputable evidence the accident had not damaged his confidence when finishing sixth to Massini's Maguire in the Ballymore Properties Hurdle at the Festival, and later winning at Cheltenham's April meeting. He has the ability to win over a variety of distances.

▶▶Staying hurdlers

Alan King's 163-rated **Blazing Bailey** made a bold attempt to become the first five-year-old to win the World Hurdle, finishing third to Inglis Drever after mistakes at the final two flights. He will be more of a force this time around, and there's no doubt he has strengthened up during his summer break.

Plenty of potential point-scorers from the Emerald Isle

Alan Sweetman with a rundown of some of Ireland's contenders for top honours over hurdles and fences

▶▶Chasers

Ireland's leading two-mile chaser **Nickname** would only become a credible contender for the Queen Mother Champion Chase in the event of genuinely soft ground for the Festival. Martin Brassil's French-bred gelding is an ideal sort for a typical Irish winter and enjoyed an exceptional 2006-07 season, winning six of his seven races. He should again be a significant point-scorer on the domestic scene, having consistently proved himself superior to his contemporaries.

In Nickname's absence, **Mansony** was able to record a fine victory in a Punchestown Grade 1 race that provided further proof that the former 2m champion **Newmill** is not the force he was. Mansony looks capable of further success at a high level, while last season's best novices such as **Schindlers Hunt** and **Gemini Lucy** have the potential to become major players.

▶▶Staying chasers

Injury has blighted the careers of Irish-trained Cheltenham Gold Cup winners **Kicking King** and **War Of Attrition**, and the complexion of the 2007-08 season will be significantly influenced by whether or not the pair can return to recapture past glories.

As outstanding domestic competitor **Beef Or Salmon** reaches the twilight of his career, there will be considerable focus on **In Compliance**. He had looked destined for the

top when winning the John Durkan Memorial last December, but did not run again until the Punchestown festival, where his third placing behind a couple of British raiders left a question-mark about his stamina.

The Gold Cup fifth **Cane Brake** will aim to build to build on last season's momentum, established in major handicap chases, and **Snowy Morning**, beaten ten lengths by the brilliant Denman in the Royal & SunAlliance Chase, is potentially the most interesting graduate from the novice ranks.

Offshore Account, who relegated a below-par Snowy Morning to fourth when underlining his rate of improvement with a Grade 1 win at Punchestown, should also take his career to a higher level.

The recent history of the Grand National has involved a massive revival in Irish fortunes, a trend maintained when Gordon Elliott saddled the former British-trained **Silver Birch** to a wonderful victory last season. The Tom Taaffe-trained **Slim Pickings** is one of the more obvious names for the 2008 shortlist, along with former Irish Grand National winner **Point Barrow**, who fell at the first when one of the main fancies for this year's race.

▶▶Hurdlers

The hurdling division has provided rich pickings for a group of top-class Irish performers over the course of several seasons. **Hardy Eustace** and **Brave Inca** took the starring roles during that period, and a strong supporting cast placed Ireland in an unprecedented position of supremacy. For a while last winter, it looked as if this era was about to end, and then along came a dark-horse in the shape of **Sublimity** to take on the championship mantle. Sure to have a campaign explicitly geared to the defence of his title, Sublimity is unlikely to have more than one or two races in the lead-up to Cheltenham.

Though the impression of an old order passing was confirmed when **Silent Oscar** recorded a shock Grade 1 victory at Punchestown, the fact that the Harry Rogers-trained gelding is an eight-year-old, the same age as runner-up **Macs Joy**, who has been around at the top level for a long period, implies that further improvement is by no means guaranteed.

Several younger horses have arrived on the scene, including the Dermot Weld-trained **Bobs Pride**, a former Group 3 winner on the Flat whose late-season handicap victories at Fairyhouse and Punchestown were indicative of rapid improvement. His form ties in with the similarly progressive **Farmer Brown**, an emphatic winner of the Galway Hurdle.

The Irish novice scene presented a somewhat confused picture by the end of last season. The lightly-raced **Ebaziyan** won the Supreme Novices' at Cheltenham in decisive fashion before ending on a major low in a Punchestown race in which the highly-regarded **Clopf** was merely a workmanlike winner and one of the other main fancies **De Valira** was a faller. Though the evidence is inconclusive, all three should make an impact in the senior ranks.

The latter part of last season proved a major anti-climax for the Noel Meade-trained

Iktitaf, whose pre-Christmas exploits had suggested serious Champion Hurdle claims. He will begin the new season with plenty to prove, while his stablemate **Harchibald** has a mountain to climb in order to rehabilitate himself.

▶▶Staying hurdlers

Former two-time Champion Hurdle winner **Hardy Eustace** is set to make a transition to the staying division. Last winter's campaign showed that the old warrior no longer has the pace to beat the top two-milers, but there is no real sign that a major decline has set in.

There is a crying need for new blood in Irish staying hurdles, and one who could fit the bill is **Black Harry**, who was lying second when falling at the final flight in the Brit Insurance Novices' Hurdle.

Only one of the 14-strong field for the 2007 Ladbrokes World Hurdle was trained in Ireland, pretty much summing up a lack of serious talent. Nor can much encouragement be derived from the Grade 1 Champion Stayers' Hurdle at Punchestown won by the British-trained mare Refinement. Runner-up **Powerstation** is a talented enough sort, but well short of genuine championship standard on the evidence of his second placing in the Coral Cup off a mark of 139.

Essex, the former Pierse Hurdle and Totesport Trophy winner, finished fourth in the Punchestown event on his first attempt at three miles. It is a shade worrying that his stamina appeared to give out but he has looked in good order on the Flat since undergoing a palate operation. Having had a light campaign last season, he could yet become a force in the division.

'The Tom Taaffe-trained Slim Pickings is one of the more obvious names for a 2008 shortlist, along with former Irish Grand National winner Point Barrow, who fell at the first when one of the main fancies for this year's race'

An abundance of talent in the chasing division

Andrew King reports from the West Country, where there are high hopes of plenty of big-race success

▶▶Chasers

Well Chief bounced back from over a year on the sidelines when impressively winning the Game Spirit Chase at Newbury and went to Cheltenham a warm order for the Champion Chase, but hit the deck at an early stage.

He was sent on a retrieval mission at Aintree but failed to really sparkle for whatever reason. However, he is still highly regarded at Pond House and will again have the Champion Chase as his main objective this time. He is likely to start off in the Tingle Creek Chase at Sandown and be guided towards Cheltenham from there.

At his recent owners' day, Paul Nicholls insisted he was keen on the chances of **Twist Magic** over the winter as the five-year-old has come back from his summer break a stronger and better individual. It is hard to fault the gelding's record over fences, as he would definitely have been involved in the finish of the Arkle but for pitching over on landing two out when still going ominously well. He then went to Aintree and made fools of a Grade 1 field. Given that that was only his fourth outing over fences, there is surely more to come and he will pay to follow.

Granit Jack was found to be suffering from stomach ulcers after a couple of lamentable efforts last winter but, once that ailment was treated, he started to live up to his lofty reputation in France when going close in the Supreme Novices' Hurdle at the Festival. Having won over fences in his native country,

the grey will have to take on handicap company in chases this time, and he is going to pay to follow in that sphere. He should be included in lists.

The Paddy Power Gold Cup at Cheltenham's November three-day meeting is the first bonus race and Nicholls could provide the answer to this always intriguing affair. **New Little Bric** will be one of several entries for the valuable prize from the yard and, come the day, he could well be their favoured representative. Although he will have no problems in getting further than the 2m4½f trip, he possesses a decent turn of foot which is always required in the race and he is one to keep on the right side.

▶▶Staying chases

The obvious pair for everyone's lists are the Cheltenham Gold Cup hero **Kauto Star** and the young pretender from the same camp, **Denman**, who looked mighty impressive when landing the Royal & SunAlliance Chase.

Nicholls is hoping to keep them apart until they go head to head in chasing's Blue Riband next March, but he will have his work cut out, as there are only so many options for the pair, and if the weather intervened as it did last winter, he is in for a headache or two.

Kauto Star looks certain to run in two of the bonus contests culminating in a tilt at the Gold Cup, and the same applies to Denman. Kauto Star's early-season target is the King George at Kempton on Boxing Day, a race where he had

Detroit City: high hopes that a breathing operation will have a positive effect

to survive his usual bad blunder in the closing stages, but for a horse to make that sort of error and then win the way he did, he is obviously something very special and it is going to take a good horse to lower his colours.

Denman is likely to get his season off to a cracking start in the Charlie Hall Chase at Wetherby, and then he could be primed for a tilt at the Hennessy Gold Cup in late November before taking whichever route is chosen to Prestbury Park at the Festival.

Last term, the Charlie Hall went the way of **Our Vic** in impressive style, and the Pipe team once again intend starting their enigmatic chaser off in that contest. The way he finished full of running behind Taranis at Cheltenham over 2m5f last March suggested connections may have been better off letting him take his chance in the Gold Cup. He is a tremendously talented performer who always seems to nick a major prize, and it is worth putting him in some lists, as there is bound to be an upset or two along the way before the competition draws to a close.

▶▶Hurdlers

Don't all fall over laughing at once, but the dark horse from the area for the top hurdles bonus races is **Ouninpohja**, who has thrived during his summer at the Paul Nicholls yard.

Last season he managed to get his awkward head in front once for his present trainer, but on other occasions reverted to his old tricks of getting there on the bridle before virtually snatching defeat from certain victory. This resulted in him being called all manner of unkind names, but the horse possesses the latent talent to do well this term and it is definitely worth including him in a few lists, as the plan is to campaign him from October, with a tilt at the Champion Hurdle very much in mind next March.

Detroit City went into last season's Champion as a short-priced favourite, but proved a major flop when never looking likely to follow up his win in the Triumph the year before. The thoroughly lacklustre effort had connections scratching their heads, especially after he appeared to down tools at Aintree the following month. His season rests on whether a breathing operation over the summer has had the desired effect. He is a smart performer on his day and merits respect this winter.

▶▶Staying hurdlers

One look at last season's World Hurdle will illustrate this region's prospects in this division – two rank outsiders from the David Pipe yard and the supplemented Natal, who disappointed in seventh. This is not staying hurdler country.

Some trends and ideas to help bag plenty of points

Ben Hutton on what it takes to win some of the season's top races – including two new bonus events

▶▶Paddy Power Gold Cup

Hindsight is a wonderful thing, but when it comes to the first bonus race of the Ten To Follow jumps campaign, a bit of aftertiming could just help you land a cool 50 points-plus as the competition kicks off.

The one thing that recent Paddy Power, or Thomas Pink Gold Cup, winners have in common is that they have all been real class acts. The seven-year rollcall of winners reads as follows: Exotic Dancer, Our Vic, Celestial Gold, Fondmort, Cyfor Malta, Shooting Light and Lady Cricket.

This magnificent seven clearly illustrate that this is no run-of-the-mill Grade 3 handicap that is landed by a chaser simply taking his turn to win a top prize; it takes a seriously good horse to win the Paddy Power.

However, this is where the problem arises. If we could spot this seriously good horse in advance, we'd all be millionaires, but it isn't impossible, as the last three winners had all dropped hints that they could turn out to be top-class, or had done so little wrong that we couldn't rule out the progress to become top-class. Striking a line through those who have already shown their limitations will ensure that the vast majority of runners can be discarded.

Possible contenders who fit the bill this time around are **L'Antartique**, **Private Be**, **Not Left Yet**, **Ofarel D'Airy** and **Oedipe**, none of whom we've got to the bottom of yet.

Put a gun to my head and Not Left Yet would be of greatest interest, closely followed

by Oedipe and Ofarel D'Airy. Not Left Yet's form closely resembles that of stablemate Celestial Gold, with the pair both having the strange preparation of a run in the 4m National Hunt Chase at the Festival, and the Pipe yard obviously has a prolific record in the race.

▶▶Arkle Trophy

The addition of the Arkle as a 50-point bonus race has opened up a further avenue of analysis for Ten To Followers.

In the past, 2m novice chasers have had to run up a serious sequence to produce an adequate number of points to justify their places in a list, and given that there are so many possible different Arkle winners at the start of the season, relative to the likes of the Gold Cup and the Champion Hurdle, it hasn't seemed worth the risk. My Way De Solzen winning four races for 69 points, and Voy Por Ustedes winning five for 77 (fair totals but not massively impressive given all their hard work) ram home this point.

This time around, however, it could be worth taking that risk by sticking in a speedy novice chaser, as there are an extra 25 points to play for in the Arkle, as well as 12 for the runner-up. The other positive point when it comes to selecting a 2m type is that top-class hurdling form tends to translate well to fences when it comes to winning the Arkle. Recent winners My Way De Solzen, Well Chief and Moscow Flyer are proof of this, and the likes of

Silverburn: looks an obvious pick for the Royal & SunAlliance Chase

Contraband and Azertyuiop were also pretty handy over hurdles.

One prospect who stands out above all others, to these eyes at least, is Grade 1-winning novice hurdler **Glencove Marina**. The Willie Mullins-trained five-year-old looks to have any amount of potential and can only improve on what he did last season, as there was more than a hint of greenness about him. Although he stays further than 2m, connections have hinted at aiming him for the Arkle, but he should score plenty of points regardless of the distance he is campaigned over.

As for other possibles, **Wins Now** has the stamp of a chaser but was pretty hot over hurdles nevertheless. It's always worth remembering how well French- and German-bred five-year-olds tend to fare in the Arkle, and it will be worth looking at the *Racing Post* Stable Tours for Nicholls, Pipe and King to see what is heading in that direction. **Poquelin** and **Predateur**, trained by Nicholls, are two to keep an eye on, as is the transfer window when there's some more proven form.

▶▶Royal & SunAlliance Chase

The Arkle is not the only novice chase at the Cheltenham Festival to be souped up for the Ten To Follow, but the Royal & SunAlliance Chase is not approached with the same enthusiasm as its shorter compatriot.

The last two winners of the race, Denman and Star De Mohaison, have scored a relatively paltry 64 and 76 points respectively, and even with some extra bounty on offer this season, the search for a staying star could easily be pointless.

The reason for this is that (last year's winner Denman excluded) SunAlliance winners have tended to show very little over hurdles, which makes the list of possible scorers pretty unmanageable on the whole, at least until the transfer window, whereas with the Arkle we have a more compacted group to consider.

That said (and advised), for those who desperately want to allocate one of their spots to a SunAlliance horse, **Black Harry** and **Silverburn** are the obvious picks, but **Hairy Molly** would be mine if forced into it. After winning the Cheltenham bumper in 2006, he never really looked at home over hurdles last season, and this big horse could have his talent rekindled by the switch to fences.

▶▶Gold Cup

The title of this section shouldn't really be 'Gold Cup', more like 'A Dig At Denman'. The last four horses to win the Cheltenham Gold Cup, namely Kauto Star, War Of Attrition, Kicking King and Best Mate, all had excellent Grade 1 form over 2m prior to winning the

Bewleys Berry is one to keep in mind for the Grand National

Festival's feature, and arriving at Prestbury Park in March with a stamina question mark hanging over you now seems a prerequisite as opposed to a negative.

Given this recent trend, Denman is fully expected to be too slow to be capable of winning the Gold Cup. Although he may score points during the season, he also looks to lack the speed for the King George and leaving him out completely is a highly recommended tactic.

Others who seem to lack the speed to win a modern-day Gold Cup are **Star De Mohaison, Neptune Collonges, Aces Four, Trabolgan** and **The Listener**.

▶▶**Grand National**

I've got the National sussed. You have to have been laid out for it. Or at least that's what the last five years of evidence suggests. The connections of Silver Birch, Numbersixvalverde, Hedgehunter, Amberleigh House and Monty's Pass all managed to protect their respective handicap marks by running their charges over hurdles, or adopting the recent novel approach of targeting cross-country chases.

What doesn't pay off is protecting a handicap mark by not running a horse, as the last five winners had all run at least four times in the season prior to their National success, and all bar Hedgehunter raced within 32 days

of Aintree (Hedgehunter was 49). The message is therefore clear: don't wrap them in cotton wool, keep them battle-hardened and keep them away from the clutches of the handicapper. Being trained in Ireland tends to help as well.

Further evidence to support these theories comes from last season's runner-up and third home, with McKelvey having been campaigned over hurdles, and Slim Pickings suffering a mid-season loss of form to keep his rating down – another novel way of doing things.

Putting this into practice on the morning of Grand National Saturday is pretty difficult, but applying it months in advance is nigh-on impossible, which is why the January transfer window is so appealing in this instance. If you're in contention for the big prize with the Cheltenham Festival out of the way, having a National horse in your list will definitely get the adrenalin going, and it should be possible to spot one at the beginning of 2008 that's been laid out for the race.

It doesn't do any harm to pinpoint a few prime candidates now, and **Slim Pickings**, **Sir Frederick** and **Bewleys Berry** should all be watched closely. However, the one I really like is **Kings Advocate**, rated 131, who might have to win a race to make the cut, but who should pick up a few points along the way nevertheless.

My Way De Solzen so popular with the leading trainers

Laura Stephens with the word from the handlers on their biggest hopes and what they like from elsewhere

Nicky Henderson
Home: 1205 **Jack The Giant**
Away: 1307 **My Way De Solzen**

Jack The Giant finished third in the Arkle and up until that point he'd done everything right by winning all his races over fences. He's a gorgeous big horse and I think there's plenty still to come. He loves fast ground and I think he can only improve. Because of him I've chosen **My Way De Solzen**. For the winner of the World Hurdle to come back and win the Arkle the following year is incredible and gives him so many options.

Howard Johnson
Home: 1462 **Tidal Bay**
Away: 1112 **Denman**

Based on **Tidal Bay**'s performance last season, in which he ended the season by winning the Grade 2 novices' hurdle at Aintree, I think he should progress really well. He's a very good horse with huge prospects. I like to think he could be anything.

    Denman has everything you could ask for in a horse. He has size and scope, he stays, he jumps and he's honest. That's what you call a proper racehorse.

Philip Hobbs
Home: 1429 **Snap Tie**
Away: 1307 **My Way De Solzen**

Snap Tie ran second in two very good bumpers at Newbury and Cheltenham last season and is the type of horse to improve for having had the summer off. He'll now go novice hurdling.

    I won't make the obvious choice of Kauto Star. I think **My Way De Solzen** could be even better over three miles than he was when he won the Arkle over two at last year's Cheltenham Festival.

Alan King
Home: 1459 **Theatre Girl**
Away: 1221 **Kauto Star**

Theatre Girl was useful in bumpers last season, especially when finishing second at Aintree behind Turbo Linn, who has gone on to do so well on the Flat. She's an exciting prospect and will go novice hurdling.

    Kauto Star is an obvious choice but he was phenomenal last season. He will be tough to beat in whatever races he runs in, but I suppose we will have to take him on with a few of ours. He's a class act.

Iktitaf: could show the benefit of a wind operation this season

Carl Llewellyn
Home: 1384 **Quartano**
Away: 1307 **My Way De Solzen**

Quartano won his first two bumpers for us and he's done very well over the summer. He's bigger and stronger, has a good attitude and jumps well. I think he could go all the way to the top.

My Way De Solzen showed what a good horse he was by winning the World Hurdle then coming back to win the Arkle the following year. He has all the attributes of a Gold Cup winner waiting to happen.

Noel Meade
Home: 1193 **Iktitaf**
Away: 1058 **Bobs Pride**

We gave **Iktitaf** a hobday wind operation at the end of last season. If it was a success, I think it could really help him quite a lot in his races.

Dermot Weld's **Bobs Pride** never stopped improving last season. He came off the Flat and ended the season winning the big two-mile handicap hurdle at Punchestown. I think he's the type of horse who could be anything.

Willie Mullins
Home: 1049 **Black Harry**
Away: 1307 **My Way De Solzen**

Black Harry ran very well last season but he was a little bit too free in his style of running. I'm hoping that when he goes over fences he won't be like that. He's a fine big chasing type who can carry weight and stay the trip.

My Way De Solzen looked to have a lot of potential when winning the Arkle last season. He's obviously very speedy but he also stays.

Ferdy Murphy
Home: 1416 **Shouldhavehadthat**
Away: 1296 **Money Trix**

Shouldhavehadthat looks smart. He has good form, jumps well and will go novice chasing. I think two miles will be the optimum trip for him. We usually have staying types but he looks sharp. We're pleased with what he's shown us so far.

Money Trix is going novice chasing and I'm sure he'll be decent. I chose According To John from Nicky Richards' stable last year who did well and I'd say Money Trix is an even higher class of horse.

Paul Nicholls
Home: 1476 **Twist Magic**
Away: 1307 **My Way De Solzen**

Twist Magic is an exciting two-mile chaser who will go for the Champion Chase at Cheltenham in March. The plan is to start off in the Haldon Gold Cup (now the William Hill Gold Cup Chase) in October.

I've always been a fan of **My Way De Solzen**. I don't know what the plan is for him this season but it will be interesting if they step him up in trip and aim him at the Ryanair Chase.

Charlie Swan
Home: 1333 **One Cool Cookie**
Away: 1442 **Straw Bear**

One Cool Cookie won the Powers Gold Cup at Fairyhouse last April. I think going right-handed he could pick up a few nice races again this season. The plan is to start with him either at Gowran Park or at Punchestown in October.

Straw Bear obviously wasn't right in the Champion Hurdle last year where he really disappointed. He's a decent horse with a lot of ability and I can see him running well in the two-mile races in Britain.

Jonjo O'Neill
Home: 1136 **Exotic Dancer**
Away: 1445 **Sublimity**

Exotic Dancer's the best we've got. If we just got rid of Kauto Star we could be winning plenty of races. He's a year older and as a result stronger and he'll be going for all the good races again.

Sublimity is very good and young at seven. I think it will be very hard to find a hurdler to beat him this season.

Tom Taaffe
Home: 1320 **Ninetieth Minute**
Away: 1161 **Glencove Marina**

Ninetieth Minute won his bumper well at Clonmel, winning by seven lengths. That was his only start, and he's still only four. He looks the sort to do well as he travels and has been jumping well at home. He's still improving.

Willie Mullins' **Glencove Marina** was a top novice hurdler last season who kept on improving. He looks to have what it takes.

David Pipe
Home: 1362 **Pauillac**
Away: 1315 **New Little Bric**

Pauillac's a lovely four-year-old who was at one stage favourite for the Triumph Hurdle. I'm not 100 per cent sure that he'll go over fences this season but whatever he does he has summered well, filled out and grown. He's had only six runs and is definitely open to improvement.

Again, **New Little Bric** has had only five runs in Britain. He's big, he jumps and he travels. I think he'll improve again this season especially when he's stepped up in trip.

'He's summered well, filled out and grown. He's had only six runs and is definitely open to improvement'

David Pipe on one-time Triumph Hurdle favourite Pauillac

Names to note from the men in the saddle

Laura Stephens talks to ten of the leading riders about their biggest hopes for the months ahead – both at home and away

 ### Mark Bradburne
Home: 1063 **Briery Fox**
Away: 1221 **Kauto Star**

It was very disappointing when **Briery Fox** was brought down early on in the Topham. At least he showed he took to the fences as he jumped round perfectly without me. The plan this season will be for him to step up in trip and run in the Becher Chase.

You just can't get away from **Kauto Star**. He's the reigning Gold Cup winner and he's versatile over any trip. I should think that most jockeys would love to get the ride on him.

 ### Graham Lee
Home: 1416 **Shouldhavehadthat**
Away: 1296 **Money Trix**

Shouldhavehadthat is an ex-Nicky Henderson horse. I beat him at Uttoxeter and Mick Fitzgerald was really cross. Now that I have ridden him at home I can see why he wasn't very happy, he's a really nice horse.

Nicky Richards' trains **Money Trix** and the form looked very good when he was second to Black Jack Ketchum at Aintree in 2006. He's had a year off since and I presume he'll go novice chasing. He could be anything.

 ### Paddy Brennan
Home: 1032 **Ashley Brook**
Away: 1197 **Inglis Drever**

I'm looking forward to riding **Ashley Brook**. I think he was very unlucky when he fell at the last in the Champion Chase at the Cheltenham Festival. This will be the first year that he's stepped up in trip and I think it will be the making of him.

I won't be riding **Inglis Drever**, but what with Mighty Man being injured, I don't think there's anything in the 3m hurdling division that can get to within five lengths of him.

 ### Jamie Moore
Home: 1016 **Altilhar**
Away: 1491 **Wichita Lineman**

Altilhar is still only four and he progressed really nicely last season including when he was second behind Gaspara in the Fred Winter at the Cheltenham Festival. I think he'll appreciate a step up in trip. I think Dad will aim him at the big handicap hurdles over two to two and a half miles.

Wichita Lineman looked very good last season as a novice and I think he could go right to the top of the staying hurdle division.

'There's nothing that can get within five lengths of him'
Paddy Brennan on dual World Hurdle winner Inglis Drever

Tony McCoy
Home: 1491 **Wichita Lineman**
Away: 1339 **Osana**

Wichita Lineman proved he was a top-class staying novice hurdler last season by winning the Brit Insurance at the Cheltenham Festival. Whether he goes chasing or hurdling he will be very hard to beat and I look forward to riding him.

Dave Pipe's **Osana** ran in some good novice hurdles last season and he looks just the sort to make a decent two-mile chaser if they decide to send him over fences.

Tom Scudamore
Home: 1155 **Gaspara**
Away: 1221 **Kauto Star**

Gaspara was amazing last season, especially her run in the Aintree Hurdle behind Al Eile which was just superb. This year should be especially good for her as there's the new mares' hurdle at the Cheltenham Festival. She's one of many exciting horses at Pond House.

Kauto Star was outstanding last season as he proved he was champion from 2m to 3m2f. He's won all the big races and is the one we all have to beat but hopefully we'll find something.

Timmy Murphy
Home: 1077 **Celestial Gold**
Away: 1221 **Kauto Star**

I think **Celestial Gold** is pretty good. He won the Betfair Bowl at Aintree the year before last but he's been off the track since then. He's very talented but is prone to injury. If he stays right he's one to really look forward to riding in all the big 3m chases.

Kauto Star will no doubt be opposing Celestial Gold, but what can I say? He's an absolute machine.

Sam Thomas
Home: 1315 **New Little Bric**
Away: 1221 **Kauto Star**

I don't know whether I'll get to ride him again this season but last year I rode **New Little Bric** to win on his first start in this country from France. I can see him winning plenty of races and he's still only a young horse.

Obviously **Kauto Star** is the class horse out there and there doesn't seem to be anything that can possibly beat him. There's no reason why he can't win this season's Gold Cup and keep winning it in the future.

Tom O'Brien
Home: 1152 **French Saulaie**
Away: 1053 **Blue Splash**

It's only the top riders who can choose which horses they want to ride and I tend to take what I can get, but one horse who I hope to ride is **French Saulaie** for my boss Philip Hobbs. He was very keen in his younger days but now he's learnt to settle he could be very good. I think the plan for him is to go over fences.

Peter Bowen's **Blue Splash** will make a good staying chaser. He did very well as a novice and I think he can still improve.

Robert Thornton
Home: 1307 **My Way De Solzen**
Away: 1018 **Amaretto Rose**

The world is at **My Way De Solzen**'s feet. I think the plan is to go for the intermediate chase at Carlisle which Monet's Garden won last year followed by the King George, the Pillar Property Chase (now the Letheby and Christopher Chase) and then the Gold Cup.

It's difficult to choose a horse I won't ride, considering I think I'll also win the Champion Hurdle and the World Hurdle! After riding her at Ascot I think **Amaretto Rose** will be awesome when she goes novice chasing.

How to enter

From the list of 500 horses starting on page 35, select ten to follow in jumps races during the period of the competition – November 16, 2007 to April 5, 2008 inclusive. Each list of ten horses costs £10 or €16 to enter. There are three ways to enter

online **totetentofollow.co.uk**
www.totetentofollow.co.uk Entries accepted up to 8.00pm Thursday 15 November. If you have previously registered online with Ten to Follow, just 'login' with your username and password to access your details. New online entrants – select 'register' complete your details, including your chosen username and password, then follow the instructions to enter and pay with your bank card or credit card. You can monitor your entry online and will also have the opportunity to make online substitutions during the January transfer window

telephone **0871 200 2030 (RoI +44871 200 2030)**
Entries accepted up to: 8.00pm Thursday, November 15. Follow the prompts to enter and pay with your bank card or credit card. You can monitor your entry online or by telephone and will also have the opportunity to make online substitutions at: www.totetentofollow.co.uk during the January transfer window

post **PO Box 116, Wigan, WN3 4WW**
Entries accepted up to: 8.00pm Thursday, November 15. Each horse has a reference number, write the reference numbers - not the horse names - clearly on the entry form, using a blue or black ballpoint pen – NOT a felt tip. Only horses contained in the list are eligible and must be entered by their reference numbers. Entries containing horse names are not accepted.

Should a selection be duplicated in any one line, points will only be awarded once with the repeated selection disregarded. Where a selection number is illegible, capable of dual interpretation or is not contained in the prescribed list, the selection will be void and the remaining selections will count. Entries containing less than ten selections count for the number of selections made.

Where more than ten selections are stated in one line, the first ten selections will count with the remainder disregarded.

You may enter as many lists as you wish

although each entry must be made on an official entry form. Photocopied entry forms are accepted for multiple entries. Each entry form must contain the name, address and telephone number of the entrant. Multiple entries in the name of a syndicate must also contain the name and address of the organiser.

Completed entry forms must be accompanied by cheque/crossed postal order payable to: Totesport for the amount staked in £ or €. Payment in other currencies is not accepted. Cash should only be sent by guaranteed delivery. Where the remittance is insufficient to cover the number of entries required, the amount received will be allocated to entries in the order of processing with any remaining entries void.

mini-leagues
For entries made online – friends, families and pubs, clubs etc can set-up their own mini-league, where in addition to being entered in the Ten to Follow competition you will also be able to view your own private leaderboard containing the scores and positions of other entries in your mini-league. To set-up a mini-league you will need to appoint a member of your group as the organiser, who when completing his/her online entry will need to register a name for your mini-league. After completing an entry in the competition and registering a mini-league name, the organiser will be provided with a PIN which will be required to gain future access to the mini-league leader board. The organiser then advises the PIN to other members of the group who will need to input this when making their online entries.

substitutions
During the transfer window which opens at 9.00am Sunday, January 6 until 6.00pm on Friday, January 11, all entrants have the opportunity to replace up to two selections in each entry line with substitute selections from the original list of 500 horses. The cost of substituting a horse during the transfer window is £2.50 per selection per list, with a maximum of two selections per list. Points scored by substituted selections up to the close of the transfer window will continue to count and points scored by the replacement (substitute) selection will qualify for points from the day following the close of the transfer window.

Scoring and prize-money

1. Selections count when winning jump races under the Rules of Racing in Great Britain or Ireland during the period of the competition – November 16, 2007 to April 5, 2008.

2. Winning selections will be awarded points as follows:

   ▶▶**25** points in a race worth £30,000 or more to the winner

   ▶▶**20** points in a race worth £25,000 and up to £29,999 to the winner;

   ▶▶**15** points in a race worth £15,000 and up to £24,999 to the winner;

   ▶▶**12** points in a race worth £10,000 and up to £14,999 to the winner;

   ▶▶**10** points in a race worth less than £10,000 to the winner.

   Prize-money will be taken as the published racecard penalty value to the winner. For races in Ireland, prize-money published in € will be converted to £ at the official BHB conversion rate. The rate for 2007 is €1.48 to £1 and will be subject to change from January 1, 2008. In the event of a dead-heat, points will be divided by the number of horses dead-heating with fractions rounded down. No points will be awarded for a walkover. The official result on the day will be used for the calculation of points with any subsequent disqualifications disregarded.

3. An additional 25 points will also be awarded to the winner and 12 points to the runner-up in each of these races:

   ▶▶Paddy Power Gold Cup (Cheltenham, November 17)
   ▶▶Hennessy Cognac Gold Cup (Newbury, December 1)
   ▶▶King George VI Chase (Kempton, December 26)
   ▶▶AIG Europe Champion Hurdle (Leopardstown, January 27)
   ▶▶Hennessy Cognac Irish Gold Cup (Leopardstown, Feb 10)
   ▶▶Totesport Trophy (Newbury, February 9)
   ▶▶Racing Post Chase (Kempton, February 23)
   ▶▶Smurfit Kappa Champion Hurdle (Cheltenham, March 11)
   ▶▶Irish Independent Arkle Trophy (Cheltenham, March 11)
   ▶▶Queen Mother Champion Chase (Cheltenham, March 12)
   ▶▶Royal & SunAlliance Chase (Cheltenham, March 12)
   ▶▶Ladbroke World Hurdle (Cheltenham, March 13)
   ▶▶Ryanair Festival Trophy Chase (Cheltenham, March 13)
   ▶▶Totesport Cheltenham Gold Cup (Cheltenham, March 14)
   ▶▶John Smith's Grand National (Aintree, April 5)

   Any of the above races rescheduled to take place outside the dates of the competition will not count.

5. Bonus points according to the official Tote win dividend odds, including a £1 unit stake, will be awarded as follows to winning selections:

   ▶▶£4 to £7 ....4 points
   ▶▶Over £7 up to £11............7 points
   ▶▶Over £11 up to £16........11 points
   ▶▶Over £16 up to £22 ......16 points
   ▶▶Over £22 up to £29 ......22 points
   ▶▶Over £29 up to £37 ......29 points
   ▶▶Over £37.......................37 points

In the event of no Tote win dividend being declared, the starting price will determine any bonus points. Should neither a Tote win dividend nor a starting price be returned, bonus points will not apply. The leaderboard will be published in the *Racing Post* each Tuesday and Friday of the contest and also at **www.totetentofollow.co.uk**. The Ten to Follow competition is operated as a pool by the Tote. Entry forms are available from Totesport, the *Racing Post*, selected Trinity Mirror publications and at **www.totetentofollow.co.uk**. All stake money, including additional stakes from substitutions, will be aggregated and paid out in dividends after a 30 per cent deduction to cover administration/expenses etc. The minimum gross pool (before deductions) will be £1 million guaranteed. £50,000 will be allocated for the four monthly and Cheltenham Festival dividends, with the balance divided as follows to the overall winners:

   ▶▶WINNER................................70%
   ▶▶2nd...10%
   ▶▶3rd 5%
   ▶▶4th..4.5%
   ▶▶5th...3%
   ▶▶6th..2.5%
   ▶▶7th 2%
   ▶▶8th..1.5%
   ▶▶9th 1%
   ▶▶10th......................................0.5%

Monthly dividends of £10,000 each will be paid at the end of December, January, February and March to the entrant with most points during the month. A dividend of £10,000 will be paid to the entrant accumulating most points in the races scheduled to form the Cheltenham Festival meeting (March 11-14). In the event of the complete Cheltenham Festival meeting being abandoned and not rescheduled during the period of the competition, the special dividend will revert to the overall pool. In the event of a tie for any places, dividends for the places concerned will be shared.

The rules

1. You must be aged 18 or over to enter.
2. Selections can only be changed during the transfer window.
3. The names of winners/leaders will be published in the *Racing Post* and at: www.totetentofollow.co.uk. Any disagreement with the published list must be made in writing and received within five days of the publication date at: Tote Ten to Follow, PO Box 116, Wigan WN3 4WW or e-mail at: totetentofollow@totesport.com.

Claims received after this date or telephone enquiries cannot be considered.

4. Neither the Tote, nor the publishers of the *Racing Post* and Trinity Mirror, accept any responsibility for non-receipt of entries. Proof of posting will not be taken as proof of delivery.
5. Members of staff or their immediate families of the Tote or the *Racing Post* are not eligible to enter.
6. In all cases the decision of the Tote is final.

VIP PRIZE
UP FOR GRABS

▶▶All entries – internet, telephone or post – received before midnight Wednesday, November 14 will be automatically entered into a prize draw with the winning entrant receiving *two VIP hospitality packages for the Cheltenham Festival on Wednesday March 12, 2008 including: Club Enclosure Badges, lunch with wine, afternoon tea, complimentary bar in a private box Plus £50 totepool betting voucher*. Totesport terms and conditions apply. No cash alternative.

ENTRY FORM

EACH SELECTION REQUIRES A FOUR-DIGIT NUMBER. NUMBERS ARE LISTED FROM PAGE 35 ONWARDS		EXAMPLE			
	1	1	0	8	9
	2	1	2	2	4

ENTRY ONE				ENTRY TWO				ENTRY THREE				ENTRY FOUR			
1				1				1				1			
2				2				2				2			
3				3				3				3			
4				4				4				4			
5				5				5				5			
6				6				6				6			
7				7				7				7			
8				8				8				8			
9				9				9				9			
10				10				10				10			

ENTRY FIVE				ENTRY SIX				ENTRY SEVEN				ENTRY EIGHT			
1				1				1				1			
2				2				2				2			
3				3				3				3			
4				4				4				4			
5				5				5				5			
6				6				6				6			
7				7				7				7			
8				8				8				8			
9				9				9				9			
10				10				10				10			

COMPLETE IN CAPITAL LETTERS

NUMBER OF ENTRIES [____] Each entry costs £10 or €16

SURNAME _ FORENAME _ _ _ _ _ _ _ (Mr/Ms/Mrs/Miss)

SYNDICATE NAME (if applicable) _ (max 20 characters)

ADDRESS _

_ POSTCODE _ _ _ _ _ _ _ _ _ _ _ _

TELEPHONE (Day) _ _ _ _ _ _ _ _ _ _ _ _ _ _ _ _ _ _ (Evening) _ _ _ _ _ _ _ _ _ _ _ _

I enclose cheque/postal order made payable to 'Tote Credit Ltd' for £ _ _ _ _ _ _ or € _ _ _ _ _ _

SEND COMPLETED ENTRY FORM TO:

TOTE TEN TO FOLLOW, PO BOX 116, WIGAN WN3 4WW.

Entries must be received by Thursday, November 15, 2007

From time to time we may send you details of other offers. If you prefer not to receive details please tick box ☐

How to read the profiles of the 500 horses in this year's Ten to Follow competition

The number to put on your entry form

Age, colour, sex, sire, dam, dam's sire

Trainer

Career form figures to August 31, 2007

1136 Exotic Dancer (Fr)

7 b g Turgeon - Northine (Northern Treat)

J O'Neill   Sir Robert Ogden

PLACINGS: /F2873/331F/2112121-   **RPR 177+c**

Starts	1st	2nd	3rd	4th	Win & Pl
18	7	4	3	-	£494,553

	4/07	Aint	3m1f Cls1 Gd2 Ch good	£85,530
	1/07	Chel	3m1¹/₂f Cls1 Gd2 Ch heavy	£57,288
149	12/06	Chel	2m5f Cls1 Gd3 131-157 Ch Hcap soft	£85,530
139	11/06	Chel	2m4¹/₂f Cls1 Gd3 123-149 Ch Hcap gd-sft	£62,722
	12/05	Chel	2m5f Cls2 Nov Ch gd-sft	£9,864
	10/03	Autl	1m7f Hdl 3yo v soft	£13,091
	10/03	Autl	1m7f Hdl 3yo holding	£16,208

Owner

Current Racing Post Rating

Career wins

Tremendous performer who improved out of all recognition last season for the combination of extreme waiting tactics and cheekpieces, and would be Britain's leading chaser were it not for the dominance of Kauto Star; scooped Cheltenham's Paddy Power and Boylesports.com Gold Cups before Christmas before going on to establish himself the second-best stayer around; underlined his credentials for the Festival showpiece by winning the Cotswold Chase at Cheltenham by 18l from Our Vic with a performance full of authority that proved 3m-plus to be well within his capabilities; had played second fiddle to Kauto Star in the King George at Kempton on Boxing Day, and did so again in the Gold Cup, although he reduced the gap from 8l to 2¹/₂l (3m2¹/₂f, good to soft, 18 ran); saved his very best for last in the Grade 2 Betfair Bowl at Aintree, where he recorded a Racing Post Rating of 177 (Kauto Star won the Gold Cup with RPR of 175) in slamming My Will by 13l; prone to the odd jumping error, but did his connections proud last season in a campaign that saw his official mark rise from 139 to 172; will have to contend with Paul Nicholls' champion again this term, but is not far behind him strictly on figures and would not have to improve much to be bang there. *'Kauto Star is a great horse and a great champion, but we still think we are capable of beating him at some point.' (Barry Simpson, racing manager to owner Sir Robert Ogden)*

Profile of the horse, including significant going and distance information, trainer quote and, where appropriate, its prospects for the coming season

1000 A New Story (Ire)

9 b g Fourstars Allstar - Diyala (Direct Flight)

M Hourigan (Ir)   Storey's Over Syndicate

PLACINGS: 112833R333/035244U0-   RPR **138**c

Starts	1st	2nd	3rd	4th	Win & Pl
46	8	9	4		£120,422
103	11/05 Cork	3m4f 103-131 Ch Hcap heavy			£20,777
91	11/05 Limk	2m4f 91-121 Ch Hcap heavy			£9,066
98	10/05 Clon	3m 87-111 Hdl Hcap soft			£6,371
84	4/04 Tram	2m4f 73-92 Hdl 5-6yo Hcap yld-sft			£4,866
77	3/04 Dpat	2m6f Nov 75-91 Hdl Hcap yld-sft			£4,380

Former Cork National winner who has made the frame in several valuable long-distance handicap chases in the last couple of seasons, and deserves to win another one; mixed hurdles and chase outings last term, and ran his best race when ³/₄l second to Point Barrow in the Pierse Leopardstown Handicap Chase in January, leading at the last and just run out of it close home (3m, soft to heavy, 19 ran); hampered and unseated three out in the Irish National (well held and making no impression at the time) before finishing 11th of 13 finishers in the Scottish equivalent at Ayr; has been placed in a Thyestes Chase and an Irish National, among other big races, and will surely get his head in front one day; likes soft ground.

1001 Abragante (Ire)

6 b g Saddlers' Hall - Joli's Girl (Mansingh)

D Pipe   D A Johnson

PLACINGS: 23803P2P/F1U112341-1   RPR **147**+h

Starts	1st	2nd	3rd	4th	Win & Pl
19	6	3	3	1	£58,591
140	5/07 Hayd	2m7¹/₂f Cls2 126-152 Hdl Hcap good			£15,658
125	4/07 Chel	3m Cls2 109-135 Hdl Hcap good			£10,334
116	12/06 Tntn	2m7¹/₂f Cls3 94-120 Ch Hcap gd-sft			£6,506
105	12/06 Extr	2m6¹/₂f Cls4 90-114 Hdl Hcap soft			£5,205
105	11/06 Hayd	2m4f Cls3 105-116 Ch Hcap good			£9,759
	3/05 Weth	2m Cls6 NHF 4-6yo gd-sft			£2,016

Smart and consistent staying handicapper who mixed chasing with hurdling last season; not entirely straightforward and often doesn't find as much at the end of his races as looks likely, but that did not fail to stop him winning five times and finishing no worse than fourth when completing; saved his best for last, following up a win over hurdles at Cheltenham in April by scoring in the competitive Long Distance Handicap at Haydock the following month, staying on late to deny Chilling Place by a neck despite a 15lb rise in the handicap; raised another 8lb for that success, so starts the new campaign with a career-high mark over hurdles, although he is rated some 23lb lower over fences, so looks well treated in that sphere and will surely be sent in search of valuable prizes at around 3m. *'He scared himself over fences last season when unseating at Ascot. He doesn't find much off the bridle and needs to be kidded along.' (David Pipe, trainer)*

1002 Acambo (Ger)

6 gr g Acambaro - Artic Lady (No Pass No Sale)

D Pipe   D A Johnson

PLACINGS: 11350/11P6-   RPR **150**+h

Starts	1st	2nd	3rd	4th	Win & Pl
9	4		1	-	£151,621
136	12/06 Asct	2m Cls1 List 113-139 Hdl Hcap gd-sft			£84,510
128	5/06 Hayd	2m Cls1 Gd3 117-147 Hdl Hcap good			£42,765
118	12/05 Wind	2m Cls3 109-135 Hdl Hcap gd-sft			£16,796
	11/05 Tntn	2m1f Cls5 Mdn Hdl gd-fm			£5,439

Developed into a smart 2m handicap hurdler last season and is now expected to make a smooth transition to chasing; suffered a few defeats at short prices before springing something of a surprise to win last year's Swinton Hurdle at Haydock, but proved that success no fluke when returning to action seven months later and winning a hugely competitive renewal of the Ladbroke Hurdle at Ascot, snugly holding Tarlac by 2l; pulled up when going for a big-race double in the Totesport Trophy at Newbury in February, but returned to something approaching his best when sixth in a Listed handicap at Aintree in April; something of an in-and-out performer, but should be seen to better effect over fences, and likely to be mentioned as an Arkle contender during the next few months.

1003 According To John (Ire)

7 br g Accordion - Cabin Glory (The Parson)

N Richards   Sir Robert Ogden

PLACINGS: 34/1111/11443-   RPR **151**+c

Starts	1st	2nd	3rd	4th	Win & Pl
9	6	-	1	2	£60,070
	12/06 Kels	2m6¹/₂f Cls3 Nov Ch heavy			£7,157
	11/06 Carl	2m4f Cls3 Nov Ch heavy			£7,807
123	4/06 Ayr	3m¹/₂f Cls2 Nov 123-129 Hdl Hcap gd-sft			£11,711
	3/06 Carl	3m1f Cls4 Nov Hdl heavy			£3,083
	1/06 Ayr	2m6f Cls4 Nov Hdl soft			£2,928
	12/05 Newc	3m Cls4 Nov Hdl heavy			£3,116

Smart novice chaser last season; left two disappointing efforts in Graded company behind him when finishing 13¹/₂l third behind Denman at 66-1 in the Royal & SunAlliance Chase at Cheltenham in March (3m1/₂f, good to soft, 17 ran), where he seemed to relish the end-to-end gallop and stern test of stamina, and may have been closer but for a mistake at the second-last; has always been held in high regard by his trainer, and although he will need to brush up on his jumping, he should be competitive in handicaps off his chase mark of 140 (best RPR over fences is 151); Hennessy is an obvious early-season target, and the way he stayed on powerfully up the Cheltenham hill suggests he will have no problem staying the 3m2¹/₂f trip; possibly better going left-handed. *'He's a great big horse who should keep improving and he ideally wants ground on the soft side of good.' (Nicky Richards, trainer)*

1004 Aces Four (Ire)

8 ch g Fourstars Allstar - Special Trix (Peacock I)

F Murphy   The DPRP Aces Partnership

PLACINGS: /0/24331131/F11241F-   **RPR 162+c**

Starts	1st	2nd	3rd	4th	Win & Pl
19	4	3	2		£89,189

4/07	Aint	3m1f Cls1 Nov Gd2 Ch good	£45,616
11/06	Newc	3m Cls3 Nov Ch gd-sft	£6,494
11/06	Newc	2m4f Cls4 Ch good	£3,838
4/06	Prth	3m¹/₂f Cls3 Nov Hdl gd-fm	£7,807
3/06	Ayr	2m4f Cls4 Nov Hdl good	£3,253
2/06	Ludl	3m Cls4 Mdn Hdl good	£3,904

Progressed no end in his first season chasing, making up into a classy animal; impressed with his bold front-running style when winning his first two races over fences, and improved again when runner-up to Patsy Hall at Cheltenham in December (3m2f, soft, 5 ran); sent off 25-1 for the Royal & SunAlliance Chase at the Cheltenham Festival (3m1f, good to soft, 17 ran), but was the only one to make a race of it with Denman in the second half of the contest, jumping boldly from the front, and still had every chance prior to stumbling badly three out and weakening to finish 13¹/₂l fourth (would have finished second but for mistake); confirmed that promise when winning the Grade 2 Mildmay Novices' Chase at Aintree, springing off the good ground to beat Arkle fourth Faasel by 8l (value for more); would have followed up in a Grade 1 at the Punchestown festival, but fell at the last when 1l up on Offshore Account (3m1f, good, 7 ran); handles soft, but ideally wants good ground; stays well, and looks destined for bigger and better things. *'It'll be the Peterborough Chase followed by the King George and then we'll decide between the Ryanair or Gold Cup.' (Ferdy Murphy, trainer)*

1005 Adamant Approach (Ire)

13 b g Mandalus - Crash Approach (Crash Course)

W Mullins (Ir)   Greenstar Syndicate

PLACINGS: 1F67512157411315-129   **RPR 153h**

Starts	1st	2nd	3rd	4th	Win & Pl
56	12	9	4	10	£248,779

	7/07	Klny	2m1f Ch gd-yld	£9,237
	4/07	Fair	3m Hdl gd-fm	£13,196
140	1/07	Leop	3m 114-144 Hdl Hcap sft-hvy	£14,955
136	12/06	Punc	2m4f 110-136 Hdl Hcap heavy	£12,347
135	9/06	List	2m3f 121-147 Ch Hcap sft-hvy	£19,062
	9/06	Klny	2m4f Hdl yield	£13,469
	5/06	Navn	2m4f Hdl heavy	£6,672
	3/03	Cork	2m4f Nov Ch gd-yld	£9,286
	12/02	Punc	2m Ch heavy	£6,773
117	1/02	Leop	2m 102-126 Hdl Hcap yld-sft	£48,252
	10/01	Fair	2m Mdn Hdl good	£5,565
	2/00	Leop	2m NHF 5-6yo yield	£4,140

Ultra-tough and versatile veteran who remains a force to be reckoned with in handicaps over both fences and hurdles; retained his form remarkably well in a long campaign last season, and has won six times since September 2006; gained his biggest success in that sequence at Listowel last September,

but his best effort came when 4l third behind Oscar Park in the Pertemps Final at the Cheltenham Festival in March (3m, good to soft, 24 ran), staying on after being given plenty to do; won twice more after that, a hurdle at Fairyhouse and a chase at Killarney, but disappointing in two outings at the Galway festival; shows no real signs of slowing down, though, and no doubt he can pay his way again as he switches codes.

1006 Afrad (Fr)

6 gr g Linamix - Afragha (Darshaan)

N Henderson   The Not Afraid Partnership

PLACINGS: 312/2451803/F21323-   **RPR 142+h**

Starts	1st	2nd	3rd	4th	Win & Pl
16	3	4	4	1	£43,816

	12/06	Chep	2m3¹/₂f Cls4 Ch soft	£4,880
127	12/05	Sand	2m4¹/₂f Cls3 118-135 Hdl Hcap gd-sft	£6,717
	12/04	Newb	2m¹/₂f Cls4 Nov Hdl 3yo good	£3,549

Useful hurdler/chaser, although not as talented as half-brother and stablemate Afsoun; didn't look at all natural when tackling fences last season, gaining his sole win from four attempts at Chepstow on Welsh National day, where he beat Ballybough Jack by 24l only after several rivals hit the deck in the home straight (would probably not have won otherwise); reverted to hurdles afterwards, and posted better form in finishing 1³/₄l third behind Verasi in the Lanzarote Hurdle at Kempton (2m5f, soft, 17 ran) and 8l second to Labelthou in Haydock's Grade 2 Rendlesham Hurdle (2m7¹/₂f, heavy, 6 ran); has an advantageous mark over fences (133 opposed to 143) and connections might be tempted to try to iron out his jumping problems and exploit it; needs dig in the ground.

1007 Afsoun (Fr)

5 b g Kahyasi - Afragha (Darshaan)

N Henderson   Trevor Hemmings

PLACINGS: 21153/1F1233-   **RPR 165h**

Starts	1st	2nd	3rd	4th	Win & Pl
11	4	2	3	-	£168,273

	1/07	Hayd	2m Cls1 Gd2 Hdl heavy	£28,510
143	11/06	Newb	2m¹/₂f Cls1 List 123-143 Hdl Hcap soft	£17,106
	2/06	Hntg	2m¹/₂f Cls2 Nov Hdl 4yo gd-fm	£16,265
	12/05	Chel	2m1f Cls2 Nov Hdl 3yo gd-sft	£13,779

High-class hurdler who goes chasing this season; won twice over the smaller obstacles last term (the Gerry Feilden Hurdle at Newbury and Haydock's Champion Hurdle trial), but ran his best races in defeat in championship company in the spring; stayed on up the hill in the Champion Hurdle at Cheltenham to finish 3¹/₄l third behind Sublimity (2m¹/₂f, soft, 10 ran), and filled the same spot the following month in the Aintree Hurdle, possibly not seeing out the trip as strongly as course specialist Al Eile (2m4f, good, 11 ran); has won in heavy ground, but doesn't need it that way (going was not as soft as officially described at the Festival); had reportedly schooled well over fences even before his last hurdles campaign, so every reason to believe he will take to his new challenge and make up into a serious Arkle challenger.

1008 Air Force One (Ger)

5 ch h Lando - Ame Soeur (Siberian Express)

C Mann   Brian Walsh (Co Kildare)

PLACINGS:	F/5112-				RPR **139**h

Starts	1st	2nd	3rd	4th	Win & Pl
5	2	1	-	-	£27,891
	1/07	Ludl	2m5f Cls4 Nov Hdl good		£3,578
	12/06	Leic	2m4¹/₂f Cls3 Nov Hdl soft		£6,263

Very progressive novice hurdler last season, and looks an excellent prospect now that he goes chasing; won minor events at Leicester and Ludlow at around 2m4f, but best effort when a staying-on 12l second to Wichita Lineman in the Grade 2 Brit Insurance Hurdle at the Cheltenham Festival (3m, good to soft, 20 ran); has plenty of stamina, and connections hope he will prove good enough to return to the Festival for the SunAlliance Chase.

1009 Aitmatov (Ger)

6 b g Lomitas - Atoka (Kaiseradler)

N Meade (Ir)   John O'Meara

PLACINGS:	7/321212214-				RPR **139**+h

Starts	1st	2nd	3rd	4th	Win & Pl
10	3	4	1	1	£52,244
	4/07	Fair	2m4f Nov Gd2 Hdl good		£21,114
	12/06	Navn	2m4f Nov Hdl heavy		£7,148
	10/06	Gway	2m Mdn Hdl 5yo sft-hvy		£6,195

Consistent performer in good novice hurdles in Ireland last season, never finishing out of the first four in his last nine outings; gained the best of his three successes in a Grade 2 contest at Fairyhouse in April, looking very much at home on good ground at the end of a long season, and beating Davorin by 5¹/₂l (2m4f, 8 ran); had earlier been runner-up behind Clopf and Kazal in other Graded events, but rather disappointing on his final start at the Punchestown festival when only fourth, beaten 23l, behind Glencove Marina; should make his mark in above-average novice chases.

1010 Al Eile (Ire)

7 b g Alzao - Kilcsem Eile (Commanche Run)

J Queally (Ir)   M A Ryan

PLACINGS:	01/963371/146/7541-3				RPR **161**+h

Starts	1st	2nd	3rd	4th	Win & Pl
19	6	1	3	2	£347,501
	4/07	Aint	2m4f Cls1 Gd1 Hdl good		£91,232
	1/06	Hayd	2m Cls1 Gd2 Hdl heavy		£28,510
	4/05	Aint	2m4f Cls1 Gd1 Hdl good		£87,000
	4/04	Aint	2m¹/₂f Cls1 Nov Gd1 Hdl 4yo good		£63,800
	11/03	Chel	2m¹/₂f Cls2 Nov Hdl 3yo good		£12,852
	9/03	List	2m Hdl 3yo gd-fm		£8,065

High-class hurdler; had muscle problems before

Christmas, but returned to form in style in April by winning the Grade 1 Aintree Hurdle for the second time in three years, beating Gaspara by 1¹/₂l (2m4f, good, 11 ran); effective between 2m and 2m4f, but the longer trip definitely suits, and no question he is a horse who comes to life on a flat track granted some good ground, especially in the spring; ran a fine race on the Flat in June, finishing fourth behind Juniper Girl in the Northumberland Plate on ground that would have been too testing for him; main targets are likely to be the Grade 1 Hatton's Grace Hurdle at Fairyhouse in December and the Aintree Hurdle.

1011 Albertas Run (Ire)

6 b g Accordion - Holly Grove Lass (Le Moss)

J O'Neill   Trevor Hemmings

PLACINGS:	110/14111-				RPR **135**+h

Starts	1st	2nd	3rd	4th	Win & Pl
8	6			1	£74,120
128	4/07	Aint	3m¹/₂f Cls1 List 128-150 Hdl Hcap good		£28,510
115	3/07	Sand	2m4¹/₂f Cls1 Nov Gd3 106-132 Hdl 4-7yo Hcap heavy		£34,212
107	1/07	Hntg	2m5¹/₂f Cls4 97-115 Hdl Hcap soft		£3,253
	10/06	Uttx	2m Cls4 Nov Hdl 4-6yo good		£3,904
	1/06	Hayd	2m Cls6 NHF 4-6yo good		£1,713
	11/05	Hayd	2m Cls6 NHF 4-6yo gd-sft		£1,932

Dual bumper winner who was progressive over hurdles last season and promises to make a decent staying novice chaser; improved with each of his five starts, winning four times along the way, most notably at Aintree in a competitive handicap, making light of a 13lb rise in the weights from his previous win to beat Lyes Green by ¹/₂l, with a further 1¹/₄l back to stablemate Refinement, who did no harm to the form by winning Punchestown's Grade 1 Champion Stayers' Hurdle next time out; raised a total of 29lb for his success last season, and likely to be switched to fences now.

1012 Alderburn

8 b g Alderbrook - Threewaygirl (Orange Bay)

H Daly   Mrs D P G Flory

PLACINGS:	3/713362/41F17B/P11-				RPR **153**+c

Starts	1st	2nd	3rd	4th	Win & Pl
18	5	2	3	1	£45,863
135	3/07	Newb	3m Cls3 116-135 Ch Hcap good		£9,395
129	12/06	Kemp	3m Cls3 124-135 Ch Hcap gd-sft		£12,526
120	2/06	Hntg	3m Cls3 Nov 103-124 Ch Hcap good		£7,807
	12/05	Leic	2m4¹/₂f Cls4 Ch good		£4,935
	12/04	Wind	2m4f Cls4 Mdn Hdl soft		£3,621

Smart staying handicap chaser who must have good ground to show his best; raced just three times last season, flopping on his seasonal reappearance, but winning the next two off long breaks; beat Yardbird by 1l at Kempton over Christmas (3m, good to soft, 10 ran) and defied a 6lb rise in the weights at Newbury in late March, where he lobbed along in rear until advancing from halfway and galloping clear up the straight to beat Alexanderthegreat by 3l (3m, good, 17 ran); that left him looking very well handicapped for the Betfred Gold Cup at Sandown at the end of April, but he was denied a crack at the big prize when picking up a knee infection on the eve of the race; up to a mark of 147 now (raised 12lb from Newbury), so will need to improve, but the Hennessy at the Berkshire venue in November could be an early target if we get a dry autumn.

1013 Alexander Taipan (Ire)

7 b g Taipan - Fayafi (Top Ville)
W Mullins (Ir)   Noel O'Callaghan
PLACINGS: 4/121476/22U1F1-07   RPR **152**c

Starts	1st	2nd	3rd	4th	Win & Pl
15	4	3	-	2	£80,039

137	4/07	Punc	2m5f Nov 116-137 Ch Hcap good	£46,081
	1/07	Fair	2m1f Ch heavy	£8,871
	11/05	Punc	2m4f Mdn Hdl soft	£7,841
	5/05	Punc	2m NHF good	£4,901

No great shakes over hurdles, but developed into a smart novice chaser last season, and should pay his way in handicaps/Graded events at around 2m4f; won twice, putting up his best effort to date when humping top weight to victory in a valuable novices' handicap chase at the Punchestown festival, prevailing by a neck from Anothercoppercoast; might well have won the Grade 1 Dr P J Moriarty Novice Chase at Leopardstown in February (2m5f, heavy, 10 ran) but for falling at the last when 1l down and challenging Mister Top Notch; down the field when returned to hurdles in a couple of Graded events at Auteuil in May/June, so unlikely trainer will focus much on the smaller obstacles; if there is some room for improvement, it is in his jumping (failed to complete twice last season and makes the odd mistake); acts well on heavy.

1014 Alfie Flits

5 b g Machiavellian - Elhilmeya (Unfuwain)
G A Swinbank   Dom Flit
PLACINGS: 1114/

Starts	1st	2nd	3rd	4th	Win & Pl
4	3	-	-	1	£8,152

2/06	Carl	1m6f Cls6 NHF 4yo soft	£2,056
1/06	Sthl	2m Cls6 NHF 4yo gd-sft	£2,056
12/05	Weth	1m6f Cls6 NHF 3yo heavy	£2,172

Smart form in bumpers in 2005/06, culminating in an excellent fourth to Pangbourne in the valuable event at Aintree's Grand National meeting; has since run solely on the Flat, winning twice in Listed company over 1m4f, but a shade disappointing at up to 1m6f in 2007; set to go novice hurdling this winter, with his trainer believing he is at his best on flat tracks; will start off being aimed at some weak contests in the north before a crack at something more valuable; has the engine to do well if taking to jumping, and likely to be seen to best effect on goodish ground.

1015 All Star (Ger)

7 b g Lomitas - Alte Garde (Garde Royale)
N Henderson   Lynn Wilson, Nick Wilson, Martin Landau
PLACINGS: 71646/4215005/13405-   RPR **133**+c

Starts	1st	2nd	3rd	4th	Win & Pl
19	3	2	1	3	£47,080

11/06	Asct	2m1f Cls2 Ch gd-sft	£12,526
118	11/05	Hntg	2m4¹/₂f Cls3 98-118 Hdl Hcap good	£13,812
104	12/04	Tntn	2m1f Cls3 89-115 Hdl Hcap good	£6,126

Useful hurdler (RPR of 140) who didn't reach quite the same level in his first season over fences, but remains open to improvement; got his chase career off to a good start in a decent 2m1f beginners' event at Ascot in November, where he jumped well and came through from the rear to beat subsequent multiple winner Flying Enterprise by 1³/₄l; did not go on from that, however, being soundly beaten in two Graded novice chases (made mistakes) and flopping in the Coral Cup at Cheltenham before a decent fifth of 16 in a handicap chase at the Punchestown festival; reserves his best efforts for good ground, so could easily pop up somewhere in the autumn or spring off what looks a fair mark of 130; goes well fresh, likes right-handed tracks and stays 2m4f.

1016 Altilhar (USA)

4 b g Dynaformer - Al Desima (Emperor Jones)
G L Moore   H R Hunt
PLACINGS: 161214-   RPR **130**+h

Starts	1st	2nd	3rd	4th	Win & Pl
6	3	1	-	1	£41,184

128	3/07	Asct	2m Cls2 Nov 104-130 Hdl 4yo Hcap good	£12,526
	1/07	Ludl	2m Cls4 Nov Hdl 4yo gd-sft	£3,578
	11/06	Fknm	2m Cls4 Nov Hdl 3yo good	£5,205

Former 1m2f handicapper on the Flat who made a good start to his hurdling career, racking up three wins in his first season; improved on previous form to finish runner-up to handicap snip Gaspara in the Fred Winter Juvenile Novices' Handicap Hurdle at the Cheltenham Festival (2m1/2f, good to soft, 24 ran), having lots of ground to make up running down the hill, but staying on to excellent effect (beaten 5l); rewarded for that effort when carrying 11st 10lb to victory in a novice handicap at Ascot before not disgraced when 7³/₄l fourth behind Emmpat off an 8lb higher mark in the Grade 2 Scottish Champion Hurdle at Ayr, keeping on after getting outpaced (would have preferred a stronger gallop); likely to prove best at around 2m; best efforts over hurdles have come on good/good to soft, but won on the Flat on good to firm; usually blinkered; looks one for good handicaps. *'I think he was very, very unlucky at Cheltenham – he should have won a minute there.' (Gary Moore, trainer)*

1017 Always Waining (Ire)

6 b g Unfuwain - Glenarff (Irish River)

P Bowen   Peter J Douglas Engineering

PLACINGS: 1/740P771/24P41131-1   **RPR 145+c**

Starts		1st	2nd	3rd	4th	Win & Pl
21		8	1	1	5	£73,078
134	5/07	Uttx	3m Cls2 118-144 Ch Hcap good			£19,014
126	4/07	Ayr	3m1f Cls2 Nov 116-126 Ch Hcap gd-fm			£12,989
121	3/07	Newb	2m6½f Cls3 Nov 113-129 Ch Hcap good			£5,855
	1/07	Tntn	2m3f Cls4 Ch soft			£3,904
110	4/06	Bang	3m Cls3 95-120 Hdl Hcap gd-sft			£6,181
	2/05	Uttx	2m4½f Cls3 Nov Hdl soft			£9,296
	2/05	MRas	2m1½f Cls3 Nov Hdl 4yo good			£4,833
	1/05	Uttx	2m Cls4 Nov Hdl 4yo heavy			£3,445

Progressive staying chaser; won four of his last five during his novice campaign, taking his form up a couple of notches on his last two starts; kept on strongly to beat Get My Drift by 6l in a 3m1f novices' handicap at Ayr, and followed up off an 8lb higher mark in a quite valuable 3m handicap at Uttoxeter in May, beating the very smart Joaaci by 1½l; those two runs – and a Racing Post Rating of 145 – mark him down as a potential candidate for good long-distance handicap chases this season off his official figure of 142.

1018 Amaretto Rose

6 b m Alflora - Teenero (Teenoso)

N Henderson   Weatherbys Racing Club

PLACINGS: 10/1113-   **RPR 148+h**

Starts		1st	2nd	3rd	4th	Win & Pl
6		4	-	1	-	£39,820
	1/07	Hayd	2m Cls1 Nov Gd2 Hdl heavy			£17,106
	12/06	Asct	2m Cls4 Nov Hdl gd-sft			£5,205
	10/06	Wwck	2m Cls6 NHF 4-6yo good			£2,056
	2/06	Towc	2m Cls5 NHF 4-6yo soft			£2,602

Really classy mare over hurdles last season; propelled to the head of the market for the Supreme Novices' with crushing victories at Ascot and Haydock, ploughing through the deep mud to beat Astarador by 18l at the latter venue in January; started 2-1 favourite for the big event at the Cheltenham Festival, and looked set to land the spoils when cruising in the front rank racing down the final hill, but had nothing more to give from the last and finished 3¼l third behind Ebaziyn (2m1½f, soft, 22 ran); could be more to come.

1019 Ambobo (USA)

7 b g Kingmambo - Bold Bold (Sadler's Wells)

M Brassil (Ir)   S Mulryan

PLACINGS: 111211/2190/7-   **RPR 108c**

Starts		1st	2nd	3rd	4th	Win & Pl
11		6	2	-	-	£92,161
	2/06	Mars	2m3f Hdl v soft			£8,938
	1/05	Chel	2m4½f Cls1 Nov Gd2 Hdl gd-sft			£17,400
	11/04	Engh	2m1½f List Hdl 4yo v soft			£25,352
	9/04	Chol	2m1f Hdl 4yo good			£12,169
	8/04	Claf	2m1f Hdl 4yo holding			£7,099
	8/04	Gram	2m1½f Hdl 4yo good			£2,704

Classy hurdler when trained in France by Arnaud Chaille-Chaille, showing his best form when beating Brewster by 2½l in a Grade 2 novice hurdle at Cheltenham in January 2005; switched to Ireland last term, but saw the track only once in a Grade 2 novice chase at Naas in February, coming 20l last of seven finishers behind Benefit Night; not the biggest horse ever to go chasing, and a bit to prove now, but should not be written off as a lost cause just yet; best at around 2m4f on soft ground.

1020 Amstecos (Ire)

7 b g Presenting - Mrs Doeskin (Buckskin)

B Hamilton (Ir)   Sean Macklin

PLACINGS: 5/01/111-   **RPR 135+h**

Starts		1st	2nd	3rd	4th	Win & Pl
6		4	-	-	-	£13,709
	3/07	Ayr	2m4f Cls4 Nov Hdl soft			£2,928
	2/07	Fair	2m Mdn Hdl heavy			£4,669
	5/06	Prth	2m1½f Cls5 Nov NHF 4-6yo soft			£2,193
	12/05	DRoy	2m NHF 4-7yo yld-sft			£3,921

Northern Ireland-trained gelding who is unbeaten in two bumpers and two novice hurdles since December 2005, and looks a cracking prospect for 3m novice chases; held up by niggling problems last autumn, but got off the mark first time over timber in February when responding to pressure to beat Monoceros by 2l at Fairyhouse (2m, heavy, 15 ran); missed possible targets at Cheltenham, and instead went to Ayr for a fair contest over 2m4f in March, where he travelled well before knuckling down to beat the smart staying chaser Ossmoses by a neck, giving 4lb to the runner-up (soft, 9 ran, pair pulled 16l clear of the third); well-made sort who has always looked likely to excel over fences, and his trainer will be itching to get going with him this autumn; clearly suited by soft ground, and could well make up into a Graded-class performer.

1021 An Accordion (Ire)

6 b g Accordion - Jennie's First (Idiot's Delight)

D Pipe   B A Kilpatrick

PLACINGS: 111/2113-   **RPR 144+c**

Starts		1st	2nd	3rd	4th	Win & Pl
4		2	1	1	-	£18,553
	1/07	Font	2m6f Cls3 Nov Ch soft			£7,701
	11/06	Leic	2m7½f Cls4 Mdn Ch good			£5,332

Half-brother to smart handicap chaser Horus and a winner of three point-to-points who improved with each of his four starts under rules last season and looks an interesting contender for staying handicap chases; followed a win in a maiden chase by landing a novice contest, but showed his best form in defeat on his handicap debut at Cheltenham in January, finishing third behind Flying Enterprise despite making plenty of jumping errors (2m5f, heavy, 10 ran); needs to brush up his technique, but packed full of potential and likely to take higher rank this term.

1022 Andreas (Fr)

7 b g Marchand De Sable - Muscova Dancer (Muscovite)

P Nicholls   Trevor Hemmings

PLACINGS: 0/F11F/1261F3/3331F-   **RPR 160+c**

Starts	1st	2nd	3rd	4th	Win & Pl
21	1	1	7		£125,190
143	3/07	Chel	2m³/₂f Cls1 Gd3 132-158 Ch Hcap gd-sft		£48,467
119	2/06	Ludl	2m Cls3 100-119 Hdl Hcap good		£5,205
	5/05	NAbb	2m¹/₂f Cls3 Nov Ch gd-fm		£6,104
119	4/05	Chel	2m¹/₂f Cls3 107-133 Ch Hcap good		£9,526
	3/05	Tntn	2m¹/₂f Cls3 Ch gd-fm		£5,493
	12/03	Cagn	2m2f Hdl 3yo good		£8,104
	7/03	Divo	2m Hdl 3yo good		£2,805

Consistent 2m handicap chaser who last season finally got a deserved reward for his efforts over fences by winning the Grand Annual Chase at the Cheltenham Festival; had been favourite for that contest the previous year when falling at the fourth, but got it right in March from a 1lb lower mark when beating Hasty Prince by 3l despite a ponderous leap at the second-last; looked sure to be in the shake-up at a valuable handicap at Aintree's Grand National meeting the following month, but fell at the third-last when still going well; has reportedly had various niggling problems since that tumble, so might not be seen until the second half of the season, when decent ground would again make him of interest in the spring festival handicaps.

1023 Another Promise (Ire)

8 b g Presenting - Snape (Strong Gale)

F Murphy   Geoff Hubbard Racing

PLACINGS: 55/47152/4/11F21151-   **RPR 154c**

Starts	1st	2nd	3rd	4th	Win & Pl
17	6	2	-	2	£99,592
	4/07	Punc	2m Nov Gd1 Ch good		£46,081
	1/07	Hntg	2m¹/₂f Nov Gd2 Ch soft		£14,255
126	12/06	Newc	2m4f Cls3 100-126 Ch Hcap soft		£9,395
105	10/06	Kels	3m1f Cls4 79-105 Ch Hcap gd-sft		£4,554
95	9/06	Hexm	3m1f Cls5 73-95 Ch Hcap gd-fm		£3,083
90	12/04	Wwck	2m3f Cls4 Nov 72-90 Hdl Hcap heavy		£3,621

Exciting prospect who had a terrific first season's chasing; biggest success came when winning the Grade 1 Swordlestown Cup Novice Chase over 2m at the Punchestown festival in April, staying on well from the last to beat reliable yardstick Royal Shakespeare by 3¹/₂l, and impressing with a solid round of jumping; had found things happening a bit too quickly in the Arkle Trophy at the Cheltenham Festival on his previous start (2m, soft, 13 ran), but by no means disgraced to finish fifth, beaten 13l by My Way De Solzen; had earlier in the season proved his effectiveness over further, finishing runner-up in the Rehearsal Chase at Newcastle in November (3m, good to soft, 11 ran), and easily bagging a 2m4f handicap chase back at the same venue; acts on any ground, and connections seem hell-bent on sticking to the minimum trip with him. *'He's probably going to stay down the 2m route. We'll aim him*

at the Tingle Creek and Champion Chase.' (Ferdy Murphy, trainer)

1024 Anothercoppercoast (Ire)

7 ch g Presenting - Parsee (Persian Mews)

P Roche (Ir)   Mrs E Queally

PLACINGS: 136/21034/3183632-   **RPR 142c**

Starts	1st	2nd	3rd	4th	Win & Pl
14	2	2	5	1	£46,317
	11/06	Cork	2m4f Nov Ch heavy		£12,122
	11/05	Punc	2m NHF 5yo soft		£5,391

Cork novice chase winner last season, but posted his best efforts in defeat; was twice placed at huge odds in Grade 1s in Ireland, finishing 21l third behind Cailin Alainn at Leopardstown over Christmas (3m, heavy, 11 ran) and 21l third behind One Cool Cookie at Fairyhouse in April (2m4f, good, 11 ran); finished with a neck second to Alexander Taipan in a novices' handicap chase at the Punchestown festival; definitely races to be won with him off his chase mark in the low 130s, seems to handle all types of ground, and may improve further when stepped up to distances beyond 3m.

1025 Aran Concerto (Ire)

6 b g Zaffaran - Frizzball (Orchestra)

N Meade (Ir)   John Corr

PLACINGS: 161115-   **RPR 146+h**

Starts	1st	2nd	3rd	4th	Win & Pl
6	4	-	-	-	£106,182
	2/07	Leop	2m2f Nov Gd1 Hdl heavy		£46,622
	12/06	Navn	2m4f Nov Gd1 Hdl heavy		£44,828
	11/06	Navn	2m Mdn Hdl soft		£6,672
	10/06	Naas	2m3f NHF 4-7yo yld-sft		£4,766

Highly touted hurdler who added substance to the hype - up to a point - in his novice campaign last winter; won two small-field Grade 1s in heavy ground in Ireland, beating Footy Facts by 7l at Navan in December (2m4f) and stablemate Leading Run by 3l at Leopardstown in February (2m2f), doing it very easily both times; was one of the Irish bankers of the Cheltenham Festival in the Ballymore Properties Novices' Hurdle (started 5-2 favourite), but was racing in a big field on ground faster than he had encountered before, and those two factors probably forced the mistakes that had him on the back foot from an early stage, so in the end he did well to finish 10¹/₂l fifth behind Massini's Maguire (2m5f, good to soft, 15 ran); has received treatment since for a sprained hock, but reported fine at the time of writing and poised to embark on a novice chase campaign; has always looked a chaser in the making, and while his trainer may regret saying it, he is on record as touting this one as a potential Cheltenham Gold Cup winner. *'He's well balanced, he's got gears, stamina and he settles well – he's the real deal.' (Noel Meade, trainer)*

1026 Aranleigh (Ire)

5 b g Insan - Lexy Lady (Strong Gale)

A Mullins (Ir)   John P McManus

PLACINGS: 13-   **RPR 135+b**

Starts	1st	2nd	3rd	4th	Win & Pl
2	1		1		£10,724
	1/07	Fair	2m NHF 4-6yo heavy		£5,369

Nicely bred type who showed classy form in bumpers last season, and has the potential to make his presence felt in the top novice hurdles; defeated the highly touted Mad Fish by 5l (pair a distance clear) on his debut at Fairyhouse in January, coping well with the heavy ground, leading 3f out and rallying when tackled in the straight to stretch away; was subsequently sold to J P McManus, and sent off 8-1 for the Champion Bumper at the Cheltenham Festival (2m, good to soft, 24 ran), where he ran well to finish 2³/4l third behind Cork All Star (stayed on strongly after short of room 5f out); looks a good prospect for novice hurdles.

1027 Arcalis

7 gr g Lear Fan - Aristocratique (Cadeaux Genereux)

J H Johnson   Andrea & Graham Wylie

PLACINGS: 11431/1P595/4465541-   **RPR 157h**

Starts	1st	2nd	3rd	4th	Win & Pl
17	5			4	£174,007
	4/07	Sand	2m¹/₂f Cls2 Hdl gd-fm		£20,283
	11/05	Newc	2m Cls1 Gd1 Hdl soft		£45,072
	3/05	Chel	2m¹/₂f Cls1 Nov Gd1 Hdl good		£58,000
	12/04	Newc	2m Cls4 Nov Hdl good		£3,523
	12/04	Ayr	2m Cls3 Nov Hdl good		£4,765

Former Supreme Novices' Hurdle winner, but has struggled to break into the top echelon since; comfortably turned over in a string of small-field Graded hurdles last season, but his handicap mark slowly came down, and that allowed him to run a big race under 11st 2lb in the County Hurdle at the Cheltenham Festival, where he led at the last and kept on at one pace to finish 2¹/4l fifth behind Pedrobob (2m1f, good to soft, 28 ran); fourth in the Aintree Hurdle before ending a long losing run by dead-heating with Penzance for a decent conditions hurdle at Sandown in April; won't be winning any Champion Hurdles now, but could well win a competitive handicap.

1028 Arctic Echo

8 b g Alderbrook - Arctic Oats (Oats)

G A Swinbank   R P Dineen

PLACINGS: 1139/23/111430-   **RPR 132h**

Starts	1st	2nd	3rd	4th	Win & Pl
12	5		3	1	£18,369
	1/07	Catt	3m1¹/₂f Cls4 Nov Hdl soft		£3,333
	12/06	Sedg	2m5¹/₂f Cls4 Nov Hdl soft		£2,928
	5/06	Hexm	2m4¹/₂f Cls4 Mdn Hdl good		£3,083
	10/04	Hexm	2m¹/₂f Cls6 NHF 4-6yo gd-fm		£1,855
	9/04	Hexm	2m¹/₂f Cls6 NHF 4-6yo gd-fm		£1,904

Staying hurdler who bears all the hallmarks of a useful novice chaser in the making; won three times over hurdles, the pick being a 13l defeat of Ellerslie George at Catterick, before a step up in grade; no match for Chief Dan George at Wetherby, but a good third behind the smart Bedlam Boy at Newcastle before a below-par run in Listed handicap company at Aintree's Grand National meeting; seems best going left-handed on soft ground. *'He wants 3m and some cut in the ground.' (Bill Haigh, assistant trainer)*

1029 Ardaghey (Ire)

8 b/br g Lord Americo - Mrs Pepper (Lancastrian)

N Twiston-Davies   D J & S A Goodman

PLACINGS: 1441/36P21UF0/1P062-   **RPR 147+c**

Starts	1st	2nd	3rd	4th	Win & Pl
17	4	2	1	2	£35,912
130	10/06	Chel	3m¹/₂f Cls3 104-135 Am Ch Hcap gd-sft		£6,026
	2/06	Towc	3m¹/₂f Cls4 Ch soft		£4,120
	2/05	Leic	2m4¹/₂f Cls3 Nov Hdl 4-7yo heavy		£5,512
	10/04	Uttx	2m Cls6 NHF 4-6yo good		£1,883

Handicap chaser who is typical of his trainer's charges, in that his long suit is stamina and easy going brings out the best in him; reappearance outing appeared to herald a successful season ahead, as he outclassed his rivals in an amateurs' race at Cheltenham, but earned an 11lb jump in the weights for that and failed to cope with new mark; Hennessy run can be forgotten (saddle slipped, pulled up) but he struggled on next two starts until handicapper showed a little leniency, and produced his best effort on his final start when 9l second to Simon (subsequent Racing Post Chase winner) in the Sky Bet Chase at Southwell (3m1f, soft, 10 ran); likely to find opportunities away from the top level when conditions are in his favour.

1030 Armaturk (Fr)

10 ch g Baby Turk - Armalita (Goodland)

P Nicholls   Trevor Hemmings

PLACINGS: 3936/1512P63/22U30B-   **RPR 161+c**

Starts	1st	2nd	3rd	4th	Win & Pl
49	13	8	10	4	£318,563
153	12/05	Ling	2m Cls2 128-153 Ch Hcap soft		£18,859
148	10/05	Ling	2m Cls1 List 122-148 Ch Hcap good		£17,400
154	11/04	Chel	2m Cls2 136-162 Ch Hcap good		£17,400
148	10/04	Ling	2m Cls1 List 124-148 Ch Hcap gd-sft		£17,850
138	1/04	Donc	2m¹/₂f Cls2 115-140 Ch Hcap soft		£13,640
	2/03	Winc	2m5f Cls2 Ch gd-sft		£11,980
	4/02	Aint	2m Cls1 Nov Gd1 Ch good		£46,500
	2/02	Wwck	2m¹/₂f Cls1 Nov Gd2 Ch soft		£18,000
	12/01	Newb	2m2¹/₂f Cls3 Nov Ch good		£5,905
	10/01	Kemp	2m Cls2 Hdl gd-sft		£6,890
	4/01	Kemp	2m Cls3 Nov Hdl 4yo good		£3,939
	4/01	Plum	2m Cls4 Nov Hdl 4yo heavy		£2,513
	1/01	Pau	2m¹/₂f Hdl 4yo soft		£6,305

High-class if exposed chaser between 2m and 2m4f who is often forced to run in Pattern contests to avoid lumping huge weights in handicap company and therefore finds it difficult to win; drew a blank in six starts last season, but ran some big races in defeat, none more so than at Cheltenham in

November when beaten only 3l by Rubberdubber, to whom he was conceding 17lb (2m, good, 9 ran); that effort was one of the very best of his career, according to Racing Post Ratings, so he is clearly no back-number, but with a handicap mark that does not relent because of his consistency, it's not easy to see where the next win will come from.

1031 Arteea (Ire)

8 b g Oscar - Merric (Electric)

M Hourigan (Ir)   Michael O'Flaherty

PLACINGS: 3212314/431441286/3-   **RPR 133c**

Starts	1st	2nd	3rd	4th	Win & Pl
22	5	3	4	4	£103,133
	1/06	Naas	2m3f Nov Ch soft		£9,653
	10/05	Gway	2m1f Nov Gd3 Ch soft		£25,245
	3/05	Naas	2m Nov Hdl yld-sft		£6,861
	12/04	Limk	2m3f Mdn Hdl 5yo heavy		£6,326
	4/04	Fair	2m NHF 4-5yo yield		£27,711

Grade 3 winner and Grade 1-placed in novice chases two seasons ago, his best effort a $^3/_4$l second to the ill-fated Missed That at Leopardstown in January 2006 (2m1f, yielding to soft, 7 ran); raced just once last season, finishing 19l last of three finishers behind Justified in a Listed chase at Limerick last October; better than that, and despite his long absence, is reported in tip-top condition by his trainer at the time of writing; looks a candidate for good 2m handicap chases on easy ground on the pick of his form, though that is obviously from some time ago.

1032 Ashley Brook (Ire)

9 ch g Magical Wonder - Seamill (Lafontaine)

K Bishop   Mrs E K Ellis

PLACINGS: 12135/112421/32/12F-   **RPR 164c**

Starts	1st	2nd	3rd	4th	Win & Pl
21	7	6	3	2	£201,076
124	1/07	Chel	2m1f Cls2 115-130 Hdl Hcap heavy		£16,265
	4/05	Aint	2m Cls1 Nov Gd1 Ch good		£63,800
	11/04	NAbb	2m5^1/$_2$f Cls3 Nov Ch good		£10,199
	11/04	Extr	2m1^1/$_2$f Cls3 Nov Ch gd-sft		£10,192
	12/03	Tntn	2m3^1/$_2$f Cls4 Nov Hdl good		£2,744
	11/03	Extr	2m1f Cls3 Nov Hdl good		£4,056
	1/03	Ludl	2m Cls6 NHF 4-6yo soft		£1,607

Very talented, bold-jumping, front-running chaser whose progress has been hampered over the years by sore shins; returned from 14 months on the sidelines to romp away with a handicap hurdle at Cheltenham in January, presaging a return to the big time; was put in his place by another returnee, Well Chief, in the Game Spirit Chase at Newbury the following month, but took his chance anyway in the Champion Chase in March, and was in the process of running a cracker – rallying to mount a renewed challenge to Voy Por Ustedes – when crashing out at the last; emerged battered and unbowed from that crunching fall, and trainer reported his legs to be standing up especially well as he began to return to work this summer; likely to have a run over hurdles before a possible tilt at

the King George over 3m at Christmas, after which a decision on his Cheltenham Festival target will be made; very courageous, and looks the sort to come out fighting again despite his setbacks; bounces off good ground.

1033 Aztec Warrior (Ire)

6 b g Taipan - Eurocurrency (Brush Aside)

Miss H Knight   Mrs T P Radford

PLACINGS: 342614/5P141201-   **RPR 137c**

Starts	1st	2nd	3rd	4th	Win & Pl
14	4	2	1	3	£39,416
	4/07	Font	2m6f Cls3 Nov Ch gd-fm		£5,637
	1/07	Winc	2m5f Cls3 Nov Ch soft		£6,665
	11/06	Folk	2m5f Cls3 Nov Ch good		£7,807
	3/06	Sand	2m^1/$_2$f Cls4 Nov Hdl soft		£5,205

Useful chaser with plenty of physical scope to improve; won novice events at Folkestone, Wincanton and Fontwell last season, posting his best figures at the second venue when eased down to beat Opera De Coeur by 5l; best effort in defeat came in the Grade 1 Scilly Isles Novices' Chase at Sandown in February, where he lost his good early position and dropped to last at halfway, but kept on gamely to finish 8l second to New Little Bric (2m4^1/$_2$f, good to soft, 4 ran); only real flop came at the Cheltenham Festival, where he finished well beaten in the Jewson Novices' Handicap Chase; trainer has long seen him as a potential three-miler, so could be more to come when he steps up to that sort of trip; generally good jumper who could make up into a contender for races like the Racing Post Chase; may be best right-handed.

1034 Ballistraw (Ire)

8 ch g Carroll House - Well Over (Over The River)

M Hickey (Ir)   M W Hickey

PLACINGS: 216/11221/0412-   **RPR 147c**

Starts	1st	2nd	3rd	4th	Win & Pl
9	3	3	-	1	£53,435
123	12/06	Punc	2m4f 103-131 Ch Hcap heavy		£13,020
	3/06	Gowr	3m Hunt Ch soft		£7,148
	12/05	Limk	2m6f Mdn Hunt Ch heavy		£5,391

Former hunter chaser who did well for his tiny yard in good handicap chases in the first half of last season; scored by a neck at Punchestown in December before a cracking effort in the valuable Paddy Power Chase at Leopardstown over Christmas, where he challenged Cane Brake on the run-in but failed by ^{1}/$_2$l to overhaul the subsequent Gold Cup fifth (3m, heavy, 28 ran, was getting just 6lb from the winner when jockeys' allowance taken into account); wasn't seen out again owing to a few niggly problems, but reportedly well over those now (would have been ready to run at the Punchestown festival, but ground was too firm); lightly raced, and no surprise to see him doing well in handicaps, given that he is a brother/half-brother to smart sorts Red Devil Robert and Lord

Of The River; should be out again in November, with connections keen to bring him back in the softest race they can find for him (now rated 137).

1035 Ballyagran (Ire)

7 b g Pierre - Promalady (Homo Sapien)
N Meade (Ir)   Kevin C O'Sullivan
PLACINGS: 11/213U674F/O25114-2   **RPR 139c**

Starts	1st	2nd	3rd	4th	Win & Pl
16	4	3	1	2	£78,224

10/06	Rosc	2m Nov Gd3 Ch sft-hvy	£20,203
9/06	List	2m3f Ch sft-hvy	£8,340
10/05	Cork	2m Nov Hdl gd-yld	£10,157
4/05	Gowr	2m NHF soft	£4,411

Lightly raced chaser with plenty of scope for improvement; clear-cut winner of an admittedly very weak Grade 3 novice chase at Roscommon last October, where he led before the straight and stayed on well to beat Some Timbering by 7l; comfortably held in fourth behind Gemini Lucy in a much more legitimate Listed event at Punchestown a fortnight later, but was then confined to his box for the winter by lameness; came good in time to make his handicap debut in the Galway Plate in August, and ran a blinder to finish 3l second to Sir Frederick (2m6f, good to yielding, 22 ran); has a future in big handicap chases if he can stay free of injury; suited by cut in the ground.

1036 Ballycassidy (Ire)

11 br g Insan - Bitofabreeze (Callernish)
P Bowen   R Owen & P Fullagar
PLACINGS: 50F1/4U20P5P0U6-1659   **RPR 146+c**

Starts	1st	2nd	3rd	4th	Win & Pl
58	15	9	6	1	£271,308

132	5/07	Kels	2m6½f Cls3 109-133 Ch Hcap gd-fm	£12,526
140	4/06	Prth	3m Cls2 119-140 Ch Hcap good	£18,789
124	6/05	Worc	3m Cls2 105-131 Hdl Hcap gd-fm	£12,696
138	5/05	Kels	3m1f Cls2 114-140 Ch Hcap gd-fm	£17,936
	12/03	Newb	3m Cls3 Nov Ch gd-fm	£10,280
	11/03	Newb	3m Cls1 Nov Gd2 Ch gd-sft	£23,450
	10/03	Aint	3m1f Cls3 Nov Ch good	£11,675
	9/03	MRas	2m6½f Cls3 Nov Ch gd-fm	£8,700
127	7/03	MRas	2m4f Cls2 114-140 Ch Hcap gd-fm	£40,600
	7/03	Strf	3m Cls3 Nov Ch gd-fm	£5,852
	6/03	NAbb	2m5½f Cls3 Nov Ch gd-fm	£6,224
	1/02	Hntg	3m2f Cls1 Nov Gd2 Hdl gd-sft	£12,128
113	6/01	Strf	3m3f Cls3 99-117 Hdl Hcap gd-fm	£3,666
	5/01	Strf	2m6½f Cls3 Nov Hdl good	£3,900
	5/01	Hrfd	3m2f Cls4 Mdn Hdl good	£2,800

Veteran handicap chaser; didn't really spark for most of last season, but not for the first time in his career came good when the ground firmed up in the spring; ran well until unshipping his rider at Becher's second time round in the Grand National, and was a respectable sixth of 23 in the Scottish equivalent at Ayr a week later; had dropped to a very favourable mark by that stage, and duly got back to winning ways at Kelso in May, rallying after an error 2 out to lead on the run-in and beat Scots Grey by 3½l; undone by the unseasonably wet weather in the summer, but had showed by that

stage that he retained enough ability and enthusiasm to prolong his career in good handicaps; likely to have one more crack at the National next spring, and connections will be hoping for some fast ground en route.

1037 Bambi De L'Orme (Fr)

8 gr g True Brave - Princesse Ira (Less Ice)
I Williams   Mr & Mrs John Poynton
PLACINGS: UF23/1740B/52P37511-   **RPR 145+c**

Starts	1st	2nd	3rd	4th	Win & Pl
35	7	6	4	2	£155,686

137	4/07	Ayr	2m Cls2 122-142 Ch Hcap gd-fm	£18,789
130	4/07	Aint	2m Cls1 Gd3 128-154 Ch Hcap good	£39,014
	5/05	Wwck	2m½f Cls2 Ch gd-fm	£10,114
	2/04	Newc	2m½f Cls4 Ch good	£4,739
	5/03	Nant	2m1½f Hdl 4yo v soft	£11,221
	11/02	Sbri	1m7f Hdl 3yo heavy	£3,239
	9/02	Vire	2m Hdl 3yo good	£2,945

Consistent 2m chaser who falls between two stools – just too high in the weights for ordinary handicaps, but not of the class required for the top events; very well suited by a flat track and ran well in defeat at Newbury in November when 1³/4l runner-up to handicap snip Saintsaire (2m1f, soft, 9 ran); generally better in second half of the season and produced a decent showing in the Grand Annual at Cheltenham, when fifth behind Andreas (2m1/2f, good to soft, 23 ran); that heralded a return to his best in the Grade 3 Red Rum Chase at Aintree where, off his lowest rating for two years, he found more than can sometimes be the case on the run-in to beat Marshall Hall by 1¹/2l; 2m is his trip and fast conditions bring out the best in him. *'Aintree suits him.' (Ian Williams, trainer)*

1038 Barbers Shop

5 b g Saddlers' Hall - Close Harmony (Bustino)
N Henderson   The Queen
PLACINGS: 1/3122U-1   **RPR 130+h**

Starts	1st	2nd	3rd	4th	Win & Pl
7	3	2	1	-	£15,240

6/07	Sthl	2m1f Cls4 Hdl good	£3,253
12/06	Asct	2m6f Cls3 Mdn Hdl good	£6,263
3/06	Winc	2m Cls6 Mdn NHF 4-6yo soft	£1,713

Useful hurdler who looks to have the scope to improve over fences this season; officially rated 136 over the smaller obstacles at the time of writing, having won a maiden event at Ascot last December (beat Pantalaimon by 5l) and an intermediate contest at Southwell in June (sent off odds-on, and saw off Mister Benedictine comfortably enough); in between was runner-up to Secret Ploy at Kempton before a 1-4 defeat at Market Rasen and a spill at Bangor; slightly tricky customer who can hang under pressure, but remains unbeaten in completed starts on good ground; probably best at around 2m4f. *'He's a chaser really.' (Nicky Henderson, trainer)*

1039 Baron Windrush

9 b g Alderbrook - Dame Scarlet (Blakeney)

N Twiston-Davies   The Double Octagon Partnership

PLACINGS: U16216/P4PUP/PP5P11-   **RPR 148 + c**

Starts	1st	2nd	3rd	4th	Win & Pl
24	7	1	1	1	£175,733

131	3/07	Uttx	4m1¹/₂f Cls1 List 122-148 Ch Hcap soft £57,020
121	2/07	Wwck	3m5f Cls3 109-135 Ch Hcap heavy £6,506
129	1/05	Wwck	3m5f Cls1 Gd3 126-152 Ch Hcap soft £66,700
	11/04	Aint	3m1f Cls2 Nov Ch gd-sft...£17,015
	10/04	Strf	3m Cls3 Ch soft £6,812
	3/04	Weth	3m1f Cls4 Nov Hdl gd-sft £3,472
	3/04	MRas	2m6f Cls4 Nov Cond Hdl good £3,689

Long-distance handicap chaser who emerged from a prolonged period when his form figures resembled a bad rack at Scrabble to win his last two starts of the season; made the most of the handicapper's leniency to win a run-of-the-mill Warwick handicap (3m5f, heavy, 6 ran) off a career-low mark, and defied a 10lb hike in the attritional Midlands National at Uttoxeter next time out, utilising his bottomless stamina to run out a 12l winner from D'Argent; starts this campaign 12lb higher, which may bring his little spree to an end; the Welsh National looks a logical objective.

1040 Battle Cry

6 b/br g Accordion - Miss Orchestra (Orchestra)

N Twiston-Davies   Hamsard Ltd

PLACINGS: 13FP29P-   **RPR 126h**

Starts	1st	2nd	3rd	4th	Win & Pl
7	1	1	1	-	£4,656

	10/06	Worc	2m Cls6 NHF 4-6yo gd-sft...£1,713

Useful novice hurdler, and a similar type to stablemate Imperial Commander, although not yet in the same class; promising effort in a Cheltenham bumper in November when 10l third behind subsequent Champion Bumper winner Cork All Star (2m1¹/₂f, good to soft, 11 ran); went hurdling after that, but failed to complete in three of five starts, although not disgraced in the Ballymore Properties Novices' Hurdle at the Cheltenham Festival when ninth behind Massini's Maguire (2m5f, good to soft, 15 ran); still a novice over hurdles (went closest to winning when second to Duc De Regniere at Kempton), but trainer tends to send his youngsters chasing and this one could make a name for himself over fences.

1041 Beau Michel (Fr)

5 b g Saint Preuil - Rosacotte (Rose Laurel)

P Nicholls   C G Roach

PLACINGS: 114712-   **RPR 124h**

Starts	1st	2nd	3rd	4th	Win & Pl
6	3	1	-	1	£28,937

115	2/07	Winc	2m6f Cls3 111-130 Hdl Hcap soft......................£17,536
	10/06	Extr	2m1f Cls3 Nov Hdl good..£5,205
	5/06	Worc	2m Cls6 NHF 4-6yo gd-sft...£1,713

Brother to smart Irish performer Marcus Du Berlais,

and likely to come into his own when sent novice chasing this term; won three of his six starts last season, steadily improving along the way and following a bumper win with victories over hurdles at Exeter and Wincanton; showed his best form in defeat on his final start when sporting first-time blinkers and chasing home Abragante in a decent little handicap at Cheltenham in April, seeming to appreciate the longer trip on his first try over 3m, although he was reportedly distressed after that run; not one of the stable stars, but useful and sure to win more races. *'He'll be better given 3m over fences.' (Paul Nicholls, trainer)*

1042 Bedlam Boy (Ire)

6 br g Broken Hearted - Evening Fashion (Strong Gale)

N Richards   T Ambler

PLACINGS: 34/42F113-   **RPR 138 + h**

Starts	1st	2nd	3rd	4th	Win & Pl
8	2	1	2	2	£18,483

123	2/07	Newc	2m4f Cls2 Nov 109-135 Hdl Hcap heavy...............£9,395
	2/07	Hexm	2m¹/₂f Cls5 Mdn Hdl soft £1,627

Progressed well in novice hurdles last season, and goes straight over fences now; came back a better horse following a mid-season break, winning in testing conditions at Hexham and Newcastle, and finishing 11¹/₂l third behind Tidal Bay in the Grade 2 Mersey Novices' Hurdle at Aintree in April (2m4f, good, 10 ran); more relaxed now, and should have few problems picking up a couple of run-of-the-mill chases in the north; should he impress, the Grade 1 Feltham Novices' Chase at Kempton on Boxing Day is a race his trainer has in mind en route to an assignment at Cheltenham. *'Jumping fences will be his game.' (Nicky Richards, trainer)*

1043 Beef Or Salmon (Ire)

11 ch g Cajetano - Farinella (Salmon Leap)

M Hourigan (Ir)   B J Craig

PLACINGS: 2P/2110U32/21212108-   **RPR 172c**

Starts	1st	2nd	3rd	4th	Win & Pl
41	17	7	5	1	£933,041

	2/07	Leop	3m Gd1 Ch heavy £79,054
	12/06	Fair	2m2f Hdl heavy...£8,578
	11/06	DRoy	3m Gd1 Ch yld-sft...£60,345
	2/06	Leop	3m Gd1 Ch yield £75,724
	12/05	Leop	3m Gd1 Ch yld-sft...£69,149
	12/04	Leop	3m Gd1 Ch sft-hvy £68,662
	11/04	DRoy	3m Gd1 Ch soft £60,141
	4/04	Punc	3m1f Gd1 Ch good £76,056
	12/03	Cork	2m Gd2 Ch yld-sft...£21,104
	12/03	Punc	2m4f Gd1 Ch yield £37,987
	2/03	Leop	3m Gd1 Ch yld-sft...£67,597
	12/02	Leop	3m Gd1 Ch heavy £59,816
	12/02	Cork	2m Gd3 Ch soft £15,915
	11/02	Cork	2m4f Gd2 Ch heavy £21,933
	1/02	Gowr	2m2f Hdl heavy..£7,975
	1/02	Cork	2m NHF soft £4,868
	11/01	Clon	2m NHF soft £4,173

Top-class staying chaser over a number of seasons, and looked just about as good as ever in a campaign that yielded two more Grade 1 victories last winter; lowered the colours of War Of Attrition in a thrilling finish at Down Royal last November (prevailed by a neck) and brought the house down at Leopardstown in February when winning his third Hennessy Cognac Gold Cup; looked to face an impossible task when turning for home well adrift of The Listener, but kept battling away in the style that had brought him his Down Royal victory and got up on the run-in to beat the grey raider by ^{3}/4l; also finished runner-up twice at the top level, behind Kauto Star in the Betfair Chase at Haydock, and The Listener in the Lexus Chase at Leopardstown over Christmas; also won a minor hurdle race in mid-season, but ended his campaign by flopping for the umpteenth time in the Cheltenham Gold Cup and running below par at Punchestown; raring to go again this winter, and will have his usual campaign in the top events at Down Royal and Leopardstown, but won't be going to Cheltenham this time; can remain a potent force in small-field, heavy-ground chases in Ireland.

1044 Berings Express (Fr)

4 b g Bering - Ess Express (Subotica)

J O'Neill — Mrs Gay Smith

PLACINGS: 10- — **RPR 106+b**

Starts	1st	2nd	3rd	4th	Win & Pl
2	1	-	-	-	£2,055
	11/06	Wwck	1m6f Cls6 NHF 3yo good £2,056		

Promising novice hurdle prospect, who raced twice in bumpers last season for French trainer Nicolas Clement; made the journey across the Channel worthwhile on his debut at Warwick last November where he was always travelling well and came home in front to beat Helens Vision by 1^1/2l, with 6l back to Theatre Girl in third, who scored next time out; unable to build on that promising start, finishing down the field in the Champion Bumper at Cheltenham on his only other start, although he was beaten only around 23l; bought privately during the summer, and surprising if he fails to make his presence felt over hurdles.

1045 Berwick Law (Ire)

5 ch g Snurge - Cruby Hill (Prince Rupert)

L Lungo — Mr & Mrs Raymond Anderson Green

PLACINGS: 11- — **RPR 116+b**

Starts	1st	2nd	3rd	4th	Win & Pl
2	2	-	-	-	£3,083
	3/07	Ayr	2m Cls6 NHF 4-6yo heavy £1,370		
	12/06	Ayr	2m Cls6 NHF 4-6yo heavy £1,713		

Unbeaten bumper horse who is set to go novice hurdling; gained both his successes in heavy ground at Ayr, beating Scrappie by 11l in a poor contest in December, and Mey Clouds by a bloodless 15l in an equally dire affair in March; hard to imagine many ropier fields being assembled than the two he saw off, but scored without breaking sweat, and will surely be placed

to win some weak novice hurdles in the north before tackling something better; impossible to say how he will handle better ground.

1046 Bewleys Berry (Ire)

9 ch g Shernazar - Approach The Dawn (Orchestra)

J H Johnson — Andrea & Graham Wylie

PLACINGS: 11/121FP/1236P/429F- — **RPR 146+c**

Starts	1st	2nd	3rd	4th	Win & Pl
15	4	3	1	1	£70,527
	11/05	Weth	3m1f Cls4 Ch gd-sft £3,855		
	1/05	Donc	3m^1/2f Cls1 Nov Gd2 Hdl good £18,150		
	12/04	Hexm	2m^1/2f Cls4 Nov Hdl heavy £3,585		
	4/04	Gowr	2m2f NHF yld-sft............................£5,596		

Smart staying handicap chaser whose bold-jumping style has swiftly turned him into something of a specialist over the big National fences at Aintree; ran his best race in a light campaign in the Becher Chase there last November, when he cut out most of the running, but was headed at the last and kept on at the same pace to finish 8l second to Eurotrek (3m2f, good, 21 ran); ran a lacklustre race in heavy ground at Haydock in February, but the spark was back in the Grand National, where he was again bowling along at the head of affairs and still looked to hold every chance when falling at Becher's second time round (good, 40 ran); stays well and likes good ground, and current mark of 138 is likely to be looked after en route to another crack at the Becher and Grand National.

1047 Bible Lord (Ire)

6 ch g Mister Lord - Pharisee (Phardante)

A Turnell — M Tedham

PLACINGS: 51/60211- — **RPR 135+c**

Starts	1st	2nd	3rd	4th	Win & Pl
5	2	1	-	-	£19,342
122	3/07	Ling	2m4^1/2f Cls3 Nov 99-125 Ch Hcap gd-sft £10,021		
	3/07	Kemp	2m4^1/2f Cls3 Nov Ch heavy £7,793		

Winning Irish point-to-pointer who made considerable progress in first season under Rules; made a good impression in defeat at Kempton when runner-up, beaten 8l, to Limited Edition (2m4^1/2f, good to soft, 5 ran) and ran almost to that level back at the same track when ploughing through the mud for a 15l defeat of previous winner Il Duce in March; stepped up on that in his first handicap at Lingfield when helping to force the pace and drawing clear from the third-last, having 6l to spare over Dunsfold Duke; has shown his best form on ground no worse than good to soft, and although he acts in the mud, is probably better out of it; crying out for 3m and scope for considerable improvement at that trip given his relative inexperience.

1048 Billyvoddan (Ire)

8 b g Accordion - Derryclare (Pollerton)

H Daly   Trevor Hemmings

PLACINGS: 1223124/13419U/513P-   **RPR 160+c**

Starts	1st	2nd	3rd	4th	Win & Pl
22	5	3	6	2	£117,446

139	12/06	Asct	3m Cls1 List 130-153 Ch Hcap gd-sft £39,438
	1/06	Leic	2m4¹/₂f Cls3 Nov Ch gd-sft £7,516
	11/05	Hntg	2m4¹/₂f Cls3 Nov Ch good £7,498
	1/05	Donc	2m3¹/₂f Cls3 Nov Hdl 4-7yo good £5,785
	5/04	Uttx	2m4¹/₂f Cls4 Nov Hdl gd-sft £3,575

Developed into a high-class staying chaser in a light campaign last term, and his success - and consequent rising handicap mark - means he will have to compete in Graded chases this winter; needed the run on his reappearance last autumn, and duly improved to spring a 25-1 surprise (in first-time blinkers) in the valuable Silver Cup Handicap Chase at Ascot in December, where he recovered from being badly impeded early on to lead 4 out, and drew clear to slam Zabenz by 12l (3m, good to soft, 18 ran); was next seen out in the Ryanair Chase at the Cheltenham Festival in March, where he ran a cracker to finish ³/₄l third behind Taranis (2m5f, good to soft, 9 ran); that appeared to set him up for a really good crack at the Grand National under 11st 4lb, but he ran abysmally at Aintree and was pulled up early on the second circuit; now rated 159, so it looks like his handicapping days are over; needs decent ground, and races like the Peterborough Chase and King George could be on the agenda in the first half of the season.

1049 Black Harry (Ire)

7 b/br g Flemensfirth - Raise An Ace (Buckskin)

W Mullins (Ir)   Sean O'Driscoll

PLACINGS: 1/05311F-   **RPR 148h**

Starts	1st	2nd	3rd	4th	Win & Pl
7	3	-	1	-	£22,280

	1/07	Fair	3m Nov Hdl heavy....................................£10,997
	1/07	Naas	2m3f Mdn Hdl sft-hvy...............................£4,669
	12/05	Leop	2m NHF 5yo yld-sft....................................£5,881

Dour staying type who appeals as the sort to make his mark in novice chases this season, with the Royal & SunAlliance Chase a realistic target; took a while to develop into a smart novice hurdler last season, but eventually got on to the scoresheet at Naas and Fairyhouse in January, and was the only one to pose a threat to Wichita Lineman from two out in the Brit Insurance Novices' Hurdle at the Cheltenham Festival, where he would almost certainly have finished second but for falling at the last (3m, good to soft, 20 ran); comes from a good jumping family (related to smart chaser Yorkshire Edition) and likely to come into his own once he jumps a fence; handles very testing ground.

1050 Black Jack Ketchum (Ire)

8 b g Oscar - Cailin Supreme (Supreme Leader)

J O'Neill   Mrs Gay Smith

PLACINGS: 11/11111/15F2-   **RPR 164+h**

Starts	1st	2nd	3rd	4th	Win & Pl
11	8	1	-	-	£169,279

	12/06	Chel	2m5¹/₂f Cls1 Gd2 Hdl soft.........................£22,808
	4/06	Aint	3m¹/₂f Cls1 Nov Gd1 Hdl gd-sft.................£51,318
	3/06	Chel	3m Cls1 Nov Gd2 Hdl good £42,765
	12/05	Chel	3m Cls1 Nov Gd2 Hdl gd-sft.....................£17,106
	11/05	Chel	2m5f Cls2 Nov Hdl gd-sft £10,898
	10/05	Uttx	2m6¹/₂f Cls4 Nov Hdl gd-sft £3,360
	7/04	Worc	2m Cls6 NHF 4-6yo good £1,868
	6/04	Worc	2m Cls6 NHF 4-6yo good £1,873

Winner of the Brit Insurance Novices' Hurdle at the Cheltenham Festival the season before last in a campaign that stretched his unbeaten run to seven, but scored only once last term in what was a frustrating campaign; spent last summer as hot ante-post favourite for the World Hurdle, but after beating Blazing Bailey to win a Grade 2 at Cheltenham on his return in December, he did his pretensions to that crown no favours when beaten a distance by that same rival back at Cheltenham the following month (on unsuitably testing ground) before falling at the third in the race itself, for which he was sent off 2-1 favourite; headed to Aintree after that, but found course specialist Mighty Man too hot to handle in the Grade 2 Liverpool Hurdle and went down by 13l, failing to match the winner's speed in the closing stages after looking a potent threat on the turn into the home straight (3m1f, good, 6 ran); still only lightly raced, stays over hurdles and could yet banish the memory of that downbeat campaign, although the air of invincibility that once surrounded him has now been shattered; would be interesting if dropped back to 2m. *'He just can't pick up on heavy ground.' (Jonjo O'Neill, trainer)*

1051 Blazing Bailey

5 b g Mister Baileys - Wannaplantatree (Niniski)

A King   Three Line Whip

PLACINGS: 11232/012413F-   **RPR 163+h**

Starts	1st	2nd	3rd	4th	Win & Pl
12	4	3	2	1	£131,858

	1/07	Chel	3m Cls1 Gd2 Hdl heavy............................£34,212
147	11/06	Hayd	2m Cls2 127-147 Hdl 4yo Hcap gd-sft £19,518
	2/06	Font	2m2¹/₂f Cls4 Nov Hdl 4yo good £3,253
	1/06	Font	2m2¹/₂f Cls4 Nov Hdl 4yo soft.....................£4,554

Smart juvenile hurdler two seasons ago (third in the Triumph Hurdle), and developed into a leading stayer in open company last term; won over 2m on his reappearance before good efforts in defeat in the Relkeel Hurdle at Cheltenham (second to Black Jack Ketchum) and Long Walk Hurdle at Ascot (3¹/₂l fourth behind Mighty Man); really announced himself, though, with a magnificent victory in the Cleeve Hurdle at Cheltenham in January, where he devoured the closing hill to beat Inglis Drever by 4l; was getting 8lb from the runner-up that day, and could not confirm the placings on better ground and at level weights in the World Hurdle in March, finishing 4³/4l third behind Howard Johnson's ace (3m, good to soft, 14 ran); took quite a heavy fall at Aintree on his final outing; will return this season for the top staying hurdles, and with another year on his back should again be a contender when the ground is soft.

1052 Blue Shark (Fr)

5 b/br g Cadoudal - Sweet Beauty (Tip Moss)

N Henderson   Trevor Hemmings

PLACINGS: 5/23311/

Starts	1st	2nd	3rd	4th	Win & Pl
6	2	1	2	-	£71,518
	12/05	Chep	2m¹/₂f Cls1 Gd1 Hdl 3yo gd-sft		........£28,510
	11/05	Autl	2m2f List Hdl 3yo Hcap v soft		........£25,532

Ex-French hurdler who made a huge impression on his sole British start in December 2005, but has been off the track since with knee problems; had won in Listed company for Bernard Secly before his switch to Nicky Henderson, and announced himself as a serious Triumph Hurdle prospect by romping away with the Grade 1 Finale Hurdle at Chepstow, racing up with the pace throughout and drawing clear from 2 out to beat Turko by 8l (classy sorts Fair Along and Twist Magic comfortably seen off); subsequent absence is an obvious cause for concern, but he has the potential to make up into a very interesting novice chase prospect; yet to race on anything like fast ground, and likely to remain best with plenty of cut, and over further than 2m.

1053 Blue Splash (Fr)

7 b g Epervier Bleu - Harpyes (Quart De Vin)

P Bowen   Walters Plant Hire Ltd

PLACINGS: 73543/122141-   RPR **141+c**

Starts	1st	2nd	3rd	4th	Win & Pl
11	3	2	2	2	£32,133
	2/07	Newc	3m Cls2 Nov Ch heavy		........£12,526
	1/07	Extr	3m1¹/₂f Cls3 Nov Ch heavy		........£7,807
103	10/06	Aint	3m¹/₂f Cls3 Nov 90-105 Hdl Hcap good		........£6,506

Brother to Feltham winner Ungaro, and a promising long-distance chaser in his own right; won two heavy-ground novice events last season, beating Dream Alliance by 12l at Exeter on New Year's Day, and landing the odds in all-the-way fashion at Newcastle in February, despite jumping out to his right; took on better rivals on good to soft going in a Grade 2 event at Wetherby in between, and probably posted a similar level of form in finishing 8¹/4l fourth behind Heltornic; real stayer who ought to be contesting some good handicap chases over 3m-plus this winter, and his trainer is keen on a tilt at the Welsh National at Chepstow over Christmas; has won on good ground over hurdles.

1054 Blueberry Boy (Ire)

8 b g Old Vic - Glenair Lady (Golden Love)

P Stafford (Ir)   Joseph E Keeling

PLACINGS: P133/211240/1436F-   RPR **140c**

Starts	1st	2nd	3rd	4th	Win & Pl
15	4	2	3	2	£79,303
	11/06	Punc	2m Nov Gd2 Ch soft		........£26,938
	12/05	Punc	2m Nov List Hdl soft		........£18,468
	11/05	Punc	2m Hdl soft		........£7,841
	12/04	Leop	2m NHF 5yo sft-hvy		........£6,083

Former useful novice hurdler who ran well in some of the top novice chases in Ireland last season; made the best possible start to his chasing career by winning a Grade 2 event over 2m at Punchestown last November, staying on well to beat Gemini Lucy by 2¹/2l; not disgraced in Grade 1 company at Fairyhouse next time, when 13l fourth behind Cailin Alainn (2m4f, heavy, 10 ran), and that was followed by an 11l third to Schindlers Hunt in another Grade 1 at Leopardstown (2m1f, soft to heavy, 9 ran); suffered a bad overreach when disappointing on his next run at Navan, and fell on his final start at the Punchestown festival; will be starting in handicaps at around 2m.

1055 Blythe Knight (Ire)

7 ch g Selkirk - Blushing Barada (Blushing Groom)

J Quinn   Maxilead Limited

PLACINGS: 1321-   RPR **151+h**

Starts	1st	2nd	3rd	4th	Win & Pl
4	2	1	1	-	£37,356
	4/07	Aint	2m¹/₂f Cls1 Nov Gd2 Hdl good		........£31,361
	11/06	Bang	2m1f Cls4 Nov Hdl gd-sft		........£2,928

Classy sort on the Flat, and put his speed to good use in novice hurdles last season; posted much his best effort when scarcely coming off the bridle to beat Osana by 2l in a Grade 2 event at Aintree's Grand National meeting (2m1¹/2f, good, 8 ran); that was a marked step up on his previous efforts, but he continued to thrive on the Flat, and won a Group 3 event at Epsom on Derby day; best hurdles form so far has been on speed-favouring tracks, so it's likely that connections will want to see how he handles Cheltenham before firming up plans to train him for the Champion Hurdle.

1056 Bob Bob Bobbin

8 gr g Bob Back - Absalom's Lady (Absalom)

C Tizzard   Mrs Sarah Tizzard

PLACINGS: 233114/5U34112P/14P-   RPR **152+c**

Starts	1st	2nd	3rd	4th	Win & Pl
20	6	3	3	4	£63,632
134	11/06	Bang	3m¹/₂f Cls3 114-135 Ch Hcap gd-sft		........£10,141
	1/06	Chep	3m Cls3 Nov Ch soft		........£7,701
	1/06	Chep	3m2¹/₂f Cls4 Ch soft		........£4,127
	2/05	Wwck	2m3f Cls4 Nov Hdl 4-7yo heavy		........£3,991
	1/05	Folk	2m6¹/₂f Cls4 Nov Hdl soft		........£3,484
	10/04	Chep	2m¹/₂f Cls6 NHF 4-6yo soft		........£1,974

Reliable and consistent staying chaser; looked an

improved horse last season when winning at Bangor, showing plenty of resolution to see off Distant Thunder, and then stepped up on that form when fourth in the Rehearsal Chase at Newcastle off a career-high mark of 142, beaten 3l by Neptune Collonges (3m, good to soft, 11 ran); Welsh National was next on the agenda, but he injured his withers at the 11th hour and didn't return until out of his depth and pulled up behind Kauto Star in the Cheltenham Gold Cup; has reportedly made a full recovery and the Rehearsal and Welsh National are again the plan; stays 3m3f and probably further, and very effective in the mud, although left-handed tracks suit him best.

1057 Bob Hall (Ire)

6 b g Sadler's Well - Be My Hope (Be My Native)
J O'Neill   John P McManus

PLACINGS: 8/121/31522-   **RPR 148+c**

Starts	1st	2nd	3rd	4th	Win & Pl
9	3	3	1	-	£43,554
12/06	Leic	2m4¹/₂f Cls4 Ch good			£5,205
1/06	Navn	2m Nov Hdl sft-hvy			£6,672
11/05	Fair	2m2f Mdn Hdl 4yo heavy			£5,881

Lightly raced, unexposed and interesting chaser at around 2m5f; won only one of his five races over fences last season after arriving from David Wachman in Ireland, but there was a lot to like about the way he hammered Scottish Champion Hurdle winner Genghis by 27l at Leicester in December, jumping precisely and coming home as he liked; didn't win again, but he finished a very promising second in L'Antartique in the Jewson handicap at the Cheltenham Festival, failing by only 2l to reel in the winner (2m5f, good to soft, 19 ran); starts the season rated 8lb higher than he was there, but is very likely to be ahead of the handicapper and is open to plenty more improvement after only five starts over fences; looks an ideal sort for the Paddy Power Gold Cup, the first bonus race in this competition.

1058 Bobs Pride (Ire)

5 b g Marju - Vyatka (Lion Cavern)
D Weld (Ir)   R Blacoe

PLACINGS: 52/121d411-   **RPR 139+h**

Starts	1st	2nd	3rd	4th	Win & Pl
8	3	2	-	1	£57,382
124	4/07	Punc	2m 105-133 Hdl Hcap good		£32,990
114	4/07	Fair	2m Nov 86-116 Hdl Hcap good		£9,897
	9/06	List	2m Mdn Hdl 4yo sft-hvy		£6,672

Group 3 winner in his Flat days and has taken well to hurdles; decent form in the mud before Christmas, including when 1³/₄l runner-up to subsequent Grade 1 winner Hide The Evidence at Roscommon (2m, soft to heavy, 18 ran), but that was surpassed in two runs on good ground after a four-month break; 3l defeat of Top The Charts at Fairyhouse was followed by an equally comfortable

victory off a 10lb higher mark in a valuable handicap hurdle at the Punchestown festival, where he was always travelling strongly before coming away to beat Bien Bronze by 3l (probably value for more); starts the campaign 14lb higher again, but has bags of scope, and likely to thrive at around 2m on decent ground. *'He's rapidly improving and he's going to go right to the top over hurdles.' (Dermot Weld, trainer)*

1059 Border Castle

6 b g Grand Lodge - Tempting Prospect (Shirley Heights)
Miss V Williams   D E Harrison

PLACINGS: 13244/1P5-0   **RPR 133+h**

Starts	1st	2nd	3rd	4th	Win & Pl
9	2	1	1	2	£22,348
118	12/06	Chel	2m1f Cls3 109-135 Hdl Hcap soft		£12,526
	12/05	Hayd	2m Cls3 Nov Hdl soft		£5,400

Useful handicap hurdler; produced a career-best on reappearance, making the most of a relatively lenient mark at Cheltenham in December when given a patient ride, taking it up at the last and keeping on in good style to beat Pilca by 3¹/₂l; ran a stinker next time, but much better on his return from a two-and-a-half-month break when – blinkered first time – he stayed on strongly to finish 11¹/₂l fifth behind the progressive Gaspara in Sandown's Imperial Cup (2m1/₂f, heavy, 17 ran); blinkers left off when well down the field in the Swinton Hurdle at Haydock in May; goes well in the mud and very well when fresh (would be interesting if blinkered again).

1060 Bothar Na (Ire)

8 ch g Mister Lord - Country Course (Crash Course)
W Mullins (Ir)   Mrs Michael O'Dwyer

PLACINGS: 44/55115UPP8-6642292   **RPR 145+c**

Starts	1st	2nd	3rd	4th	Win & Pl
24	5	3	-	5	£114,888
127	9/06	List	3m 111-135 Ch Hcap sft-hvy		£62,328
121	8/06	Tral	2m4f 102-130 Ch Hcap yield		£20,203
	5/05	Kbgn	3m1f Hunt Ch soft		£4,411
	5/05	Wxfd	3m Hunt Ch gd-fm		£4,411
	5/05	Limk	3m Hunt Ch soft		£4,901

Handicap chaser who has made the trip to Aintree in the last two seasons, and the Grand National is likely to be on the agenda again this term; was in good form last autumn, winning at Tralee (fortunate to score, left in the lead at the last) and in the Kerry National at Listowel, where he stayed on really well in testing ground to beat Pearly Jack by 2l; ran okay when fifth in the Munster National at Limerick (3m, yielding to soft, 11 ran), but form then took a bit of a nosedive, including when failing to complete in the Hennessy and the Grand National (fourth in the Fox Hunters' in 2006) and down the field in the Galway Plate; starts the season on a good mark of 133 (last win came off 127).

1061 Boychuk (Ire)

6 b g Insan - Golden Flower (Highland Chieftain)

P Hobbs
Mrs D L Whateley

PLACINGS: 911113343/31212253-
RPR **147**+c

Starts	1st	2nd	3rd	4th	Win & Pl
17	6	3	5	1	£98,311

11/06	Newb	3m Cls1 Nov Gd2 Ch gd-sft	£19,957
10/06	Extr	2m7¹/₂f Cls4 Ch gd-fm	£4,554
11/05	Chel	2m¹/₂f Cls1 Nov Gd2 Hdl gd-sft	£17,106
10/05	Extr	2m1f Cls4 Nov Hdl gd-sft	£4,264
10/05	Extr	2m1f Cls4 Nov Hdl firm	£4,290
7/05	Klny	2m1f NHF 4yo firm	£4,411

Smart novice chaser last season, and one for handicaps at around 3m this winter; high point came when beating Gungadu by 1¹/₂l in a Grade 2 event at Newbury's Hennessy meeting, where he needed to be hard driven in the straight, but responded well to get on top on the long run-in (3m, good to soft, 5 ran); failed to win again, but was highly tried on occasions, and didn't run far below his Newbury best when 10l second to Ungaro in the Grade 1 Feltham Chase at Kempton on Boxing Day (3m, good to soft, 6 ran); not as good in the spring following a mid-season break (twice beaten at odds-on), but might be worth a second look for the Hennessy given his course form, although his stamina for the job remains open to question.

1062 Briareus

7 ch g Halling - Lower The Tone (Phone Trick)

A Balding
Miss E J Lambourne

PLACINGS: 211/2016/21-
RPR **144**+c

Starts	1st	2nd	3rd	4th	Win & Pl
9	4	3	-	-	£82,968

12/06	Asct	2m3f Cls1 Nov Gd2 Ch good	£22,536
2/06	Winc	2m1 Gd2 Hdl gd-sft	£39,914
4/05	Newb	2m¹/₂f Cls4 Nov Hdl good	£4,602
3/05	Kemp	2m Cls3 Nov Hdl gd-sft	£5,170

Classy hurdler (sixth to Brave Inca in the 2006 Champion Hurdle) whose novice chase campaign came to an end just as it was getting going last term; second to Killaghy Castle first time out, but stepped up on that to win a Grade 2 novice chase at Ascot in December, where he shrugged off a blunder at the first to make almost all the running and beat Knight Legend and Royal Shakespeare by 3l and a short head (first run over as far as 2m3f, classy Natal back in fourth); was touted as a potential Arkle candidate, but suffered a suspensory strain and was not seen out again; reportedly on the way back now, and a mark of 144 looks something to go to war with in good handicap chases (150 over hurdles); comes alive on good ground. *'He's much better in a smaller field with a bit of daylight.' (Andrew Balding, trainer)*

1063 Briery Fox (Ire)

9 ch g Phardante - Briery Gale (Strong Gale)

H Daly
Vicky Reed, Helen Plumbly, Jane Trafford

PLACINGS: 2/11413/42102/1843B-
RPR **139**+c

Starts	1st	2nd	3rd	4th	Win & Pl
14	4	2	2	3	£40,085

128	10/06	Worc	2m4¹/₂f Cls3 112-129 Ch Hcap gd-sft	£13,012
	12/05	Fknm	3m¹/₂f Cls3 Nov Ch good	£8,073
	2/05	Fknm	2m4f Cls3 Nov Hdl 4-7yo good	£5,528
	11/04	Winc	2m Cls6 NHF 4-6yo good	£2,268

Lightly raced handicap chaser, ideally suited by 2m4f-3m on decent ground; made a winning reappearance last October in a handicap at Worcester, beating the in-form Nayodabayo by 1¹/₂l; disappointing on his next two starts, so was given a mid-season break, and returned with a cracking 6³/₄l third behind Rambling Minster at odds of 40-1 in the valuable Agfa Diamond Handicap Chase at Sandown in February (3m¹/₂f, good to soft, 18 ran); rested again before a crack at the Topham Chase at Aintree, but was brought down at the third; has shown he can compete for good prizes off his current mark (134), and could pop up in a big race when fresh and racing on decent ground.

1064 Buena Vista (Ire)

6 b g In The Wings - Park Special (Relkino)

D Pipe
M Archer & the late Jean Broadhurst

PLACINGS: 6416/11112336/116F-
RPR **149**c

Starts	1st	2nd	3rd	4th	Win & Pl
16	7	1	2	1	£80,500

	1/07	Hrfd	2m Cls3 Nov Ch heavy	£6,376
	12/06	Extr	2m3¹/₂f Cls2 Nov Ch soft	£13,012
128	7/05	MRas	2m1¹/₂f Cls2 108-131 Hdl Hcap good	£20,300
	6/05	NAbb	2m1f Cls3 Nov Hdl gd-fm	£5,538
	6/05	Strf	2m¹/₂f Cls3 Nov Hdl gd-fm	£6,125
	5/05	Hrfd	2m1f Cls4 Nov Hdl gd-fm	£3,936
	1/05	Donc	2m¹/₂f Cls6 Mdn NHF 4-6yo good	£2,408

Former smart hurdler (finished third in the Supreme Novices') who proved himself just as effective over fences last season and should now do well in handicap company between 2m and 2m4f; won novice chases either side of the new year, doing slightly better at Hereford in January when just coming out on top after a pulsating battle with Chief Yeoman over the last and up the home straight; below-par against the best 2m novices in the Arkle at Cheltenham when sixth behind My Way De Solzen, and is almost certainly better than that; could well prove best when there is not quite so much emphasis on speed, and would be most interesting if lining up for the Paddy Power Gold Cup. *"He basically wants a fast-run race on decent ground." (David Pipe, trainer)*

1065 Burntoakboy

9 b g Sir Harry Lewis - Sainte Martine (Martinmas)

R Newland   Dr R D P & Mrs L J Newland

PLACINGS: 0327449/892352117-94   **RPR 138+h**

Starts		1st	2nd	3rd	4th	Win & Pl
35		4	4	3	8	£75,311
128	3/07	Chel	2m5f Cls1 Gd3 127-151 Hdl Hcap gd-sft £45,616
119	1/07	Leic	2m4¹/₂f Cls3 98-119 Hdl Hcap soft £6,263
	3/04	Punc	2m Mdn Hdl soft £5,839
	7/03	Klny	2m1f NHF 5-7yo sft-hvy £4,032

Formerly a moderate sort on the Flat in Ireland, but transformed by his new trainer into a very smart handicap hurdler at around 2m5f last season; arrived at the Cheltenham Festival for the Coral Cup on the back of an emphatic success at Leicester from a mark of 119, and showed that he was still very well treated when defying a rise of 9lb to hand a 3l beating to Powerstation, with a further 5l back to the third; raised another 12lb for that fine effort, and failed to trouble the judge in two further starts over hurdles, and one over fences at Uttoxeter in May; expected by his trainer to make his mark as a novice chaser, although his two forays in that sphere have offered little encouragement, and he would probably struggle off his revised mark if tried again over hurdles.

1066 Butler's Cabin (Fr)

7 b g Poliglote - Strictly Cool (Bering)

J O'Neill   John P McManus

PLACINGS: 22/4337/311143011-   **RPR 145+c**

Starts		1st	2nd	3rd	4th	Win & Pl
15		5	2	4	2	£167,223
135	4/07	Fair	3m5f 131-159 Ch Hcap good £95,608
	3/07	Chel	4m1f Cls2 Nov Am Ch gd-sft £30,010
112	10/06	Chel	2m4¹/₂f Cls3 106-132 Ch Hcap good £10,960
112	10/06	Aint	2m4f Cls3 98-120 Ch Hcap good £9,998
105	10/06	Hrfd	2m3f Cls4 85-110 Ch Hcap gd-fm £5,205

Very smart handicap chaser who found plenty of improvement in the spring for a step up to extreme distances and looks tailor-made for races like the Welsh National; won three on the bounce last October at around 2m4f and ran well in fourth behind stablemate Exotic Dancer in the Paddy Power Gold Cup, but really came into his own when stepped up in trip; sent off at 33-1 for the 4m1f National Hunt Chase at the Cheltenham Festival, but belied those odds with a ³/₄l defeat of Character Building, who had won two of his previous three races; collapsed with oxygen deficiency after that battling win, but bounced back less than a month later to win the Irish Grand National from a 12lb higher mark, holding Nine De Sivola by 1l; upped another 14lb for that success, so far from well treated, but is still young and lightly raced and so open to further improvement. *'He's a superb jumper.' (Jonjo O'Neill, trainer)*

1067 Bywell Beau (Ire)

8 b g Lord Americo - Early Dalus (Mandalus)

G A Charlton   W F Trueman

PLACINGS: 3/6422S5P/203121147-   **RPR 147+h**

Starts		1st	2nd	3rd	4th	Win & Pl
24		3	5	4	4	£35,285
	3/07	Kels	2m2f Cls1 Nov Gd2 Hdl heavy £19,957
	2/07	Kels	2m¹/₂f Cls4 Nov Hdl soft £2,602
	12/06	Kels	2m¹/₂f Cls4 Mdn Hdl heavy £2,535

Former long-standing maiden hurdler who improved out of all recognition last term when dropped back to 2m and allowed to bowl along in front; won three times by very wide margins at Kelso, most notably beating Mohayer by 23l in an admittedly weak Grade 2 contest in March (2m2f, heavy, 9 ran); faced much sterner opposition in another Grade 2 at Aintree the following month, but certainly wasn't disgraced, leading until two out and keeping on once headed to finish 15¹/₂l fourth behind Champion Hurdle prospect Blythe Knight (2m¹/₂f, good, 8 ran); below par in Grade 1 company at the Punchestown festival, when unable to lead and fading to finish seventh behind Clopf; goes chasing now, and could easily make up into a contender for Graded events, possibly even the Arkle; effective from 2m-2m4f and handles soft ground well.

1068 Cailin Alainn (Ire)

8 br m Mister Lord - Royal Toombeola (Royal Fountain)

C Byrnes (Ir)   Dewdrop Racing Syndicate

PLACINGS: 70311/1111FF-   **RPR 149+c**

Starts		1st	2nd	3rd	4th	Win & Pl
11		6	-	1	-	£137,634
	12/06	Leop	3m Nov Gd1 Ch heavy £33,621
	12/06	Fair	2m4f Nov Gd1 Ch heavy £44,828
	11/06	Clon	2m4f List Ch heavy £17,959
	10/06	Cork	2m4f Nov Ch good £11,673
	4/06	Fair	2m4f Nov Gd3 Hdl gd-yld £23,346
	4/06	Tram	2m Mdn Hdl good £5,719

Classy mare who took charge of some of Ireland's top novice chases in the first half of the season; won four on the bounce, culminating in heavy-ground Grade 1 successes in December at Fairyhouse (beat Schindlers Hunt by ³/₄l) and Leopardstown (comfortable 4¹/₂l triumph over Patsy Hall); had her sights raised further when taking on established aces in the Letheby & Christopher Chase at Cheltenham in January, and was still travelling well with the likes of Exotic Dancer and Our Vic when crashing out at the third-last; returned to Cheltenham in March for a crack at Denman in the Royal & SunAlliance Chase, but fell again, this time at about halfway; a bit to prove, but still unexposed, and a mark of 142 gives her every chance of doing some damage in good handicaps; equally at home on good and heavy ground.

1069 Callherwhatulike (Ire)

6 b m Old Vic - Fleece Alley (Brush Aside)

R Tyner (Ir)   Fifteen To Eight Syndicate

PLACINGS: P21158/422212-   **RPR 137**h

Starts	1st	2nd	3rd	4th	Win & Pl
9	2	4		1	£27,198
	1/07	Navn	2m7f Mdn Hdl heavy		..........£5,603
	3/06	Gowr	2m2f NHF yield		..........£4,766

Very consistent in bumpers and novice hurdles last
season and showed considerable improvement
towards the end of the campaign; string of
frustrating runner-up spots before the turn of the
year was followed by a breakthrough at Navan,
when battling gamely in the heavy ground to beat
Bill's Folly by 2l; better again came a month later
at Naas when, in Grade 2 company, she was the
only one to make a race of it with Kazal
(completing a four-timer and also subsequent
winner), eventually giving best by 1^1/4l but with
16l back to the third (2m4f, heavy, 10 ran);
proved her versatility as regards trip, effective
between 2m2f and 2m7f, but has shown definite
preference for testing ground; goes over fences
now and may be force to be reckoned with in
mares-only races.

1070 Cane Brake (Ire)

8 b g Sadler's Wells - Be My Hope (Be My Native)

T Taaffe (Ir)   Mount Temple Two Racing Synd

PLACINGS: 1146/424PP58P/2115P-   **RPR 161**c

Starts	1st	2nd	3rd	4th	Win & Pl
25	7	3	2	3	£209,475
142	12/06	Leop	3m 114-142 Ch Hcap heavy		..........£74,897
129	11/06	Navn	3m 119-147 Ch Hcap soft		..........£44,897
	12/04	Limk	2m4f Nov Gd2 Ch heavy		..........£24,331
	12/04	Navn	2m4f Nov Ch soft		..........£13,754
	11/04	Cork	2m4f Nov Ch soft		..........£11,920
	10/04	Gway	2m6f Ch heavy		..........£9,169
	1/04	Fair	2m4f Mdn Hdl 5yo soft		..........£6,317

High-class staying chaser who was completely
revitalised by a change of stables last season;
landed a valuable handicap at Navan off a mark of
129 in November, and then defied a 13lb rise in
desperate conditions in the Paddy Power Chase at
Leopardstown, powering home under top weight
to beat Ballistraw by ^{1}/2l; given a break, he
reappeared in the Cheltenham Gold Cup and ran
the race of his life to finish fifth behind Kauto Star,
staying on strongly up the hill to be beaten only 11l
(3m2^1/2f, good to soft, 18 ran), suggesting that
he has a future in top conditions chases; made no
show when pulled up in the Irish National on
his final outing, but the ground was a bit fast for
him; worth his place in all the big races over
3m-plus, especially when the mud is flying, and
there will be plenty of options for him in
Ireland; is surely weighted out of handicaps now,
though.

1071 Caracciola (Ger)

10 b g Lando - Capitolina (Empery)

N Henderson   P J D Pottinger

PLACINGS: P3P/019585/820465-00   **RPR 142**h

Starts	1st	2nd	3rd	4th	Win & Pl
30	6	4	3	1	£101,443
132	10/05	Ling	2m^1/2f Cls3 110-135 Hdl Hcap soft		..........£10,192
	12/03	Kemp	2m Cls2 Nov Ch good		..........£10,496
	12/03	Hayd	2m Cls3 Nov Ch soft		..........£8,988
122	11/03	Sand	2m^1/2f Cls3 98-124 Hdl Hcap good		..........£5,499
	2/03	Newb	2m^1/2f Cls3 Nov Hdl good		..........£7,384
	12/02	Newb	2m^1/2f Cls3 Mdn Hdl good		..........£4,739

Smart handicapper over both hurdles and fences,
but campaigned exclusively over the smaller
obstacles last season; didn't win, but was placed in
a valuable handicap at Ascot in October (2l second
to Desert Quest, 2m, good to firm, 15 ran) and the
Totesport Trophy at Newbury in February (3l fourth
to Heathcote, 2m1/2f, soft, 20 ran); also ran a
cracker in the County Hurdle at the Cheltenham
Festival, where he was hard ridden to jump the last
upsides the leader, and kept on well to finish a
close sixth behind Pedrobob in a blanket finish
(2m1f, good to soft, 28 ran); well below that form
in the Scottish Champion Hurdle and Swinton
Hurdle, but that should ensure he starts the new
season on a fair mark; can continue to acquit
himself well in big-field handicaps if time doesn't
catch up with him.

1072 Caribou (Fr)

5 b g Epervier Bleu - Cardoudalle (Cadoudal)

O Sherwood   It Wasn't Us

PLACINGS: 0141/322411-   **RPR 131+**c

Starts	1st	2nd	3rd	4th	Win & Pl
10	4	2	1	2	£32,434
	4/07	Prth	3m Cls2 Nov Ch soft		..........£11,430
	2/07	Leic	2m Cls4 Ch soft		..........£5,070
	4/06	MRas	2m1^1/2f Cls4 Nov Hdl 4yo soft		..........£4,554
	12/05	Leic	2m Cls3 Nov Hdl 3yo soft		..........£5,673

Smart novice chaser last season, and potentially
a decent staying handicapper; educated in small-
field novice and beginners' chases before getting
off the mark at the fifth attempt in a four-runner
event at Leicester, where he stayed on resolutely to
hold off Spidam by 2^1/2l; ridden with more
restraint than usual when tackling 3m for the
first time on his final start at Perth in April, and
seemed to relish the test of stamina and testing
conditions as he outstayed Lankawi to score by
3^1/2l; has gained all four of his wins in soft
ground, and connections are eyeing an audacious
tilt at the Hennessy with him. *'Now we know
he stays 3m-plus, it has opened up
loads of options.' (Oliver Sherwood,
trainer)*

1073 Carthalawn (Ire)

6 ch g Foxhound - Pohutakawa (Affirmed)

C Byrnes (Ir)   Joe Soap Syndicate

PLACINGS: 52222210/53F173F1F3-   **RPR 147c**

Starts	1st	2nd	3rd	4th	Win & Pl
22	4	8	3		£50,868
113	2/07	Naas	2m 100-130 Ch Hcap sft-hvy		£8,171
	10/06	Gowr	2m1f Ch gd-yld		£6,672
	4/06	Cork	2m Mdn Hdl 4-5yo gd-yld		£5,719
	8/05	Tral	2m NHF 4yo yld-sft		£4,411

Smart 2m chaser who was much improved in the spring following a mid-season break; gained an easy success at Naas in February, and then ran a good race in the Grand Annual at the Cheltenham Festival, where he was still travelling well about 5l off the leaders when making a mistake and coming down at the third-last; departed too soon there to be sure how he would have fared, but probably would have gone very close on the evidence of his final outing, when 6$^{1}/_{2}$l third behind Another Promise in a Grade 1 novice chase at the Punchestown festival in April (2m, good, 7 ran); raised to an official mark of 140 for the start of this season (only 110 over hurdles), and sure to be campaigned with handicaps in mind this winter.

1074 Casey Jones (Ire)

6 b g Oscar - Arborfield Brook (Over The River)

N Meade (Ir)   Ms Gillian Burke

PLACINGS: 1/51223531-   **RPR 132+h**

Starts	1st	2nd	3rd	4th	Win & Pl
9	3	2	2	-	£35,774
	4/07	Punc	3m Nov Hdl good		£10,997
	11/06	DRoy	2m6f Mdn Hdl yld-sft		£7,148
	4/06	Gowr	2m NHF yld-sft		£4,289

Decent hurdler with the scope to make up into a smart staying chaser this season; ran well in Graded novice events over timber throughout last winter, notably finishing 9l second to Footy Facts at Navan in November (2m4f, soft, 9 ran), 6$^{1}/_{4}$l third behind Kazal at Naas in January (2m4f, soft to heavy, 8 ran) and 6$^{1}/_{4}$l third behind stablemate Aitmatov at Fairyhouse in April (2m4f, good, 8 ran); stepped up to 3m for the first time at the Punchestown festival, and benefited from having his sights lowered to non-Graded company when beating Emma Jane by $^{1}/_{2}$l (good, 24 ran); expected to prove better over fences.

1075 Catch Me (Ger)

5 br g Law Society - Calcida (Konigsstuhl)

E O'Grady (Ir)   J P O'Shea

PLACINGS: 112U3F-   **RPR 148+h**

Starts	1st	2nd	3rd	4th	Win & Pl
6	2	1	1	-	£30,875
	11/06	Naas	2m Hdl 4yo yld-sft		£6,672
	10/06	Naas	2m Mdn Hdl 4yo soft		£4,766

Smart Flat stayer, who developed into one of

Ireland's leading novice hurdlers last season; won twice at Naas last autumn, but really signalled his promise in the Ballymore Properties Novices' Hurdle at Cheltenham, for which he was sent off at 7-1 and finished third, less than 2l behind Massini's Maguire after being left short of room on the run-in; was in the process of running another cracker in the Grade 1 Champion Novice Hurdle at Punchestown when falling at the last, so has to prove that tumble has not dented his confidence, but will be highly tried this term and capable of notching plenty of points in Graded contests in Ireland during the winter. *'We'll be aiming him at the better hurdle races to see if he is good enough.' (Edward O'Grady, trainer)*

1076 Cave Hill (Ire)

5 b g Dr Massini - Eurogal (Strong Gale)

Miss H Knight   Trevor Hemmings

PLACINGS: 1/1-   **RPR 113b**

Starts	1st	2nd	3rd	4th	Win & Pl
1	1	-	-	-	£1,626
	11/06	Hrfd	2m1f Cls6 NHF 4-6yo soft		£1,627

Former Irish point-to-point winner who won his only start in a bumper for new connections last season; that debut victory came at Hereford last November, where he was sent off an unfancied 16-1 shot, but showed real guts to beat Greenbridge by a head, the pair pulling well clear of the third; second and third boosted the form by winning next time, with Greenbridge going on to contest valuable events at Newbury and Aintree, so the winner was probably an above-average sort; nice prospect for novice hurdles. *'He's a 3m chaser in the making, and it looks to me like he'll go on any ground.' (Henrietta Knight, trainer)*

1077 Celestial Gold (Ire)

9 br g Persian Mews - What A Queen (King's Ride)

D Pipe   D A Johnson

PLACINGS: /2111/13321/1137/U1/

Starts	1st	2nd	3rd	4th	Win & Pl
11	5	1	3	-	£254,116
	4/06	Aint	3m1f Cls1 Gd2 Ch good		£85,530
142	11/04	Newb	3m2$^{1}/_{2}$f Cls3 Gd3 137-163 Ch Hcap good		£69,600
136	11/04	Chel	2m4$^{1}/_{2}$f Cls1 Gd3 134-160 Ch Hcap good		£63,800
	4/04	Chel	3m1$^{1}/_{2}$f Cls2 Nov Ch gd-fm		£11,137
	11/03	Towc	2m6f Cls4 Nov Ch gd-sft		£2,947

Top-class chaser who missed last season with heat in a leg, but would be a major player in the top events at 3m-plus if returning to his best; last seen when earning a Racing Post Rating of 171 with a 7l demolition of former Gold Cup runner-up Take The Stand in the Grade 2 Betfair Bowl at Aintree in April 2006, having unshipped his rider at the half way stage in the Cheltenham showpiece on his previous start; clearly difficult to train having had only 11 career starts, but has achieved plenty for one so lightly raced, including a memorable Paddy Power Gold Cup/Hennessy Gold Cup double in his second season over fences; has a lengthy absence to overcome as well as having to prove that he retains his old ability, but would be a force to be reckoned with if his time on the sidelines has not taken its toll. *'He'll be back for the top-class races this season and is very exciting.' (David Pipe, trainer)*

1078 Celtic Son (Fr)

8 b g Celtic Arms - For Kicks (Top Ville)

D Pipe   D A Johnson

PLACINGS: 12111123P/124420/PP-

Starts	1st	2nd	3rd	4th	Win & Pl
24	7	4	1	3	£82,478
	11/05	Winc	2m5f Cls1 Nov Gd2 Ch good		£19,957
	2/05	Kemp	3m¹/₂f Cls3 Nov Hdl gd-sft		£4,983
121	1/05	Wwck	3m1f Cls2 109-135 Hdl Hcap soft		£14,019
105	1/05	Newb	3m¹/₂f Cls4 84-110 Cond Hdl Hcap gd-sft		£3,780
105	1/05	Tntn	3m¹/₂f Cls4 83-105 Hdl Hcap gd-sft		£3,965
98	1/05	Extr	2m6¹/₂f Cls4 Nov 74-100 Hdl Hcap gd-sft		£3,850
	2/03	Thur	2m NHF 4yo sft-hvy		£3,584

High-class novice chaser in 2005/06, but failed to sparkle in two outings in the second part of last season; pulled up in both the Racing Post Chase and in a speculative crack at the Grand National, looking a shadow of the horse who made a stunning chasing debut at Wincanton in November 2005 with a textbook round of jumping that saw him promoted to the front of the ante-post market for that season's SunAlliance Chase; worth another chance between 2m4f and 3m and remains relatively unexposed, having raced only eight times over fences. *'He's a bit of an in-and-out performer.' (David Pipe, trainer)*

1079 Central House

10 b g Alflora - Fantasy World (Kemal)

D Hughes (Ir)   John F Kenny

PLACINGS: 3113414R3/242326257-   RPR **156+c**

Starts	1st	2nd	3rd	4th	Win & Pl
45	11	13	8	4	£371,723
	2/06	Punc	2m Gd2 Ch yield		£23,795
	12/05	Cork	2m Gd2 Ch heavy		£27,702
	11/05	Navn	2m Gd2 Ch soft		£20,777
	2/05	Naas	2m Gd2 Ch soft		£30,011
	1/05	Fair	2m1f Gd2 Ch heavy		£23,085
	12/04	Leop	2m1f Gd1 Ch soft		£32,042
	12/03	Leop	2m1f Nov Gd1 Ch soft		£42,208
	11/03	Fair	2m1f Ch soft		£8,442
	12/02	Cork	2m Nov Hdl soft		£7,408
	11/02	Clon	2m Mdn Hdl 5yo soft		£3,810
	11/02	Punc	2m NHF 4-5yo soft		£4,445

Solid chaser who has been scrapping it out in Graded events in Ireland and Britain for a number of seasons, but endured his first winless campaign last winter; that was mainly due to the emergence of Nickname, as he finished second to Martin Brassil's ace on no fewer than four occasions; got closest when beaten ³/₄l at Navan last October (2m, yielding to soft, 5 ran), and was subsequently beaten by 14l at Leopardstown's Christmas

meeting, 7l at Punchestown in February and 13l back at Navan over 2m4f in March; hard to see him winning a Grade 1 nowadays, but capable of winning further down the ladder, although he will inevitably bump into Nickname a lot of the time; has gained all his wins at around 2m on soft ground.

1080 Cerium (Fr)

6 b g Vaguely Pleasant - Tantatura (Akarad)

P Nicholls   B Fulton, T Hayward, S Fisher & L Brady

PLACINGS: 2/119148/11310P/19P-   RPR **154+c**

Starts	1st	2nd	3rd	4th	Win & Pl
16	7	1	1	1	£118,646
144	11/06	Asct	2m3f Cls1 Gd2 128-146 Ch Hcap soft		£39,914
139	2/06	Winc	2m Cls2 Nov 122-142 Ch Hcap good		£12,642
	11/05	Aint	2m Cls2 Nov Ch gd-sft		£10,451
	10/05	Wwck	2m¹/₂f Cls3 Nov Ch good		£7,101
	2/05	Winc	2m Cls3 Nov Hdl gd-sft		£5,184
	11/04	Chel	2m¹/₂f Cls1 Nov Gd2 Hdl 3yo good		£17,400
	10/04	Kemp	2m Cls3 Mdn Hdl 3yo gd-sft		£9,329

Formerly a smart 2m novice chaser who bounced back to form at the start of last season having disappointed at the end of his previous campaign; showed the benefit of a wind operation to score on his return to action in a Grade 2 limited handicap at Ascot in November, where he hit the front two out and stayed on well to beat Knowhere by 2¹/₂l; failed to spark on his other two starts, however, beating only three home in the Boylesports.com Gold Cup at Cheltenham before pulling up in the Grade 1 Ascot Chase; clearly talented on his day, but hard to predict and a rating of 154 (10lb higher than at the start of last season) will not make things particularly easy.

1081 Character Building (Ire)

7 ch g Accordion - Mrs Jones (Roselier)

J Quinn   Mrs E Wright

PLACINGS: 322241/21412P-   RPR **141+c**

Starts	1st	2nd	3rd	4th	Win & Pl
12	3	5	1	2	£31,131
120	2/07	MRas	2m4f Cls3 Nov 96-120 Ch Hcap soft		£9,759
	12/06	Wwck	3m2f Cls4 Ch soft		£3,904
	4/06	Sedg	2m4f Cls4 Nov Hdl gd-fm		£3,253

Progressive novice chaser last season, and a candidate for good long-distance handicaps; looked a natural over fences when winning at Warwick and Market Rasen, but his main target was the 4m1f National Hunt Chase at the Cheltenham Festival; started 7-1 there, and looked the likely winner when he challenged at the last, but threw away his chance by hanging right on the run-in and had to give best to subsequent Irish National winner Butler's Cabin; started 6-1 for the Scottish National the following month, but ran a stinker and was pulled up (hated the fast ground); can be expected to put that run behind him when encountering easier conditions this season.

1082 Chelsea Harbour (Ire)

7 b g Old Vic - Jennyellen (Phardante)

T Mullins (Ir)   Mrs Paul Duffin

PLACINGS: 626610U2/178F4114U0-   RPR **136**c

Starts	1st	2nd	3rd	4th	Win & Pl
21	4	2	-	2	£54,043
	1/07	Naas	3m Nov Gd2 Ch heavy		£24,193
109	1/07	Naas	2m4f 95-116 Ch Hcap sft-hvy		£8,171
	5/06	Punc	2m4f Hdl soft		£8,101
108	2/06	Thur	2m6f 79-109 Hdl Hcap yld-sft		£5,957

Stepped up on his hurdling form in his first season chasing, and appeals as the sort to fare well in staying handicaps; took time to find his feet over fences, scoring on his fifth attempt in a Naas handicap, and followed that up by winning a Grade 2 at the same track, staying on dourly to beat O'Muircheartaigh by 5^1/2l (3m, heavy, 8 ran); upped to Grade 1 company and not entirely disgraced when fourth of 10 behind Mister Top Notch in the Dr PJ Moriarty Novice Chase (2m5f, heavy) at Leopardstown, outpaced before keeping on over a trip on the short side; let down by jumping in the SunAlliance Chase and then may have found ground on the fast side in the Irish National. *'His spring target is either the Irish or Grand National.' (Thomas Mullins, trainer)*

1083 Chief Dan George (Ire)

7 b g Lord Americo - Colleen Donn (Le Moss)

J Moffatt   Maurice W Chapman

PLACINGS: 692P422/3334F111181-   RPR **156**h

Starts	1st	2nd	3rd	4th	Win & Pl
23	5	3	5	4	£101,605
	4/07	Aint	3m^1/zf Cls1 Nov Gd1 Hdl good		£54,169
	2/07	Hayd	2m7^1/zf Cls1 Nov Gd2 Hdl heavy		£17,186
	2/07	Weth	3m1f Cls1 Nov Gd2 Hdl gd-sft		£15,473
	12/06	Ayr	2m5^1/zf Cls4 Nov Hdl heavy		£3,083
	12/06	Hexm	3m Cls4 Mdn Hdl heavy		£3,448

High-class novice hurdler last season, and looks the type to develop into a live World Hurdle candidate; made rapid progress since joining current connections in October 2006, his finest moment coming when springing a 20-1 surprise in the Grade 1 Sefton Novices' Hurdle at Aintree in April; scored by 4l from Cheltenham Festival winner Wichita Lineman (Ballymore Properties winner Massini's Maguire another 27l back in fourth), benefiting from a strong pace and leading after the last, having been held up; tweaked a muscle in his quarters when eighth behind Wichita Lineman on his previous start, but had earlier racked up a four-timer, including Grade 2 events at Wetherby and Haydock; revels in a test of stamina and acts very well on heavy ground, and will prove a tough rival granted those conditions. *'He's in great form, and looks in better nick this year than last. We'll start him off in the Great Yorkshire Hurdle, followed by the Long Walk and then the World Hurdle.' (James Moffatt, trainer)*

1084 Chilling Place (Ire)

8 ch g Moscow Society - Ethel's Dream (Relkino)

P Hobbs   M J Tuckey

PLACINGS: 136P/125F01/UF0022-2   RPR **149**c

Starts	1st	2nd	3rd	4th	Win & Pl
19	5	4	1	-	£56,364
	4/06	Extr	2m3^1/zf Cls3 Nov Ch gd-sft		£7,157
	10/05	Extr	2m1^1/zf Cls3 Ch gd-sft		£5,395
	12/04	Chel	2m1f Cls2 Nov Hdl 4-6yo good		£10,092
	11/04	Extr	2m1f Cls3 Nov Hdl gd-sft		£5,785
	10/04	Winc	2m Cls3 Nov Hdl good		£5,135

Winning novice chaser in 2005/06, but jumping problems in the early part of last season saw him revert to hurdles in the second half of the campaign; ran with credit in decent handicaps in the spring, when he battled against a rising mark; 5l second to stablemate French Saulaie at Cheltenham in April (2m5^1/2f, good, 9 ran), and ten days later went down fighting again to Oslot off a 3lb higher mark at Sandown, beaten 1^1/4l (2m4^1/2f, good to firm, 17 ran); up another 3lb, but went closest of all to a deserved win at Haydock in May, when a neck second to Abragante over 2m7^1/2f, the longest trip he has tried (good, 19 ran); that should open up more opportunities, and he could yet improve in handicap hurdles (now rated 144) or chases (142) at around 3m.

1085 Christdalo (Ire)

7 ch m Glacial Storm - Benbradagh Vard (Le Bavard)

D Pipe   D A Johnson

PLACINGS: 81211/1/P1436122-   RPR **129+**h

Starts	1st	2nd	3rd	4th	Win & Pl
9	3	2	1	1	£22,004
	2/07	Folk	2m6^1/zf Cls4 Nov Hdl heavy		£3,578
	12/06	Chep	3m Cls4 Mdn Hdl soft		£3,253
	5/05	Tipp	2m2f NHF yld-sft		£4,901

Multiple Irish point-to-point winner who should do well in mares' only novice chases at around 3m this term; spent last season gaining experience over hurdles, winning twice and reaching the frame on four of her other six starts, doing best of all on her final outing when coming home 6l second to Silver Charmer in a Listed handicap at Cheltenham (2m5^1/2f, good, 18 ran); no surprise to see her notch up a sequence in a division often short of quality.

1086 Church Island (Ire)

8 ch g Erins Isle - Just Possible (Kalaglow)

M Hourigan (Ir)   B J Craig

PLACINGS: 3521111UU21P/797994-   PR **140**c

Starts	1st	2nd	3rd	4th	Win & Pl
30	6	4	1	1	£94,178
	2/06	Navn	3m Nov Gd2 Ch sft-hvy		£23,795
	11/05	Chel	3m^1/zf Cls2 Nov Hdl gd-sft		£10,572
	10/05	Clon	3m Nov Ch soft		£9,311
	10/05	Tipp	2m4f Nov Gd3 Ch yld-sft		£20,777
	9/05	Kbgn	2m4f Ch gd-fm		£5,391
	12/04	Punc	2m Mdn Hdl soft		£6,569

Good novice chaser two seasons ago, when the

pick of his five successes was an 8l defeat of Celtic Son at Cheltenham in November 2005 (3m¹/₂f, good to soft, 7 ran); struggled in handicap company for most of last season, but returned to form on good ground when 4³/₄l fourth behind Butler's Cabin in the Irish Grand National at Fairyhouse in April, putting up a bold effort from the front and still in front jumping the last (3m5f, 29 ran); looks reasonably treated on the pick of his form on decent ground, and could well be aimed at one of the Nationals again.

1087 Clarnazar (Ire)

5 b g Shernazar - Legal Countess (Legal Circles)

N Meade (Ir)   Killcross Syndicate

PLACINGS: P111-   **RPR 110+h**

Starts	1st	2nd	3rd	4th	Win & Pl
2	2	-	-	-	£10,007
	12/06	Limk	2m6f Mdn Hdl yld-sft £6,195
	12/06	Dpat	2m2f NHF 4-7yo sft-hvy £3,812

Promising, unbeaten hurdler whose campaign was cut short by injury midway through last season; had started his career with a 6l bumper success at Downpatrick and a maiden hurdle victory at Limerick on Boxing Day, where despite a slipping saddle he rallied when challenged over the last two to beat Callherwhatulike by ¹/₂l (2m6f, yielding to soft, 18 ran); that form worked out quite well, with plenty of future winners coming out and the runner-up subsequently Grade 2-placed, but he himself went lame and wasn't seen again; lacks experience, but has the scope to go on to better things, either over hurdles or if switched to fences.

1088 Classic Fiddle

5 ch m Classic Cliche - Fiddling The Facts (Orchestra)

N Henderson   Mrs E Roberts

PLACINGS: 11/121-   **RPR 122+h**

Starts	1st	2nd	3rd	4th	Win & Pl
5	4	1	-	-	£12,274
	3/07	Bang	2m1f Cls4 Nov Hdl heavy £3,253
	1/07	Hrfd	2m4f Cls4 Nov Hdl 4-7yo heavy £2,958
	4/06	Chel	2m1f Cls4 NHF 4-6yo good £3,578
	3/06	Plum	2m2f Cls6 Mdn NHF 4-6yo soft................... £1,713

Progressive mare out of former classy staying chaser Fiddling The Facts; has been beaten just once in two bumpers and three novice hurdles, when not surprisingly unable to concede 7lb to subsequent Aintree Hurdle runner-up Gaspara at Chepstow in February (2m4f, soft, 7 ran); got the job done either side of that defeat, beating Trigger The Light by 1¹/₂l in gritty fashion at Hereford, and rounding off with a 23l thumping of Gunnasayso in a moderate heavy-ground race at Bangor in March; has done little wrong, and almost certainly better to come when she tackles fences; not out of the question that she could develop into a SunAlliance contender, having been brought along slowly to date.

1089 Classified (Ire)

11 b g Roselier - Treidlia (Mandalus)

D Pipe   D A Johnson

PLACINGS: 1/2114/9/U11FP21-P63   **RPR 140c**

Starts	1st	2nd	3rd	4th	Win & Pl
24	12	2	1	2	£187,813
	4/07	Chel	3m1¹/₂f Cls2 Nov Ch good £12,526
	12/06	Font	2m6f Cls3 Nov Ch gd-sft........................... £6,506
	12/06	Tntn	2m7¹/₂f Cls4 Ch gd-sft............................... £5,530
	2/03	Font	2m4f Cls1 Gd2 Hdl gd-sft £23,200
	1/03	Chel	2m5¹/₂f Cls1 Gd1 Hdl gd-sft £44,625
	4/02	Aint	2m6f Cls1 Nov Gd2 Hdl good £29,000
	2/02	Sand	2m6f Cls2 Nov Hdl soft............................. £7,215
	1/02	Wwck	2m5f Cls1 Nov Gd2 Hdl soft £12,000
	12/01	Newb	2m5f Cls1 Nov Gd1 Hdl good £16,660
	12/01	Plum	2m5f Cls4 Nov Hdl good............................ £2,545
	12/01	Towc	2m Cls6 NHF 4-6yo heavy £2,261
	10/01	Gowr	2m4f NHF good £5,565

Former winner of the Grade 1 Cleeve Hurdle who developed into a smart staying chaser in his first season over fences last term; won three of his nine races, but actually showed his best form in defeat, returning a Racing Post Rating of 140 when chasing home Patman Du Charmil at Warwick (3m¹/₂f, good) and when third behind Keenan's Future at Newton Abbot (3m2¹/₂f, good to soft, conceding 26lb to the winner); dismounted after crossing the line on his latest start, but is reportedly well, lightly raced and open to improvement.

1090 Cleni Boy (Fr)

5 b g Panoramic - Kailasa (RB Chesne)

N Meade (Ir)   D P Sharkey

PLACINGS: 531/13351-   **RPR 134+h**

Starts	1st	2nd	3rd	4th	Win & Pl
8	3	-	3	-	£27,717
	1/07	Thur	2m6f Nov Hdl soft £7,470
	9/06	Gway	2m Mdn Hdl 4-5yo good £6,195
	4/06	Punc	2m NHF 4yo good £7,625

Showed smart novice hurdle form last season, and has the potential to do well in handicaps or over fences; won his maiden at Galway before twice finishing 6l third behind Hide The Evidence, including in Grade 1 company at Fairyhouse in December (2m, heavy, 9 ran); ran his only bad race at Leopardstown over Christmas (nothing came to light), but back to winning ways when stepped up to 2m6f at Thurles in January, where he looked a stayer over the trip; should be more to come.

1091 Clopf (Ire)

6 b g Dr Massini - Chroma (Supreme Leader)

E O'Grady (Ir)   Bernard Anthony Heffernan

PLACINGS: 116/1121-   **RPR 139+h**

Starts	1st	2nd	3rd	4th	Win & Pl
7	5	1	-	-	£90,152
	4/07	Punc	2m Nov Gd1 Hdl good £46,081
	11/06	Navn	2m Nov Gd3 Hdl yld-sft £16,612
	10/06	Clon	2m Nov Hdl 4-5yo soft £6,910
	3/06	Limk	2m3f NHF 5-7yo soft £5,957
	2/06	Limk	2m NHF 5-7yo soft £4,766

Highly regarded 2m hurdler who spent the summer

at around 25-1 for the Champion Hurdle, a race for which his trainer believes he is a genuine candidate, but one for which he will have to find substantial improvement to stand any chance of winning; beaten only once last term in a campaign restricted to racing in Ireland (found lame before the Supreme Novices' at Cheltenham), and capped that near faultless campaign by winning the Grade 1 Champion Novice Hurdle at Punchestown, where he got going again at the final flight after looking in trouble two out and got up to beat Rindoon by 1¹/₂l; earned a Racing Post Rating of 137 for his final success, and given that Ebaziyan (who finished last in that race) had notched 150 for winning the Supreme Novices', he clearly has some way to go if he is to justify his trainer's ambitions, although could have plenty of point-scoring opportunities in Graded races in Ireland during the winter. *'He's a natural jumper and might be better on better ground.' (Edward O'Grady, trainer)*

1092 Cloudy Lane

7 b g Cloudings - Celtic Cygnet (Celtic Cone)

D McCain   Trevor Hemmings

PLACINGS: 21F21121/361201U-   **RPR 135+c**

Starts	1st	2nd	3rd	4th	Win & Pl
15	6	4	1	-	£69,340
124	3/07	Chel	3m¹/₂f Cls2 123-139 Am Ch Hcap gd-sft		£33,011
	12/06	Newc	3m Cls4 Ch soft		£3,904
124	4/06	Hayd	2m4f Cls2 Nov 104-130 Hdl 4-8yo Hcap gd-sft		£13,012
	2/06	Hayd	2m4f Cls4 Nov Hdl 4-7yo soft		£4,554
	1/06	Hayd	2m4f Cls4 Nov Hdl 4-7yo soft		£4,554
	5/05	Sthl	2m1f Cls6 NHF 4-6yo good		£2,037

Promising chaser; gave his trainer the biggest win of his burgeoning career when winning the Kim Muir as a novice at the Cheltenham Festival in March, leading four out and responding to all his experienced rider's urgings to beat Parsons Legacy by ³/₄l (3m¹/₂f, good to soft, 24 ran); attempted to follow up off a 7lb higher mark in the Irish Grand National at Fairyhouse the following month, but was weakening out of things when badly hampered and unseating his rider at the third-last; likes a bit of decent ground, and with further improvement he can win another good handicap; stays well.

1093 Comply Or Die (Ire)

8 b g Old Vic - Madam Madcap (Furry Glen)

D Pipe   D A Johnson

PLACINGS: 11214/1211F2P6/4P/

Starts	1st	2nd	3rd	4th	Win & Pl
15	6	3	-	2	£120,624
	11/04	Chel	3m¹/₂f Cls2 Nov Ch good		£12,971
	11/04	Winc	2m5f Cls1 Nov Gd2 Ch good		£20,825
	10/04	Bang	2m4¹/₂f Cls3 Ch good		£6,906
	12/03	Chel	3m1¹/₂f Cls1 Nov Gd2 Hdl gd-sft		£17,400
	10/03	Plum	2m5f Cls4 Nov Hdl gd-fm		£3,423
	10/03	Chep	2m¹/₂f Cls3 Nov Hdl gd-fm		£3,663

Runner-up to Trabolgan in the 2005 SunAlliance Chase at the Cheltenham Festival, but has been absent from the racecourse for the best part of two years; was last seen when failing to complete in the Welsh National in 2005, but had earlier made a decent seasonal reappearance in the Hennessy Gold Cup at Newbury, finishing fourth behind his old rival after appearing to hold every chance between the final two fences (3m2¹/₂f, good, 19 ran); impossible to say how he will fare after such a long layoff, but connections are upbeat and keen to have a crack at the valuable staying chases, so every indication that he is somewhere near back to his best.

1094 Convincing

4 b c Selkirk - Hot Thong (Jarraar)

J Murphy (Ir)   John Joseph Murphy

PLACINGS: 10110-1   **RPR 128h**

Starts	1st	2nd	3rd	4th	Win & Pl
6	4	-	-	-	£53,676
	6/07	List	2m Hdl good		£9,763
	2/07	Leop	2m Gd2 Hdl 4yo heavy		£24,193
	1/07	Punc	2m Gd3 Hdl 4yo heavy		£14,955
	12/06	Fair	2m Mdn Hdl 3yo heavy		£4,766

Nothing special on the Flat (won twice over 7f) but made up into a decent juvenile hurdler last season, and while he'll probably struggle at the highest level, appeals as the type to do well in valuable handicaps; tally of four wins from six starts over jumps is impressive, the highlights being narrow victories in a Grade 3 at Punchestown in January (beat Majestic Concorde) and a Grade 2 at Leopardstown in February (by a neck over Financial Reward), showing battling qualities to win all out on both occasions; reportedly had a temperature when beaten at Leopardstown in December, and only other defeat came in the Triumph Hurdle at the Cheltenham Festival, finishing 14th when conditions were probably on the fast side (2m1f, good to soft, 23 ran); likely to prove best around 2m. *'He's very, very tough.' (John Murphy, trainer)*

1095 Cooldine (Ire)

5 b g Beneficial - Shean Alainn (Le Moss)

W Mullins (Ir)   Mrs Violet O'Leary

PLACINGS: 1170-   **RPR 130b**

Starts	1st	2nd	3rd	4th	Win & Pl
3	1	-	-	-	£4,668
	2/07	Fair	2m NHF 4-6yo heavy		£4,669

Winning point-to-pointer who showed some decent form in bumpers last season in the Florida Pearl colours; started favourite on his debut, and was all out to win a Fairyhouse bumper, before stepping up on that form when seventh behind Cork All Star in the Champion Bumper, running better than 50-1 SP had suggested and only 5³/₄l behind the winner (2m1f, good to soft, 24 ran); somewhat disappointing when only 12th in Grade 1 company at the Punchestown festival (2m, good, 19 ran), but probably found conditions on the fast side; likely to need a test of stamina at the minimum trip and will stay 2m4f; related to winning jumpers (dam, winning hurdler over 2m5f, sister to useful staying hurdler/chaser Brackenfield) and has the size and scope to do well over hurdles.

1096 Copsale Lad

10 ch g Karinga Bay - Squeaky Cottage (True Song)

N Henderson   Swallow Partnership

PLACINGS: 1/U24B3/12123/PP105-   RPR **145+h**

Starts	1st	2nd	3rd	4th	Win & Pl
21	5	3	3	1	£81,403
125	2/07	Newb	3m¹/₂f Cls3 108-130 Hdl Hcap soft		£6,263
	12/05	Ling	2m4¹/₂f Cls3 Nov Ch soft		£8,318
	10/05	Ling	2m4¹/₂f Cls4 Ch good		£4,290
	4/04	Chel	2m5¹/₂f Cls2 Nov Hdl 5-7yo gd-fm		£17,400
	1/04	Extr	2m3f Cls4 Nov Hdl soft		£3,796

Very smart chaser who contested some of last season's biggest handicaps, but was short of luck; started off in the Paddy Power Gold Cup (sent off second-favourite), but was badly hampered by a faller at the 8th fence and lost all chance (eventually pulled up); jumped badly left at Ascot next time (pulled up again), but bounced back off an 18lb lower mark over hurdles at Newbury in February, beating a competitive field by 5l and more; that persuaded connections to have a tilt at the Coral Cup at the Cheltenham Festival, for which he was sent off favourite, but he was never able to get competitive and trailed in 16th behind Burntoakboy; back over fences for his final outing in a valuable handicap at Aintree, and at least managed to complete in finishing 17l fifth behind Reveillez (3m1f, good, 18 ran); starts the season on a mark of 141 (2lb lower than last year) and could kick off in the Old Roan at Aintree or the Paddy Power again.

1097 Cork All Star (Ire)

5 b g Fasliyev - Lucky State (State Dinner)

Mrs J Harrington (Ir)   Cathal M Ryan

PLACINGS: 11115-   RPR **138+b**

Starts	1st	2nd	3rd	4th	Win & Pl
5	4	-	-	-	£50,168
	3/07	Chel	2m¹/₂f Cls1 Gd1 NHF 4-6yo gd-sft		£28,510
	11/06	Chel	2m¹/₂f Cls1 List NHF 4-6yo gd-sft		£8,553
	8/06	Gway	2m NHF 4-7yo good		£8,340
	7/06	Cork	2m NHF 4-5yo firm		£4,766

Leading bumper horse last season, and an obvious candidate for top novice hurdle honours this winter; hosed up in a competitive Listed bumper at Cheltenham's Open meeting in November, and spent most of the winter as favourite for the big one at the Festival in March; had been usurped from that position by Mad Fish come post time, but that didn't stop him running out a 1¹/₄l winner from outsider Sophocles, battling on gamely after leading 2f out; lost his unbeaten record with a below-par fifth behind Mick The Man at the

Punchestown festival, not helped by pulling hard in the early stages, and possibly finding the ground a little quicker than ideal; will no doubt have a return to Cheltenham for the Supreme Novices' as his long-term target, and ought to be up to winning plenty along the way.

1098 Cornish Sett (Ire)

8 b g Accordion - Hue 'N' Cry (Denel)

P Nicholls   Peter Hart

PLACINGS: 1141/2142217F/01726-   RPR **150+c**

Starts	1st	2nd	3rd	4th	Win & Pl
20	7	5	-	2	£126,159
	11/06	Chel	3m¹/₂f Cls2 Ch gd-sft		£15,658
140	3/06	Newb	2m4f Cls1 List 125-144 Ch Hcap gd-fm		£39,205
	11/05	Newb	2m1f Cls3 Ch good		£7,059
	4/05	Ayr	2m Cls2 Nov Hdl good		£12,041
113	1/05	Chel	2m1f Cls3 Nov 91-114 Hdl Hcap good		£10,005
	12/04	Chep	2m¹/₂f Cls4 Mdn Hdl soft		£3,491
	5/04	Ludl	2m Cls6 NHF 4-6yo good		£3,189

Very smart chaser who was upped in trip last season and proved just as effective at 3m-plus as he had previously done over shorter; there had been question marks over his resolution in the past, but he put up a most determined display in a four-runner graduation chase at Cheltenham in November, knuckling down well to beat Fundamentalist by a neck, with a distance back to It Takes Time in third; did not score again, but did well to chase home Simon on unsuitably soft ground in the Racing Post Chase at Kempton in February before failing to see out the marathon 3m5¹/₂f trip in the Betfred Gold Cup at Sandown; starts the season with a mark of 144, so not that badly treated on his best form and might be able to pick up another decent handicap or two.

1099 Cracking Cliche

5 ch m Classic Cliche - Calametta (Oats)

Miss V Williams   Mrs R F Knipe

PLACINGS: 24F-   RPR **103b**

Starts	1st	2nd	3rd	4th	Win & Pl
3	-	1	-	1	£1,717

From a successful family and showed plenty of promise in three starts in bumpers last season; led 5f out until headed by the winner 1f out on debut when 4l second to Isn't That Lucky at Fontwell (1m6f, good, to soft, 12 ran); ran to a similar level in a better race at Sandown when a one-paced fourth, 10¹/₂l behind Swaythe (2m¹/₂f, heavy, 14 ran); going well and close up when fell 5f out in a competitive mares' bumper at Aintree won by the excellent Turbo Linn (2m1f, good, 20 ran); goes over hurdles now and should be capable of success, especially against her own sex; versatile as regards ground preference and likely to stay 2m4f.

1100 Crocodiles Rock (Ire)

5 b g Heron Island - That's The Bonus (Executive Perk)

J O'Neill   John P McManus

PLACINGS: 5116-   RPR **132+b**

Starts	1st	2nd	3rd	4th	Win & Pl
4					£15,327
	2/07	Newb	2m¹/₂f Cls1 Gd2 NHF 4-6yo soft		£11,404
	12/06	Newb	2m¹/₂f Cls4 NHF 4-6yo soft		£3,253

One of last season's leading bumper performers, and likely to take high rank in novice hurdles this term; won two races at Newbury last season, including a Grade 2 contest won in previous years by the likes of Iris's Gift and Cornish Rebel and last season featuring seven previous winners; showed a game attitude there to rally and beat Just A Thought by 1l, and was staying on in the closing stages of the Champion Bumper at Cheltenham on his only other start, where he finished sixth, beaten less than 5l; could well be suited by a step up in trip this term, and difficult to see him not being competitive at a decent level over hurdles. *'He's tough, he gallops and he loves soft ground.' (Jonjo O'Neill, trainer)*

1101 Crossbow Creek

9 b g Lugana Beach - Roxy River (Ardross)

M Rimell   Mark Rimell

PLACINGS: 11453/31BF3P/8311P-9   RPR **157+c**

Starts	1st	2nd	3rd	4th	Win & Pl
28	7	2	4	4	£106,797
145	10/06	Asct	2m1f Cls1 List 124-145 Ch Hcap gd-fm		£19,957
134	10/06	Kemp	2m Cls2 110-136 Ch Hcap good		£12,526
	11/05	Tntn	2m¹/₂f Cls3 Ch gd-fm		£5,514
126	1/05	Kemp	2m Cls2 119-144 Hdl Hcap good		£9,119
115	1/05	Kemp	2m Cls3 109-133 Hdl Hcap good		£29,000
	2/04	Ludl	2m Cls4 Mdn Hdl good		£4,033
	2/03	Weth	2m Cls6 NHF 4-6yo gd-sft		£2,436

Versatile performer who bounced back from a lean spell to do well over fences last autumn; won a pair of 2m handicaps, beating Cossack Dancer by 5l at Kempton and following up off an 11lb higher mark at Ascot with a 1¹/₄l defeat of subsequent big-race winner Demi Beau; not seen again until the Red Rum Handicap Chase at Aintree in April, but ran no sort of race there, before posting some decent efforts on the Flat (including a win on the AW at Kempton); ideally wants a strongly run race at around 2m on decent ground, although life will be tough in chases off his current mark of 153; rated 21lb lower over hurdles, though, and connections are keen to exploit what looks a lenient mark. *'I trained him for the Galway Hurdle in August but the ground went against him – he must have fast ground. The plan is to explore other options by switching him between hurdles and chases.' (Mark Rimell, trainer)*

1102 Crow Wood

8 b g Halling - Play With Me (Alzao)

J Quinn   Mrs Marie Taylor

PLACINGS: 13410/21638-   RPR **148h**

Starts	1st	2nd	3rd	4th	Win & Pl
10	3	1	2	1	£79,637
140	11/06	Winc	2m Cls1 Gd2 140-160 Hdl Hcap good		£28,644
124	2/06	Muss	2m Cls2 106-132 Hdl Hcap gd-fm		£18,789
	10/05	Uttx	2m Cls4 Nov Hdl good		£3,395

Useful 2m hurdler; expertly placed to win the Grade 2 Elite Hurdle at Wincanton off a mark of 140 last November, making all and showing a smart turn of foot to beat Desert Quest by ¹/₂l (2m, good, 6 ran); put in his place by the likes of Straw Bear and Detroit City on his next two starts, but returned in the spring to finish 4³/₄l eighth to Pedrobob in the County Hurdle at the Cheltenham Festival (2m1f, good to soft, 28 ran); ideally suited by good ground on a flat track at around 2m, and has the ability to pick up another decent handicap.

1103 Crozan (Fr)

7 b g Sassanian - La Guyonniere (Silver Rainbow)

N Henderson   Trevor Hemmings

PLACINGS: 0/563672/14PP/2PF4-   RPR **156c**

Starts	1st	2nd	3rd	4th	Win & Pl
18	1	2	1	2	£46,428
	11/05	Chel	2m4¹/₂f Cls2 Nov Ch gd-sft		£10,428

Rather hit-and-miss chaser who tends to show his smartest form first time when fresh; posted a career-best effort first time out last season in a good graduation chase at Ascot in December, just coming off worse by a short head in a tremendous scrap from the last with Tamarinbleu (2m5¹/₂f, good to soft, 6 ran); duly flopped 14 days later at Haydock, so was given a break until the Cheltenham Festival; sported first-time blinkers in the Ryanair Chase, in which he bowled along in a clear lead and was going nicely ahead of the closing pack when clipping the top of the fourth-last and coming down; impossible to say how he would have fared from that point, and his subsequent below-par fourth behind Monet's Garden at Aintree should not be read too literally, as Cheltenham may have taken the edge off him; would be no surprise to see him head for the Paddy Power Gold Cup, but would need to improve to defy a mark of 150.

1104 Cuchulains Son (Ire)

5 b g Bob Back - Gallic Approach (Toulon)

W Mullins (Ir)   John J Brennan

PLACINGS: 924-131   RPR **128b**

Starts	1st	2nd	3rd	4th	Win & Pl
6	2	1	1	1	£12,931
	8/07	Baln	2m1f NHF 4-7yo yield		£4,202
	5/07	Rosc	2m4f NHF 5-7yo good		£4,435

Nicely bred type who showed decent form in

bumpers last season and should pay his way in staying novice hurdles; stepped up considerably on first two efforts when fourth in Punchestown's Grade 1 Paddy Power Champion Bumper in April (2m, good, 19 ran), keeping on and beaten only 4½l; up in trip and easily landed the odds at Roscommon on his next start, always travelling well and asserting in the straight; again odds-on, but done no favours when short of room over 1f out in Listowel event (also had to come from a fair way back) on his next start; by Bob Back, a good influence for stamina, and his dam is a half-sister to Irish National winner Feathered Leader, so has excellent chance of staying 3m; a good-ground horse according to his trainer.

1105 D'Argent (Ire)

10 gr g Roselier - Money Galore (Monksfield)

A King   Nigel Bunter

PLACINGS: /351115P/F852U/1PP2-   **RPR 145c**

Starts	1st	2nd	3rd	4th	Win & Pl
22	6	3	1	-	£137,486
135	12/06	Chel	3m1½f Cls1 131-156 Ch Hcap soft		.............£57,020
	1/04	Wwck	3m½f Cls2 Nov Ch gd-sft		.............£14,040
	12/03	Wwck	3m½f Cls3 Nov Ch good		...............£6,929
	12/03	Wwck	3m2f Cls4 Nov Ch good		...............£3,484
	3/02	Extr	2m3f Cls4 Nov Hdl good		...............£2,842
	3/02	Donc	2m4f Cls4 Nov Hdl soft		...............£3,122

Mud-loving staying chaser; made a spectacular return from 629 days on the sidelines when winning a valuable handicap chase at Cheltenham last December, always racing up with the pace and really digging deep after a mistake 3 out to hold the late thrust of New Alco by a short head; pulled up on his next two starts, at his beloved Warwick and in the William Hill Handicap Chase at the Cheltenham Festival, but returned to form just four days after the latter event in the Midlands Grand National at Uttoxeter, finishing 12l second to Baron Windrush (4m1½f, soft, 18 ran but only seven finished); missed the Scottish National because of fast ground; real battler when he is on his game, and still capable of running well in top events off his current mark of 141.

1106 Dancing Bay

10 b g Suave Dancer - Kabayil (Dancing Brave)

N Henderson   Elite Racing Club

PLACINGS: 6010/2025/U3620/21P-   **RPR 129c**

Starts	1st	2nd	3rd	4th	Win & Pl
23	5	5	1	1	£85,024
128	2/07	Fknm	3m½f Cls4 Ch gd-sft		...............£4,332
122	3/04	Newb	2m½f Cls2 108-133 Hdl Hcap gd-sft		.....£12,442
	12/03	Hexm	2m½f Cls3 98-124 Hdl Hcap soft		.....£5,824
	2/03	Plum	2m5f Cls3 Nov Hdl soft		...............£6,858
	1/03	Plum	2m Cls3 Nov Hdl soft		...............£5,590

Grand servant whose list of placed efforts in big races includes a Chester Cup, Queen Alexandra Stakes and Doncaster Cup on the Flat, and a Swinton Hurdle, Coral Cup and National Spirit Hurdle over jumps; belatedly had his sights turned to chasing last season, and needed luck on his side to gain his first win in three years at Fakenham in February, where he was 4l down going to the last in a beginners' chase, but inherited the spoils when The Cool Guy came down; had earlier finished a decent second to Glasker Mill at Fontwell, but rounded off with a disappointing flop at Kempton (jumped left); not easy to win with, and a chase mark of 135 means he probably needs to be right on his game to make his mark in handicaps; likes a little ease in the ground.

1107 De Soto

6 b g Hernando - Vanessa Bell (Lahib)

J O'Neill   P A Deal

PLACINGS: 32/4/711445-   **RPR 144h**

Starts	1st	2nd	3rd	4th	Win & Pl
9	2	1	1	3	£38,582
	12/06	Kemp	2m Cls2 Nov Hdl gd-sft		...............£8,768
	12/06	Tntn	2m1f Cls3 Nov Hdl gd-sft		...............£7,807

Lightly raced sort who was highly regarded by former trainer Paul Webber and looks an interesting novice chase prospect for his new handler after changing hands for 360,000gns at Doncaster's May sale; finished second to Missed That in the 2005 Champion Bumper at Cheltenham and scored twice last season in novice hurdles; ultimately found out at the top level (finished fourth in the Supreme Novices' at Cheltenham and fifth in the Grade 2 Top Novices' Hurdle at Aintree), but his 5l beating of Blythe Knight at Kempton on Boxing Day reads well as that rival is now being aimed at the Champion Hurdle and there was 21l back to the well regarded Kicks For Free in third; might yet deliver what he promised a couple of seasons back.

1108 De Valira (Ire)

5 ch g Shantou - Valira (Nijinsky)

M O'Brien (Ir)   D Mac A'Bhaird

PLACINGS: 1/211201F-   **RPR 136h**

Starts	1st	2nd	3rd	4th	Win & Pl
8	4	2	-	-	£70,137
	4/07	Fair	2m Nov Gd2 Hdl gd-fm		.............£26,392
	12/06	Leop	2m Nov Gd2 Hdl heavy		.............£22,448
	12/06	Fair	2m2f Mdn Hdl 4-5yo heavy		...............£6,433
	3/06	Leop	2m NHF 4yo yield		...............£6,433

Half-brother to the high-class Valiramix, and last season proved himself a smart 2m hurdler with a future; highly tried and rewarded that approach with a pair of victories in Grade 2 company, both by a neck and both worthy of a Racing Post Rating of 136; probably claimed the most notable scalp when winning on only his second start over hurdles at Leopardstown in December, getting the better of Catch Me, who was unbeaten at the time; beaten around 15l in the Supreme Novices' Hurdle at the Festival and fell at the fourth on his only other outing at the top level; has plenty of ground to make up on last season's leading 2m novices if he is to challenge for honours at the top level, but has a fine attitude and looks sure to win more races. *'He's got gears and he stays well.' (Denis Cullen, assistant trainer)*

1109 Degas Art (Ire)

4 b g Danehill Dancer - Answer (Warning)

J H Johnson   Andrea & Graham Wylie

PLACINGS: 11103-   RPR **141 + h**

Starts	1st	2nd	3rd	4th	Win & Pl
5	3	-	1	-	£44,480
	2/07	Muss	2m Cls2 Nov Hdl 4yo good		£9,395
	11/06	Aint	2m¹/₂f Cls2 Nov Hdl 3yo good		£9,759
	10/06	Weth	2m Cls1 Nov List Hdl 3yo soft		£11,404

Smart juvenile hurdler last season, and expected to improve further as he strengthens up; went to Cheltenham unbeaten in three starts, notably beating Katchit by 1¹/₂l at Wetherby on his jumps debut in October (received 8lb) and subsequent Ebor winner Purple Moon by 12l at Musselburgh in February; started 7-1 at the Festival, but the strong pace forced him into mistakes at the head of affairs, and he was backtracking quickly from two out, eventually finishing 12th behind the much-improved Katchit; took on his old rival again at Aintree, and posted his best Racing Post Rating in finishing 12l third (2m¹/₂f, good, 12 ran); official hurdles mark of 144 means he will have to improve to make his mark in handicaps, but the best should be yet to come. *'He's a flat-track horse who didn't like the hills at Cheltenham.' (Graham Wylie, owner)*

1110 Demi Beau

9 b g Dr Devious - Charming Life (Sir Tristram)

E Williams   Cunningham Racing

PLACINGS: 0F/050/231FP/21P94-0   RPR **151 + c**

Starts	1st	2nd	3rd	4th	Win & Pl
21	4	2	1	3	£117,350
136	11/06	Asct	2m1f Cls2 133-156 Ch Hcap soft		£74,364
121	12/05	Ludl	2m Cls3 95-121 Ch Hcap good		£6,369
118	12/03	Chel	2m1f Cls3 115-130 Hdl Hcap good		£16,066
	1/03	Donc	2m¹/₂f Cls4 Nov Hdl gd-sft		£3,562

Handicap chaser who endured a season of two halves, and never regained his form after long midwinter break; employed forcing tactics on his reappearance and almost lasted home at Ascot when 1¹/₄l runner-up to Crossbow Creek (2m1f, good to firm, 6 ran); stepped up on that to post best RPR of his life over the same course and distance next time, making most on ground officially soft but likely better than that (not thought to be in his favour) to beat Hasty Prince by 2l in a very valuable handicap; absent until the Grand Annual Chase at the Cheltenham Festival, when he ran a stinker and was pulled up behind Andreas (2m1/2f, good to soft, 23 ran); better

when fourth behind Dempsey at Sandown (2m, good to firm, 8 ran) when unable to set the pace, but well beaten over hurdles on his final outing; best on fast ground at around 2m in smallish fields when able to dictate, and will be kept to right-handed tracks from now on.

1111 Dempsey (Ire)

9 b g Lord Americo - Kyle Cailin (Over The River)

C Llewellyn   Mrs T Brown

PLACINGS: 9FP21U13/12B/U4U121-   RPR **168 + c**

Starts	1st	2nd	3rd	4th	Win & Pl
25	9	3	2	1	£213,798
	4/07	Sand	2m Cls1 Gd2 Ch gd-fm		£57,020
153	2/07	Sand	2m Cls2 Gd3 134-155 Ch Hcap gd-sft		£28,510
142	1/06	Sand	2m Cls2 117-142 Ch Hcap gd-sft		£12,526
	3/05	Sand	2m Cls3 Nov Ch gd-sft		£7,020
	1/05	Ludl	2m Cls4 Ch gd-sft		£4,440
	4/04	Winc	2m Cls4 Nov Hdl good		£3,595
	12/03	Folk	2m1¹/₂f Cls4 Nov Hdl 4-6yo gd-sft		£2,604
	11/03	Folk	2m1¹/₂f Cls4 Nov Hdl 4-6yo good		£3,010
	10/03	Hrfd	2m1f Cls6 NHF 4-6yo gd-fm		£1,519

Former dodgy jumper who developed into a high-class 2m chaser last season, and will go for all the top races this term; has always gone best on right-handed tracks, and proved the point with two all-the-way wins at Sandown, landing a Grade 3 handicap under 11st 10lb in February, and beating Hoo La Baloo by 7l in the Grade 2 Celebration Chase on the final day of the season; in between ran a cracker in the Champion Chase at the Cheltenham Festival, leading two out and staying on after he was headed at the last to finish 1¹/₂l second to Voy Por Ustedes (2m, good to soft, 10 ran); set to start off in the Haldon Gold Cup at Exeter, with races like the Tingle Creek, Champion Chase and Celebration Chase his obvious targets thereafter; unsuited by extremes of ground, and looks a much safer conveyance now than he was in his younger days.

1112 Denman (Ire)

7 ch g Presenting - Polly Puttens (Pollerton)

P Nicholls   Mrs M Findlay & P K Barber

PLACINGS: 1/11112/11111-   RPR **165 + c**

Starts	1st	2nd	3rd	4th	Win & Pl
10	9	1	-	-	£211,011
	3/07	Chel	3m¹/₂f Cls1 Gd1 Ch gd-sft		£96,934
	2/07	Newb	3m Cls2 Nov Ch soft		£11,711
	11/06	Newb	2m4f Cls2 Nov Gd2 Ch heavy		£19,957
	11/06	Chel	2m4¹/₂f Cls2 Nov Ch gd-sft		£12,526
	10/06	Extr	2m1¹/₂f Cls3 Nov Ch good		£10,410
	2/06	Bang	3m Cls3 Nov Hdl good		£6,831
	1/06	Chel	2m4¹/₂f Cls1 Nov Gd1 Hdl gd-sft		£22,808
	11/05	Winc	2m6f Cls3 Nov Hdl good		£5,010
	10/05	Winc	2m6f Cls4 Nov Hdl good		£3,435

An outstanding talent who was beaten only once over hurdles (in the SunAlliance at Cheltenham), and last season won all five starts over fences, establishing himself as the best staying novice in the land and sounding a warning to the owner of stablemate Kauto Star; capped his memorable campaign over fences with a most impressive success in the SunAlliance Chase, in which he was sent off 6-5 favourite and never gave his followers a cause for concern as he oozed class and came home 10l clear of Snowy Mountain; had earlier faced only one serious task when pitched against Don't Push It at Cheltenham in November, but although he was not overwhelmingly impressive, he found plenty on the run-in to defeat that progressive rival by ³/4l; has always been held in huge regard by both his owner and trainer (sent off favourite on all but one of his starts), and although he has well over a stone to find strictly on figures, he starts the season at a best-priced 6-1 for the Gold Cup (as short as 4-1); given that plenty of improvement is likely after only five starts over fences, he could well give his stablemate and reigning champion a good run for his money at Cheltenham in March, with other top races likely to come his way en route to a crack at the main prize. *'I have in my mind that he'll go for the Charlie Hall at Wetherby, but I will try to keep him apart from Kauto Star as long as I can.' (Paul Nicholls, trainer)*

1113 Desert Air (Jpn)

8 ch g Desert King - Greek Air (Ela-Mana-Mou)

D Pipe   Mrs Belinda Harvey

PLACINGS: 6407/214004/0313P00-   **RPR 138+c**

Starts	1st	2nd	3rd	4th	Win & Pl
27	4	3	3	3	£95,676
	2/07	Plum	2m1f Cls4 Ch heavy		£3,920
132	1/06	Sand	2m¹/2f Cls1 List 123-149 Hdl Hcap soft		£57,020
122	10/04	Extr	2m3f Cls3 104-125 Hdl Hcap good		£5,031
	1/03	Tntn	2m1f Cls3 Nov Hdl soft		£4,531

Former winner of the Ladbroke Hurdle who proved himself a useful chaser in the first part of last season; showed his best form when winning a little novice contest at Plumpton in February, justifying odds-on favouritism to beat the frustrating Spidam by 5l; switched back to hurdles after a below-par display over fences at Wincanton, but failed to make a mark at Cheltenham, Aintree or Sandown; on something of a recovery mission now, over both fences and hurdles, but undeniably talented at around 2m on testing ground, if not always inclined to put his best foot forward.

1114 Desert Quest (Ire)

7 b g Rainbow Quest - Jumilla (El Gran Senor)

P Nicholls   Mrs M Findlay

PLACINGS: 221U113110/12930-   **RPR 164+h**

Starts	1st	2nd	3rd	4th	Win & Pl
15	6	3	2		£144,032
144	10/06	Asct	2m Cls2 118-144 Hdl Hcap gd-fm		£49,576
131	3/06	Chel	2m1f Cls1 Gd3 122-147 Hdl Hcap good		£37,063
127	3/06	Newb	2m¹/2f Cls3 108-127 Hdl Hcap good		£9,395
120	12/05	Donc	2m¹/2f Cls2 111-136 Hdl Hcap gd-sft		£10,545
114	12/05	Tntn	2m3¹/2f Cls3 94-120 Hdl Hcap good		£4,827
	10/05	Tntn	2m3¹/2f Cls3 Nov Hdl firm		£5,493

Classy 2m hurdler who capped a progressive

campaign the season before last with victory in the County Hurdle at the Cheltenham Festival; unable to land a blow when trying to do the double last March, albeit from a 30lb higher mark, but had done well earlier in the campaign; won the William Hill Handicap Hurdle at Ascot on his seasonal return, appreciating the quick surface to beat Caracciola by 3l, a performance that saw him cut to as short as 10-1 for the Champion Hurdle, and he did well in the Elite Hurdle at Wincanton in November as he was conceding 23lb to the progressive Crow Wood when going down by only ¹/2l (2m, good, 6 ran); ultimately had his target changed at the Festival, and was always going to have it all to do on ground that wasn't ideal and from top weight; has yet to win from a mark higher than 144, so likely to struggle in handicaps, but will reportedly try his hand at chasing this season, with connections eyeing further success. *'He's the fastest hurdler you've seen since Istabraq.' (Harry Findlay, owner)*

1115 Detroit City (USA)

5 gr g Kingmambo - Seattle Victory (Seattle Song)

P Hobbs   Terry Warner

PLACINGS: 81111/11160-   **RPR 166+h**

Starts	1st	2nd	3rd	4th	Win & Pl
10	7	-	-	-	£306,609
	2/07	Sand	2m¹/2f Cls1 List Hdl soft		£17,106
	12/06	Chel	2m1f Cls1 Gd2 Hdl soft		£114,040
148	11/06	Chel	2m¹/2f Cls1 Gd3 125-148 Hdl Hcap gd-sft		£37,063
	4/06	Aint	2m¹/2f Cls1 Nov Gd1 Hdl 4yo good		£68,424
	3/06	Chel	2m1f Cls1 Gd1 Hdl 4yo good		£57,020
	2/06	Sand	2m¹/2f Cls3 Nov Hdl 4yo good		£5,205
	1/06	Newb	2m¹/2f Cls4 Nov Hdl 4yo gd-sft		£2,928

High-class hurdler, but one whose reputation was severely dented by two poor runs in the spring; charged to Champion Hurdle favouritism last term with three straight wins, bolting up in a handicap at Cheltenham, getting the better of Hardy Eustace by 1l in the Bula Hurdle in December, and overcoming a blunder at the last to beat Straw Bear by a couple in the Agfa Hurdle at Sandown in February (2m1/2f, soft, 6 ran); all three wins were characterised by a willingness to find more after coming off the bridle, but it was a very different story in the Champion Hurdle in March, where he was ridden along after a slow jump at the second, lost touch from three out and trailed in 19l sixth behind Sublimity (2m1/2f, soft, 10 ran); upped in trip for the 2m4f Aintree Hurdle the following month, and started favourite again, but was again in trouble from an early stage and trailed in a very long last behind Al Eile; no questioning his class (winner of a Triumph Hurdle and a Cesarewitch), but impossible to know what to expect when he returns for the top hurdle events this season, although he has been treated for a breathing problem, which connections believe could put him right back on track.

1116 Dom D'Orgeval (Fr)

7 b g *Belmez - Marie D'Orgeval (Bourbon)*
D Pipe   A J White & Mrs A Underhill
PLACINGS: 5/325111354/3431103-   **RPR 149h**

Starts	1st	2nd	3rd	4th	Win & Pl
31	9	4	5	2	£177,670

	2/07	Hexm	3m1f Cls3 Nov Ch soft	£6,397
	1/07	Fknm	3m¹/₂f Cls4 Ch gd-sft	£5,205
136	2/06	Uttx	2m4¹/₂f Cls2 118-136 Hdl Hcap heavy	£18,591
132	1/06	Ling	2m3¹/₂f Cls1 Gd2 125-145 Hdl Hcap heavy	£22,808
123	12/05	Ling	2m3¹/₂f Cls2 111-132 Hdl Hcap soft	£9,845
109	1/05	Uttx	2m Cls3 109-128 Hdl Hcap heavy	£10,179
91	10/04	Strf	2m¹/₂f Cls4 77-99 Hdl Hcap soft	£4,875
85	9/04	NAbb	2m1f Cls4 79-105 Hdl Hcap good	£4,150
81	7/04	NAbb	2m3f Cls4 73-100 Hdl Hcap gd-fm	£3,010

Very smart hurdler (finished third in the Coral Cup at Cheltenham) who transferred much of that ability to fences last season and will be interesting in staying handicaps this term; finished in the frame in three starts in France over hurdles last summer before starting his campaign in Britain with a third behind Inglis Drever in the Grade 2 Long Distance Hurdle at Newbury, the best effort of his career according to Racing Post Ratings (3m1/2f, soft, 5 ran); switched from Nick Williams to his new trainer after that fine effort, and duly won his first two starts over fences before getting outclassed behind Denman in the SunAlliance Chase at Cheltenham; plenty of signs on his final start, though, that he can bag a decent prize when finishing third behind Aces Four in the Grade 2 Mildmay Novices' Chase at Aintree (3m1f, good, 10 ran), especially as he has a little in hand over fences compared to his handicap mark over hurdles. *'He's one for the big staying chases this season.' (David Pipe, trainer)*

1117 Don't Push It (Ire)

7 b g *Old Vic - She's No Laugh Ben (Alleged)*
J O'Neill   John P McManus
PLACINGS: 3/11/1211F5-   **RPR 159+c**

Starts	1st	2nd	3rd	4th	Win & Pl
9	5	1	1	-	£38,126

	2/07	Chep	2m1¹/₂f Cls3 Nov Ch soft	£5,855
	12/06	Chel	2m5f Cls2 Nov Ch soft	£12,526
	10/06	Strf	2m4f Cls4 Ch soft	£5,205
	12/05	Hayd	2m4f Cls3 Nov Hdl 4-7yo soft	£5,237
	9/05	MRas	2m1¹/₂f Cls6 NHF 4-6yo good	£1,960

High-class novice chaser between 2m and 2m5f last season who spent the summer quoted between 16-1 and 33-1 for the Champion Chase; would have had a big say in the outcome of the Arkle Trophy at Cheltenham but for tipping up at the second-last with Twist Magic, and had earlier laid down solid credentials for a bold show in that contest by winning three of his four races en route to the Festival; made subsequent SunAlliance Chase winner Denman pull out all the stops at Cheltenham in November before going down by just ³/4l (lost ground with a blunder at the third-last) and impressed with a 23l rout of Phar Bleu at Chepstow in February; had possibly had enough for

the season when beating only one home in the Grade 1 Maghull Chase at Aintree and is way better than that effort; starts the new campaign with a mark of 149, which would give him a chance in the big handicaps, with the Ryanair Chase at Cheltenham an alternative to the 2m crown. *'He's very highly strung and he even sweats at home on the gallops.' (Jonjo O'Neill, trainer)*

1118 Double Default (Ire)

6 ch g *Beneficial - Over The Risc (Over The River)*
N Richards   Sir Robert Ogden
PLACINGS: 01/2211-   **RPR 131h**

Starts	1st	2nd	3rd	4th	Win & Pl
4	2	2	-	-	£7,922

	4/07	Hexm	3m Cls4 Nov Hdl soft	£3,083
	3/07	Ayr	2m4f Cls4 Mdn Hdl soft	£2,928

Former Irish point-to-point winner who developed into a smart novice hurdler last season and should go on to better things over fences; had to narrowly settle for second-best behind Chief Dan George on his first two starts over hurdles in December, although that was no disgrace given the winner's subsequent Grade 1-winning exploits; brought back to the track in the spring, and won twice at odds-on in soft ground, at Ayr and Hexham, although it was hard work getting the better of Jack The Blaster on the latter occasion; has raced only on soft or heavy ground and stays 3m no problem, so the plan is to build up his confidence with a couple of wins in novice chases in the north before looking at bigger targets in the second half of the season.

1119 Double Eagle

5 b g *Silver Patriarch - Grayrose Double (Celtic Cone)*
D McCain   Dr G M Thelwall Jones
PLACINGS: 1943312-   **RPR 125+h**

Starts	1st	2nd	3rd	4th	Win & Pl
7	2	2	2	1	£18,879

	2/07	Carl	2m4f Cls4 Nov Hdl soft	£2,741
	10/06	Carl	2m1f Cls6 NHF 4-6yo soft	£1,713

Progressive novice hurdler last season, and everything points to him coming into his own in 3m novice chases this term; took four attempts to break his duck, doing so with a 4l defeat of Camden George at Carlisle in February (2m4f, soft, 17 ran); started 33-1 for the Grade 3 EBF Novices' Hurdle Final at Sandown the following month, but belied those odds to hit the front approaching two out, and kept on at the same pace to finish 4l second to Albertas Run (2m4¹/2f, heavy, 16 ran); looks all stamina, and will surely improve on his already decent form over fences this winter, especially granted plenty of cut in the ground. *'He's already jumped fences at home and is a 3m chaser in the making.' (Donald McCain, trainer)*

1120 Dream Alliance

6 ch g Bien Bien - Rewbell (Andy Rew)

P Hobbs   The Alliance Partnership

PLACINGS: 4/23116F/5124361-   **RPR 145+c**

Starts		1st	2nd	3rd	4th	Win & Pl
14		4	2	2	2	£48,023
129	4/07	Prth	3m Cls2 113-138 Ch Hcap soft £25,052
	11/06	Extr	2m7¹/₂f Cls3 Nov Ch gd-sft £7,807
	2/06	Hayd	2m4f Cls4 Nov Hdl 4-7yo heavy £4,554
	1/06	Chep	2m4f Cls4 Mdn Hdl soft £3,416

Progressive young chaser who looks set to contest good staying handicaps this season; won a 3m novice chase at Exeter in November before a string of defeats in class 3 events, often being turned over at short odds; looked to be losing his way when well beaten in a novices' handicap at Ascot in March, but changed all that by beating established chasers in some style in a valuable contest at Perth at the end of April, always racing prominently and quickly asserting from four out to beat Lothian Falcon and Iron Man by 8l and 11l (3m, soft, 15 ran); that form has a very solid look to it, so a 13lb hike in the weights may not stop him making his mark in even better company; likes a right-handed track and ease in the ground, so something like the Badger Ales Trophy at Wincanton might appeal as an early target. *"We've all backed him at 100-1 to win the Cheltenham Gold Cup before 2009" (Janet Volkes, part-owner)*

1121 Duc De Regniere (Fr)

5 b g Rajpoute - Gladys De Richerie (Le Pontet)

N Henderson   Sir Peter & Lady Gibbings

PLACINGS: 3110-   **RPR 137+h**

Starts		1st	2nd	3rd	4th	Win & Pl
4		2	1	1	-	£21,135
	2/07	Kemp	2m5f Cls4 Nov Hdl gd-sft £4,554
	12/06	Newb	2m¹/₂f Cls2 Nov Hdl gd-sft £12,526

Ex-French gelding who looks an exciting prospect for novice chases this season; won his first two novice hurdles in Britain last season, beating the smart Osana by 2¹/₂l at Newbury in December (getting 5lb from the runner-up) and pushed out to beat Battle Cry and Wyldello by 4l and 7l over 2m5f at Kempton in February; trainer was initially reluctant to go to Cheltenham, but he took his chance, only to finish well down the field behind Massini's Maguire in the Ballymore Properties Hurdle; is much better than that run suggests, and the best should still be to come over fences; could develop into a serious Royal & SunAlliance contender. *'It's a case of he will be a very good horse rather than he is a very good horse. I can't believe he won't be a 3m chaser.' (Nicky Henderson, trainer)*

1122 Dun Doire (Ire)

8 b g Leading Counsel - Yes Boss (Carlingford Castle)

A Martin (Ir)   Dunderry Racing Syndicate

PLACINGS: 30/151111117/0F251P-   **RPR 144+c**

Starts		1st	2nd	3rd	4th	Win & Pl
25		9	1	1	-	£140,248
	3/07	DRoy	3m2f Ch yld-sft £9,338
129	3/06	Chel	3m¹/₂f Cls1 Gd3 121-146 Ch Hcap gd-sft £45,616
115	1/06	Gowr	3m 115-138 Ch Hcap gd-yld £44,828
103	1/06	Fair	3m1f 95-113 Ch Hcap sft-hvy £8,340
93	12/05	Navn	2m4f 81-113 Ch Hcap soft £9,066
85	12/05	Hayd	2m4f Cls3 Nov 85-110 Ch Hcap soft £5,556
79	11/05	Weth	2m4¹/₂f Cls4 Nov 79-102 Ch Hcap soft £3,855
92	5/05	Limk	3m 81-94 Hcap soft £5,146
82	2/05	Navn	2m4f 76-99 Hdl Hcap heavy £6,126

Cheltenham Festival winner in 2006 (beat Juveigneur in the William Hill Handicap Chase) and will have his campaign geared around the Becher Chase and Grand National this season; that was also the case last term, but he fell early on in the Becher and was never a factor in the National, tailed off as early as the fifth fence; was predictably quietly campaigned in between, but did finish second over hurdles at Navan in December, and prepped for Aintree by winning a conditions chase at Down Royal, beating Romaha by ³/4l; needs to convince that he is in love with the National fences, but connections are keen to go back there with him.

1123 Dunbrody Millar (Ire)

9 b/br g Lord Americo - Salt Mills (Proverb)

P Bowen   Dundon Else Partnership

PLACINGS: F1215P4/PPS33444021-   **RPR 133+c**

Starts		1st	2nd	3rd	4th	Win & Pl
45		5	6	6	4	£158,784
129	4/07	Aint	2m5¹/₂f Cls2 129-155 Ch Hcap good £62,630
120	2/06	Sand	3m¹/₂f Cls2 117-143 Ch Hcap gd-fm £28,184
101	1/06	Plum	3m5f Cls3 101-125 Ch Hcap soft £18,789
93	12/05	Font	3m2¹/₂f Cls4 68-94 Ch Hcap soft £4,014
	3/04	Limk	3m Mdn Hdl yld-sft £6,083

Handicap chaser who is lit up by the big fences on Aintree's Grand National course; finished fourth in the 2006 Topham, third in last season's Becher, and gained a deserved first victory there in the latest renewal of the Topham in April, where he led approaching 2 out and galloped on powerfully to beat Theatre Knight by 6l from 17lb out of the handicap (2m5¹/2f, good, 29 ran); ran there because he missed the cut for the Grand National, but has been raised to a new mark of 133, and connections will be keen to sneak him into the big one at the bottom of the weights, as he is a stone better round Aintree than anywhere else; has won on soft and good to firm going, and is a previous winner of the Sussex National over 3m5f, so should have the stamina for the job.

1124 Duty (Ire)

4 b g Rainbow Quest - Wendylina (In The Wings)

K O'Brien (Ir)   D J Sharkey

PLACINGS: 21105-   **RPR 132+h**

Starts	1st	2nd	3rd	4th	Win & Pl
5	2	1	-	-	£24,365
	2/07	Fair	2m Gd3 Hdl 4yo heavy		£15,395
	2/07	Gowr	2m Mdn Hdl 4yo heavy		£6,070

Smart performer over middle distances on the Flat who proved himself an equally useful 2m hurdler last season and should now do well in handicaps; won his first two races over jumps, notably a Grade 3 contest at Fairyhouse in February, where he appreciated the testing ground to beat subsequent winner J'y Vole by 6l; seemingly outclassed at both the Cheltenham and Punchestown festivals, but the ground at either would not have been ideal, and there is almost certainly better to come.

1125 Earth Planet (Ire)

5 b g Kayf Tara - Arctic Rose (Jamesmead)

P Nicholls   R M Penny

PLACINGS: 123-   **RPR 115b**

Starts	1st	2nd	3rd	4th	Win & Pl
3	1	1	1		£8,133
	10/06	Chep	2m¹/₂f Cls6 NHF 4-6yo good		£1,713

Smart bumper performer last season who should make a decent impression in the novice hurdle ranks; got off the mark first time up at Chepstow in October (slightly fortuitous as the likely looking winner wandered about) before earning place money behind highly regarded Seven Is My Number and Crocodiles Rock at Ascot and Newbury; showed a tendency to hang on his last two starts, but that was probably just inexperience, and he should be winning races over hurdles. *"He's an exciting novice hurdler who enjoys good ground." (Paul Nicholls trainer)*

1126 Ebaziyan (Ire)

6 gr g Daylami - Ebadiyla (Sadler's Wells)

W Mullins (Ir)   Peter Garvey

PLACINGS: 2118-   **RPR 150+h**

Starts	1st	2nd	3rd	4th	Win & Pl
4	2	1			£73,697
	3/07	Chel	2m¹/₂f Cls1 Nov Gd1 Hdl soft		£68,424
	2/07	Thur	2m Mdn Hdl 6yo yld-sft		£3,969

Decent 1m4f performer on the Flat for John Oxx, but better over hurdles, and sprang a shock when winning the Supreme Novices' at the Cheltenham Festival at odds of 40-1; seemingly no fluke about that success, as he was cruising behind the leaders before quickening up on the run-in and striding away to post an authoritative 3l win over Granit Jack; that was a huge improvement on his previous runs, when second at Cork and driven out for a narrow success at Thurles; was sent off second-favourite to rack up the hat-trick in the Grade 1 Champion Novice Hurdle at the Punchestown festival, but trailed in a dismal last of eight finishers behind Clopf (2m, good); had reportedly had a setback after Cheltenham, and found the ground too fast, so the effort is probably best ignored; a bit to prove, but a return to his best could see him develop into a legitimate Champion Hurdle contender.

1127 Echo Point (Ire)

7 b g Luso - Lady Desart (Buckskin)

N Richards   The Border Reivers

PLACINGS: 1/12/41U341-2   **RPR 138+c**

Starts	1st	2nd	3rd	4th	Win & Pl
10	4	2	1	2	£30,495
	4/07	Prth	2m Cls3 Nov Ch gd-sft		£7,807
	12/06	Sedg	2m4f Cls4 Ch soft		£4,120
	10/05	Sedg	2m1f Cls4 Nov Hdl 4-6yo gd-sft		£3,679
	2/05	Fair	2m NHF 4-6yo soft		£5,881

Talented, but inconsistent, front-running novice chaser last season; made all to win at Sedgefield (2m4f) and Perth (2m), doing best at the latter track in April when beating Chief Yeoman by 8l on good to soft going; jumped well on the whole there (made costly errors at times last term), and that will be an important factor in his immediate future, which lies in handicap chases in the north; best when there is plenty of give underfoot, and suited by sharp tracks.

1128 Ellerslie Tom

5 br g Octagonal - Tetravella (Groom Dancer)

P Bowen   Don Jones

PLACINGS: 246/21031111437-6533   **RPR 141+h**

Starts	1st	2nd	3rd	4th	Win & Pl
22	5	2	4	3	£50,113
124	9/06	Bang	2m1f Cls3 112-133 Hdl Hcap gd-fm		£10,410
	8/06	Strf	2m¹/₂f Cls3 Nov Hdl gd-fm		£6,263
	8/06	NAbb	2m1f Cls4 Nov Hdl gd-fm		£4,888
	8/06	Bang	2m1f Cls4 Nov Hdl gd-fm		£4,554
108	5/06	Kels	2m2f Cls3 106-124 Hdl Hcap gd-fm		£9,481

Very useful young handicap hurdler; won four in a row in the summer of 2006, and returned to good form in handicaps in the spring; not beaten far in sixth behind Leslingtaylor in the Swinton Hurdle at Haydock, and was cruelly denied in the valuable Summer Hurdle at Market Rasen in July, where he led between the last two but tired inside the last 150 yards to be beaten two short heads by Kings Quay and Prince Ary, giving weight to both (2m1¹/₂f, soft, 17 ran); that run showed he is not merely a good-ground performer, and could well convince connections to keep him on the go through the winter this time, unlike last season, when he did not race between September and the end of March.

Kauto Star and Ruby Walsh cross the line to win the King George at Kempton

Crowds in the packed stands watch the action in the Paddy Power Gold Cup

Runners and riders storm down the track in the Grand National

The media scrum surrounds Halcon Genelardais after his Welsh National win

Gaspara wins at Chepstow in a season that included Cheltenham success

Racing Demon after his win in the Peterborough Chase at Huntingdon

1129 Emmpat (Ire)

9 b g Bigstone - Nordic Abu (Nordico)

C Swan (Ir)　　　　　　　　　　　　　　Michael D Mee

PLACINGS: 72/33F/11B5/4411-0PP　　　　RPR **141**+h

Starts	1st	2nd	3rd	4th	Win & Pl
17	4	1	3	2	£120,355
134	4/07	Ayr	2m Cls1 Gd2 134-151 Hdl Hcap gd-fm		£39,438
120	4/07	Fair	2m 112-140 Hdl Hcap gd-fm		£57,095
	6/05	Tipp	2m4f Nov Hdl good		£7,351
	6/05	Gowr	2m Mdn Hdl gd-fm		£4,901

Useful 2m hurdler; hit a rich vein of form on fast ground when returning from a mid-season break in the spring, winning a valuable handicap hurdle at Fairyhouse, and following up 11 days later with a 4l defeat of Ouninpohja in the Grade 2 Scottish Champion Hurdle at Ayr; went backwards after that, although he was probably unlucky to encounter such easy conditions in the summer; good handicapper, but scoring opportunities likely to be few and far between because of his ground preference.

1130 Emotional Moment (Ire)

10 b g Religiously - Rosceen Bui (Phardante)

T Taaffe (Ir)　　　　　　　　　　　　Watercork Syndicate

PLACINGS: 1P/7422167/P9235430-　　　　RPR **144**h

Starts	1st	2nd	3rd	4th	Win & Pl
49	13	3	4	6	£237,405
	1/06	Gowr	3m Gd3 Hdl yield		£17,959
	2/05	Navn	3m Gd3 Hdl heavy		£23,085
	1/05	Gowr	3m Gd3 Hdl sft-hvy		£18,468
	12/04	Leop	3m Gd2 Hdl heavy		£22,923
	1/04	Leop	2m5f Nov Gd3 Ch soft		£22,887
	12/03	Thur	2m Ch good		£5,377
	2/03	Navn	3m Gd2 Hdl yld-sft		£21,104
114	12/02	Navn	2m 107-130 Hdl Hcap yld-sft		£11,963
106	11/02	DRoy	2m 105-131 Hdl Hcap heavy		£25,920
99	10/02	Wxfd	2m 87-107 Hdl Hcap yld-sft		£5,291
85	1/02	Gowr	2m1f 77-111 Hdl Hcap heavy		£7,620
76	1/02	DRoy	2m 64-85 Hdl Hcap soft		£3,810
69	12/01	Limk	2m 66-91 Hdl Hcap soft		£6,121

Smart 2m4f-3m hurdler who hasn't won since January 2006, and could benefit from a drop in the weights, as his current rating forces him to compete in Graded events; runner-up to Rosaker, beaten 6l, at Navan in November (2m4f, yielding to soft, 10 ran) and that heralded a run of decent efforts that peaked in January at Gowran, when outpaced between the last two in a Grade 3 event he had won for the two previous years, eventually finishing 9¹/₄l fourth behind the high-class Celestial Wave (3m, heavy, 8 ran); also third over fences behind Back In Front at Thurles (3m, heavy, 7 ran); loves the mud and stays 3m well, but not likely to be improving at his age. *'I've always said that he is a bit short of being a Grade 1 winner.' (Tom Taaffe, trainer)*

1131 Eric's Charm (Fr)

9 b g Nikos - Ladoun (Kaldoun)

O Sherwood　　　　　　　　　　　M St Quinton & P Deal

PLACINGS: 5/1132124/F1216/P12/

Starts	1st	2nd	3rd	4th	Win & Pl
18	8	4	1	1	£105,308
128	3/06	Sand	3m¹/₂f Cls3 114-128 Ch Hcap soft		£7,807
	3/05	Kemp	2m4¹/₂f Cls3 Nov Ch gd-sft		£8,054
	12/04	Folk	3m1f Cls4 Ch good		£4,238
	2/04	Kemp	2m5f Cls3 Nov Hdl good		£6,220
	12/03	Hrfd	2m3¹/₂f Cls3 Nov Hdl gd-sft		£3,809
	11/03	Ling	2m3¹/₂f Cls3 Nov Hdl 4-6yo good		£4,303
	3/03	Hntg	2m¹/₂f Cls6 NHF 4-6yo good		£2,009
	2/03	Font	2m2¹/₂f Cls6 NHF 4-6yo gd-sft		£1,939

Developed into a smart staying chaser in 2005/06, when he was runner-up to Lacdoudal off a mark of 140 in the Betfred Gold Cup at Sandown on his final start (3m5¹/2f, good to firm, 18 ran); fast ground at Sandown took its toll, however, as he suffered a leg injury that forced him to miss the whole of last season; has reportedly made a full recovery and is back in full training, and handicapper has given him a chance by dropping him to 137; has a decent strike-rate in chases (three wins from eight starts) and the plan is to go wherever he can get a soft surface; seems effective at trips upwards of 2m4f, while has an affinity for Sandown and Kempton, where in five starts (three at Sandown, two at Kempton) he has never finished out of the first two; may be one for the Racing Post Chase.

1132 Essex (Ire)

7 b g Sadler's Wells - Knight's Baroness (Rainbow Quest)

M O'Brien (Ir)　　　　　　　　　　　　　B P S Syndicate

PLACINGS: 11/3110/2544/514-1　　　　RPR **150**h

Starts	1st	2nd	3rd	4th	Win & Pl
14	6	1	1	3	£215,576
	7/07	Tipp	2m Gd3 Hdl heavy		£30,791
	4/07	Fair	2m4f List Hdl gd-fm		£15,395
144	2/05	Newb	2m¹/₂f Cls3 114-139 Hdl Hcap gd-sft		£72,500
125	1/05	Leop	2m 114-136 Hdl Hcap sft-hvy		£55,780
	4/04	Fair	2m Hdl 4yo yield		£10,315
	2/04	DRoy	2m Mdn Hdl 4yo yield		£4,866

Former Totesport Trophy winner who missed most of last term after chipping a knee bone, but returned in the spring and won two of his three races; had little problem overcoming Sweet Kiln in a Listed race over 2m4f at Fairyhouse in April (first try at the trip) and then added a Grade 3 success at Tipperary in July to his CV, beating Star Wood by 5l, with 24l back to Al Eile in third; tried over 3m between those efforts, and acquitted himself well by finishing fourth behind Refinement, beaten only around 6l; has always come up shy of the best, and likely to continue doing so, but is still lightly raced over hurdles and should have no trouble holding his own in Ireland, especially now that more options have been opened up with proof that he stays significantly further than 2m and that a recent laser-palate operation seems to have had a positive effect.

1133 Euro Leader (Ire)

9 b g Supreme Leader - Noreaster (Nordance)

W Mullins (Ir)   John Cox

PLACINGS: 18/4111F3F51/512166-   **RPR 134+h**

Starts	1st	2nd	3rd	4th	Win & Pl
26	10	3	1	2	£208,709

	9/06	Cork	2m4f Hdl firm £7,625
148	8/06	Gway	2m1f 120-148 Ch Hcap gd-fm £22,724
140	4/06	Punc	2m4f 116-144 Ch Hcap good £24,693
133	9/05	List	3m 106-133 Ch Hcap good................£64,096
120	8/05	Tral	2m4f 105-127 Ch Hcap yld-sft £20,777
	5/05	Punc	2m Ch gd-yld £9,234
	3/05	Limk	2m4f Ch gd-yld......................................£7,841
	12/03	Cork	2m Mdn Hdl 4-5yo yield £5,377
	10/03	Tipp	2m NHF gd-fm £8,065
	9/03	List	2m4f NHF 5-7yo good £5,825

Talented and versatile performer who excels on fast ground; put in his best effort last season when winning a seven-runner 2m1f handicap chase at Galway last August, jumping soundly and staying on strongly to beat Prince Of Pleasure by 8l; then reverted to hurdles, finishing runner-up to Maxxium in a Tralee handicap (2m1f, good, 8 ran) before landing the odds from stablemate Adamant Approach in a 2m4f conditions hurdle at Cork; Paddy Power Gold Cup was mentioned as a possible target for the first half of last season, but he wasn't seen after finishing lame when down the field in a Grade 2 chase at Gowran Park in October (2m4f, good to yielding, 8 ran); starts the season with a BHB rating of 154 over fences, so the top handicaps/Graded chases are likely to be on the agenda on his return; has won over 3m, but mostly campaigned over 2m-2m4f last season.

1134 Evelith Echo

4 b g Overbury - Sunday News'N'Echo (Trempolino)

A King   Allan Stennett

PLACINGS: 5211-   **RPR 111+b**

Starts	1st	2nd	3rd	4th	Win & Pl
4	2	1	-	-	£7,005

	4/07	Ayr	2m Cls4 NHF 4-6yo gd-fm.....................£3,253
	2/07	Kemp	2m Cls4 NHF 4-6yo soft £3,253

Dual bumper winner who is set to go novice hurdling this winter; ran with promise in fair events at Cheltenham and Haydock, and was well touted before getting off the mark at Kempton in February, where he made smooth headway from the rear from 5f out, led with 1f to run and was driven out to beat Harrisburg by 5l in soft ground; returned two months later in a good little bumper run on much quicker ground at Ayr, and kept on a roll with a battling neck defeat of previous winner Quws Law; versatile, progressive sort who should win races over hurdles.

1135 Ever Present (Ire)

9 ch g Presenting - My Grand Rose (Executive Perk)

N Richards   Ramsay Donald Brown

PLACINGS: 51245/5/3/1331/11P-   **RPR 145+c**

Starts	1st	2nd	3rd	4th	Win & Pl
14	5	1	3	1	£35,319

128	12/06	Kels	3m1f Cls2 118-144 Ch Hcap heavy....................£12,526
119	11/06	Carl	2m4f Cls3 100-119 Ch Hcap soft £6,506
	3/06	Ayr	3m1f Cls4 Ch soft..£3,708
110	4/05	Kels	2m6¹/₂f Cls3 97-123 Hdl Hcap soft £4,927
	11/02	Bang	2m1f Cls4 Nov Hdl soft.......................................£3,178

Progressive, bold-jumping, front-running staying chaser who started last season on a mark of 119 and is now rated 137 courtesy of two successes; won by 8l at Carlisle last November, and followed up the following month off a 9lb higher mark in a better event at Kelso, although he was very tired jumping the last and virtually ground to a halt on the run-in before holding off Rambling Minster by 1l (3m1f, heavy, 8 ran); was given nearly two months off to get over that exhausting effort, but was pulled up quite early on in his reappearance in the Sky Bet (Great Yorkshire) Chase at Southwell in January, with a minor niggle that sidelined him for the remainder of the season; reportedly back in good shape, and remains an interesting prospect at 3m-plus; all three chase wins to date have come in fields with fewer than nine runners.

1136 Exotic Dancer (Fr)

7 b g Turgeon - Northine (Northern Treat)

J O'Neill   Sir Robert Ogden

PLACINGS: /F2873/331F/2112121-   **RPR 177+c**

Starts	1st	2nd	3rd	4th	Win & Pl
18	7	4	3	-	£494,553

	4/07	Aint	3m1f Cls1 Gd2 Ch good £85,530
	1/07	Chel	3m1¹/₂f Cls1 Gd2 Ch heavy £57,288
149	12/06	Chel	2m5f Cls1 Gd3 131-157 Ch Hcap soft £85,530
139	11/06	Chel	2m4¹/₂f Cls1 Gd3 123-149 Ch Hcap gd-sft £62,722
	12/05	Chel	2m5f Cls2 Nov Ch gd-sft.....................................£9,864
	10/03	Autl	1m7f Hdl 3yo v soft £13,091
	10/03	Autl	1m7f Hdl 3yo holding..£16,208

Tremendous performer who improved out of all recognition last season for the combination of extreme waiting tactics and cheekpieces, and would be Britain's leading chaser were it not for the dominance of Kauto Star; scooped Cheltenham's Paddy Power and Boylesports.com Gold Cups before Christmas before going on to establish himself the second-best stayer around; underlined his credentials for the Festival showpiece by winning the Cotswold Chase at Cheltenham by 18l from Our Vic with a performance full of authority that proved 3m-plus to be well within his capabilities; had played second fiddle to Kauto Star in the King George at Kempton on Boxing Day, and did so again in the Gold Cup, although he reduced the gap from 8l to 2¹/₂l (3m2¹/₂f, good to soft, 18 ran); saved his very best for last in the Grade 2 Betfair Bowl at Aintree, where he recorded a Racing Post Rating of

177 (Kauto Star won the Gold Cup with RPR of 175) in slamming My Will by 13l; prone to the odd jumping error, but did his connections proud last season in a campaign that saw his official mark rise from 139 to 172; will have to contend with Paul Nicholls' champion again this term, but is not far behind him strictly on figures and would not have to improve much to be bang there. *'Kauto Star is a great horse and a great champion, but we still think we are capable of beating him at some point.' (Barry Simpson, racing manager to owner Sir Robert Ogden)*

1137 Faasel (Ire)

6 b g Unfuwain - Waqood (Riverman)

N Richards   Jim Ennis

PLACINGS: 11221/233822/551423-   **RPR 157 + c**

Starts	1st	2nd	3rd	4th	Win & Pl
18	5	6	3	1	£189,923

1/07	Catt	2m3f Cls4 Ch soft	£3,253
4/05	Aint	2m¹/₂f Cls1 Nov Gd1 Hdl 4yo gd-sft	£69,600
2/05	Ayr	2m Cls3 Nov Hdl heavy	£4,992
2/05	Kels	2m¹/₂f Cls4 Nov Hdl good	£3,523
1/05	Kels	2m¹/₂f Cls4 Nov Hdl soft	£3,510

Former Triumph Hurdle runner-up, but went backwards until making the switch to fences midway through last season; made a winning start over fences at Catterick, and stepped up markedly on that effort at Cheltenham when 6³/4l fourth behind My Way De Solzen in the Arkle Trophy (2m, soft, 13 ran), despite losing his early position with a blunder at the first; tackled 3m-plus for the first time in the Grade 2 Mildmay Novices' Chase at Aintree and put in some good late work to finish 8l second to Aces Four (3m1f, good, 10 ran); disappointing third behind Yes Sir back over 2m4f at Ayr on his final start; quirky sort who doesn't always find a lot under pressure, but goes well fresh; will take the handicap route over fences to start with, although connections are planning to switch him back to hurdles at some stage, as he looks potentially well-handicapped off 143.

1138 Fair Along (Ger)

5 b g Alkalde - Fairy Tango (Acatenango)

P Hobbs   Alan Peterson

PLACINGS: U11113428/03111202-   **RPR 158 + c**

Starts	1st	2nd	3rd	4th	Win & Pl
17	7	4	3	2	£178,017

12/06	Newb	2m2¹/₂f Cls3 Nov Ch gd-sft	£7,998
12/06	Sand	2m Cls1 Nov Gd2 Ch soft	£19,957
11/06	Chel	2m Cls1 Nov Gd2 Ch gd-sft	£25,780
11/05	Aint	2m¹/₂f Cls2 Nov Hdl 3yo gd-sft	£10,146
11/05	Chel	2m¹/₂f Cls1 Nov Gd2 Hdl 3yo gd-sft	£17,106
8/05	Bang	2m1f Cls4 Nov Hdl 3yo good	£3,034
7/05	Bang	2m1f Cls4 Nov Hdl 3yo gd-sft	£3,414

Former smart hurdler (second in the 2006 Triumph), but proved even better in the top 2m novice chases last season, in a campaign characterised by his bold-jumping, front-running style; made the most of his 4yo allowance to win

in Grade 2 company on his first two chase outings, beating Natal by 9l at Cheltenham and My Way De Solzen by 10l at Sandown, before completing the hat-trick with a 46l demolition of Killaghy Castle at Newbury over Christmas; was given a long break afterwards, going straight to the Arkle at the Cheltenham Festival, and probably ran his best race of all in finishing 5l second to My Way De Solzen, as he was unable to gain his usual pitch at the front and was hampered by fallers two out before staying on up the hill; no show under 10st 7lb in the County Hurdle three days later, and then found the impressive Twist Magic 5l too good off level weights at Aintree (2m, good, 6 ran); ran in the Chester Cup on the Flat the following month, and did well to finish 1¹/₂l second to Greenwich Meantime (being aimed at the Cesarewitch at the time of writing); chase mark of 154 gives him half a chance in the top 2m handicaps (possibly the Haldon Gold Cup over a shade further), but will surely be competing in Graded chases at some point; loves a bit of cut in the ground.

1139 Faucon Bleu (Fr)

4 gr g Cadoudal - Label Bleu (Pistolet Bleu)

Miss H Knight   Lady Bamford & Alice Bamford

PLACINGS: 2/13-   **RPR 118 + h**

Starts	1st	2nd	3rd	4th	Win & Pl
3	1	1	1	-	£11,311

10/06	Uttx	2m Cls4 Nov Hdl 3yo soft	£2,928

Promising ex-French jumper; ran twice in juvenile hurdles for new connections last autumn, sluicing up by 8l from Risk Runner in the soft at Uttoxeter before a very decent 12¹/₂l third behind the classy Degas Art in a better contest at Aintree (2m¹/₂f, good, 5 ran, finished well clear of the fourth); wasn't seen out again, but reportedly back on track, and could be switched to fences at this early stage in his career; looks like a stiffer test of stamina will suit as well. *'He's not big, but is athletic and has the right attitude. He likes soft ground and long-term he'll be a chaser.' (Henrietta Knight, trainer)*

1140 Field Commander (Ire)

5 b g Blue Ocean - Fern Fields (Be My Native)

M Hourigan (Ir)   Gigginstown House Stud

PLACINGS: 5640-143111   **RPR 145 + h**

Starts	1st	2nd	3rd	4th	Win & Pl
10	4	-	1	2	£37,326

8/07	Gway	2m4f Nov Hdl gd-yld	£12,756
7/07	Klny	2m1f Nov Hdl good	£6,070
7/07	Limk	2m Nov Hdl yield	£12,316
5/07	Slig	2m Mdn Hdl 5yo gd-fm	£3,969

Showed little in bumpers and over hurdles last season, but rapidly progressed into a very smart performer over timber during the summer and is expected to go for some big prizes in the spring; won four novice hurdles out of six between May and August, following up successes at Sligo, Limerick and Killarney with a 1¹/₄l defeat of Jadanli at the Galway festival, staying on strongly on his first attempt at 2m4f, and conceding 6lb and more all round; probably won't leave his box very often in the middle of winter, but likely to have all the big festivals in his sights in the spring, with the Ballymore Properties Novices' Hurdle at Cheltenham a distinct possibility (current RPR of 145 only 4lb lower than Massini's Maguire achieved at the Festival last season); improving fast. *'He's good – definitely one for the Ten to Follow lists.' (Michael Hourigan, trainer)*

1141 Financial Reward (Ire)

4 b c Fruits Of Love - Lamp Of Phoebus (Sunshine Forever)

W Mullins (Ir)   Mrs M Warde

PLACINGS: 124123822-26   **RPR 137**h

Starts	1st	2nd	3rd	4th	Win & Pl
11	2	5	1	1	£68,598
	1/07	Thur	2m Hdl 4yo soft		£6,070
	11/06	Limk	2m Mdn Hdl 3yo soft		£4,766

No great shakes on the Flat, but made up into a very useful juvenile hurdler, and is one to consider for top handicaps such as the Pierse Hurdle and Totesport Trophy; won at Limerick and Thurles, but his best efforts came when runner-up in Graded events, just pipped by Convincing in a Grade 2 at Leopardstown in February (heavy, 9 ran) and put in an even better effort when beaten only ³/₄l by Punjabi in the Grade 1 Ballymore Properties 4-y-o Hurdle at the Punchestown festival (good, 10 ran), rallying well and finishing closer to that rival than he did in the Triumph Hurdle; having his tenth race over hurdles, but showing no signs of being jaded, when runner-up to stablemate J'y Vole in a Grade 3 at Auteuil in May (very soft, 2m4f, 16 ran), caught in the last strides but seeing out the longer trip well; tough sort who seems to go on any surface.

1142 Finger Onthe Pulse (Ire)

6 b g Accordion - Quinnsboro Ice (Glacial Storm)

T Taaffe (Ir)   Conor Clarkson

PLACINGS: 1/F221312/110UF-   **RPR 147+**h

Starts	1st	2nd	3rd	4th	Win & Pl
13	5	3	1	-	£61,856
130	10/06	Naas	2m4f 116-146 Hdl Hcap soft		£17,959
122	10/06	Naas	2m4f 121-149 Hdl Hcap yld-sft		£13,693
	3/06	Navn	2m Nov Hdl 4-5yo sft-hvy		£6,672
	12/05	Leop	2m2f Mdn Hdl 4yo yield		£7,106
	1/05	Leop	2m NHF 4yo sft-hvy		£5,391

Handicap hurdler who won twice in a fortnight at Naas last October, lasting home on the second occasion by 1l from Pacolet, whereupon trainer confessed that the race had come a bit quick; was given a break and stepped up in class, but made little show in the Lanzarote Hurdle at Kempton behind Verasi, and unshipped his rider on the bend

after jumping just two flights in the Coral Cup at the Cheltenham Festival; fell at the second-last in a Listed hurdle won by Essex at Fairyhouse on his final start, but was beginning to go backwards at the time; goes chasing now, and is expected to make a good fist of his new career; relishes cut in the ground and effective at around 2m4f, although he will probably stay 3m over fences, and better for a decent break between races.

1143 Fiveforthree (Ire)

5 gr g Arzanni - What A Queen (King's Ride)

W Mullins (Ir)   Olde Crowbars Syndicate

PLACINGS: 153-   **RPR 134+**b

Starts	1st	2nd	3rd	4th	Win & Pl
3	1	-	1	-	£7,524
	2/07	Punc	2m NHF 5-6yo heavy		£5,369

Nicely bred sort (half-brother to high-class chaser Celestial Gold) who proved himself more than useful in bumpers last season, and should make his mark in novice hurdles; started favourite when winning on his debut at Punchestown in impressive fashion by 7l, and then sent over for the bumper at the Cheltenham Festival, where he ran well to finish a keeping-on fifth behind Cork All Star, faring best of the Mullins trio in the race (2m1f, good, to soft, 24 ran); sent off 6-4 favourite at Fairyhouse in April (2m, good, 14 ran) but probably found conditions on the fast side when 2¹/₂l third behind Sizing Africa; likely to need 2m4f-plus when sent hurdling.

1144 Fleet Street

8 ch g Wolfhound - Farmer's Pet (Sharrood)

N Henderson   W H Ponsonby

PLACINGS: 13133/4/100-   **RPR 134+**h

Starts	1st	2nd	3rd	4th	Win & Pl
9	3	-	3	1	£33,634
127	3/07	Newb	2m¹/₂f Cls3 110-133 Hdl Hcap gd-sft		£4,684
	1/04	Tntn	2m1f Cls4 Nov Hdl gd-sft		£4,238
	10/03	Strf	2m¹/₂f Cls3 Mdn Hdl gd-fm		£5,239

Talented jumper who has raced just five times since finishing third behind Brave Inca and War Of Attrition in the 2004 Supreme Novices' Hurdle; made his latest return from a 15-month absence in a small 2m1¹/₂f handicap hurdle at Newbury in March, and duly took full advantage of a drop in the weights to run out a 2¹/₂l winner over Swing Bill; raced twice in the space of 24 hours at the Punchestown festival the following month (handicap hurdles over 2m4f and 2m), but was unable to get competitive in either, although he had the excuse that he was slightly hampered on the former occasion; fragile sort who has had plenty of problems, but is being aimed at novice chases this season (finished fourth to Voy Por Ustedes in a novice event at Plumpton in December 2005).

1145 Flight Leader (Ire)

7 b g Supreme Leader - Stormy Petrel (Strong Gale)

C Tizzard   John & Heather Snook

PLACINGS: 625/121134-   **RPR 154h**

Starts	1st	2nd	3rd	4th	Win & Pl
9		3	2	1	1	£48,002
	1/07	Chel	2m4¹/₂f Cls2 Hdl heavy £13,152			
	12/06	Chel	3m Cls1 Nov Gd2 Hdl soft £19,957			
	10/06	Chep	3m Cls5 Mdn Hdl gd-sft £2,741			

Took high rank among staying novices last season, proving well suited by left-handed tracks and particularly Cheltenham; travelled supremely well throughout when beating Labelthou by 9l at the track in December, and then improved on that when demonstrating his tenacity in a ¹/₂l defeat of Temoin at the same track three weeks later; not disgraced behind Blazing Bailey and Inglis Drever in the Grade 2 Cleeve Hurdle in January (3m, heavy, 9 ran), nor in the Brit Insurance Novices' Hurdle at the Festival, when the drying ground went against him before finishing fourth, beaten 20l by Wichita Lineman (3m, good to soft, 20 ran); likely to do well in the staying novice chase division.

1146 Flintoff (USA)

6 ch g Diesis - Sahibah (Deputy Minister)

Miss V Williams   Andrew Flintoff & Paul Beck

PLACINGS: 42710/111P/223110-   **RPR 146+c**

Starts	1st	2nd	3rd	4th	Win & Pl
15		6	3	1	1	£28,292
122	1/07	Newb	3m Cls3 105-125 Ch Hcap heavy £5,855			
	1/07	Weth	2m4¹/₂f Cls4 Ch heavy............................£3,999			
	5/05	Ctml	2m1¹/₂f Cls4 Nov Hdl 4yo good £3,519			
	5/05	Ctml	2m6f Cls4 Nov Hdl soft..........................£3,949			
	5/05	Towc	2m5f Cls4 Nov Hdl good £4,212			
	3/05	Carl	2m1f Cls6 NHF 4-6yo gd-sft £1,981			

Big improver in his novice season over fences, and looks one for valuable handicap chases over 3m-plus; placed efforts before the turn of the year showed promise, but two heavy-ground victories in four days in January demonstrated his class; blinkered first time when winning a moderate contest at Wetherby by 26l, and repeated the dose at Newbury over 3f further, coming clear from the second-last and beating Ice Melted by 14l; up in grade and off a 13lb higher mark when well beaten in the Agfa Diamond Chase at Sandown on his final start, but given a questionable ride tactically, and the performance can be forgiven.

1147 Foligold (Fr)

5 b g Gold Away - Folidalways (Always Fair)

Mrs J Harrington (Ir)   Right G Syndicate

PLACINGS: 02116230-   **RPR 134h**

Starts	1st	2nd	3rd	4th	Win & Pl
8		3	2	1	-	£31,312
	10/06	Gway	2m4f Nov Hdl sft-hvy £8,979			
	10/06	Limk	2m2f Hdl 4yo yld-sft................................£13,469			

Useful novice hurdler last season, winning twice in

ordinary company in October before posting better form in Grade 3 events; twice placed behind Kazal in that grade, beaten 8l into second at Limerick in December (2m6f, soft to heavy, 8 ran), and getting within 1³/₄l on 7lb better terms at Leopardstown the following month (2m4f, soft, 7 ran); sported first-time blinkers as a 66-1 shot in the Ballymore Properties Novices' Hurdle at the Cheltenham Festival, but was backtracking quickly from the third-last and wound up tenth, beaten 32l by Massini's Maguire (2m5f, good to soft, 15 ran); is certainly better than that (may have found the ground too fast) and ought to hold his own in handicap hurdles if connections opt to delay a switch to fences.

1148 Footy Facts (Ire)

7 b g Oscar - Princess Henry (Callernish)

R Tyner (Ir)   Maurice Kelleher

PLACINGS: 1118/3112-   **RPR 135h**

Starts	1st	2nd	3rd	4th	Win & Pl
7		4	1	1	-	£74,092
	11/06	Navn	2m4f Nov Gd3 Hdl soft............................£17,959			
	11/06	Cork	3m Nov List Hdl gd-yld £22,448			
	3/06	Curr	2m NHF sft-hvy £13,469			
	3/06	Thur	2m NHF 5-7yo soft £4,289			

Ran just four times in novice hurdles last season (not seen out after Christmas), but improved with every start; beaten in a Grade 3 over 2m on his reappearance, but stepped up on that when sent over 3m, cruising home by 7l from Swiss Hall at Cork; better still at Navan three weeks later, back down to 2m4f, in a Grade 3 when turning in a slick round of jumping and winning unextended by 9l from Casey Jones; recorded best RPR on his final start over the same track and trip when put in his place by high-class Aran Concerto, going clear until reeled in by the winner and eventually beaten 7l (2m4f, heavy, 6 ran); versatile as regards trip and doesn't have to have mud to show his form; stays over hurdles and likely to be a force to be reckoned with in the thinly contested staying events in Ireland.

1149 Foreman (Ger)

9 ch g Monsun - Fleurie (Dashing Blade)

T Doumen (Fr)   John P McManus

PLACINGS: 1F4147/22/69131/23P-   **RPR 163+c**

Starts	1st	2nd	3rd	4th	Win & Pl
26		8	5	5	3	£335,208
	4/06	Aint	2m Cls1 Nov Gd1 Ch gd-sft £62,722			
	1/06	Ling	2m Cls1 Nov Gd2 Ch soft £19,957			
	1/04	Leop	2m Gd1 Hdl yield £63,556			
	11/03	Engh	2m2f List Hdl 4yo v soft £18,078			
	4/03	Engh	2m3f List Hdl v soft................................£20,260			
	2/03	Kemp	2m5f Cls3 Nov Hdl good..........................£6,844			
	5/02	Badn	2m¹/₂f Hdl 4yo good £6,748			
	5/02	Folk	2m1¹/₂f Cls4 Mdn Hdl good £2,870			

High-class 2m chaser (beat Voy Por Ustedes as a novice at Aintree in April 2006), but below his best in a light campaign last term; looked to be firmly on course for a strong Champion Chase bid when 6^1/2l third behind Voy Por Ustedes at Kempton over Christmas, but ran deplorably in the Game Spirit at Newbury in February, jumping slowly in rear, finding nothing when shaken up just after halfway and tailed off when pulled up three out; wasn't seen out again, so has a bit to prove now, but will be back for Graded chases this winter; no doubting his class (former Irish Champion Hurdle winner) if he can regain his best form; might need to be stepped up in distance now. *'He's not fast enough for a Champion Chase.' (Tony McCoy, rider)*

1150 Forget The Past

9 b g Past Glories - Worth Matravers (National Trust)
M O'Brien (Ir)   S Mulryan
PLACINGS: 212/10331135/114038-   **RPR 158+c**

Starts	1st	2nd	3rd	4th	Win & Pl
22	8	3	5	1	£257,868
	1/07	Thur	2m4f Gd2 Ch soft		£21,993
	1/07	Punc	2m4f Hdl heavy		£7,937
	2/06	Fair	3m1f Gd2 Ch sft-hvy		£22,448
	2/06	Gowr	2m4f Gd2 Ch soft		£22,448
	4/05	Punc	2m5f Nov Gd2 Ch soft		£25,394
	12/04	Leop	3m Nov Gd1 Ch sft-hvy		£36,444
	11/04	Punc	2m6f Nov Gd3 Ch yld-sft		£17,650
	10/04	Limk	2m4f Ch yield		£9,169

High-class chaser between 2m4f and 3m who finished third in War Of Attrition's Gold Cup; failed to repeat form as good as that last season, despite having been treated for a back problem; did best of all when putting up a superb round of jumping to win the Grade 2 Kinloch Brae Chase at Thurles in January; had been expected to take in the Ryanair Chase at the Cheltenham Festival after that, but ultimately lined up in the Gold Cup after stablemate In Compliance was ruled out of the raced; ultimately finished tenth behind Kauto Star, beaten around 18l on ground that had a little more give than ideal; overall balance of form last term was a little disappointing (including two spins over hurdles in April), but even if failing to recapture his very best, he should be a force in Ireland at just below the top level.

1151 French Opera

4 b g Bering - On Fair Stage (Sadler's Wells)
N Henderson   Lynn Wilson & Martin Landau
PLACINGS: 1-   **RPR 97+h**

Starts	1st	2nd	3rd	4th	Win & Pl
1	1	-	-	-	£1,951
	3/07	Tntn	2m1f Cls4 Mdn Hdl 4yo good		£1,952

Moderate middle-distance maiden on the Flat, but promises to do better over hurdles after winning on his debut over 2m1f at Taunton in March; didn't look a great contest at the time, but the horse he beat comfortably by 3^1/2l, Sabre Hongrois, went on to win twice, and there were a number of other subsequent winners further back, so he probably

did well to score at the first time of asking; starts the season with an official hurdles mark of 112, which looks more than fair, given that Sabre Hongrois was on 115 at the time of writing; could be one to move up through the ranks on good ground at around 2m. *'He still has some strengthening up to do.' (Nicky Henderson, trainer)*

1152 French Saulaie (Fr)

6 b g French Glory - Parade Royale (Garde Royale)
P Hobbs   Mrs R J Skan
PLACINGS: 4U2/15412021-2   **RPR 135+h**

Starts	1st	2nd	3rd	4th	Win & Pl
12	3	4		2	£49,575
120	4/07	Chel	2m5^1/2f Cls2 117-140 Hdl Hcap good		£12,213
	1/07	Hntg	2m1^1/2f Cls4 Nov Hdl 4-7yo soft		£4,554
	5/06	Worc	2m Cls4 Nov Hdl gd-sft		£3,083

Ex-French hurdler who improved rapidly on better ground in the spring at the end of his first season with Philip Hobbs; dotted up in a decent handicap over 2m5^1/2f at Cheltenham in April (beat Chilling Place by 5l) before running a cracker over 2m - and off a 12lb higher mark - in the valuable Swinton Hurdle at Haydock, where he was hampered at the fifth but put in a strong late run to finish 1^1/2l second to the progressive novice Leslingtaylor (good, 23 ran); clearly on the up, and while another 3lb rise to an official mark of 135 will not help his cause, he should be up to competing in the top 2m handicaps this season, although a switch to fences would come as no surprise (is a half-brother to a winning chaser in France).

1153 Full House (Ire)

8 br g King's Theatre - Nirvavita (Highest Honor)
P Webber   The Chamberlain Addiscott Partnership
PLACINGS: F1U3P3F1/F1P681/PF6-   **RPR 148+c**

Starts	1st	2nd	3rd	4th	Win & Pl
23	5	-	5	-	£52,526
133	4/06	Sand	2m4^1/2f Cls2 116-138 Ch Hcap good		£12,526
129	10/05	Weth	2m4^1/2f Cls2 109-135 Ch Hcap gd-fm		£9,281
120	4/05	Sand	2m4^1/2f Cls3 Nov 101-127 Ch Hcap good		£12,441
	6/04	Strf	2m4f Cls3 Ch gd-fm		£5,746
98	2/04	Asct	2m^1/2f Cls3 95-116 Hdl Hcap good		£4,771

Versatile sort who is equally at home in a handicap chase or at the most prestigious meetings on the Flat; needs fast ground, so tends to stay in his box through the depths of winter, but looked as good as ever over fences when 13l sixth behind Dempsey in the Grade 2 Celebration Chase at Sandown in April (2m, good to firm, 8 ran); ran on into the summer on the Flat, scoring at Goodwood in May and landing a famous success in the Ascot Stakes at Royal Ascot the following month; still improving on that evidence, and could pick up a decent 2m handicap chase during the months of the Ten to Follow competition if there is a bit of fast ground somewhere.

1154 Fundamentalist (Ire)

9 b g Supreme Leader - Run For Shelter (Strong Gale)

N Twiston-Davies   Gripen

PLACINGS: 121/112U/4FF0/2056P-   **RPR 151 + c**

Starts	1st	2nd	3rd	4th	Win & Pl
16	4	3	-	1	£126,538

	11/04	Chel	2m Cls1 Nov Gd2 Ch good	£30,250
	9/04	Prth	2m4½f Cls3 Nov Ch good	£7,385
	3/04	Chel	2m5f Cls1 Nov Gd1 Hdl good	£58,000
	2/04	Kemp	3m½f Cls3 Nov Hdl good	£4,953

Once a potential top-notcher but now not, and seems to be a horse without a trip; looked on the way back when a very encouraging neck runner-up to Cornish Sett on his reappearance in a graduation chase at Cheltenham last November (3m½f, good to soft, 4 ran), bowling along in front in typical fashion and rallying up the hill after a mistake at the last; showed precious little, though, in four starts between 2m4f and 3m2f after that; has at least tumbled down the handicap and is 19lb below his peak assessment, which may offer connections a scrap of encouragement; possibly best fresh but hasn't won for almost three years and his inclusion in any list would be an act of considerable faith.

1155 Gaspara (Fr)

4 b f Astarabad - Gaspaisie (Beyssac)

D Pipe   M C Pipe

PLACINGS: 36/5137F62211112-   **RPR 146 + h**

Starts	1st	2nd	3rd	4th	Win & Pl
15	5	3	2		£164,608

130	3/07	Chel	2m½f Cls1 Nov List 119-140 Hdl 4yo gd-sft	£42,765
126	3/07	Sand	2m½f Cls1 List 113-132 Hdl Hcap heavy	£34,212
	2/07	Chep	2m4f Cls4 Nov Hdl 4-7yo soft	£2,733
	1/07	Tntn	2m3½f Cls4 Nov Hdl soft	£3,904
	6/06	Autl	2m1½f Hdl 3yo v soft	£13,903

Hugely progressive filly between 2m1f and 2m4f over hurdles last season after arriving from France; improved with each of her five starts, claiming her biggest payday when following success in the Imperial Cup at Sandown by winning the Fred Winter Juvenile Hurdle at the Cheltenham Festival, where she put up a most game, front-running performance to beat Altilhar unchallenged by 5l; probably did best of all when tasting defeat for the only time, however, coping admirably with the step up to top company in the Grade 1 Aintree Hurdle and going down to course specialist Al Eile by only 1½l (2m4f, good, 11 ran); that effort suggested she was right up there with the cream of last season's juvenile hurdlers, and she will surely take plenty of beating in the build-up to a crack at the new mares' hurdle race at the Festival, although she also has the option of novice chasing. *'She's not very big, but she's all heart and gives her best every time.' (David Pipe, trainer)*

1156 Gazza's Girl (Ire)

7 b/br m Norwich - Miss Ranova (Giacometti)

Mrs J Harrington (Ir)   Patrick McCooey

PLACINGS: 050421117/31U3F1250-   **RPR 143c**

Starts	1st	2nd	3rd	4th	Win & Pl
21	5	2	2	1	£95,426

	1/07	Thur	2m4f Nov Gd3 Ch soft	£20,674
	10/06	Gway	2m6f Ch heavy	£8,979
104	2/06	Fair	3m Nov 96-124 Hdl Hcap sft-hvy	£29,183
96	2/06	Leop	2m2f 83-113 Hdl Hcap yield	£11,224
88	2/06	Fair	2m4f Nov 77-107 Hdl Hcap yield	£5,957

Overcame some jumping problems to post progressive form in the top staying novice chases last season; ran well in Grade 1 company before gaining her biggest success of the season in a Grade 3 mares' event at Thurles in January, where she led travelling easily at the last and drew clear to beat Sabina Park by 4l (2m4f, soft, 12 ran); finished 4l second to Snowy Morning at Navan next time, and was about the same distance behind the same rival when the pair were second and fifth behind Denman in the Royal & SunAlliance Chase at the Cheltenham Festival (3m½f, good to soft, 17 ran); looks well treated on a mark of 131, and will surely be aimed at valuable handicap chases.

1157 Gem Daly (Fr)

6 b g Nikos - Tinopasa (No Pass No Sale)

N Meade (Ir)   Patrick Nicholas McCormack

PLACINGS: P/1-   **RPR 106 + b**

Starts	1st	2nd	3rd	4th	Win & Pl
1	1	-	-	-	£5,718

	12/06	Leop	2m NHF 5yo sft-hvy	£5,719

Imposing French-bred who surprised his trainer by winning a bumper on his racecourse debut at Leopardstown's Christmas meeting last season, moving up to lead travelling well 2f out and ridden out to beat Oscar Time by 6l (2m, soft to heavy, 14 ran); missed the remainder of the season after suffering a stress fracture of a cannonbone, and Noel Meade will have been dismayed at how the form worked out, as there were certainly no stars among the vanquished; could only win as easily as he did, however, and remains an interesting candidate for novice hurdles.

1158 Gemini Lucy (Ire)

7 ch m Glacial Storm - Jodi (Phardante)

Mrs J Harrington (Ir)   Queens Prices Syndicate

PLACINGS: 0/66184/111F12201U-0   **RPR 142 + c**

Starts	1st	2nd	3rd	4th	Win & Pl
19	6	2	1	1	£111,733

135	4/07	Fair	2m1f 135-156 Ch Hcap good	£43,986
	10/06	Punc	2m2f Nov List Ch yield	£14,367
	8/06	Gway	2m1f Nov Ch gd-fm	£13,469
	7/06	Klny	2m4f Nov Ch firm	£9,877
	6/06	Punc	2m Ch gd-fm	£7,148
85	4/06	Wxfd	2m Nov 78-97 Hdl 4-6yo Hcap yield	£6,195

Smart novice chaser at up to 2m4f last season; won

four times between June and October 2006, completing the haul with a 4l defeat of Mounthenry in a Listed event at Punchestown (2m2f, yielding, 8 ran); was given a mid-winter break, and returned in even better form; finished 12l second to Nickname in a Grade 2 at Naas before blundering her way round in the Arkle (tenth behind My Way De Solzen, and reported in season afterwards), but then posted her best form to date when winning a valuable 2m1f handicap chase on good ground at Fairyhouse, where she made every yard and galloped on powerfully to slam Old Flame by 17l; started favourite for a Grade 1 contest at the Punchestown festival but unseated rider at the first, before a dismal effort over hurdles at Cork in July; hard to catch over the minimum on good ground.

1159 Getoutwhenyoucan (Ire)

7 gr g Old Vic - Galice Du Soleil (Royal Charter)

D Pipe   D A Johnson

PLACINGS: 1/P1222111P/

Starts	1st	2nd	3rd	4th	Win & Pl
7	3	3	-	-	£22,889
122	11/05	Chel	3m¹/₂f Cls4 113-129 Am Ch Hcap gd-sft..............£10,534
	8/05	NAbb	3m2¹/₂f Cls3 Ch gd-fm £6,014
102	7/05	NAbb	3m3f Cls4 76-102 Hdl Hcap gd-sft £3,293

Progressive chaser when last seen in 2005 and regarded as an ideal sort for long-distance handicaps; made his last appearance when sent off favourite and pulled up in a race won by Lacdoudal at Sandown in December that year, but had won three out of three over fences before that, culminating in an impressive 9l defeat of Bee An Bee over 3m¹/₂f at Cheltenham; has to prove that he is over the injury that ruled him out of action last season, but it's not difficult to see him scoring if able to pick up where he left off.

1160 Glasker Mill (Ire)

7 b g Old Vic - Lucey Allen (Strong Gale)

Miss H Knight   Trevor Hemmings

PLACINGS: 110/331176/1FF0-0   **RPR 140+c**

Starts	1st	2nd	3rd	4th	Win & Pl
13	4	-	2	-	£19,520
	1/07	Font	2m2f Cls4 Ch soft £5,831
	1/06	Hayd	2m4f Cls4 Nov Hdl 4-7yo heavy £4,554
	12/05	Font	2m6¹/₂f Cls4 Nov Hdl good £3,419
	2/05	Kemp	2m Cls6 NHF 4-6yo soft £3,539

Smart jumper whose season went pear-shaped after an impressive chasing debut, but remains interesting for handicaps this term; winning start over fences came at Fontwell in January, where he jumped neatly under a patient ride and asserted from the last to beat Dancing Bay and Desert Air by 3¹/₂l and a head; was immediately hailed by his trainer as a Royal & SunAlliance candidate, but two falls in the space of a week in February put paid to any such plans; showed little in a pair of

handicap hurdles in the spring, but those efforts should have restored a little of his confidence; form of his Fontwell win was franked with the second, third and fourth all scoring next time, so should not be written off; suited by cut in the ground.

1161 Glencove Marina (Ire)

5 b g Spectrum - Specifiedrisk (Turtle Island)

W Mullins (Ir)   John J Brennan

PLACINGS: 11/131-8   **RPR 144h**

Starts	1st	2nd	3rd	4th	Win & Pl
6	4	-	1	-	£88,768
	4/07	Punc	2m4f Nov Gd1 Hdl good.....................£46,081
	3/07	Thur	2m Mdn Hdl 5yo heavy £4,669
	4/06	Punc	2m NHF 4-5yo good £30,517
	2/06	Thur	2m NHF 4yo yld-sft..............................£3,812

Classy novice hurdler who made excellent strides in a short space of time last season and looks set to make his mark in novice chases; didn't make his hurdling debut until March, when easily making the odds in Thurles maiden; finished third to De Valira as favourite for a Grade 2 hurdle at Fairyhouse the following month, but stepped up a good deal on that form to land the Grade 1 Land Rover Champion Novice Hurdle at the Punchestown festival, 1l up on Catch Me when that rival fell at the last (still not entirely fluent); sent off second-favourite for Grade 2 Prix La Barka at Auteuil in May (2m5f, very soft, 15 ran) but only eighth of 11 finishers; benefited from the step up to 2m4f at Punchestown (dam half-sister to Ascot Gold Cup winner Mr Dinos), but connections believe he has the speed to make it to the top at 2m over fences, and the Arkle Chase has been pencilled in as the long-term target.

1162 Glenfinn Captain (Ire)

8 br g Alderbrook - Glenfinn Princess (Ginger Boy)

T Taaffe (Ir)   John P McManus

PLACINGS: 1/11U21/1F-   **RPR 135+c**

Starts	1st	2nd	3rd	4th	Win & Pl
8	5	1	-	-	£53,808
	10/06	Fair	2m Ch sft-hvy £5,957
	4/06	Fair	2m Nov Gd2 Hdl gd-yld £26,938
	1/06	Cork	2m2f Hdl heavy £8,578
	12/05	Fair	2m Mdn Hdl heavy £6,861
	3/05	DRoy	2m NHF sft-hvy £3,921

Promising graduate to fences in an abbreviated season last winter; jumped well when seeing off Khetaam by 8l at Fairyhouse on his chasing debut and was favourite for a Grade 1 at Leopardstown over Christmas (2m1f, soft to heavy, 9 ran), where he led and jumped well until falling at the fourth-last (race eventually won by Schindlers Hunt); relishes plenty of cut and should be effective between 2m and 2m4f; will have to take on seasoned rivals now and lacks experience, but blessed with plenty of talent and could well take high rank over fences; current handicap mark of 140 may be ripe for exploitation.

1163 Golden Child (Ire)

5 b g Supreme Leader - Native Singer (Be My Native)

N Twiston-Davies   D J & S A Goodman & R Rexton

PLACINGS: 11813-   RPR **109+h**

Starts	1st	2nd	3rd	4th	Win & Pl
5	3		1		£12,621
3/07	Kemp	2m5f Cls4 Nov Hdl heavy			£3,904
11/06	Asct	2m Cls3 NHF 4-6yo soft			£6,263
10/06	Worc	2m Cls6 NHF 4-6yo gd-sft			£2,056

From the family of classy chasers Nick Dundee and Ned Kelly, and appeals as a novice with a future over fences; won two bumpers before making his hurdling debut at Ascot when eighth behind a useful Ringaroses (2m4f, good to soft, 14 ran); showed considerable improvement after a ten-week break when sloshing through the mud to win a minor Kempton contest by 11l from Greenhill Bramble; well below that form on final outing, but fast ground to blame and he shouldn't be judged on that 49l third behind Oscardeal at Southwell (2m5f, good to firm, 10 ran); will continue over hurdles for the time being, but may be seen to considerably better advantage over fences at 3m or thereabouts, when soft ground looks a prerequisite.

1164 Grand Bleu (Ire)

4 b g Great Palm - Blue Pool (Saddlers' Hall)

F Doumen (Fr)   Uplifting Bloodstock Ltd

PLACINGS: 114-   RPR **139+h**

Starts	1st	2nd	3rd	4th	Win & Pl
3	2			1	£25,375
2/07	Hayd	2m Cls2 Nov Hdl 4yo heavy			£13,012
12/06	Fntb	1m2f Hdl 3yo v soft			£5,421

Useful juvenile hurdler last season; won a very weak five-runner renewal of the Victor Ludorum Hurdle at Haydock in February, coming home 15l clear of King's Revenge in heavy ground; missed the Cheltenham Festival, but took on Katchit at Aintree, where he looked a bit one-paced on the faster ground and finished 21l fourth behind the Triumph Hurdle winner (2m^1/2f, good, 12 ran); held in high regard, and could be interesting for Graded hurdles when the ground is riding soft; has won a hurdle race over 1m2f in France, but could be stepped up in trip at some stage.

1165 Grangeclare Lark (Ire)

6 b m Old Vic - Grangeclare Rose (Gianchi)

D Hughes (Ir)   T Hendy

PLACINGS: 4243/1111611-   RPR **140+h**

Starts	1st	2nd	3rd	4th	Win & Pl
11	6	1	1	2	£107,978
4/07	Punc	2m2f Gd3 Hdl good			£30,791
4/07	Fair	2m4f Nov Gd3 Hdl good			£22,873
12/06	Leop	2m4f List Hdl heavy			£19,081
11/06	Cork	2m Hdl 5yo sft-hvy			£8,101
11/06	DRoy	2m Nov Gd3 Hdl yld-sft			£17,959
10/06	Fair	2m NHF 4-7yo sft-hvy			£4,289

Prolific mare last season, winning five of her six starts in novice hurdles; twice successful in Grade 3 events at the direct expense of Shuil Aris in April, beating Paul Nolan's mare by a short head at Fairyhouse (2m4f, good, 14 ran) and extending the advantage to 2^1/2l on 3lb worse terms at Punchestown 17 days later (2m2f, good, 13 ran); likely to go over fences this term, and should do well (half-brother Scarthy Lad improved for a switch to the bigger obstacles); stays 2m4f and acts on good and heavy ground.

1166 Granit Jack (Fr)

5 gr g Glaieul - Line Grey (Le Nain Jaune)

P Nicholls   J Hales

PLACINGS: 71111/3212-   RPR **146+h**

Starts	1st	2nd	3rd	4th	Win & Pl
9	5	2	1		£91,642
2/07	Tntn	2m3^1/2f Cls4 Nov Hdl soft			£3,426
2/06	Pau	2m3^1/2f List Ch 4yo soft			£19,862
1/06	Pau	2m3^1/2f Ch 4yo gd-sft			£11,917
1/06	Pau	2m3^1/2f Ch 4yo heavy			£10,593
12/05	Pau	2m1f Ch 3yo soft			£10,894

Exciting chasing prospect; disappointed when beaten at short odds on his first two starts over hurdles in Britain last season, but ended with two much-improved performances after being treated for stomach ulcers; made short work of despatching inferior rivals at Taunton in February before going some way to justifying his lofty home reputation with a fine second in the Supreme Novices' Hurdle at the Cheltenham Festival, failing by only 3l to catch Ebaziyan after jumping a little big in places (2m1/2f, soft, 22 ran); very speedy type who will be pitched straight into open company over fences having already won four times in that sphere in his native France, and it would be no surprise to see him winning plenty of races at 2m4f-plus.

1167 Green Belt Flyer (Ire)

9 b g Leading Counsel - Current Liability (Caribo)

Miss V Williams   Green Belt Foresters

PLACINGS: /8746412FP230/8851P-   RPR **144+c**

Starts	1st	2nd	3rd	4th	Win & Pl
34	7	3	3	5	£78,815
130	3/07	Newb	3m Cls3 110-130 Ch Hcap soft		£10,021
119	10/05	Naas	2m3f 98-129 Ch Hcap soft		£9,234
	3/05	Naas	2m Nov Ch yld-sft		£8,331
	1/05	Tram	2m Ch sft-hvy		£5,146
122	2/04	Naas	2m 91-122 Hdl Hcap yield		£9,169
	12/03	Gowr	2m Nov Hdl 4-6yo yield		£6,273
	6/03	Baln	2m Mdn Hdl 4-5yo sft-hvy		£4,705

Handicap chaser who took some time to settle into his first season for Venetia Williams, but eventually returned to best; well down the field over 2m and 2m1f, but was stepped up to 3m for the first time after a seven-week break at Newbury in March, and looked revitalised, strolling home by 9l from Harrycone Lewis after his handicap rating had dropped to a lenient mark; obviously it went straight back up and he was never at the races when pulled up in Reveillez's race at Aintree (3m1f, good, 18 ran); appears better with cut in the ground but probably effective from 2m4f upwards; likely to need a little mercy from the handicapper, but has the ability to win races.

1168 Greenhope (Ire)

9 b g Definite Article - Unbidden Melody (Chieftain)

N Henderson   Lynn Wilson, Giles Wilson & Martin Landau

PLACINGS: 84/0202163/51P/004-0   **RPR 144c**

Starts		2nd	3rd	4th	Win & Pl
23	6	2	2	2	£96,498
132	3/06 Chel	2m¹/₂f Cls1 Gd3 126-147 Ch Hcap good			£42,765
	2/05 Plum	2m1f Cls3 Ch soft			£7,228
122	12/03 Kemp	2m Cls3 97-123 Hdl Hcap good			£6,206
	12/01 Kemp	2m Cls2 Nov Hdl 3yo good			£7,053
	11/01 Chel	2m¹/₂f Cls2 Nov Hdl 3yo good			£8,619
	11/01 Asct	2m¹/₂f Cls3 Nov Hdl 3yo good			£4,875

Useful 2m chaser whose finest hour came when gaining an emotional success in the 2006 Grand Annual at the Cheltenham Festival; rarely fired on all cylinders in a light campaign last season, but showed there was still fire in the belly when 6³/4l fourth behind Bambi De L'Orme in a Grade 3 handicap chase at Aintree in April, off an 8lb higher mark than his Festival-winning one (2m, good, 15 ran); no show in a handicap hurdle at Uttoxeter on his final outing; winning prospects probably depend on the handicapper cutting him some slack, but he is still open to a little progress after just nine starts over fences; best on good ground, and likes to go from the front.

1169 Gungadu

7 ch g Beneficial - Tsarella (Mummy's Pet)

P Nicholls   Mrs M Findlay & P K Barber

PLACINGS: 31/11/312127/1211F-   **RPR 151+c**

Starts		2nd	3rd	4th	Win & Pl
11	5	3	1	-	£82,798
	2/07 Asct	3m Cls1 Nov Gd2 Ch gd-sft			£22,808
	1/07 Wwck	3m¹/₂f Cls2 Nov Ch heavy			£12,793
	10/06 Chel	3m¹/₂f Cls2 Nov Ch good			£12,572
	2/06 Winc	2m6f Cls2 Nov Hdl gd-sft			£8,768
	11/05 Chep	2m4f Cls4 Nov Hdl gd-sft			£3,103

Very smart staying novice chaser last season who looks ideal for long-distance handicap chases; sent off at odds-on for his first four starts over fences, winning three times and putting up his best visual display at Warwick in January when slamming In Accord by 25l before going to Ascot and defeating Wee Robbie by 4l in the Grade 2 Reynoldstown Chase; suffered defeat at the hands of Boychuk at Newbury in November and ended his season with a fall in the four-miler at the Cheltenham Festival, a race for which he was sent off the 2-1 favourite and was still in contention when blundering; at home on testing ground, and races like the Welsh National and Totesport Classic Chase should be up his street, especially if his tendency to make the odd severe jumping mistake can be ironed out.

1170 Hairy Molly (Ire)

7 b g Shernazar - Ballilaurenka (Buckskin)

J Crowley (Ir)   F T B Syndicate

PLACINGS: 213112/310-   **RPR 128+h**

Starts	1st	2nd	3rd	4th	Win & Pl
9	4	2	2	-	£53,291
2/07 Naas	2m3f Mdn Hdl sft-hvy				£5,603
3/06 Chel	2m¹/₂f Cls1 Gd1 NHF 4-6yo good				£22,808
2/06 Naas	2m3f NHF sft-hvy				£4,766
1/06 Naas	2m3f NHF soft				£4,289

Champion Bumper winner two seasons ago, but progress over hurdles last winter was hampered by minor setbacks; just needed the run behind the smart Scotsirish at Leopardstown in January, and duly improved to win a maiden hurdle at Naas in February, relishing a step up to 2m3f and asserting on the run-in to beat the decent Knowledge Box by 3l (soft to heavy); stepped up to 3m for the Brit Insurance Novices' Hurdle at the Cheltenham Festival, but didn't jump well and trailed in 11th behind Wichita Lineman; will be given a run or two over hurdles this autumn, but the plan is to switch to chasing at some point; big horse who could really come into his own over fences, and obviously has Royal & SunAlliance Chase potential; well served by soft/heavy ground.

1171 Halcon Genelardais (Fr)

7 ch g Halcon - Francetphile (Farabi)

A King   Ian Payne & Kim Franklin

PLACINGS: 45/2211/F41115/113P-   **RPR 165+c**

Starts	1st	2nd	3rd	4th	Win & Pl
17	7	2	1	2	£192,919
147	12/06 Chep	3m5¹/₂f Cls1 Gd3 130-151 Ch Hcap soft			£57,020
133	11/06 Hayd	2m7¹/₂f Cls2 131-157 Hdl Hcap gd-sft			£62,630
	2/06 Extr	3m1¹/₂f Cls3 Nov Ch soft			£10,058
	2/06 Weth	3m1f Cls1 Nov Gd2 Ch soft			£18,461
	1/06 Wwck	3m¹/₂f Cls2 Nov Ch soft			£12,793
	3/05 Uttx	2m4¹/₂f Cls4 Nov Hdl gd-sft			£4,732
	2/05 Font	2m6¹/₂f Cls4 Nov Hdl gd-sft			£3,504

High-class long-distance chaser who pulled off a perfectly executed plan when winning the Welsh National last Christmas; went to Chepstow on the back of a very valuable handicap win over hurdles at Haydock (beat Irish Wolf by 1¹/4l), but proved himself even better over fences with an impressive victory at the Welsh venue, where he jumped well, led 3 out and ran on strongly to beat Mon Mome by 4l; loved the soft ground there, and was thought capable of stepping up to Gold Cup class if testing conditions prevailed, but he was a remote third behind Exotic Dancer in the Letheby and Christopher Chase at Cheltenham in January, and was a bitter disappointment in first-time blinkers in the Festival showpiece, being tailed off when pulled up 3 out; clearly a lot better than that, and with just seven chase starts behind him, he may yet have more to come; might be tricky to place, as My Way De Solzen would appear to be his stable's number one contender for the top chases if the ground is soft.

1172 Harchibald (Fr)

8 b g Perugino - Dame D'Harvard (Quest For Fame)

N Meade (Ir)   D P Sharkey

PLACINGS: 15/431112/21312/455-   RPR **146**h

Starts	1st	2nd	3rd	4th	Win & Pl
25	8	5	3	4	£371,357

	12/05	Chel	2m1f Cls1 Gd2 Hdl gd-sft	£42,765
	10/05	Tipp	2m Gd1 Hdl soft	£46,170
	12/04	Kemp	2m Cls1 Gd1 Hdl gd-sft	£58,000
	11/04	Newc	2m Cls1 Gd1 Hdl good	£43,500
	11/04	Punc	2m Gd2 Hdl yld-sft	£21,547
119	2/04	Leop	2m 103-130 Hdl Hcap good	£10,086
	4/03	Punc	2m Hdl 4yo good	£11,607
	12/02	Fair	2m Mdn Hdl 3yo soft	£5,503

One-time top-class 2m hurdler who won three Grade 1 events in 2004/05, but was heartbreakingly outbattled by Brave Inca in the 2005 Champion Hurdle at Cheltenham; returned from injury last season and managed just three starts, all of them producing disappointing outcomes; didn't handle testing conditions at Tipperary in October or Gowran in February (has never run well in very soft ground), but should have done better on his favoured good going at the Punchestown festival, where he failed to pick up at all and finished 13^1/$_2$l fifth behind Silent Oscar; has been freshened up over the summer, and connections can only hope he rediscovers his best form on fast ground. *'He was basically in training for two years solid and needed a complete break. He's had that over the summer and come back fresh and well.'* (Noel Meade, trainer)

1173 Hard Act To Follow (Ire)

8 ch g Shernazar - Lauren's Gem (Over The River)

J H Johnson   Andrea & Graham Wylie

PLACINGS: 1/11P/1-   RPR **140**+c

Starts	1st	2nd	3rd	4th	Win & Pl
5	4	-	-	-	£18,643

10/06	Weth	2m7^1/$_2$f Cls5 Ch good	£3,253
1/06	Carl	3m1f Cls3 Nov Hdl heavy	£6,506
12/05	Ayr	2m4f Cls3 Nov Hdl soft	£4,964
3/05	DRoy	2m NHF 5-7yo yld-sft	£3,921

Lightly raced gelding whose novice chase campaign was cut short after one impressive win; that success came on good ground at Wetherby last October, where he made all, drew clear on the bit from three out and was eased down to beat King Of Confusion by 38l, with the rest strung out at very wide intervals (2m7^1/$_2$f, 7 ran); was a good novice hurdler the season before that, winning three on the bounce before being pulled up behind Black Jack Ketchum at the Cheltenham Festival; has a worrying absence to overcome, and lacks experience, but connections will no doubt seek to build him up in graduation chases before tackling something better.

1174 Hardy Eustace (Ire)

10 b g Archway - Sterna Star (Corvaro)

D Hughes (Ir)   Laurence Byrne

PLACINGS: /123311/17323/12143-   RPR **166**+h

Starts	1st	2nd	3rd	4th	Win & Pl
30	11	7	5	1	£911,282

1/07	Leop	2m Gd1 Hdl soft	£67,568
11/06	Asct	2m3^1/$_2$f Cls1 Gd2 Hdl soft	£56,340
12/05	Punc	2m4f Hdl soft	£8,409
3/05	Chel	2m1^1/$_2$f Cls1 Gd1 Hdl good	£174,000
2/05	Gowr	2m Gd2 Hdl heavy	£27,702
4/04	Punc	2m Gd1 Hdl good	£67,606
3/04	Chel	2m1^1/$_2$f Cls1 Gd1 Hdl good	£174,000
3/03	Chel	2m5f Cls1 Nov Gd1 Hdl good	£58,000
12/02	Leop	2m4f Nov Hdl heavy	£11,963
12/02	Fair	2m Nov Gd1 Hdl sft-hvy	£27,914
4/02	Fair	2m NHF 4-5yo yield	£24,141

High-class hurdler whose six Grade 1 successes include two in the Champion Hurdle, in 2004 and 2005; looked in great heart in the run-up to Cheltenham last season, slamming Mighty Man by 11l over 2m4f at Ascot, going down fighting to Detroit City in the Bula (conceding 4lb to the winner) and bringing the house down by winning the Irish Champion Hurdle at Leopardstown in January, where he defied his advancing years in gritty, front-running style to outbattle Brave Inca on the run-in by 3l (2m, soft, 8 ran); started 3-1 to regain his Cheltenham crown at the age of ten, but was never travelling with the same enthusiasm and was fighting a losing battle from two out, eventually finishing 3^1/$_2$l fourth behind Sublimity; closed out with an 8^1/$_4$l third behind Silent Oscar at the Punchestown festival, a run that convinced connections that his future now lies over further; likely to remain a force in Graded hurdles in Ireland, and if he is to go to Cheltenham, it will probably be for the World Hurdle. *'Staying races will give him more of a chance.'* (Dessie Hughes, trainer)

1175 Harris Bay

8 b g Karinga Bay - Harristown Lady (Muscatite)

Miss H Knight   Mrs G M Sturges & H Stephen Smith

PLACINGS: /9P4007/1131P1/11PP-   RPR **141**+c

Starts	1st	2nd	3rd	4th	Win & Pl
18	7	-	2	1	£70,407

126	11/06	Asct	3m Cls2 118-137 Ch Hcap gd-sft	£31,315
88	10/06	Towc	2m5f Cls4 Nov 76-102 Hdl Hcap good	£3,253
116	4/06	Sand	2m4^1/$_2$f Cls3 Nov 102-123 Ch Hcap good	£12,700
109	2/06	Leic	2m7^1/$_2$f Cls3 109-125 Ch Hcap soft	£8,142
102	12/05	Sand	2m4^1/$_2$f Cls3 Nov 99-108 Ch Hcap soft	£6,783
88	11/05	Towc	2m3^1/$_2$f Cls4 Nov 77-101 Ch Hcap soft	£4,050
	1/04	Ludl	2m Cls6 NHF 4-6yo gd-sft	£2,723

Useful handicap chaser who has had wind operations, and always races in a tongue tie; made a winning return last season over hurdles at Towcester, and that set him up for a career-best success in a valuable 3m handicap chase at Ascot in November, where he came through in the straight after a patient ride to beat Lou Du Moulin Mas and Tango Royal by 1^1/$_2$l and 2^1/$_2$l (officially good to soft ground, but race was run in a downpour); has always been somewhat fragile, though, and was pulled up in his two subsequent starts in other valuable contests, where he got behind in big fields and appeared to sulk; progressive before those flops, and he may yet have more to give in small fields with cut in the ground.

1176 Hasty Prince

9 ch g Halling - Sister Sophie (Effervescing)

J O'Neill   John P McManus

PLACINGS: 13/436600791/525227-   **RPR 147+c**

Starts	1st	2nd	3rd	4th	Win & Pl
31	6	5	4	1	£177,200
138	4/06	Sand	2m4¹/₂f Cls2 115-138 Hdl Hcap gd-fm £12,526
	12/04	Ludl	2m4f Cls3 Nov Ch gd-sft.................................£8,174
	4/04	Sand	2m¹/₂f Cls2 Hdl good £40,600
131	11/03	Chep	2m4f Cls2 119-140 Hdl Hcap gd-fm £17,400
	3/03	Donc	2m3¹/₂f Cls3 Hdl gd-sft £6,754
	1/03	Hntg	2m¹/₂f Cls4 Nov Hdl soft £3,668

Very smart handicap chaser at around 2m but kept finding one too good last season and could do with some help from the handicapper; ran four times over fences (and twice over hurdles), finishing second three times, probably doing just about best of all in the Grand Annual at the Cheltenham Festival, where he led two from home only to get collared on the run-in and eventually go down by 3l to Andreas (2m, good to soft, 23 ran); was racing from a mark of 137 there and was raised 6lb for his effort, so likely to continue finding life tough; consistent, but has won only once over fences – a novice contest nearly three years ago – a record that speaks for itself.

1177 Heads Onthe Ground (Ire)

10 br g Be My Native - Strong Wings (Strong Gale)

E Bolger (Ir)   John P McManus

PLACINGS: 22/3PP/0P29/1123411-   **RPR 145+c**

Starts	1st	2nd	3rd	4th	Win & Pl
22	3	9	2	2	£58,809
126	3/07	Chel	3m7f Cls2 124-150 Ch Hcap soft £28,184
	2/07	Punc	3m Ch soft £7,003
	1/03	Navn	2m6f Mdn Hdl soft £4,929

Nothing special over regulation fences, but last season became yet another from his yard to excel when switched to the cross-country arena; twice beat subsequent Grand National hero Silver Birch in that sphere, triumphing by 10l at Punchestown in February, and following up with a 3¹/₂l defeat of his compatriot over 3m7f at the Cheltenham Festival; had earlier finished third behind stablemate Spot Thedifference at Cheltenham's December meeting, so was clearly progressing at a rate of knots in the second half of the campaign; probably has a few years ahead of him yet, and will surely have his season geared towards a Festival repeat in March. *'He didn't have much weight at the Festival – it remains to be seen whether he can do it again with a lot more on his back.' (Enda Bolger, trainer)*

1178 Heathcote

5 b g Unfuwain - Chere Amie (Mr Prospector)

G L Moore   B Siddle & B D Haynes

PLACINGS: 1211/0378291-7   **RPR 133+h**

Starts	1st	2nd	3rd	4th	Win & Pl
12	4	2	1	-	£116,376
126	2/07	Newb	2m¹/₂f Cls1 Gd3 124-146 Hdl Hcap soft £85,530
	4/06	Towc	2m Cls4 Nov Hdl 4yo gd-sft £4,437
	2/06	Plum	2m Cls3 Nov Hdl 4yo gd-sft £5,205
	12/05	Ling	2m¹/₂f Cls3 Nov Hdl 3yo soft.......................£5,179

Smart handicap hurdler; took everyone by surprise when winning the Totesport Trophy at Newbury in February, defying odds of 50-1 to lead approaching the last and beat Overstrand and subsequent County Hurdle hero Pedrobob by a neck and 2l; that was a huge improvement on anything he had achieved before; flopped in France on his final outing (2m6f probably too far), but has had only 12 starts over hurdles, and is probably capable of a bit better; starts the season on a mark of 133, 7lb higher than at Newbury.

1179 Hedgehunter (Ire)

11 b g Montelimar - Aberedw (Caerwent)

W Mullins (Ir)   Trevor Hemmings

PLACINGS: F/9240611/04222/599-   **RPR 109c**

Starts	1st	2nd	3rd	4th	Win & Pl
35	5	14	2	4	£776,908
144	4/05	Aint	4m4f Cls1 Gd3 134-155 Ch Hcap gd-sft £406,000
	2/05	Fair	3m1f Gd3 Ch soft..£16,160
129	1/04	Gowr	3m 127-155 Ch Hcap soft £34,331
115	2/03	Punc	3m4f 115-143 Ch Hcap sft-hvy.....................£13,506
	2/02	Clon	3m Mdn Hdl heavy £4,868

One of the finest Aintree horses of the modern era, winning the 2005 Grand National and finishing runner-up in 2006, while also having the class to finish second to War Of Attrition in the 2006 Gold Cup at Cheltenham; came nowhere near matching those exploits last season, running only three times in all; prepared for another tilt at Aintree with a couple of runs in minor events over hurdles, finishing down the field both times; well fancied for the Grand National, being sent off 9-1, but could make no impression under his welter 11st 12lb burden, finishing ninth of 12 finishers; another crack at the National is sure to be on the cards, but he is likely to be burdened with plenty of weight once again, and won't race much en route.

1180 Heez A Dreamer (Ire)

7 b g Naheez - Tuitestown (Orchestra)

Miss V Williams   James Drummond

PLACINGS: 1/2F4P/21361315-   **RPR 143+c**

Starts	1st	2nd	3rd	4th	Win & Pl
8	3	1	2	-	£30,986
	2/07	Extr	2m3¹/₂f Cls3 Nov Ch heavy £7,036
	1/07	Font	2m6f Cls3 Nov Ch soft £8,348
	11/06	Uttx	2m6¹/₂f Cls4 Ch heavy................................£5,704

Encouragingly progressive in his first season under

Rules, and has the scope to improve; produced his best form in novice chases after the turn of the year, first when making the most of rivals' jumping shortcomings at Fontwell, then when plugging on gamely for third in a Grade 2 at Wetherby in February, beaten 6¹/₂l by Heltornic (3m1f, good to soft, 7 ran); beat moderate rivals at Exeter, and then ran a cracker in the William Hill Trophy at the Cheltenham Festival, staying on gamely up the hill past beaten horses for fifth, 10¹/₂l behind Joes Edge (3m¹/₂f, good to soft, 23 ran); likely to be seen to best advantage in the mud over 3m-plus; starts the campaign on a very reasonable mark (1lb below Cheltenham run).

1181 Heltornic (Ire)

7 ch m Zaffaran - Majestic Run (Deep Run)

M Scudamore   Stephen W Molloy

PLACINGS: /F1F1446069/132711F-   **RPR 146+c**

Starts	1st	2nd	3rd	4th	Win & Pl
20	6	2	2	2	£122,677
124	2/07	Hayd	3m4¹/₂f Cls1 Nov Gd2 Ch Hcap heavy	...........£71,275
	2/07	Weth	3m1f Cls1 Nov Gd2 Ch gd-sft	...............£17,408
	10/06	Worc	2m7¹/₂f Cls3 Ch gd-sft	.........................£7,807
	1/06	Hayd	2m6f Cls4 Nov Hdl soft	...........................£4,554
	11/05	Ling	2m7f Cls4 Nov Hdl heavy	..........................£3,380
	2/05	Fknm	2m Cls7 NHF 4-7yo good	..........................£2,237

Progressive staying chaser who won three times last season; the highlight was winning the valuable Grade 3 Red Square Vodka Gold Cup Chase at Haydock in February, where she powered through the mud under an aggressive ride from Tom Scudamore to beat L'Aventure by 1¹/₄l; might well have won the William Hill Trophy at Cheltenham (3m¹/₂f, good to soft, 23 ran) on her final start of the season had she not failed to negotiate the tricky downhill fence 2 out; starts this season the same mark of 136, and after just seven outings over fences is expected to figure prominently in the top long-distance handicap chases this term; Hennessy and the Welsh National could be targets.

1182 Heron's Flight (Ire)

5 b/br g Heron Island - Beau's Trout (Beau Charmeur)

N Meade (Ir)   All Four One Syndicate

PLACINGS: 4/21511-   **RPR 126+h**

Starts	1st	2nd	3rd	4th	Win & Pl
6	3	1	-	1	£21,983
	3/07	Naas	2m Nov Hdl heavy	....................£7,470
	1/07	Punc	2m Mdn Hdl heavy	...................£7,470
	12/06	Fair	2m NHF 4yo heavy	....................£5,719

Useful hurdler who was not overfaced during his novice campaign, and should have more to give over hurdles or fences this season; got off the mark in a 2m Punchestown maiden hurdle in January that threw up lots of future winners (beat Montana Bay by 2¹/₂l), after which he was rested for two months; returned at Naas in similarly heavy conditions in March, and did his own bit for form by rallying to beat Earth Magic by 1l (2m, 19

ran); has been campaigned like a horse whose best days lie ahead of him, and sure to have his sights raised this term; yet to race on anything like good ground, or at distances beyond 2m.

1183 Hi Cloy (Ire)

10 b g Be My Native - Thomastown Girl (Tekoah)

M Hourigan (Ir)   Mrs S McCloy

PLACINGS: /231146313/6532365P-   **RPR 158+c**

Starts	1st	2nd	3rd	4th	Win & Pl
39	9	6	10	3	£358,094
	4/06	Aint	2m4f Cls1 Gd1 Ch good	............£85,932
	12/05	Leop	2m1f Gd1 Ch yld-sft	.................£32,270
	12/05	Punc	2m4f Gd1 Ch soft	......................£46,099
	4/04	Fair	2m4f Gd1 Ch yield	....................£41,510
	3/04	Limk	3m Nov List Ch yld-sft	...........£16,046
	2/04	Leop	2m5f Nov Ch good	....................£11,920
	12/03	Limk	2m4f Nov Gd2 Ch soft	...........£21,104
	1/03	Leop	2m4f Hdl soft	............................£8,442
	12/02	Leop	2m Mdn Hdl heavy	.....................£6,773

High-class chaser whose biggest – and most recent – success came in the Grade 1 Melling Chase at Aintree in April 2006; generally below his best in a winless campaign in Grade 1 and 2 company last winter, running his best race when 2l second to Forget The Past in the Grade 2 Kinloch Brae Chase at Thurles in January (2m4f, soft, 6 ran); twice travelled to Britain in the spring, but didn't cut much ice in finishing sixth in the Ryanair Chase at Cheltenham and fifth behind Monet's Garden when bidding to repeat his Aintree heroics; effective at 2m and probably stays 3m when held up on good ground; likely to again contest Graded chases in Ireland, without being good enough to win again in Grade 1 company as he nears the age of 11.

1184 Hide The Evidence (Ire)

6 ch g Carroll House - Andarta (Ballymore)

Mrs J Harrington (Ir)   Maynard Hamilton

PLACINGS: 2/P721111704-   **RPR 146h**

Starts	1st	2nd	3rd	4th	Win & Pl
11	4	2	-	1	£57,146
	12/06	Fair	2m Nov Gd1 Hdl heavy	.............£33,621
	10/06	Cork	2m Nov Hdl good	......................£9,877
	10/06	Rosc	2m Nov Hdl 4-5yo sft-hvy	.........£5,719
	8/06	Dpat	2m2¹/₂f Mdn Hdl yield	...............£3,812

Half-brother to smart chaser Knowhere, and likely to try his hand at fences himself now; the leading 2m novice hurdler in the first half of last season, when he completed a four-timer by easily beating Clopf by 6l in the Grade 1 Royal Bond Novice Hurdle at Fairyhouse in December (2m, heavy, 9 ran); took his chance in the Irish Champion Hurdle at Leopardstown the following month, but pulled hard early on and was beaten 21l into seventh behind Hardy Eustace (2m, soft, 8 ran); started 9-1 in the Supreme Novices' at the Cheltenham Festival, but weakened tamely from two out and finished 15th, and was then 7³/₄l adrift of old rival Clopf when fourth at the Punchestown festival; a switch to fences could see a return to form.

1185 Hills Of Home (Ire)

6 b g Pasternak - Carrick Shannon (Green Shoon)

A King   Killinghurst Park Stud

PLACINGS: 1-   RPR **120+b**

Starts	1st	2nd	3rd	4th	Win & Pl
1	1	-	-	-	£1,626
	4/07	Font	2m2¹/₂f Cls6 NHF 4-6yo gd-fm		£1,627

Interesting contender for novice hurdles this winter, having made a very good impression on his sole bumper start; started 10-1 for a nine-runner contest at Fontwell in April, but won in the style of much the best horse in the race, leading 4f out and pushed out to an 18l success over outsider Bering De Lauriere; was considered for the rescheduled Aintree championship bumper the following month, but was instead roughed off for the season with all his immense promise still untapped; might start back in another bumper, and very much falls into the 'could be anything' bracket at this stage.

1186 Holly Tree (Ire)

7 br g Accordion - Lime Tree (Bulldozer)

E Sheehy (Ir)   Mrs Margaret Marshall

PLACINGS: 4BF323221323133312-9   RPR **134h**

Starts	1st	2nd	3rd	4th	Win & Pl
24	4	6	7	1	£70,244
	4/07	Limk	2m4f Nov Hdl yield		£10,997
	1/07	Limk	2m Nov Hdl heavy		£11,436
	11/06	Cork	2m Mdn Hdl sft-hvy		£7,625
	1/06	Thur	2m NHF 5-6yo yld-sft		£4,051

Tough and consistent gelding who has finished in the first three 15 times from 18 starts over hurdles; won three times last season, the most notable victory being a 6l defeat of Farmer Brown at Limerick in January (2m, heavy, 10 ran); was also placed three times in Graded company, most notably finishing 1³/4l third (promoted to second) behind Clopf in the Grade 1 Champion Novice Hurdle at the Punchestown festival in April (2m, good, 9 ran); plan is to experiment with him over fences this season, and if he takes to the larger obstacles, he is an interesting recruit to that sphere.

1187 Homer Wells (Ire)

9 b g Arctic Cider - Run And Shine (Deep Run)

W Mullins (Ir)   Mrs M McMahon

PLACINGS: 1223/40221233/0F11P-   RPR **144c**

Starts	1st	2nd	3rd	4th	Win & Pl
24	7	7	3	2	£172,875
125	2/07	Fair	3m1f Gd2 Ch heavy		£21,993
	1/07	Gowr	3m 119-147 Ch Hcap heavy		£43,919
	12/05	Fair	3m1f Ch soft		£7,351
	1/05	Naas	2m4f Nov Gd2 Hdl sft-hvy		£26,732
	12/04	Cork	3m Nov Gd3 Hdl soft		£18,338
	11/04	Naas	2m3f Mdn Hdl sft-hvy		£7,299
	1/04	Punc	2m NHF 6-7yo heavy		£4,859

Mud-loving staying chaser; stepped up on his novice chase form when winning the Thyestes Handicap Chase at Gowran in January, revelling in

the heavy ground to hit the front after three out and staying on well to fend off stablemate Livingstonebramble by 3¹/2l; followed up that victory in the Grade 2 Bobbyjo Chase at Fairyhouse the following month, underfoot conditions again up his street when leading close home to pip Jack High by 2l; conditions almost certainly too fast when pulled up in the Grand National on his final start (4m4f, good, 40 ran); starts the season on a reasonable mark (140), and must be considered for the Irish/Grand National granted suitable ground.

1188 Hoo La Baloo (Fr)

6 b g Unfuwain - Via Saleria (Arazi)

P Nicholls   The Stewart Family

PLACINGS: 12152144/33539172-2B   RPR **154c**

Starts	1st	2nd	3rd	4th	Win & Pl
21	7	4	3	2	£155,481
	3/07	Sand	3m¹/₂f Am Ch soft		£12,255
	3/06	Sand	2m Cls3 Nov Ch soft		£6,506
	12/05	Sand	2m Cls1 Nov Gd2 Ch good		£30,227
	10/05	MRas	2m1¹/₂f Cls3 Nov Ch good		£7,605
	4/05	Bord	2m2¹/₂f Hdl 4yo good		£12,255
	3/05	Bord	2m2¹/₂f Hdl 4yo gd-sft		£4,786
	2/05	Bord	2m2¹/₂f Hdl 4yo v soft		£4,426

Smart front-running chaser who is not easy to win with but showed last season that he is as capable at 3m as he is over shorter; landed his only success when winning the Grand Military Gold Cup at Sandown (where he goes particularly well), showing that the longer distance poses no problems when easily beating Cedar Chief by 13l; showed his versatility regarding distance when dropped back to 2m in the Grade 2 Celebration Chase back at Sandown in April and finishing 7l runner-up to Dempsey, and then when upped to 2m6¹/2f in the Summer Plate at Market Rasen and finishing 8l runner-up to Iron Man, to whom he was conceding 10lb; not harshly treated on a current mark of 145 (notched Racing Post Ratings in excess of 150 on two of his three most recent starts) and also goes on most types of ground, but gives the impression that he will often find one too good.

1189 Hot Weld

8 b g Weld - Deb's Ball (Glenstal)

F Murphy   S Hubbard Rodwell

PLACINGS: 12P5/1536112/PPP611-   RPR **145+c**

Starts	1st	2nd	3rd	4th	Win & Pl
23	7	4	1	1	£243,270
135	4/07	Sand	3m5¹/₂f Cls1 Gd3 135-161 Ch Hcap gd-fm		£91,232
124	4/07	Ayr	4m¹/₂f Cls1 Gd3 124-150 Ch Hcap gd-fm		£96,934
	3/06	Chel	4m1f Cls2 Nov Am Ch good		£30,010
	2/06	Muss	3m Cls4 Ch gd-fm		£3,904
	5/05	Prth	3m1¹/₂f Cls4 Hdl gd-fm		£3,474
	12/04	Newc	3m Cls4 Nov Hdl good		£3,426
	11/04	Sedg	3m3¹/₂f Cls4 Nov Hdl gd-sft		£3,348

Smart staying chaser on fast ground, and roared back from a spell in the doldrums to complete a memorable big-race double on consecutive weekends in the spring; fitted with cheekpieces for the first time when winning the Scottish Grand National at Ayr, jumping well, making all and scrapping on well when challenged by stablemate Nine De Sivola from the last to prevail by 1/2l; defied an 11lb higher mark in the Betfred Gold Cup at Sandown seven days later, not jumping as well and needing some reminders at halfway, but staying on well and 1l up when left clear at the last by the fall of Zabenz (beat the well-backed Reveillez by 3l); thorough stayer (also won the 2006 National Hunt Chase at Cheltenham) who loves fast ground; won't be producing too many fireworks in the dark winter months, but could be all the rage if the ground is quick on Grand National day.

1190 Howle Hill (Ire)

7 b g Ali-Royal - Grandeur And Grace (Septieme Ciel)

A King   Mrs J Brown,R Benton,R Devereux,R Lucas

PLACINGS: 1450/03330/25504/11-   RPR **135+c**

Starts	1st	2nd	3rd	4th	Win & Pl
18	4	2	3	2	£58,292

10/06	Wwck	2m Cls3 Nov Ch good	£6,506
5/06	Font	2m2f Cls4 Ch good	£4,554
1/04	Winc	2m Cls4 Nov Hdl gd-sft	£3,637
11/03	Weth	2m Nov List Hdl 3yo good	£13,000

Former smart hurdler (RPR of 143 at his peak) who won both his novice chase starts before his campaign was cut short last autumn; opened his account at Fontwell in May 2006, but improved on his return from a summer break when defying a penalty over 2m on good ground at Warwick in October, where he raced prominently throughout and asserted from the last to beat Nous Voila by 3l; was being aimed at the Grade 2 novice chase at Cheltenham's Open meeting after that smooth success, but didn't see the track again; back on the warpath now, and could yet be capable of climbing the ladder over fences if he returns in good heart; likely to start out in handicap chases at around 2m (yet to win beyond 2m2f).

1191 Idle Talk (Ire)

8 br g Hubbly Bubbly - Belon Breeze (Strong Gale)

D McCain   Trevor Hemmings

PLACINGS: U/141P/11324/26UUUU-   RPR **155+c**

Starts	1st	2nd	3rd	4th	Win & Pl
15	4	2	1	2	£81,197

1/06	Extr	3m1¹/₂f Cls3 Nov Ch gd-sft	£7,807
11/05	Worc	2m7¹/₂f Cls3 Ch good	£5,608
2/05	Ling	2m7f Cls3 Nov Hdl gd-sft	£5,018
10/04	Chep	3m Cls4 Mdn Hdl soft	£2,996

Handicap chaser whose jumping frailties are there for all to see in his form figures, but who is held in high regard and boasts some decent form, notably a second to Star De Mohaison in the 2006 Royal & SunAlliance Chase; got off to a good start last term (trained by Tom George at the time) when 1/2l second to My Will in a valuable handicap chase at

Cheltenham in November (3m3¹/₂f, good to soft, 12 ran); sixth in the Hennessy the following month, but then embarked on a sequence of four races where he unseated his rider, in the Letheby & Christopher Chase, Cheltenham Gold Cup, Grand National and Scottish National (joined Donald McCain before the Gold Cup); frustrating sort, but can win a decent handicap on his best form if his jumping improves; likes decent ground.

1192 Idole First (Ire)

8 b g Flemensfirth - Sharon Doll (Shahrastani)

Miss V Williams   D And J Racing Ltd

PLACINGS: 1/162614/61406/1341-   RPR **149+c**

Starts	1st	2nd	3rd	4th	Win & Pl
19	7	2	2	3	£159,818

136	3/07	Chel	2m5f Cls1 Gd3 129-155 Ch Hcap gd-sft	£57,020
128	1/07	Kemp	2m4¹/₂f Cls3 107-130 Ch Hcap gd-sft	£9,395
	2/06	Plum	2m1f Cls3 Ch gd-sft	£6,286
131	3/05	Chel	2m5f Cls1 Gd3 123-147 Hdl Hcap good	£43,500
119	12/04	Hntg	2m¹/₂f Cls3 100-121 Hdl Hcap good	£13,878
	4/04	MRas	2m3¹/₂f Cls3 Nov Hdl good	£5,038
	7/03	Strf	2m3f Cls3 Mdn Hdl good	£5,382

High-class handicap chaser who generally runs well at Cheltenham; made his habitual late reappearance at Kempton in January and showed the benefit of preparatory schooling when beating Laskari with bags in hand, jumping well and dominating his rivals; not seen to best effect in heavy ground next two starts, but produced his very best in the Racing Post Plate at the Cheltenham Festival, leading two out and being driven clear to thump Palarshan by 4l (second victory at the Festival); has been raised 9lb for that and must now compete off a career-high mark, although new-found jumping prowess offsets that rise; goes best with a little cut at around 2m4f and likely to be aimed at Cheltenham again, but hasn't been out until December at the earliest for the last three seasons, and could be one for the transfer window.

1193 Iktitaf (Ire)

6 b g Alhaarth - Istibshar (Mr Prospector)

N Meade (Ir)   Mrs P Sloan

PLACINGS: 4/1731121/11128F6-   RPR **165+h**

Starts	1st	2nd	3rd	4th	Win & Pl
15	7	2	1	1	£193,691

11/06	Punc	2m Gd1 Hdl soft	£44,828
11/06	DRoy	2m Gd3 Hdl yld-sft	£22,448
10/06	Punc	2m2f List Hdl yield	£14,367
4/06	Punc	2m Gd1 Hdl good	£42,759
12/05	Fair	2m Nov Gd1 Hdl sft-hvy	£34,574
11/05	Naas	2m Hdl 4yo heavy	£7,596
5/05	Kbgn	2m3f Mdn Hdl 4yo yield	£3,921

High-class 2m hurdler, but prone to throwing in the odd stinker; won his first three out of novice company last season, culminating in a Grade 1 success by 1¹/₄l from Asian Maze in the Morgiana Hurdle at Punchestown in November; started odds-on in a small field for another Grade 1 at

Leopardstown over Christmas, but after travelling easily throughout, he found little when let down on the run-in and finished 1¹/₄l second to Brave Inca (2m, heavy, 4 ran); worse was to follow when he finished a long last in the Irish Champion Hurdle, but took his chance nonetheless at the Cheltenham Festival, and was still swinging along on the bridle upsides Brave Inca when falling at the third-last; again disappointing, though, when sixth of eight behind Silent Oscar at the Punchestown festival; enigmatic sort who can't be trusted implicitly, but has had an operation to improve his breathing, and maybe that will give him a new lease of life in the top 2m hurdle races.

1194 Il Duce (Ire)

7 br g Anshan - Glory-Glory (Buckskin)

A King   Mrs Peter Prowting

PLACINGS: 21P1/2F60/1231PF23-1   **RPR 145+c**

Starts	1st	2nd	3rd	4th	Win & Pl
20	5	6	2		£46,662
135	5/07	Bang	2m4¹/₂f Cls3 109-135 Ch Hcap good		.........£8,458
	12/06	Tntn	2m7¹/₂f Cls3 Nov Ch gd-sft		.........£7,585
	5/06	Uttx	2m5f Cls4 Nov Ch gd-sft		.........£5,205
	4/05	Chep	2m4f Cls4 Nov Hdl gd-sft		.........£3,542
	3/05	Newb	2m5f Cls3 Nov Hdl gd-sft		.........£3,715
	12/04	Ling	2m Cls6 Mdn NHF 4-6yo stand		.........£1,876

Smart novice chaser during a busy campaign last season, and a decent prospect for handicaps this winter; placed behind classy novices Turko and Denman last autumn before an easy odds-on success when dropped in class at Taunton in December; disappointed on his next couple of starts, but returned to his best when fitted with blinkers in novice handicaps in the spring, finishing third at Cheltenham and rounding off with a 1³/₄l defeat of East Tycoon at Bangor in May; going the right way, and connections are hoping he progresses enough to get competitive in good handicaps at around 2m4f; best on good to soft ground. **'Blinkers helped sharpen his jumping.' (Alan King, trainer)**

1195 Imperial Commander (Ire)

6 b g Flemensfirth - Ballinlovane (Le Moss)

N Twiston-Davies   Our Friends In The North

PLACINGS: 1/146173-   **RPR 135+h**

Starts	1st	2nd	3rd	4th	Win & Pl
6	2	-	1	1	£18,075
	1/07	Newc	2m4f Cls4 Nov Hdl soft		.........£2,928
	10/06	Chel	2m¹/₂f Cls4 NHF 4-6yo gd-sft		.........£3,578

Chaser in the making who did as well as could have been hoped for over hurdles; won a Cheltenham bumper on his debut under Rules, and then took on quality opposition all season; 25-1 when seventh behind Massini's Maguire in the Ballymore Properties Novices' Hurdle at the Cheltenham Festival, racing prominently to two out (2m5f, good to soft, 15 ran), and stepped up on that on his final outing in a Grade 1 at Aintree back

over 3m, where he was one-paced over last two when third, 22l behind Chief Dan George (good, 10 ran); came with a reputation from the point-to-point field and should be well suited by 3m over fences, especially with cut in the ground; trainer does well with this type and no surprise if he is a big contender for novice honours next March.

1196 In Compliance (Ire)

7 b g Old Vic - Lady Bellingham (Montelimar)

M O'Brien (Ir)   S Mulryan

PLACINGS: 71212/31123/113-   **RPR 167+c**

Starts	1st	2nd	3rd	4th	Win & Pl
13	6	3	3	-	£145,564
	12/06	Punc	2m4f Gd1 Ch heavy		.........£44,828
	11/06	DRoy	2m4f Gd3 Ch yld-sft		.........£22,448
	3/06	Leop	2m5f Nov Ch yld-sft		.........£11,673
	2/06	Fair	2m4f Ch sft-hvy		.........£8,979
	1/05	Punc	2m Mdn Hdl 5yo sft-hvy		.........£6,377
	11/04	Fair	2m NHF 4yo soft		.........£5,839

High-class chaser at around 2m4f who is yet to race outside Ireland and looks a good thing to pick up more valuable Graded prizes in his homeland this winter; won a Grade 3 at Down Royal on his return in November, but really showed off his talent at Punchestown the following month when rising to the challenge of his first Grade 1 by beating former Cheltenham Gold Cup winner War Of Attrition by 2¹/₂l; seemed not to stay the 3m1f trip when 10¹/₂l third behind Neptune Collonges on his final start, so given his stamina limitations, the Gold Cup looks out of the question; still lightly raced and open to further improvement, and more success at the highest level looks on the cards. **'He handles testing ground but also goes well on goodish ground.' (Michael O'Brien, trainer)**

1197 Inglis Drever

8 b g In The Wings - Cormorant Creek (Gorytus)

J H Johnson   Andrea & Graham Wylie

PLACINGS: 124/221112/11F/1213-   **RPR 169+h**

Starts	1st	2nd	3rd	4th	Win & Pl
18	10	5	1	1	£549,504
	3/07	Chel	3m Cls1 Gd1 Hdl gd-sft		.........£149,027
	11/06	Newb	3m¹/₂f Cls1 Gd2 Hdl soft		.........£22,808
	11/05	Newb	3m¹/₂f Cls1 Gd2 Hdl good		.........£22,808
	10/05	Weth	3m1f Cls1 Gd2 Hdl soft		.........£22,808
	3/05	Chel	3m Cls1 Gd1 Hdl good		.........£116,000
	2/05	Winc	2m Cls1 Gd2 Hdl gd-sft		.........£37,700
	1/05	Hayd	2m Cls1 Gd2 Hdl heavy		.........£23,200
	1/04	Wwck	2m5f Cls1 Nov Gd1 Hdl gd-sft		.........£21,700
	12/03	Sand	2m4¹/₂f Cls1 Nov Gd2 Hdl gd-sft		.........£14,500
	11/03	Aint	2m4f Cls3 Nov Hdl good		.........£7,027

Terrier of a staying hurdler who came back from a tendon injury to reclaim his World Hurdle crown at the Cheltenham Festival in March; had built up to the big meeting with a neck defeat of Irish Wolf at Newbury in November and a 4l second to Blazing Bailey in the Cleeve Hurdle in January, but turned the form round with Alan King's charge on 8lb better terms in March, overcoming mistakes to lead soon after the second-last and battling on tenaciously to beat Mighty Man by ^{3}/$_4$l (3m, good to soft, 14 ran); that race seemed to leave its mark at Aintree the following month, where he could finish only 22l third behind Mighty Man on level terms again; real battler who loves the Cheltenham hill, and his main target will be a third success in the World Hurdle in March; is helped by cut in the ground, and needs his races spaced out.

1198 Irish Raptor (Ire)

8 b/br g Zaffaran - Brownskin (Buckskin)

N Twiston-Davies   Mrs Caroline Beresford-Wylie

PLACINGS: /PU8469/31UU21271U7-   **RPR** 146+c

Starts	1st	2nd	3rd	4th	Win & Pl
17	3	2	1	1	£28,416

125	2/07	Sand	3m²/₂f Cls3 105-129 Ch Hcap soft......................£9,395
110	12/06	Newb	3m Cls3 Nov 110-125 Ch Hcap soft £6,506
93	10/06	Winc	3m1¹/₂f Cls4 Nov 68-94 Ch Hcap gd-sft £5,205

Consistent performer in a busy novice campaign over fences last season; won off a mark of 93 at Wincanton in October, before overcoming what threatened to be a crisis of jumping confidence to keep producing the goods as his mark rose; made all to beat Heltornic by 8l in the Newbury mud in December, and then almost defied an 11lb hike in open company when digging very deep and beaten just ¹/₂l by Tango Royal at the same track (3m, good to soft, 7 ran); down in class when wide-margin winner at Sandown in February, but showing the signs of an arduous campaign at Cheltenham (under pressure when unseating three out in the William Hill Handicap Chase) and Aintree (seventh behind Dunbrody Millar over the National fences); possible contender for the Grand National itself, although front-running style will always mean he has a hard race.

1199 Irish Wolf (Fr)

7 b h Loup Solitaire - Erins Run (Irish River)

P Bowen   The Hacking Partnership

PLACINGS: 1243/1331227752-0123   **RPR** 150+h

Starts	1st	2nd	3rd	4th	Win & Pl
21	5	5	5	1	£71,343

129	6/07	Worc	2m7f Cls4 Ch good.......................................£3,578
114	10/06	Aint	3m¹/₂f Cls3 104-130 Hdl Hcap good £9,759
108	8/06	MRas	2m3¹/₂f Cls3 98-114 Hdl Hcap gd-fm £5,530
	11/05	Hntg	2m¹/₂f Cls4 82-108 Cond Hdl Hcap good £3,314
	8/05	Sthl	2m1f Cls4 Nov Hdl gd-fm............................£3,393

Very smart staying hurdler who posted a Racing Post Rating of 150 on four occasions last season; did it three times in handicaps (including when second to Halcon Genelardais in a very valuable event at Haydock in November), but really caught the eye when just pipped by subsequent World Hurdle winner Inglis Drever in a Grade 2 contest at Newbury's Hennessy meeting (3m1²/₂f, soft, 5 ran); wasn't getting any respite from the handicapper, so had his attentions turned to chasing in the summer, but after scraping home on

his debut at Worcester, he was a beaten favourite at Hexham and Newton Abbot, turned over by horses who had been vastly inferior over hurdles; yet to convince he is as good over the bigger obstacles, but undoubtedly classy if getting it all together; has gained all his wins on good or fast ground.

1200 Iron Man (Fr)

6 ch g Video Rock - Key Figure (Fast Topaze)

P Bowen   R Owen & P Fullagar

PLACINGS: 52/26P1554U088U3-110   **RPR** 154+c

Starts	1st	2nd	3rd	4th	Win & Pl
29	6	2	2	2	£96,356

134	7/07	MRas	2m6¹/₂f Cls1 List 126-144 Ch Hcap soft £37,063
126	5/07	Strf	2m5¹/₂f Cls2 120-132 Ch Hcap good £12,526
125	11/06	MRas	2m6¹/₂f Cls3 104-125 Ch Hcap soft....................£9,759
	1/06	Carl	2m Cls3 Nov Ch heavy £6,506
	2/05	Sand	2m¹/₂f Cls3 Nov Hdl 4yo gd-sft £5,421
	11/04	Ayr	2m Cls3 Nov Hdl 3yo soft...........................£4,716

Very smart handicap chaser, formerly trained by Howard Johnson; ended a lengthy losing run at Stratford in May, and that proved the springboard to a performance that eclipsed anything he had done before; made almost all the running to capture one of the highlights of the British summer jumps season, the Summer Plate at Market Rasen in July, galloping on relentlessly in the straight to beat Hoo La Baloo by 8l and posting a Racing Post Rating almost a stone better than anything he had previously achieved; showed a different side to his character when running out at the sixth fence in the Galway Plate; will continue to be aimed at some of the biggest handicaps in the British calendar, with the Paddy Power Gold Cup at Cheltenham a possible target in the autumn; likes soft ground.

1201 It Takes Time (Ire)

13 b g Montelimar - Dysart Lady (King's Ride)

D Pipe   D A Johnson

PLACINGS: 1742/474P6/33402-523   **RPR** 142+c

Starts	1st	2nd	3rd	4th	Win & Pl
43	11	6	8	5	£317,805

	2/05	Ling	2m4¹/₂f Cls1 Gd1 Ch gd-sft.........................£59,500
	1/03	Hayd	2m6f Cls2 Nov Ch gd-sft...........................£16,640
	4/02	Sand	3m Cls2 Hdl good..................................£29,000
134	12/01	Chel	3m Cls2 119-143 Hdl Hcap good £8,572
126	11/01	Chel	3m1¹/₂f Cls2 116-144 Hdl Hcap good £27,716
118	11/01	NAbb	2m6f Cls3 103-118 Hdl Hcap soft....................£4,820
111	2/01	Font	2m6¹/₂f Cls3 97-121 Hdl Hcap gd-sft £5,489
	1/01	Donc	3m1¹/₂f Cls3 Nov Hdl good............................£3,752
	10/00	Extr	2m3f Cls3 Nov Hdl soft...............................£3,445
	1/00	Leop	2m2f NHF yield.......................................£3,588
	12/99	Leop	2m NHF 5yo sft-hvy £4,313

Consistent handicap chaser at 2m4f upwards, but has won only once since January 2003; can usually be relied upon to run his race and proved the point during the summer with a couple of decent efforts at Market Rasen, most notably in June when conceding 23lb to King Of The Arctic and going down by only a head after getting caught close home (2m6^1/2f, good to soft, 6 ran); unlikely to find any improvement now he is entering the veteran stage, but goes on most ground and should continue to acquit himself well in decent company. *'He's slightly vulnerable to younger, less exposed horses who might still be ahead of their handicap marks.' (David Pipe, trainer)*

1202 Itsa Legend

8 b g Midnight Legend - Onawing Andaprayer (Energist)

A King   The We're A Legend Partnership

PLACINGS: 128/F4123-   **RPR 135+h**

Starts	1st	2nd	3rd	4th	Win & Pl
8	2	2	1	1	£22,465

1/07	Tntn	3m^1/₂f Cls4 Nov Hdl soft	£3,904
2/04	Kemp	2m Cls6 NHF 4-6yo gd-sft	£2,468

Lightly raced gelding who returned from almost three years off through injury last term, and delighted connections by making his mark in good novice hurdles; took three starts to get back to winning ways in minor company at Taunton, but best judged on his last two efforts; finished 15l second to subsequent Grade 1 winner Chief Dan George in a good contest at Haydock (3m, heavy, 7 ran), and had that rival in behind when 18l third (at 100-1) in the Brit Insurance Novices' Hurdle at the Cheltenham Festival, keeping on but no match for the easy winner Wichita Lineman (3m, good to soft, 20 ran); needs plenty of cut in the ground nowadays, and could be interesting if his attentions are switched to fences this term.

1203 J'y Vole (Fr)

4 b f Mansonnien - J'y Reste (Freedom Cry)

W Mullins (Ir)   Hammer & Trowel Syndicate

PLACINGS: 1952125-17   **RPR 127h**

Starts	1st	2nd	3rd	4th	Win & Pl
9	3	2	-	-	£85,639

5/07	Autl	2m3^1/₂f Gd3 Hdl 4yo v soft	£39,527
2/07	Fair	2m Hdl 4yo heavy	£6,536
10/06	Autl	2m1^1/₂f Hdl 3yo v soft	£17,214

Ex-French performer who made up into a decent juvenile hurdler last season, showing a preference for mud, and can be expected to pick up some decent contests when conditions are in her favour; always travelling well in the heavy ground when making a winning debut for Willie Mullins at Fairyhouse in February, and posted a similar effort when runner-up to Duty in a Grade 3 back at the same track (2m, heavy, 13 ran); far from disgraced when fifth behind Katchit in the Triumph Hurdle, when conditions probably weren't testing enough, before winning a Grade 3 hurdle at Auteuil in May (2m4f) from stablemate Financial Reward, rallying in gutsy fashion on the run-in to get up close home; seventh behind Good Bye Simon in a Grade 1 at the French track in June; nice type whose immediate future lies in good handicap hurdles.

1204 Jack High (Ire)

12 br g Erdelistan - Lyntim (Fidel)

T Walsh (Ir)   Ms B Ross, M McShane, D Montgomery & W Moore

PLACINGS: /3945351U9/700472F4-   **RPR 142c**

Starts	1st	2nd	3rd	4th	Win & Pl
47	8	3	9	5	£272,691

3/06	DRoy	3m2f Ch heavy	£9,545
129 4/05	Sand	3m5^1/₂f Cls1 Gd3 129-155 Ch Hcap good	£87,000
113 11/04	Navn	3m 112-136 Ch Hcap heavy	£40,799
3/04	Navn	2m4f Ch yld-sft	£6,813
118 2/03	Fair	3m Nov 93-121 Hdl Hcap yld-sft	£21,104
110 12/02	Leop	3m 99-127 Hdl Hcap heavy	£11,963
11/02	Naas	2m3f Mdn Hdl soft	£5,715
10/01	Dpat	2m2f NHF yld-sft	£2,921

Grand old staying chaser whose biggest win came in the 2005 Betfred Gold Cup at Sandown; failed to win last season, but ran admirably in defeat, especially after Christmas; showed his best form for a year when keeping on gamely for fourth, 3^1/₂l behind Point Barrow, in a valuable event at Leopardstown (3m, soft to heavy, 19 ran), just lacking a change of pace from the last; matched that level of form at Fairyhouse six weeks later when ground down after the last by Homer Wells and beaten 2l in the Grade 2 Bobbyjo Chase (3m1f, heavy, 7 ran); early faller in the Grand National before turning in an uncharacteristically average round of jumping on unsuitable ground in the Betfred, plugging on for a never-in-it fourth behind Hot Weld (3m5^1/₂f, good to firm, 10 ran); no new tricks expected, but may pick up a race or two in the mud.

1205 Jack The Giant (Ire)

5 b g Giant's Causeway - State Crystal (High Estate)

N Henderson   Hanbury Syndicate

PLACINGS: 123/211136-   **RPR 154+c**

Starts	1st	2nd	3rd	4th	Win & Pl
9	4	2	2	-	£61,072

12/06	Kemp	2m Cls1 Nov Gd2 Ch gd-sft	£18,246
11/06	Wwck	2m Cls3 Nov Ch 4yo good	£6,506
11/06	Navn	2m Cls3 Ch gd-fm	£6,506
2/06	MRas	2m1^1/₂f Cls4 Nov Hdl 4yo good	£4,229

Promising chaser who competed at the highest level in 2m novice company last season; won his first three, dotting up at Sandown and Warwick before claiming the scalp of Twist Magic in a Grade 2 at Kempton over Christmas, where he rallied after a mistake down the back to collar Paul Nicholls' charge at the last and score by 1^1/₄l (2m, good to soft, 6 ran); that was strong form, and he confirmed the promise with an excellent display in the Arkle in March, where he led at a strong pace and battled on once headed on the home turn to finish 6l third behind My Way De Solzen (2m, soft, 13 ran); took on many of the same rivals at Aintree the following month, but his jumping fell apart and he trailed in last of six behind Twist Magic; will need to improve a lot to make up into a championship contender, but could have a future in the top 2m handicap chases.

1206 Jacks Craic (Ire)

8 b g Lord Americo - Boleree (Mandalus)

J Spearing   BBB Computer Services

PLACINGS: P4221211F/564P3420P-   **RPR 141+c**

Starts	1st	2nd	3rd	4th	Win & Pl
34	4	8	5	4	£81,738
134	4/06	Aint	2m Cls1 Gd3 132-158 Ch Hcap good		£39,914
125	3/06	Newb	2m1f Cls3 108-125 Ch Hcap gd-sft		£6,506
120	2/06	Sand	2m Cls3 111-130 Ch Hcap soft		£9,395
103	1/05	Folk	2m1¹/₂f Cls4 79-105 Hdl Hcap soft		£3,494

Smart 2m handicap chaser who suffered at the hands of the handicapper after winning the Grade 3 Red Rum Handicap Chase at Aintree in April 2006; drew a blank last term, but hinted in the second half of the campaign that the ability was still there, notably when 6³/₄l fourth behind Madison Du Berlais at Southwell in January (2m, soft, 9 ran) and 11l second to Magic Sky at Newbury in March (2m1f, soft, 7 ran); likes to be held up so suited by truly run races, although his jumping looked a little suspect at times last term; now 2lb lower than in the Red Rum, so weighted to win.

1207 Jaunty Times

7 b g Luso - Jaunty June (Primitive Rising)

H Daly   J B Sumner

PLACINGS: 2243/114827/62113P7-   **RPR 138c**

Starts	1st	2nd	3rd	4th	Win & Pl
20	4	5	4	2	£47,385
	1/07	Hntg	3m Cls3 Nov soft		£6,506
120	12/06	Asct	3m Cls3 Nov 111-130 Ch Hcap gd-sft		£15,658
111	12/05	Wwck	2m5f Cls3 99-125 Hdl Hcap soft		£4,853
	11/05	Towc	2m5f Cls3 Nov Hdl 4-6yo soft		£5,842

Decent novice chaser last season; won at Ascot (a novice handicap) and Huntingdon (beat Only Vintage by a short head) either side of the new year, but posted his best form in February in the Grade 2 Reynoldstown Novices' Chase back at Ascot, where he was pushed along with six to jump but kept on to finish 7¹/₂l third behind Gungadu (3m, good to soft, 7 ran); disappointing on his last two outings, when pulled up in heavy ground in the Midlands National at Uttoxeter and well beaten behind Aces Four in a Grade 2 novice chase at Aintree (started 40-1); handicaps over 3m-plus on easy ground will be his game.

1208 Jazz D'Estruval (Fr)

10 gr g Bayolidaan - Caro D'Estruval (Caramo)

N Richards   Ashleybank Investments Limited

PLACINGS: 1/123/1123/1/33-   **RPR 144h**

Starts	1st	2nd	3rd	4th	Win & Pl
11	5	2	4	-	£70,425
128	12/05	Hayd	2m4f Cls2 119-145 Hdl Hcap soft		£13,585
	1/05	Hayd	2m6f Cls2 Nov Ch heavy		£18,095
	12/04	Ayr	2m5¹/₂f Cls2 Nov Ch heavy		£10,254
117	5/03	Prth	3m¹/₂f Cls3 95-120 Hdl Hcap good		£5,470
	4/01	Prth	2m4¹/₂f Cls3 Mdn Hdl heavy		£2,814

Talented, but fragile, ten-year-old who has raced

just 11 times over hurdles and fences in six seasons, but has never finished out of the first three; races over hurdles these days (developed an aversion to open ditches), and did well in a couple of Haydock handicaps last autumn, finishing third behind Halcon Genelardais over 3m in November and third again behind United over 2m4f in December; wasn't seen out again, and seems to be at his best fresh, as his career record on his first start of the season reads 11113; connections are targeting a valuable race in France in October before making further plans. *'He's one of the most talented I've ever trained.'* (Nicky Richards, trainer)

1209 Jazz Messenger (Fr)

7 b g Acatenango - In The Saltmine (Damister)

N Meade (Ir)   R S T Syndicate

PLACINGS: 2112733/31159-   **RPR 164h**

Starts	1st	2nd	3rd	4th	Win & Pl
12	4	2	3	-	£100,331
	12/06	Kemp	2m Cls1 Gd1 Hdl gd-sft		£57,020
	12/06	Thur	2m List Hdl soft		£16,679
	1/06	Navn	2m Hdl soft		£6,672
	1/06	Navn	2m Mdn Hdl sft-hvy		£4,765

High-class 2m hurdler; stepped up markedly on anything he had achieved before when winning the Grade 1 Christmas Hurdle at Kempton on Boxing Day, where he was left in the lead by Afsoun's fall at the fifth, and responded to his rider's urgings to repel all boarders and beat Noble Request by 4l; probably wasn't far off that level of form when 10l fifth behind Hardy Eustace in the Irish Champion Hurdle at Leopardstown the following month (2m, soft, 8 ran), after which he was given a break; returned for a first crack at 2m4f in the Aintree Hurdle on Grand National day, but was beaten a long way in ninth, and was found to have suffered a small fracture; now reported to be '100 per cent', so it's all systems go for a lightish campaign building up to a repeat tilt at the Christmas Hurdle.

1210 Jered (Ire)

5 ch g Presenting - La Noire (Phardante)

N Meade (Ir)   G McGrath

PLACINGS: 16-   **RPR 112+b**

Starts	1st	2nd	3rd	4th	Win & Pl
2	1	-	-	-	£6,069
	4/07	Fair	2m NHF 5-6yo gd-fm		£6,070

Smart bumper performer last season, and expected to do well over hurdles; made a winning debut in a 23-runner bumper at Fairyhouse in April, beating subsequent Grade 1 fourth Cuchulains Son by ³/₄l (2m, good to firm); upped in class and started favourite under a penalty at the Punchestown festival, but pulled hard early and couldn't muster anything more inside the last furlong, eventually finishing sixth of 24 behind Meadow Vale; can be forgiven that run, and should rebuild this winter.

1211 Joaaci (Ire)

7 b g Presenting - Miss Sarajevo (Brush Aside)

D Pipe   D A Johnson

PLACINGS: 61112F/1BFP/P1149P-2   **RPR 151c**

Starts	1st	2nd	3rd	4th	Win & Pl
15	5	2	-	1	£45,157

	1/07	Hrfd	3m2f Cls4 Nov Hdl heavy	£2,928
	12/06	Hrfd	3m2f Cls4 Nov Hdl soft	£3,253
143	1/06	Chel	3m2¹/₂f Cls2 123-143 Ch Hcap gd-sft	£16,910
112	4/05	Ayr	3m3¹/₂f Cls3 94-115 Ch Hcap good	£7,007
	3/05	Chep	3m Cls4 Ch heavy	£3,819

Talented handicap chaser at 3m-plus on his day but had to be switched to hurdles last season to regain the winning thread after finding the going too tough over fences; won two novice contests at Hereford either side of the new year, but was then found out in better company in that sphere as well; finally looked as though he might be coming out of the woods when finishing second to Always Waining in a handicap chase at Uttoxeter in May (3m, good, 12 ran), recording a Racing Post Rating of 151, although he now has to overcome an official mark of 147 and could find life tough once more.

1212 Joes Edge (Ire)

10 b/br g Supreme Leader - Right Dark (Buckskin)

F Murphy   Chemipetro Limited

PLACINGS: 22P11/2U044076/781P-   **RPR 140+c**

Starts	1st	2nd	3rd	4th	Win & Pl
28	7	6		2	£194,769

130	3/07	Chel	3m¹/₂f Cls1 Gd3 130-150 Ch Hcap gd-sft	£48,467
132	4/05	Ayr	4m1f Cls1 Gd3 132-163 Ch Hcap good	£70,000
127	4/05	Aint	2m4f Cls2 Nov 101-129 Am Ch Hcap good	£19,198
	11/04	Ayr	2m4f Cls3 Nov Ch soft	£8,050
	2/04	Carl	2m4f Cls4 Nov Hdl good	£3,933
	1/04	Asct	2m4f Cls3 Nov Hdl 4-7yo soft	£5,460
	4/02	Carl	2m1f Cls6 NHF 4-6yo good	£2,499

Smart staying chaser, winner of the 2005 Scottish National; went on a long losing run after that Ayr success, but usually comes good in the spring, and did so to spring a 50-1 shock in the William Hill Handicap Chase at the Cheltenham Festival, getting up in the last stride to prevail in a finish of short heads from Juveigneur and Distant Thunder; started co-favourite for the Grand National, but it wasn't his day, and he was well adrift when pulled up lame after the 20th; needs a good test at 3m and stays very well; acts on good and soft ground, and still not badly handicapped on a mark of 137.

1213 Just Classic

7 gr g Classic Cliche - Misty View (Absalom)

D Pipe   D A Johnson

PLACINGS: 1/

Starts	1st	2nd	3rd	4th	Win & Pl
1	1	-	-	-	£1,918

	4/04	Font	2m2¹/₂f Cls6 NHF 4-6yo good	£1,918

Intriguing sort; has not seen a racecourse since making a winning debut in a bumper at Fontwell

in April 2004 in which four of those in behind have since won races, but remains in training and is held in some regard; has a huge absence to overcome, but with the right trainer to pick up where he left off, and should be winning at 2m4f-plus over hurdles. *'He's a massive horse with lots of potential.' (David Pipe, trainer)*

1214 Justified (Ire)

8 b/br g Leading Counsel - Monkeylane (Monksfield)

E Sheehy (Ir)   Braybrook Syndicate

PLACINGS: 1181/11U1312/13P252-   **RPR 157+c**

Starts	1st	2nd	3rd	4th	Win & Pl
23	10	6	2	1	£268,479

	10/06	Limk	2m1f List Ch yld-sft	£19,062
	4/06	Fair	2m4f Gd1 Ch gd-yld	£45,517
	1/06	Newb	2m1f Cls3 Nov Ch gd-sft	£7,807
	11/05	Punc	2m Nov Gd2 Ch soft	£27,702
	10/05	Punc	2m2f Nov List Ch gd-yld	£14,774
	3/05	Fair	2m Nov Gd2 Hdl soft	£27,702
	1/05	Punc	2m Nov Gd2 Hdl sft-hvy	£25,394
	12/04	Punc	2m Nov List Hdl soft	£13,754
	10/04	Gway	2m Mdn Hdl 5yo heavy	£6,326
	4/04	Slig	2m NHF 5yo sft-hvy	£3,893

High-class Irish chaser over 2m-2m4f; ran well in Grade 1 company last season, notably finishing fifth behind Voy Por Ustedes in the Champion Chase at Cheltenham, and 1¹/₄l second to Mansony in the equivalent (albeit weaker) race at the Punchestown festival in April; tried 3m once, but looked to not stay the trip in finishing third behind Beef Or Salmon and War Of Attrition at Down Royal; did win a Listed chase at Limerick on his return, beating Tumbling Dice by 7l; just below the top bracket on all known evidence, but plenty of races for him in Ireland, and should pay his way again; trainer believes he is over a back problem that troubled him on occasions. *'I've never had him better so am really looking forward to seeing what he can do this season.' (Dusty Sheehy, trainer)*

1215 Justpourit (Ire)

8 b g Glacial Storm - Gale Choice (Strong Gale)

D Hughes (Ir)   Hanged Man's Five Syndicate

PLACINGS: 31324614/52212U3857-   **RPR 136+c**

Starts	1st	2nd	3rd	4th	Win & Pl
24	8	8	3	2	£50,450

	1/07	Fair	2m5f Ch heavy	£7,003
	4/06	Fair	2m4f Hdl good	£8,979
	11/05	Navn	2m Mdn Hdl soft	£6,861

Just one win (in heavy ground at Fairyhouse) from ten starts in novice chases last term, but showed decent form against Graded opposition and looks one for handicap chases at around 2m4f; finished 1¹/₂l second to Hear The Echo in a Grade 2 novice event at Leopardstown in January (2m5f, soft to heavy, 7 ran) and ran to about the same level of form when 9¹/₂l third behind Young Desperado in another Grade 2 at Navan in February (2m, heavy, 6 ran); started 66-1 for the Royal & SunAlliance

Chase at Cheltenham, and not disgraced in finishing eighth of 14 finishers behind Denman; disappointing on his last two starts, but a chase mark of 129 gives connections plenty to work with.

1216 Juveigneur (Fr)

10 ch g *Funny Baby - Azurea (On My Way)*

N Henderson   Trevor Hemmings

PLACINGS: 22102/FP2FP/32312P7-   **RPR 156c**

Starts	1st	2nd	3rd	4th	Win & Pl
34	6	10	4	-	£187,846
128	2/07	Plum	2m5f Cls4 Nov Hdl heavy £4,554
	3/05	Chel	3m¹/₂f Cls2 117-133 Am Ch Hcap good £29,000
	11/04	Drtl	2m4f Ch Hcap soft £8,789
	9/04	Crao	2m4f Ch good £5,408
	11/02	Drtl	2m4f Ch 5yo soft £3,354
	5/02	Mesl	2m1¹/₂f Ch 5yo good £2,945

Very smart staying chaser with a string of grand efforts in the top handicaps to his name; hasn't won over fences since landing the Kim Muir at the Cheltenham Festival in 2005, but has since been placed in a Betfred Gold Cup, a Hennessy, a Welsh National and the last two versions of the William Hill Handicap Chase at the Festival; no match for State Of Play at Newbury or Halcon Genelardais at Chepstow in the first half of last season, but went heartbreakingly close at Cheltenham in March when nailed right on the line by Joes Edge (3m¹/₂f, good to soft, 23 ran); flopped in the Irish National and the Betfred Gold Cup in the spring, so has been dropped a couple of pounds, but won't find life getting any easier as he nears the age of 11; very game and reliable, and deserves to win another good prize; likes cut in the ground.

1217 Kalca Mome (Fr)

9 b g *En Calcat - Belle Mome (Grand Tresor)*

P Hobbs   Miss I D Du Pre

PLACINGS: 2/7F0623106/4128206-   **RPR 147c**

Starts	1st	2nd	3rd	4th	Win & Pl
40	11	7	2	3	£130,933
135	12/06	Chel	2m¹/₂f Cls2 124-146 Ch Hcap soft......................£12,526
131	2/06	Hayd	2m Cls2 119-145 Ch Hcap heavy £16,265
124	2/05	Wwck	2m Cls2 117-143 Hdl Hcap heavy £13,585
129	2/05	Donc	2m3f Cls3 107-133 Ch Hcap good £10,247
	3/04	Sand	2m Cls3 Nov gd-sft £10,008
	1/04	Hayd	2m Cls3 Nov Ch heavy £10,004
	12/03	Hrfd	2m Cls4 Nov Ch gd-sft £2,587
	11/03	NAbb	2m¹/₂f Cls4 Nov Ch good £2,990
114	3/03	Winc	2m Cls3 109-123 Hdl Hcap soft.........................£12,557
	1/03	Tntn	2m1f Cls4 Nov Hdl soft.......................................£4,531
	11/02	Hayd	2m Cls3 Nov Hdl 4-7yo good £4,381

Smart 2m-2m4f handicap chaser who posted the best form of his life last season; came from off the pace and driven out to beat Bohemian Spirit by 2l over 2m¹/₂f at Cheltenham in December, showing a clear liking for the soft ground; had to compete off higher marks in better grade afterwards, and was not disgraced to finish runner-up to Kenzo at Hereford in December (beaten 1l) and to the well-handicapped Nozic at Chepstow in February

(beaten 12l); looks in the grip of the handicapper (starts the new season 7lb higher than his last winning mark), but could pick up a race on a going day.

1218 Kandjar D'Allier (Fr)

9 gr g *Royal Charter - Miss Akarad (Akarad)*

A King   Let's Live Racing

PLACINGS: 00/1132/3P8417/710F-   **RPR 142+c**

Starts	1st	2nd	3rd	4th	Win & Pl
40	7	4	4	4	£149,397
132	12/06	Hayd	3m Cls2 121-140 Ch Hcap heavy £19,518
108	3/06	Chep	2m4f Cls3 100-122 Hdl Hcap good....................£5,530
125	12/04	Wind	2m4f Cls3 104-125 Ch Hcap soft £6,910
115	12/04	Plum	2m4f Cls3 100-117 Ch Hcap gd-sft......................£5,343
	5/03	Autl	2m5¹/₂f Ch Hcap v soft £29,610
	11/02	Autl	2m1¹/₂f Ch 4yo heavy £13,546
	4/02	Autl	2m1¹/₂f Ch 4yo v soft £12,368

Smart handicap chaser who loves the mud; disappointed first time out last season when bidding to improve on his 2005 third in the Paddy Power Gold Cup, but bounced back the following month to gain a first win over 3m in the Tommy Whittle Chase at Haydock, leading 2 out and battling on gamely through the heavy ground to beat top-weight Wild Cane Ridge by ¹/₂l; hopelessly tailed off, though, when returning to Haydock next time in the Red Square Vodka Gold Cup, and was a casualty on the first circuit in the Grand National on his final outing; starts the season on a mark of 138 (6lb higher than his last winning rating), so will need to improve again to make his mark.

1219 Kasbah Bliss (Fr)

5 b g *Kahyasi - Marital Bliss (Double Bed)*

F Doumen (Fr)   Henri De Pracomtal

PLACINGS: 13321F/1313453-56   **RPR 154+h**

Starts	1st	2nd	3rd	4th	Win & Pl
15	4	1	5	1	£214,083
	10/06	Autl	2m3¹/₂f Gd3 Hdl 4yo v soft.................................£40,345
	9/06	Autl	2m2f List Hdl 4yo v soft £26,483
	2/06	Sand	2m¹/₂f Cls1 Nov Gd2 Hdl 4yo soft......................£15,966
	9/05	Autl	2m2f List Hdl 3yo v soft £18,723

Talented hurdler who gained his only British win when beating Blazing Bailey in a Grade 2 novice event at Sandown in February 2006; not disgraced in two visits to Britain last term, finishing 2³/₄l fourth behind Taranis under 11st 9lb in a handicap back at Sandown in February (2m6f, soft, 16 ran) and 17l fifth behind Inglis Drever in the World Hurdle at the Cheltenham Festival (3m, good to soft, 14 ran); a bit hit and miss in France afterwards, but his trainer has always stressed that he was still something of a baby, and is expected to prove more of a force in the top staying hurdles with another year under his belt; remains one for the World Hurdle shortlist, and his cause will be helped by ease in the ground.

1220 Katchit (Ire)

4 b g Kalanisi - Miracle (Ezzoud)

A King   D S J P Syndicate

PLACINGS: 11211111-   **RPR 154+h**

Starts	1st	2nd	3rd	4th	Win & Pl
8	7	1	-		£206,578
	4/07	Aint	2m¹/₂f Cls1 Nov Gd1 Hdl 4yo good		£74,126
	3/07	Chel	2m1f Cls1 Gd1 Hdl 4yo gd-sft		£68,424
	1/07	Chel	2m1f Cls1 Nov Gd2 Hdl 4yo heavy		£17,106
	12/06	Chel	2m1f Cls2 Hdl 3yo soft		£12,526
	11/06	Chel	2m¹/₂f Cls1 Nov Gd2 Hdl 3yo gd-sft		£17,106
	10/06	Chep	2m¹/₂f Cls4 Nov Hdl 3yo good		£3,253
	9/06	MRas	2m1¹/₂f Cls2 Nov Hdl 3yo good		£9,759

Remarkable hurdler who won seven out of eight as a juvenile last season, and begins the new campaign as one of the favourites for the Champion Hurdle; capped his prolific campaign with a stunning Grade 1 double in the Triumph Hurdle at Cheltenham (beat Liberate by 9l) and the Anniversary 4-Y-O Hurdle at Aintree (beat Punjabi by 4l), putting to rest suggestions that his early-season form (which included two Grade 2 wins) would not hold up at the end of a long season; met with his sole defeat at the hands of Degas Art at Wetherby at the end of October, but was beaten only 1¹/₂l giving the winner 8lb; quality of his efforts received a further advertisement when Punjabi won a Grade 1 at Punchestown at the end of the season, so he goes into the new campaign as clearly the best of his generation; enthusiastic worker who has won on heavy and good, and is very tough, so could find the improvement required to trouble Sublimity at the top of the tree. *'I'd imagine we'll start somewhere like the Bula.' (Alan King, trainer)*

1221 Kauto Star (Fr)

7 b g Village Star - Kauto Relka (Port Etienne)

P Nicholls   Clive D Smith

PLACINGS: 2353/112/21F/111111-   **RPR 184+c**

Starts	1st	2nd	3rd	4th	Win & Pl
21	12	4	2	-	£846,548
	3/07	Chel	3m2¹/₂f Cls1 Gd1 Ch gd-sft		£242,335
	2/07	Newb	3m Cls1 Gd2 Ch soft		£28,510
	12/06	Kemp	3m Cls1 Gd1 Ch gd-sft		£114,040
	12/06	Sand	2m Cls1 Gd1 Ch soft		£79,828
	11/06	Hayd	3m Cls1 Gd1 Ch soft		£114,040
167	10/06	Aint	2m4f Cls1 Gd2 147-167 Ch Hcap good		£28,510
	12/05	Sand	2m Cls1 Gd1 Ch soft		£71,275
	12/04	Newb	2m2¹/₂f Cls3 Nov Ch gd-sft		£8,840
	5/04	Autl	2m3¹/₂f Gd3 Hdl 4yo v soft		£38,028
	9/03	Autl	2m2f List Hdl 3yo v soft		£20,260
	5/03	Autl	1m7f Hdl 3yo v soft		£12,468
	4/03	Engh	1m7f Hdl 3yo v soft		£11,221

Britain's highest-rated chaser and champion of all three distance divisions after a terrific campaign in which he was unbeaten in six starts; earned Racing Post Ratings between 174 and 184 each time he ran and did not have to be at his very best to win the Cheltenham Gold Cup on his final start, capping a tremendous season and winning the Betfair Million with a 2¹/₂l beating of Exotic

Dancer; jumped very well there apart from making what has become a characteristic blunder at the final fence, just as he had done before beating the same rival in the King George at Kempton on Boxing Day and when getting the better of L'Ami by a neck in the Aon Chase at Newbury in February; put up his best effort, according to the figures, when making his debut over 3m in the Grade 1 Betfair Chase at Haydock in November, a performance that laid down his credentials as a player for the season's biggest prizes as he slammed Beef Or Salmon by 17l without having to be asked a serious question; showed his versatility after that stunning success when dropping back to 2m and scoring a repeat of his victory the previous year in the Tingle Creek Chase at Sandown, where he won with plenty to spare from subsequent Champion Chase winner Voy Por Ustedes; will start the season with a tough task ahead of him in trying to match what he did last term, but will follow a similar route and is without a doubt the best chaser to have raced in Britain or Ireland for many a year. *'I'm aiming to have him ready for Haydock's Betfair Chase in November. That will be his first target. Depending on the ground and the situation at the time, I'd love to win the Tingle Creek for a third time with him. But I think over that trip, you'd like to see the ground on the soft side.' (Paul Nicholls, trainer)*

1222 Kawagino (Ire)

7 b g Perugino - Sharakawa (Darshaan)

J W Mullins   K J Pike

PLACINGS: 24U8U174/24268545-U2   **RPR 152+h**

Starts	1st	2nd	3rd	4th	Win & Pl
20	2	4	-	4	£46,049
108	3/06	Winc	2m Cls3 99-120 Hdl Hcap soft		£6,506
	6/04	NAbb	2m1f Cls4 Nov Hdl gd-fm		£3,385

Decent hurdler, but finds it hard to win, thanks in no small part to a stiff handicap mark; is often highly tried, and was sent off 100-1 when 18¹/₂l fifth behind Sublimity in last season's Champion Hurdle (soft, 10 ran); turned out again three days later under 10st in the County Hurdle, and picked up more prize-money when 2l fourth behind Pedrobob; another good run when 8¹/₂l fifth behind Al Eile in Aintree's Martell Hurdle (2m4f, good, 11 ran); nowhere near as good over fences, and couldfinish only second off a mark of 112 in a handicap chase at Worcester in June; without a win since March 2006, and revised hurdle rating of 152 is unlikely to make his task any easier. *'He'll start off with a run or two over hurdles then go novice chasing.' (Seamus Mullins, trainer)*

1223 Kazal (Fr)

6 ch g Villez - Moody Cloud (Cyborg)

E Griffin (Ir)   J Comerford

PLACINGS: 3/1411111-   **RPR 148+h**

Starts	1st	2nd	3rd	4th	Win & Pl
7	6	-	-	1	£123,542

3/07	Thur	2m4f Nov Gd2 Hdl heavy £32,990
2/07	Naas	2m4f Nov Gd2 Hdl heavy £21,993
1/07	Leop	2m4f Nov Gd3 Hdl soft.....................................£15,395
1/07	Naas	2m4f Nov Gd2 Hdl sft-hvy £25,512
12/06	Limk	2m6f Nov Gd3 Hdl sft-hvy £17,959
10/06	Wxfd	3m Nov Hdl heavy..£7,625

Ultra-tough novice hurdler last season, winning five straight heavy-ground Graded races between late December and early March; beat the likes of Foligold, Earth Magic, Aitmatov and Chomba Womba in gritty fashion (usually led or prominent throughout), but recorded his best Racing Post Rating when giving Callherwhatulike 10lb and a $1^1/4$l beating in the Grade 2 Johnstown Novice Hurdle at Naas in February; ground was never going to be soft enough for him at Cheltenham or Punchestown, so was put away for the season; in good heart as he prepares for a return this autumn, and there should be better days to come with him.

1224 Kelami (Fr)

9 b g Lute Antique - Voltige De Nievre (Brezzo)

F Doumen (Fr)   Halewood International Ltd

PLACINGS: 03F4313/86/18392P2P-   **RPR 149c**

Starts	1st	2nd	3rd	4th	Win & Pl
36	4	5	7	3	£240,146

	10/06	Comp	2m4f Hdl v soft...£7,614
133	3/05	Chel	3m¹/₂f Cls1 Gd3 131-157 Ch Hcap good.............£46,400
126	12/03	Kemp	3m Cls3 118-135 Ch Hcap good £23,200
	3/03	Autl	2m1¹/₂f Ch Hcap v soft £23,377

Staying handicap chaser who enjoyed his finest hour when winning the William Hill Trophy at the 2005 Cheltenham Festival; visited Britain four times last season, disappointing on three occasions but looking as good as ever in the Agfa Diamond Handicap Chase at Sandown in February, where he came from miles off the pace to lead just after the last, but was worn down on the run-in by Rambling Minster (3m1/2f, good to soft, 18 ran); tailed off when pulled up two out in the Grand National on his final outing; starts this season on the same mark as at Sandown, so can obviously win a decent handicap on a going day.

1225 Kenzo III (Fr)

9 ch g Agent Bleu - Kelinda (Pot D'Or)

N Henderson   Killinghurst Park Stud

PLACINGS: 2/1P/1P32-P   **RPR 135c**

Starts	1st	2nd	3rd	4th	Win & Pl
7	2	1	1	-	£25,284

118	12/06	Hrfd	2m3f Cls2 118-144 Ch Hcap gd-sft..................£15,845
	2/05	Ludl	3m Cls4 Ch gd-sft...£4,352

Decent handicap chaser who is lightly raced owing

to leg problems, but showed last term that he retained plenty of ability; made his first start in almost two years in a good 2m3f contest at Hereford in December, where he shrugged off his absence to make most of the running and beat Kalca Mome and Hoo La Baloo by 1l and $3/4$l; pulled up at Kempton next time, but was given a break and returned in the spring with placed efforts over 3m-plus at Newbury (third to Alderburn) and Cheltenham (beaten $1/2$l by Alexanderthegreat); was reportedly over the top when again pulled up at Aintree; clearly one who can be campaigned at the big tracks, if not in the biggest races; stays 3m well and likes decent ground.

1226 Kerryhead Windfarm (Ire)

9 br g Bob Back - Kerryhead Girl (Be My Native)

A Maguire (Ir)   James R Browne

PLACINGS: 221325462F42/032800-   **RPR 143c**

Starts	1st	2nd	3rd	4th	Win & Pl
36	4	9	3	6	£111,709

10/05	Fair	2m5¹/₂f Ch good...£7,841
1/05	Punc	2m4f Hdl heavy...£7,841
11/04	Punc	2m4f Mdn Hdl yld-sft...£7,786
3/04	Navn	2m NHF 5-7yo yield £5,353

Decent staying handicap chaser, formerly trained by Michael Hourigan but now in the care of Adrian Maguire; hasn't won since his novice days in the autumn of 2005, but looks well handicapped on his best run last season, a 4l second to subsequent Gold Cup fifth Cane Brake (in receipt of just 3lb) in the valuable Troytown Handicap Chase at Navan last November (3m, soft, 16 ran); failed to figure in three subsequent starts, however, including when well held in the Thyestes Chase and Irish Grand National; official rating of 131 makes him one to consider for staying handicap chases, and he has won on good and heavy going.

1227 Key Time (Ire)

5 b g Darshaan - Kasota (Alzao)

J H Johnson   Andrea & Graham Wylie

PLACINGS: 211-   **RPR 124+h**

Starts	1st	2nd	3rd	4th	Win & Pl
3	2	1	-	-	£7,920

2/07	Muss	2m4f Cls4 Nov Hdl good....................................£3,904
12/06	Muss	2m4f Cls4 Nov Hdl good....................................£3,253

Former Glorious Goodwood handicap winner for Sir Mark Prescott, and winner of two of his three novice hurdles for new connections last winter; needed the experience behind Ellerslie George first time out, but netted two 2m4f Musselburgh wins in December and February with a minimum of fuss, beating Ferrando by 9l and Bob's Dream by 6l in all-the-way fashion; missed the end-of-season festivals, and will be an interesting and fresh contender for handicap hurdles this autumn; yet to race on anything but good ground over jumps.

1228 Kicking King (Ire)

9 b g Old Vic - Fairy Blaze (Good Thyne)

T Taaffe (Ir)   Conor Clarkson

PLACINGS: /5F1122/B12111/1231/

Starts	1st	2nd	3rd	4th	Win & Pl
23	12	6	2	-	£803,451

12/05	Sand	3m¹/₂f Cls1 Gd1 Ch good	£114,040
4/05	Punc	3m1f Gd1 Ch yld-sft	£98,936
3/05	Chel	3m2¹/₂f Cls1 Gd1 Ch good	£212,268
12/04	Kemp	3m Cls1 Gd1 Ch gd-sft	£116,000
12/04	Punc	2m4f Gd1 Ch soft	£41,197
10/04	Gowr	2m4f Gd2 Ch yield	£22,923
1/04	Leop	2m1f Nov Gd1 Ch yld-sft	£36,620
1/04	Punc	2m Nov Ch soft	£9,155
2/03	Punc	2m Nov Gd2 Hdl sft-hvy	£21,104
1/03	Cork	2m2f Hdl soft	£8,289
11/02	Naas	2m Hdl 4yo soft	£7,196
1/02	Leop	2m NHF 4yo yld-sft	£5,291

Top-class staying chaser who has won six times in Grade 1 company, most memorably defeating Take The Stand by 5l in the 2005 Cheltenham Gold Cup; off the track since winning his second King George (at Sandown) in December of that year, when he stayed on grimly to beat Monkerhostin by a neck, but sustained an injury in the process; connections hope to have him back this season, but considerable doubt still remains, and even if he does return, there is no guarantee that he will rediscover his best form after almost two years of inactivity (in fact, the odds are stacked against it); goes on any ground and stays 3m2f-plus, but a risky choice for those compiling a list, and arguably one to leave until the transfer window, as he will surely take a while to find his peak. *'There's a reasonable chance we will see him back on the racecourse. We'll give him every chance to run again.' (Conor Clarkson, owner)*

1229 Kicks For Free (Ire)

6 b g Flemensfirth - Keep The Change (Castle Keep)

P Nicholls   Trevor Hemmings

PLACINGS: 1133/112380-   RPR **135h**

Starts	1st	2nd	3rd	4th	Win & Pl
10	4	1	3	-	£43,548

11/06	Hayd	2m Cls1 Nov List Hdl gd-sft	£20,829
11/06	Winc	2m Cls3 Nov Hdl 4-6yo good	£6,506
2/06	Winc	2m Cls6 Am NHF 4-6yo good	£2,056
1/06	Winc	2m Cls6 NHF 4-6yo soft	£2,056

Well regarded sort who was top-notch in bumpers but did not quite reach the heights expected over hurdles last season, but is now likely to be seen to better effect over fences; justified odds-on favouritism on his first two starts last term, achieving most at Haydock in November when coming home in good style by 6l from Self Respect and earning a quote of 7-1 for the Supreme Novices' Hurdle in the process; ultimately finished only eighth at the Cheltenham Festival, but was beaten only around 13l for which he earned his best Racing Post Rating yet; has plenty of speed and could be difficult to stop in novice chases until the competition hots up.

1230 King Johns Castle (Ire)

8 gr g Flemensfirth - Caislain Darai (Fujiwara)

A Moore (Ir)   John P McManus

PLACINGS: 8114/3F1P523/1PU22P-   RPR **139c**

Starts	1st	2nd	3rd	4th	Win & Pl
16	3	3	2	1	£38,761

11/06	Navn	2m1f Ch yld-sft	£7,863
1/06	Naas	2m3f Mdn Hdl soft	£4,765
12/04	Gowr	2m NHF 5-7yo yld-sft	£4,380

Fair hurdler who proved better over fences last season; jumped well to win a run-of-the-mill beginners chase at Navan, but best form in defeat when 2l second to Schindlers Hunt in the Grade 1 Baileys Arkle Novice Chase at Leopardstown in January (2m1f, soft, 7 ran) and 3¹/₂l runner-up to Young Desperado in a Grade 2 back at Navan the following month (2m, heavy, 6 ran); however, also failed to complete on three occasions, breaking blood vessels when pulled up on his final start; best efforts around 2m, but has form up to 2m6f; could be a threat in handicaps if he improves his jumping.

1231 Kings Advocate (Ire)

7 b/br g Saddlers' Hall - Definitely Maybe (Brush Aside)

T Taaffe (Ir)   Conor Clarkson

PLACINGS: 8/2351/2034/3512366-   RPR **140c**

Starts	1st	2nd	3rd	4th	Win & Pl
16	2	3	4	1	£32,591

11/06	Limk	2m3¹/₂f Ch soft	£7,625
3/05	Thur	2m6f Mdn Hdl 4-6yo heavy	£3,921

Improved with experience over fences last season; won a beginners' chase at Limerick in November, before making subsequent Grade 1 winner One Cool Cookie pull out all the stops over the same course and distance in a Grade 2; went handicapping afterwards, and was sent off third-favourite for the Jewson Novices' Handicap Chase at Cheltenham (2m5f, good to soft, 19 ran), where he failed to register a threat in finishing 11l sixth to L'Antartique; lack of experience didn't stop him going off favourite for the Irish National (under just 10st) and he was not disgraced at that level when 6l sixth to Cheltenham winner Butler's Cabin (3m5f, good, 29 ran); remains on a decent mark and a likely player in major handicaps between 2m4f and 3m; has scope for further improvement.

1232 Kings Quay

5 b h Montjeu - Glen Rosie (Mujtahid)

J Quinn   Mrs Marie Taylor

PLACINGS: 1138261-1   RPR **131h**

Starts	1st	2nd	3rd	4th	Win & Pl
8	4	1	1	-	£67,241

128	7/07	MRas	2m1¹/₂f Cls2 119-145 Hdl Hcap soft	£25,052
119	4/07	Aint	2m1¹/₂f Cls1 List 114-140 Hdl Hcap good	£28,510
	9/06	Plum	2m Hdl gd-fm	£3,426
	8/06	MRas	2m1¹/₂f Cls4 Mdn Hdl good	£3,083

Beat Breeders' Cup hero Wilko on the Flat in 2004,

and progressing nicely over hurdles at the time of writing; has won two good handicaps since April, beating Diego Cao by 1l at Aintree, and defying a 9lb higher mark to short-head Prince Ary in the Summer Hurdle at Market Rasen in July (2m2f, soft, 17 ran); likes to be held up and delivered late - his last three winning margins over hurdles have been less than a length - and could still be some way in front of the handicapper; ideally suited by decent ground and big fields, which provide him with cover and a strong pace, and will be campaigned in handicaps at around 2m, with the County Hurdle a possible long-term aim.

1233 Kingscliff (Ire)

10 b g Toulon - Pixies Glen (Furry Glen)

R Alner   A J Sendell

PLACINGS: 1/112/2/421P20/4692-   **RPR 162c**

Starts	1st	2nd	3rd	4th	Win & Pl
16	5	5	-	2	£284,006
	11/05	Hayd	3m Cls1 Gd1 Ch gd-sft		£85,530
148	12/03	Chel	3m1¹/₂f Cls2 132-158 Ch Hcap good		£23,200
130	11/03	Asct	3m¹/₂f Cls2 111-137 Ch Hcap soft		£13,702
	3/03	Chel	3m2¹/₂f Cls2 Hunt Ch good		£23,200
	2/03	Winc	3m1¹/₂f Cls6 Am Hunt Ch gd-sft		£1,512

High-class staying chaser at his best, although without a win since beating Beef Or Salmon in the Betfair Bowl at Haydock in November 2005; lightly raced last season, and looked a shadow of the horse who was once placed in a King George for most of it; surprised everyone, though, with a return to form in the Grade 1 Guinness Gold Cup at the Punchestown festival, where he battled on more heartily than has often been the case in the past and finished 3¹/₂l second to Neptune Collonges (3m1f, good, 10 ran, had In Compliance and Racing Demon back in third and fourth); hard to predict at the best of times, but a repeat of that Punchestown run would make him competitive in anything just below the top level; not the greatest jumper, but stays well and suited by ease.

1234 Knight Legend (Ire)

8 b g Flying Legend - Well Trucked (Dry Dock)

Mrs J Harrington (Ir)   Lynn Wilson

PLACINGS: 315633/3F2221UF02-18   **RPR 139c**

Starts	1st	2nd	3rd	4th	Win & Pl
21	4	4	4	-	£57,720
	7/07	Tipp	3m Hdl heavy		£6,070
	1/07	Punc	2m4f Ch heavy		£7,003
	1/06	Naas	2m3f Mdn Hdl soft		£6,672
	3/05	Naas	2m NHF 4-6yo yld-sft		£4,411

Just a single novice chase win to show for a busy campaign last winter, when beating chase debutant Offshore Account by 19l in heavy ground at Punchestown in January (2m4f, 18 ran); lots of good form in defeat elsewhere, notably second places behind Briareus in a Grade 2 contest at Ascot in December (beaten 3l) and when beaten 11l by Offshore Account in a Grade 1 at the

Punchestown festival (old rival had improved a lot since their first meeting, and was better suited by 3m1f on good ground); showed his versatility when winning over hurdles at Tipperary in July, before finishing eighth in the Galway Plate; official chase mark of 137 looks to have him about right, but looks worth his place in the top handicap chases over 2m4f-3m.

1235 Knowhere (Ire)

9 b g Lord Americo - Andarta (Ballymore)

N Twiston-Davies   H R Mould

PLACINGS: 1/11/P/11F22380U-   **RPR 153+c**

Starts	1st	2nd	3rd	4th	Win & Pl
12	4	2	1	-	£90,460
	10/06	Bang	2m4¹/₂f Cls3 Nov Ch gd-sft		£8,133
	9/06	Prth	2m4¹/₂f Cls3 Nov Ch soft		£6,506
	10/04	Chep	2m4f Cls1 Nov Gd2 Ch soft		£17,400
	10/04	Hexm	2m4¹/₂f Cls4 Nov Hdl good		£3,679

Started last season as a novice over fences, but turned in his best efforts in the top handicaps with very little experience behind him; ran an absolute screamer when 1¹/₂l second to Exotic Dancer (from whom he was getting just 7lb) in the Grade 3 Boylesports.com Gold Cup at Cheltenham in December, keeping on well after pushing the pace despite a number of errors (2m5f, soft, 12 ran); trip found him out when third behind Ungaro in the Feltham at Kempton (3m, good to soft, 6 ran) and his form tailed off thereafter, including when losing his place and unseating his rider on the first circuit in the Grand National; one to watch for early, as has never won after October, and likely to pick up a couple of races over 2m4f-plus before the big guns get going. *'He looked like he'd win at two and a half miles in the Feltham, but then he ran out of petrol.' (Nigel Twiston-Davies, trainer)*

1236 L'Ami (Fr)

8 ch g Lute Antique - Voltige De Nievre (Brezzo)

F Doumen (Fr)   John P McManus

PLACINGS: F143/3324243/534270-   **RPR 163c**

Starts	1st	2nd	3rd	4th	Win & Pl
31	3	7	5	5	£309,989
	1/05	Wwck	3m¹/₂f Cls2 Nov Ch soft		£11,336
	12/04	Ling	3m Cls1 Nov Gd2 Ch gd-sft		£23,200
	11/04	Autl	2m5¹/₂f Ch Hcap v soft		£25,352

High-class staying chaser, but on a losing run that stretches back to January 2005; went closest to breaking the sequence in the Aon Chase at Newbury in February, where he threw down a determined challenge to Kauto Star on the run-in, but was a neck down as the line came (3m, soft, 6 ran, was getting 10lb from the King George and Cheltenham Gold Cup hero); elsewhere it was a tale of running well without landing a blow in the top events in Britain and Ireland, finishing third in the Betfair Chase at Haydock, fourth in the Lexus

Chase at Leopardstown and seventh in the Cheltenham Gold Cup, beaten 12^1/2l (had finished fourth behind War Of Attrition 12 months earlier); ended his season with a remote tenth behind Silver Birch under 11st 8lb in the Grand National; exposed as a stone below King George or Gold Cup class, but can pick up a Graded chase or two when the big guns are tucked up in their boxes.

1237 L'Antartique (Fr)

7 b g Cyborg - Moomaw (Akarad)

F Murphy   Mrs A N Durkan

PLACINGS: 14220/1214/4221F21U-   **RPR 155+c**

Starts	1st	2nd	3rd	4th	Win & Pl
18	6			3	£93,325
133	3/07	Chel	2m5f Cls1 Nov List 131-146 Ch Hcap gd-sft		£45,616
	12/06	Bang	2m4^1/$_2$f Cls4 Ch heavy		£5,332
	12/05	Donc	2m3^1/$_2$f Cls4 Nov Hdl good		£3,822
	11/05	Hayd	2m Cls3 Nov Hdl soft		£4,783
	9/04	List	2m NHF heavy		£7,299
	8/04	Tral	2m NHF heavy		£4,380

Decent novice chaser whose best effort by far in his first season over fences came when winning the Jewson Novices' Handicap Chase at the Cheltenham Festival; sprang a 20-1 surprise there, racing towards the rear and jumping soundly in a strongly run race before making progress to lead at the last and hold on well by 2l from Bob Hall; jumping let him down on his final start at Aintree in the 2m4f amateur riders' handicap chase, only getting to the second fence (also fell on his fifth start over fences), and made mistakes when runner-up to Dom D'Orgeval on his sixth start); Paddy Power Gold Cup back at Cheltenham looks a suitable early target; stays 3m, but best form over 2m4f, where he's suited by a strongly run race; jumping needs improving, but he has scope.

1238 L'Aventure (Fr)

8 b m Cyborg - Amphitrite (Lazer)

P Nicholls   C J Harriman

PLACINGS: 6440/641537/6782P40-   **RPR 144c**

Starts	1st	2nd	3rd	4th	Win & Pl
42	8	10	3	7	£245,353
131	12/05	Chep	3m5^1/$_2$f Cls1 Gd3 127-153 Ch Hcap gd-sft		£57,020
120	10/04	Chep	3m Cls2 120-146 Hdl Hcap soft		£12,047
	5/04	Uttx	3m Cls4 Ch gd-sft		£5,070
	1/04	Donc	2m3f Cls3 Nov Ch soft		£6,890
	1/04	Ludl	2m4f Cls4 Ch good		£4,420
	6/03	Autl	2m2f Hdl 4yo v soft		£6,545
	3/03	Engh	2m Hdl 4yo v soft		£6,545
	3/03	Engh	2m Hdl 4yo heavy		£6,545

Likeable mare who is at home over long distances in testing conditions, but is winless since landing the Welsh National in 2005; put up some decent efforts last term between some less auspicious performances, notably in the Red Square Vodka Gold Cup at Haydock in February when conjuring a late rattle to get within 1^1/4l of Heltornic and putting 15l of daylight back to Mon Mome in third (3m4^1/2f, heavy, 16 ran); was racing from her lowest-ever mark over fences on that occasion and is able to start the new campaign from the same rating after being raised a few pounds for her Haydock effort and then struggling; difficult to predict, but weighted to win and must be on the shortlist for the Welsh National again.

1239 La Dame Brune (Fr)

5 b m Mansonnien - Madame Extra (Sir Brink)

N Henderson   Mr & Mrs J D Cotton

PLACINGS: 503/115-   **RPR 125+h**

Starts	1st	2nd	3rd	4th	Win & Pl
6	2		1	-	£9,347
	12/06	Wwck	2m5f Cls4 Nov Hdl heavy		£3,904
	12/06	Hntg	2m4^1/$_2$f Cls3 Nov Hdl gd-sft		£5,205

Useful mare who looked set for bigger things when winning her first two novice hurdles last season; bolted up at Huntingdon in December, beating Knockara Luck by 19l, and followed up against a better opponent in Wyldello at Warwick three weeks later, giving 7lb to Alan King's charge and coming out on top by 1l in heavy ground; looked a potential candidate for the mares' series final or even Cheltenham after those wins, but instead appeared in a lesser event at Newbury at the beginning of March and flopped badly, trailing in a distance last of five finishers behind Master Eddy; was reportedly blowing very hard after that run, and something was clearly amiss; a bit to prove now, but retains plenty of potential over hurdles or fences.

1240 Labelthou (Fr)

8 b m Saint Preuil - Suzy De Thou (Toujours Pret)

E Lavelle   Gdm Partnership

PLACINGS: 4426/3/15112118-   **RPR 146+h**

Starts	1st	2nd	3rd	4th	Win & Pl
14	5	2	1	2	£94,989
	2/07	Hayd	2m7^1/$_2$f Cls1 Gd2 Hdl heavy		£22,808
	1/07	Wwck	2m5f Cls1 Nov Gd2 Hdl heavy		£22,808
	12/06	Sand	2m4^1/$_2$f Cls1 Nov Gd2 Hdl soft		£15,966
	11/06	Towc	2m5f Cls4 Nov Hdl soft		£3,904
	5/06	Autl	2m2f Hdl v soft		£13,903

Gritty hurdler who racked up three Grade 2 novice successes in soft/heavy ground last season; produced a power-packed performance at Sandown in December when beating subsequent Supreme Novices' Hurdle runner-up Granit Jack by 22l over 2m4^1/2f; beaten by Flight Leader at Cheltenham in December, but returned to winning ways with victories at Warwick in January (beat Zilcsh by 1^3/4l) and Haydock in February (3m, beat Afrad by 8l); those wins encouraged connections to take an audacious stab at the World Hurdle at Cheltenham (started 20-1), but she was nowhere near as effective on good to soft ground and trailed in 34l eighth behind Inglis Drever; set to go chasing now, and should do well, but needs very soft ground to show her best.

1241 Lacdoudal (Fr)

8 gr g Cadoudal - Belfaster (Royal Charter)

P Hobbs   Mrs R J Skan

PLACINGS: 24/161347221/644303-   **RPR 155c**

Starts	1st	2nd	3rd	4th	Win & Pl
33	8	8	6	5	£297,545
152	4/06	Sand	3m5¹/₂f Cls1 Gd3 133-159 Ch Hcap gd-fm		£91,232
	12/05	Sand	3m¹/₂f Cls2 Ch soft		£16,410
133	10/05	Chep	2m4f Cls1 List 127-153 Hdl Hcap soft		£26,100
138	1/05	Chel	2m5f Cls2 Nov 116-142 Ch Hcap gd-sft		£12,354
130	1/05	Kemp	2m4¹/₂f Cls2 112-138 Ch Hcap good		£12,006
	12/04	Donc	2m3f Cls4 Ch good		£5,146
	3/04	Kemp	2m Cls3 Nov Hdl good		£5,434
	12/03	Pau	2m¹/₂f Hdl 4yo heavy		£7,481

Tough and consistent handicap chaser who needs 3m-plus these days; gained his most recent success in the Betfred Gold Cup at Sandown in April 2006, beating Eric's Charm by 1¹/₄l off a mark of 152; wasn't overly punished by the handicapper and spent the whole of last season running with credit off similar sorts of marks, making the frame in the Silver Cup at Ascot (fourth behind Billyvoddan), a Listed handicap at Cheltenham on New Year's Day (fourth behind Too Forward), the Racing Post Chase (third behind Simon) and, for the second year running, a valuable 3m1f handicap at Aintree (third behind Reveillez); sole disappointing run when only 11th in the William Hill Handicap Chase at the Cheltenham Festival; thoroughly likeable sort who looks sure to continue to run well in similar contests, and could easily win another good prize on his favoured good ground in the spring.

1242 Lankawi

5 ch g Unfuwain - Zarma (Machiavellian)

P Bowen   Ms Jill Day

PLACINGS: U31244/2011122-5   **RPR 131+c**

Starts	1st	2nd	3rd	4th	Win & Pl
14	4	4	1	2	£41,070
	3/07	Sthl	2m4¹/₂f Cls3 Nov Ch gd-fm		£10,111
	3/07	Hexm	2m¹/₂f Cls3 Nov Ch soft		£5,855
	2/07	Sedg	2m4f Cls4 Ch heavy		£3,486
	11/05	Weth	2m Cls4 Nov Hdl 3yo gd-sft		£3,440

Nothing special over hurdles, but proved a revelation over fences in the second half of last season; won novice events at Sedgefield, Hexham and Southwell before an excellent effort from just out of the weights in a valuable 3m1f handicap at Aintree's Grand National meeting, where he lost no caste in finishing 7l second to the equally progressive but more experienced Reveillez (good, 18 ran, winner went on to finish second in the Betfred Gold Cup); raised 4lb for that effort, and was subsequently beaten twice, although not disgraced when fifth behind stablemate Iron Man in the Summer Plate at Market Rasen; probably needs to improve somewhat to win a good prize off his official mark of 136, but that's not impossible after just six starts over fences; seems to act on any going.

1243 Launde (Ire)

8 b g Norwich - Carbia's Last (Palm Track)

B Pollock   Dave Mee

PLACINGS: 4/2752125/1156P-   **RPR 144+c**

Starts	1st	2nd	3rd	4th	Win & Pl
11	3	2	-	-	£29,279
127	11/06	Hayd	2m Cls3 106-130 Ch Hcap gd-sft		£13,012
120	10/06	Aint	2m Cls3 103-120 Ch Hcap gd-sft		£7,807
	2/06	Leic	2m Cls4 Mdn Ch soft		£4,754

Talented front-runner with some smart form in 2m chases; began last season with all-the-way wins at Aintree and Haydock in the autumn, posting career-best figures on the latter occasion when beating Lord Rodney by 1³/₄l (2m, good to soft, 6 ran); given a mid-season break, but nowhere near as effective on his return, doing best when 10l fifth behind Madison Du Berlais in a decent contest at Southwell; dropped in the weights as a result, and starts just 2lb higher than he won off at Haydock, so every chance of a return to winning ways. *'He'll have a busy autumn, as he tends to lose his form mid-winter, so the plan is to miss Cheltenham and bring him back for Aintree and Ayr.' (Ben Pollock, trainer)*

1244 Laustra Bad (Fr)

4 b g Astarabad - Love Crazy (Loup Solitaire)

D Pipe   Mrs Sarah Ling

PLACINGS: 21344P142131-   **RPR 127+h**

Starts	1st	2nd	3rd	4th	Win & Pl
12	4	2	2	3	£66,569
	4/07	Chel	2m1f Cls2 Nov Hdl 4yo good		£8,768
	2/07	Chep	2m¹/₂f Cls4 Nov Hdl soft		£2,733
	11/06	Engh	2m1f Ch 3yo v soft		£15,890
	8/06	Claf	2m1f Hdl 3yo soft		£9,600

Useful novice hurdler in the second part of last season after arriving from France, and looks just the type to exploit the weight-for-age allowance over fences this term; has won two of his four starts in Britain, but probably showed his best form in defeat when beaten just over 5l by stablemate Gaspara in the Fred Winter Juvenile Hurdle at the Cheltenham Festival, losing out on second spot only in the shadow of the post (2m1¹/₂f, good to soft, 16 ran); has winning form over fences in France (beat Gaspara 2l last November); should do well with cut in the ground at around 2m.

1245 Le Duc (Fr)

8 b g Villez - Beberova (Synefos)

P Nicholls   The Stewart Family

PLACINGS: 739F337/02UU/0743UP-   **RPR 136+c**

Starts	1st	2nd	3rd	4th	Win & Pl
39	4	5	5	7	£181,489
131	1/05	Chel	2m5f Cls2 123-149 Ch Hcap good		£23,200
	3/04	Kels	2m1f Cls3 Nov Ch gd-sft		£5,532
	10/03	Weth	2m Cls4 Ch gd-fm		£3,990
	4/03	Aint	2m¹/₂f Cls1 Nov Gd2 Hdl 4yo good		£63,800

Classy staying handicap chaser on his day, but also

a notoriously tricky customer who is without a win since January 2005; ran three decent races last term, two of them over Cheltenham's cross-country course, coming closest to winning at the December meeting when finishing only 2³/4l down in fourth place behind old pro Spot Thedifference (3m7f, soft, 12 ran); often goes well over the National fences (has been placed in the Becher and Topham), and likely to be aimed at the National again, a race in which he has unseated his rider for the last two years; talented, and now down to his lowest-ever chase mark, but for optimists only.

1246 Le Volfoni (Fr)

6 b g *Sicyos - Brume (Courtroom)*

P Nicholls   A F Banks

PLACINGS: 1643211121F632/3646-   **RPR 152 + c**

Starts	1st	2nd	3rd	4th	Win & Pl
31	6	5	4	8	£184,610
	2/06	Font	2m4f Cls3 Nov Ch heavy		£9,626
	1/06	Plum	2m1f Cls4 Nov Ch soft		£7,543
	12/05	Hayd	2m Cls3 Nov Ch soft		£7,877
	12/05	Chep	2m¹/₂f Cls3 Ch heavy		£5,686
	4/05	Engh	2m2f List Hdl 4yo heavy		£20,425
	6/04	Autl	1m7f Hdl 3yo v soft		£14,197

Very smart novice chaser between 2m and 2m4f the season before last, who struggled a little when pitched into handicap company last term; missed the first half of the season, but returned in the new year with four decent efforts without getting his head in front; did best of all in the Racing Post Plate at the Cheltenham Festival when sent off at 16-1 and stayed on up the hill to finish 5¹/2l fourth behind Idole First (2m5f, good to soft, 23 ran); raised another 2lb for that effort to a mark of 147, so really does look handicapped to the hilt, and despite his talent, he is likely to be difficult to place.

1247 Lead On (Ire)

6 b g *Supreme Leader - Dressed In Style (Meneval)*

P Hobbs   B K Peppiatt

PLACINGS: F121-   **RPR 125 + h**

Starts	1st	2nd	3rd	4th	Win & Pl
4	2	1	-	-	£13,480
	4/07	Chel	2m1f Cls2 Nov Hdl good		£9,081
	1/07	Tntn	2m1f Cls4 Nov Hdl soft		£3,253

Likely type for novice chases this season after making a good impression over hurdles; won twice in novice company over the smaller obstacles, beating King's Revenge by 1¹/2l at Taunton in January and Nobelix by 3l in a small-field contest at Cheltenham in April; in between ran a cracker at Newbury to finish a neck second at level weights to the classy Special Envoy, the pair 7l clear (2m1/2f, good to soft, 18 ran); that winner ended the season rated 145, so this one's hurdles mark of 129 is something connections may try to exploit in the early part of the season, but he has the physique of a horse who will really thrive over

fences; likes a little dig in the ground, and although yet to race over further than 2m1f, he should be suited by a step up.

1248 Leading Authority (Ire)

6 br g *Supreme Leader - Bonnie Thynes (Good Thyne)*

C Tizzard   R G Tizzard

PLACINGS: 231/462162-   **RPR 121b**

Starts	1st	2nd	3rd	4th	Win & Pl
9	2	3	1	1	£8,534
	1/07	Extr	2m3f Cls4 Nov Hdl heavy		£2,602
	1/06	Extr	2m1f Cls6 Mdn NHF 4-6yo gd-sft		£2,056

Showed promise in bumpers before confirming that potential, to a degree, over hurdles last season; ran fourth behind subsequent Champion Bumper winner Cork All Star on his final bumper outing in November (2m1/2f, good to soft, 11 ran); best efforts in novice hurdles came in victory at Exeter, when seeing off Melba Toast by a neck, and in defeat at Chepstow, when stepped up to 3m for the first time, beaten 11l by Mark The Book (heavy, 9 ran); last four outings on heavy ground, and untried on anything faster than good to soft; goes over fences now and appeals physically as the type to thrive; likely to be out as soon as ground permits and could be one to watch for if making an early switch to novice handicaps. *'We've been waiting for this one to go over fences.' (Colin Tizzard, trainer)*

1249 Leading Man (Ire)

7 b g *Old Vic - Cudder Or Shudder (The Parson)*

F Murphy   Mrs C McKeane

PLACINGS: /72421/3154P/07146P-   **RPR 138 + c**

Starts	1st	2nd	3rd	4th	Win & Pl
18	3	2	1	5	£56,992
128	12/06	Weth	3m1f Cls1 Gd3 128-154 Ch Hcap soft		£28,510
	12/05	Weth	3m1f Cls2 Nov Ch heavy		£11,192
	4/05	Prth	2m4¹/₂f Cls3 Nov Hdl soft		£6,032

Staying handicap chaser who is regarded by his trainer as a long-term Grand National prospect; won the ten-runner Grade 3 Rowland Meyrick Handicap Chase at Wetherby on Boxing Day, clear from two out and staying on well to beat Sir Rembrandt by 8l; failed to build on that effort in subsequent races, but not entirely disgraced when fourth of nine behind The Outlier in the Peter Marsh Chase at Haydock (3m, heavy), and sixth behind Heltornic at the same track in the Red Square Vodka Gold Cup over 3m4¹/2f; ran as if out of sorts at Perth on his final start; stays well, and acts on soft/heavy ground. *'He'll be a National horse one day. He's a big, bottomless pit of a horse, who just gallops and jumps.' (Ferdy Murphy, trainer)*

1250 Leading Run (Ire)

8 b g Supreme Leader - Arctic Run (Deep Run)

N Meade (Ir) — Mrs Moira McGrath

PLACINGS: 1/111/122204- — **RPR 128h**

Starts	1st	2nd	3rd	4th	Win & Pl
10	5	3	-	1	£87,791

10/06	Punc	2m4f Mdn Hdl yield		£5,719
4/06	Punc	2m Gd1 NHF good		£44,897
2/06	Naas	2m NHF yield		£5,957
1/06	Gowr	2m NHF yield		£5,242
11/04	Navn	2m NHF 5-7yo heavy		£4,866

Former leading bumper horse who didn't quite hit the heights expected of him over hurdles last season; started with a hard-earned win at Punchestown, but had to settle for second-best on his next three outings, doing best when beaten 3l by (but absolutely no match for) stablemate Aran Concerto in a Grade 1 contest at Leopardstown in February (2m2f, heavy, 4 ran); finished well adrift behind Wichita Lineman in the 3m novice hurdle at the Cheltenham Festival (jumped right throughout), but rounded off his campaign with a better effort to finish 7¹/₂l fourth behind another stablemate, Aitmatov, in Grade 2 company at Fairyhouse (2m4f, good, 8 ran); goes chasing now, and should improve over fences, without perhaps being good enough to figure at the very highest level.

1251 Lennon (Ire)

7 b/br g Beneficial - Stradbally Bay (Shackleton)

J H Johnson — Andrea & Graham Wylie

PLACINGS: 21210/21491/111741- — **RPR 150+c**

Starts	1st	2nd	3rd	4th	Win & Pl
16	8	3	-	2	£73,269

125	4/07	Prth	2m¹/₂f Cls3 99-125 Hdl Hcap soft	£7,807
	12/06	Catt	2m Cls3 Nov Ch gd-sft	£6,506
	11/06	Aint	2m Cls2 Nov Ch good	£13,012
	10/06	Aint	2m Cls1 Nov List Ch good	£14,112
115	4/06	Prth	2m¹/₂f Cls3 95-120 Hdl Hcap good	£7,807
	12/05	MRas	2m1¹/₂f Cls3 Nov Hdl gd-sft	£4,840
	2/05	Muss	2m Cls6 NHF 4-6yo good	£2,954
	11/04	Muss	2m Cls6 Mdn NHF 4-6yo gd-fm	£2,261

Classy front-running 2m novice chaser last season; went to Cheltenham for the Arkle unbeaten in three, following up easy all-the-way defeats of Penzance (by 14l) and Opera De Coeur (eased down by 1³/₄l) on good ground at Aintree with an odds-on romp at Catterick; started 20-1 for the Arkle, but jumping errors cost him ground throughout, and he trailed in 36l seventh behind My Way De Solzen (2m, soft, 13 ran); took on many of the same rivals at Aintree, and showed himself once again to be well suited by that track with a 10¹/₂l fourth behind Twist Magic in Grade 1 company (2m, good, 6 ran); comfortable winner off an advantageous mark over hurdles on his final start at Perth; rated 144 over fences, and capable of winning a decent prize off that mark on good ground at a sharp track.

1252 Leslingtaylor (Ire)

5 b g Orpen - Rite Of Spring (Niniski)

J Quinn — Mrs Marie Taylor

PLACINGS: 11610-1 — **RPR 130+h**

Starts	1st	2nd	3rd	4th	Win & Pl
6	4	-	-	-	£61,385

126	5/07	Hayd	2m Cls1 Gd3 126-152 Hdl Hcap good	£42,765
	3/07	Newc	2m Cls4 Nov Hdl good	£2,765
	12/06	Muss	2m Cls2 Nov Hdl good	£12,526
	12/06	MRas	2m1¹/₂f Cls4 Nov Hdl gd-sft	£2,928

Smart novice hurdler last season, but saved his best performance for handicap company; that came in the valuable Swinton Hurdle at Haydock in May, where he quickened up smartly to lead on the run-in and beat French Saulaie by 1¹/₂l (2m, good, 23 ran); that was his fourth win from six starts over hurdles (supplementing novice successes at Market Rasen, Musselburgh and Newcastle), and he shows no signs of having reached the limit of his ability yet; new mark of 133 means he needs to improve again, but shrewd trainer is certain to have left a bit to work on, and he is probably still progressing physically at the age of five.

1253 Liberate

4 ch g Lomitas - Eversince (Foolish Pleasure)

P Hobbs — Mrs D L Whateley

PLACINGS: 11225- — **RPR 145+h**

Starts	1st	2nd	3rd	4th	Win & Pl
5	2	2	-	-	£36,304

11/06	Winc	2m Cls4 Nov Hdl 3yo gd-sft	£3,083
11/06	Hrfd	2m1f Cls4 Mdn Hdl 3yo gd-sft	£4,229

Classy juvenile hurdler last term, but faces a potentially difficult second season over hurdles; won his first two (at Hereford and Wincanton), but was given a break after a 1¹/₂l defeat at the hands of Poquelin at Kempton over Christmas; went fresh to the Triumph Hurdle, and ran far and away his best race to date, staying on from the rear to grab second place without ever threatening runaway winner Katchit (2m1f, good to soft, 23 ran); stepped up to 2m4f to take on older novices at Aintree, but below form in finishing a tired-looking fifth behind Tidal Bay; much better than that, but a mark of 149 demands that he show further improvement to figure in handicaps, and it could be that he is forced to try his hand in Graded hurdles or novice chases; 2m winner on the Flat, so could even be worth a try over 3m.

1254 Lightning Strike (Ger)

4 ch g Danehill Dancer - La Capilla (Machiavellian)

Miss V Williams — John Nicholls (Trading) Ltd

PLACINGS: 295- — **RPR 131h**

Starts	1st	2nd	3rd	4th	Win & Pl
3	-	1	-	-	£7,304

Fifth in the Queen's Vase at Royal Ascot in 2006,

and later beaten only 9l in the Cesarewitch, before a change of stables and switch to hurdling last spring; runner-up to prolific winner My Turn Now on debut at Huntingdon, beaten 8l (2m5f, soft, 8 ran); took his chance as a maiden in the Triumph Hurdle the following month, and improved to finish 27l ninth behind Katchit (2m1f, good to soft, 23 ran); took on the winner again on better ground at Aintree, and this time got within 21l in finishing fifth (2m1/2f, good, 12 ran); needs to improve a lot to be a candidate for top honours, but should do well in novice hurdles and handicaps between 2m and 2m4f; good ground suits, but has run well in the mud.

1255 Limerick Boy (Ger)

9 b g Alwuhush - Limoges (Konigsstuhl)
Miss V Williams   Favourites Racing III
PLACINGS: 31F21PFP/54PF/7916P-   RPR **156**+c

Starts	1st	2nd	3rd	4th	Win & Pl
28	6	2	2	1	£122,956
	12/06	Hayd	2m6f Cls3 Ch heavy		£15,802
	2/05	Kemp	2m4¹/₂f Cls1 Nov Gd2 Ch soft		£19,040
	1/05	Leic	2m Cls4 Ch gd-sft		£4,810
140	1/04	Kemp	2m Cls2 114-140 Hdl Hcap good		£29,000
	4/03	Aint	2m¹/₂f Cls1 Nov Gd2 Hdl good		£29,000
	3/03	Winc	2m Cls4 Mdn Hdl soft		£4,046

Very smart chaser, but not the most reliable and proved a one-hit wonder last season; comfortably beaten on first two starts over hurdles, but reignited his campaign on return to fences at Haydock in December, beating Royal Emperor by 16l in a peculiar heavy-ground race in which the two market leaders ran well below par; had similar ground at his favourite track, Kempton, next time out in the Racing Post Chase, but patently failed to stay 3m when sixth behind Simon; never at the races on his last start at Aintree (3m1f, good, 18 ran); best at around 2m4f-plus and seems to do well at sharp tracks on easy ground, but the handicapper may well have his measure.

1256 Limited Edition (Ire)

9 b g Parthian Springs - Rosemount Rose (Ashmore)
C Llewellyn   Malcolm C Denmark
PLACINGS: 2F58/114/P11F-   RPR **142**+c

Starts	1st	2nd	3rd	4th	Win & Pl
11	4	1			£22,887
122	2/07	Kemp	2m4¹/₂f Cls3 104-130 Ch Hcap soft		£9,800
	2/07	Kemp	2m4¹/₂f Cls4 Ch gd-sft		£5,205
	1/05	Donc	2m¹/₂f Cls4 Nov Hdl good		£3,533
	12/04	Folk	2m1¹/₂f Cls6 Nov Hdl gd-sft		£3,400

Lightly raced due to injury problems, but remains a very interesting handicap chaser at around 2m4f; won twice at Kempton last season, making all in a hot novice chase in February (beat Bible Lord by 8l, with three other next-time-out winners completing the field) and just 15 days later hacking up off a mark of 122 in a handicap, beating Fast

Forward by 36l (was 15l clear of He's The Boss when that one refused at the last); went up 13lb for that, and sent off at 10-1 for the Jewson Novices' Handicap Chase at the Cheltenham Festival, where he was a close third and still travelling well when falling four out; starts the new season on the same mark, and his copper-bottomed form makes him an obvious candidate for decent handicaps, and possibly even the Paddy Power Gold Cup; likes ease in the ground.

1257 Lindop

7 ch g Nashwan - Footlight Fantasy (Nureyev)
R Alner   R Alner
PLACINGS: 531-   RPR **129**+h

Starts	1st	2nd	3rd	4th	Win & Pl
3	1	-	1	-	£3,484
	3/07	Ling	2m¹/₂f Cls4 Mdn Hdl soft		£3,083

Progressive novice hurdler last season, and looks open to further improvement; third behind the subsequent Cheltenham Festival-placed Laustra Bad at Chepstow in February, and got off the mark over jumps at Lingfield in March, where he led 3 out and galloped to a 13l success over Edgbriar; has been brought back to the racecourse beautifully by his new trainer, having been off for four years after winning his only Flat start, and a mark of 125 gives him every chance of doing well in handicap hurdles at around 2m.

1258 Livingstonebramble (Ire)

11 b g Supreme Leader - Killiney Side (General Ironside)
W Mullins (Ir)   Favourites Racing Syndicate
PLACINGS: 2/12014/359442250U7-   RPR **146**c

Starts	1st	2nd	3rd	4th	Win & Pl
31	4	6	2	6	£91,548
128	4/06	Fair	2m1f 125-141 Ch Hcap gd-yld		£31,428
	4/05	Punc	2m2f Nov Ch yld-sft		£12,697
	11/04	Wxfd	2m4f Ch soft		£5,839
	4/02	Fair	2m4f Mdn Hdl 6yo yield		£7,196

Handicap chaser whose best effort last season came when a staying-on 3¹/₂l runner-up to stablemate Homer Wells in the Thyestes Chase at Gowran Park in January (3m, heavy, 16 ran); had his sights set high in the spring, but didn't make much impact at the Cheltenham Festival (well down the field in Racing Post Plate) and then unseated his rider at the sixth in the Grand National after being sent off at 100-1; probably found the trip on the short side and ground a bit too fast when seventh in a handicap chase at the Punchestown festival (2m4f, good, 16 ran); not as good over hurdles, but ran well when second in a handicap at Leopardstown (3m, heavy, 21 ran) in December; needs at least 3m nowadays and goes well on heavy ground.

1259 Locksmith

7 gr g Linamix - Zenith (Shirley Heights)

J H Johnson   D A Johnson

PLACINGS: 18/6640/4677032232-1   **RPR 142+c**

Starts	1st	2nd	3rd	4th	Win & Pl
29	7	5	2	4	£96,802

130	5/07	Kels	2m1f Cls3 117-135 Ch Hcap gd-fm £6,321
	4/05	Ayr	2m4f Cls1 Nov Gd2 Ch good £23,200
	4/05	Ayr	2m Cls3 Nov Ch good £9,511
	1/05	Donc	2m¹/₂f Cls2 Nov Ch good £11,492
	12/04	Plum	2m1f Cls3 Ch good £5,434
	1/04	Font	2m2¹/₂f Cls4 Nov Hdl 4yo good £3,348
	11/03	Asct	1m4f Cls6 NHF 3yo soft £2,534

Decent handicap chaser, formerly trained by Martin and David Pipe and Peter Monteith; came back to form last spring under the care of the last-named trainer, finishing 5¹/₂l third behind Bambi De L'Orme in the Grade 3 Red Rum Handicap Chase at Aintree's National meeting (2m, good, 15 ran) and runner-up to the progressive Three Mirrors at Ayr (2m4f, good to firm, 5 ran) before regaining the winning thread with an 8l defeat of Bohemian Spirit at Kelso in May (2m1f, good to firm, 5 ran); not as good over hurdles, but was placed a couple of times in handicaps last season; races almost exclusively between 2m-2m4f; versatile with regard to ground preferences.

1260 Longshanks

10 b g Broadsword - Brass Castle (Carlingford Castle)

K Bailey   Alan Halsall

PLACINGS: /1P11132/2P146/7/17-   **RPR 140+c**

Starts	1st	2nd	3rd	4th	Win & Pl
20	6	4	1	2	£75,851

130	11/06	Newb	2m6¹/₂f Cls3 110-130 Ch Hcap heavy £12,700
124	1/05	Kemp	3m Cls3 105-124 Ch Hcap good £8,970
115	12/03	Hayd	3m Cls3 102-125 Ch Hcap gd-sft £10,296
104	11/03	Ayr	2m4f Cls3 Nov 84-110 Ch Hcap gd-sft £6,734
97	11/03	Hayd	2m6f Cls4 75-101 Ch Hcap gd-sft....................£3,010
	5/03	Uttx	2m6¹/₂f Cls4 Nov Hdl soft £3,653

Handicap chaser who is lit up by the big National fences at Aintree, and was placed in the Topham Chase in 2004 and 2005; finally got into the Grand National itself in April, having missed the cut on two occasions, and did connections proud, bowling along in a prominent position until his stamina ebbed away in the second-last (finished a respectable seventh behind Silver Birch, having also bruised his foot in the run-up to the race); that was just his second start of the season, and he made sure he got into the big one by beating Schuh Shine by 11l at Newbury the previous November; quite lightly raced for a ten-year-old, and the Becher Chase over 3m3f at Aintree in November could be right up his street, before possibly being aimed at another tilt at the National; has won on good and heavy ground.

1261 Lord Henry (Ire)

8 b g Lord Americo - Auntie Honnie (Radical)

P Hobbs   Mrs Karola Vann

PLACINGS: 411/379/1101-F6   **RPR 142+c**

Starts	1st	2nd	3rd	4th	Win & Pl
12	5	-	1	1	£33,841

124	3/07	Asct	2m1f Cls3 Nov Ch good £9,395
	6/06	Hrfd	2m3f Cls4 Ch gd-fm £6,338
	5/06	Bang	2m1f Cls3 102-124 Ch Hdl Hcap good...............£6,181
	11/04	Kemp	2m Cls3 Nov Hdl 4-6yo good £4,737
	10/04	Tntn	2m3¹/₂f Cls3 Nov Hdl good £5,688

Talented but fragile 2m chaser who has made more than one comeback from injury; ran down the field in the County Hurdle at Cheltenham as a 50-1 shot (first start in nine months), but much better when winning a four-runner novice chase at Ascot a fortnight later, making all and readily seeing off the odds-on Royal Shakespeare by 7l; kept on the go for a pair of handicaps at Stratford in May and June, but fell on the first occasion and a lacklustre sixth behind Mange Tout on the other; still on the same mark of 135, and can probably score off that rating on a going day; injury problems not helped by the fact that he is best on good, fast ground.

1262 Lou Du Moulin Mas (Fr)

8 b g Sassanian - Houf (Morespeed)

P Nicholls   The Eight Amigos Racing Syndicate

PLACINGS: 62264/223408/12198P-   **RPR 138+c**

Starts	1st	2nd	3rd	4th	Win & Pl
29	3	11	3	2	£88,128

124	11/06	Newb	3m Cls3 106-125 Am Ch Hcap gd-sft £9,603
	10/06	Chel	3m1¹/₂f Cls3 Nov Hdl good £6,263
	4/04	NAbb	2m5¹/₂f Cls3 Ch good £5,876

Smart staying handicapper who had previously been tricky to win with but won two of his six races last season; came out on top in a confidence-boosting spin over hurdles at Cheltenham in October and then scored his first win over fences in 31 months at Newbury in November, thwarting Kerstino Two's bid for four on the bounce by ¹/₂l; some way below that form on his remaining three starts, so clearly not the most reliable sort, although does not look harshly handicapped on a mark of 130.

1263 Lough Derg (Fr)

7 b g Apple Tree - Asturias (Pistolet Bleu)

D Pipe   W Frewen

PLACINGS: 14601/2F13PF/32494-7   **RPR 150h**

Starts	1st	2nd	3rd	4th	Win & Pl
23	6	3	2	3	£99,776

145	12/05	Extr	2m7¹/₂f Cls3 Ch good...............................£5,927
	4/05	Chel	2m5¹/₂f Cls2 119-145 Hdl Hcap good £11,446
	12/04	Chel	2m5¹/₂f Cls2 Hdl good £12,180
	4/04	Chel	2m1f Cls2 Nov Hdl 4yo gd-fm £9,773
	1/04	Wwck	2m Cls3 Nov Hdl 4yo gd-sft £7,508
	11/03	Newb	2m¹/₂f Cls3 Nov Hdl 3yo gd-fm.....................£4,823

Smart hurdler at his best, who mixed it with the best stayers in the business last season, but is without a win since picking up a novice chase nearly two years ago; reached the frame behind the likes of Hardy Eustace, Blazing Bailey and Mighty Man twice, doing particularly well when runner-up to that rival in the Grade 1 Long Walk Hurdle at Ascot in December at 50-1 (3m1f, good to soft, 9 ran); likely to continue finding a couple too good in Graded company, but starts the new campaign with a hurdle mark of 144 (7lb lower than at the same time last year), so has been given a fair chance to get his head in front in handicap company; also has the option of reverting to fences, although he didn't progress as anticipated when sent chasing before.

1264 Lounaos (Fr)

4 b f Limnos - Luanda (Bigstone)

E Griffin (Ir)   Mrs Martina Griffin

PLACINGS: 11404-   RPR **139**h

Starts	1st	2nd	3rd	4th	Win & Pl
5	2	-	-	2	£31,820
	12/06	Leop	2m Gd2 Hdl 3yo sft-hvy		£22,448
	11/06	Navn	2m Mdn Hdl 3yo soft		£5,242

Talented filly who was very highly tried as a juvenile hurdler last season; won her first two starts, the second a Grade 2 event at Leopardstown over Christmas, and the following month was thrust into the Irish Champion Hurdle at the same track, where she ran a cracker for a 4yo filly to finish 8l fourth behind established stars Hardy Eustace, Brave Inca and Macs Joy (2m, soft, 8 ran); started 7-2 favourite for the Triumph Hurdle at the Cheltenham Festival on her next start, but was starting to struggle from the third-last and trailed in 29l tenth behind Katchit; beaten favourite again in a Grade 3 novice hurdle at Fairyhouse in April (fourth behind Grangeclare Lark), but was feeling the effects of some tough races by that stage; will run on the Flat in the autumn before a return to hurdling, when she will contest Graded events. *'She was a bit clapped out by the end of the season, but she's had a rest and is nice and fresh again.' (Eoin Griffin, trainer)*

1265 Lucifer Bleu (Fr)

8 b g Kadalko - Figa Dancer (Bandinelli)

D Pipe   A J White

PLACINGS: U175527/13/114-   RPR **149+**c

Starts	1st	2nd	3rd	4th	Win & Pl
12	4	1	1	1	£42,163
121	2/07	Winc	2m5f Cls3 107-130 Ch Hcap soft		£9,759
105	1/07	Hrfd	2m3f Cls3 94-126 Ch Hcap soft		£8,425
	4/04	Extr	2m1¹/₂f Cls4 Nov Ch gd-fm		£4,533
	5/03	Autl	2m1¹/₂f Hdl 4yo heavy		£11,221

Very lightly raced performer who shrugged off an absence of two and a half years when returning to action last season and proving himself a most progressive chaser; overcame that massive break and odds of 28-1 to score at Hereford in January,

sweeping to a 5l victory over Maletton, who had run up a hat-trick on his previous three starts; hiked 16lb for that impressive reappearance, but that failed to stop him scoring at Wincanton the following month when he beat Black Hills by 11l despite being eased considerably in the closing stages; showed a tendency to clout the odd fence en route to those successes, an issue that came to the fore again when he was sent off favourite for the Racing Post Chase at Kempton, when his stamina also seemed to give out on the soft ground over 3m as he could finish only fourth behind Simon; was racing off a mark of 124 there, having been unpenalised for his win seven days earlier, but starts this season on a mark of 143 and will not find things easy; still unexposed over fences, however, having had just five runs, and could be open to further improvement.

1266 Lyes Green

6 gr g Bien Bien - Dissolve (Sharrood)

O Sherwood   P K Gardner

PLACINGS: 8218P13/6022522-   RPR **135+**h

Starts	1st	2nd	3rd	4th	Win & Pl
14	2	5	1	-	£30,020
	3/06	Ludl	3m Cls4 Nov Hdl good		£4,554
	11/05	MRas	2m3¹/₂f Cls4 Nov Hdl heavy		£3,142

Improving handicap hurdler who was unlucky not to pick up a decent prize last season, as he finished second in four of his last five starts; best of those efforts was the last, when going down in battling fashion by ¹/₂l to Albertas Run in a Listed event at Aintree's Grand National meeting (3m¹/₂f, good, 21 ran); starts this season rated 15lb higher than at the same time last year, but still progressing, and that has persuaded connections to delay a switch to fences; most effective on good ground, and in the last two seasons has reserved his best form for March/April. *'We'll definitely be adopting more aggressive tactics this season, as they seemed to suit at Aintree.' (Oliver Sherwood, trainer)*

1267 Macs Joy (Ire)

8 b g Religiously - Snob's Supreme (Supreme Leader)

Mrs J Harrington (Ir)   Mac's J Racing Syndicate

PLACINGS: 1131154/3542121/322-   RPR **160**h

Starts	1st	2nd	3rd	4th	Win & Pl
27	9	8	4	2	£519,540
	4/06	Punc	2m Gd1 Hdl good		£89,655
	2/06	Gowr	2m Gd2 Hdl soft		£26,938
	1/05	Leop	2m Gd1 Hdl heavy		£64,007
	12/04	Leop	2m Gd1 Hdl soft		£36,620
	11/04	DRoy	2m Hdl soft		£13,754
135	5/04	Hayd	2m Cls1 Gd3 135-161 Hdl Hcap good		£40,600
123	4/04	Fair	2m 103-131 Hdl Hcap yield		£45,775
	12/03	Dpat	2m2f Mdn Hdl 4yo gd-yld		£4,481
	6/03	Tral	2m NHF 4-5yo gd-yld		£3,584

Top-class 2m hurdler over a number of seasons (won the Irish Champion in 2005, second at the

Philip Carberry celebrates after Sublimity's win in the Champion Hurdle

Katchit extends his extraordinary sequence by winning the Triumph Hurdle

My Way De Solzen powers up the Cheltenham hill to win the Arkle Trophy

It's all over as Denman kicks clear off the final bend in the SunAlliance Chase

Taranis and Ruby Walsh after their success in the Ryanair Chase

Voy Por Ustedes and Robert Thornton win the Champion Chase

Cheltenham Festival in 2006), but never quite at his best in a light campaign last term; did not reappear until the latest renewal of the Irish Champion Hurdle at Leopardstown in January, where despite not being at concert pitch after his long layoff he finished 6l third behind Hardy Eustace, flattening out on the run-in (2m, soft, 8 ran); turned over at odds of 4-9 by Newmill at Gowran Park the following month, and missed Cheltenham in March after a minor setback; fine-tuned for the Punchestown festival by finishing second to Silent Oscar on the Flat at the Curragh, but found the same horse just too good again in the ACC Bank Champion Hurdle 12 days later, going down by a neck to the much-improved winner (2m, good, 8 ran); not getting any better, but will be back to do battle in the top 2m hurdle races again this season; suited by ground on the easy side of good.

1268 Mad Fish (Ire)

5 b g Flemensfirth - Lucky Trout (Beau Charmeur)

W Mullins (Ir)   Mrs Margaret McManus

PLACINGS: 1/28-   RPR **130+b**

Starts	1st	2nd	3rd	4th	Win & Pl
2	-	1	-	-	£1,251

Point-to-point winner from a good jumping family, and showed classy bumper form last term without quite justifying the tall reputation that preceded him; made 4-7 favourite for his debut at Fairyhouse in January, but had to settle for second, beaten 5l by Aranleigh (2m, heavy, 10 ran, beat the third by a distance); was again made favourite for the Champion Bumper at the Cheltenham Festival in March, and looked the most likely winner when cruising up behind the leaders 2f out, but no response under pressure from a furlong out and eventually finished eighth, beaten 6³/4l by Cork All Star and again behind third-placed Aranleigh (2m1f, good to soft, 24 ran); obviously shows an awful lot on the home gallops, and even his bare form on the track suggests he will be a force in good novice hurdles this winter.

1269 Madison Du Berlais (Fr)

6 b g Indian River - Anais Du Berlais (Dom Pasquini)

D Pipe   Roger Stanley & Yvonne Reynolds II

PLACINGS: 2U311133/8641153173-   RPR **157+c**

Starts	1st	2nd	3rd	4th	Win & Pl
28	7	6	7	1	£135,859

146	3/07	Newb	2m4f Cls1 Gd3 131-153 Ch Hcap soft £45,616
137	1/07	Sthl	2m Cls2 117-137 Ch Hcap soft £13,012
128	1/07	Wwck	2m Cls3 110-135 Ch Hcap heavy £6,506
125	3/06	Newb	2m1f Cls3 103-129 Ch Hcap good £7,807
118	2/06	Extr	2m1¹/₂f Cls3 103-124 Ch Hcap soft............£7,829
112	2/06	MRas	2m1¹/₂f Cls4 92-115 Ch Hcap good £4,554
	8/05	Le L	2m4f Ch 4yo good £5,787

Much improved handicap chaser in the second part of last season between 2m and 2m4f; started the campaign with an official mark of 136 and ended on 151 after wins at Warwick, Southwell and in the Vodafone Gold Cup at Newbury, where he gradually crept into contention on the final circuit and eventually grabbed Nozic close home to score by a neck; far from disgraced when seventh in the Racing Post Plate at Cheltenham after a 6lb hike in the weights; sure to find life tough this term after his rapid rise up the weights, but is a progressive sort who is sure to go well in the big handicaps. *'He's a very tough horse and he loves soft ground.' (David Pipe, trainer)*

1270 Maharbal (Fr)

7 b g Assessor - Cynthia (Mont Basile)

N Henderson   The Pheasant Inn Partnership

PLACINGS: 155/791/10P-   RPR **130+h**

Starts	1st	2nd	3rd	4th	Win & Pl
9	3	-	-	-	£19,404

114	12/06	Kemp	2m5f Cls3 109-135 Hdl Hcap gd-sft £8,768
114	1/05	Extr	2m3f Cls3 88-114 Hdl Hcap gd-sft £5,281
	12/03	Newb	2m¹/₂f Cls3 Nov Hdl 3yo gd-fm............£5,077

Half-brother to smart chaser Nycteos; was kept off the track for almost two years with tendon trouble, but stripped fit on his return to run away with a decent 2m5f handicap hurdle at Kempton on Boxing Day, where he hit the front full of running 2 out and kept on well to beat Golden Bay by 5l; ran way below that form in subsequent outings off a 12lb higher mark at Cheltenham and Newbury, but both were on heavy ground that might not have suited; legs will always be a concern, and he is unlikely to be seen in action very often, but if they stand up to the pressure he could easily win one or two good novice chases this term.

1271 Mahogany Blaze (Fr)

5 b g Kahyasi - Mahogany River (Irish River)

N Twiston-Davies   Mrs Lorna Berryman

PLACINGS: 6234137U7/1650709-   RPR **136+h**

Starts	1st	2nd	3rd	4th	Win & Pl
16	2	2	2	1	£29,089

| 129 | 10/06 | Chep | 2m¹/₂f Cls2 106-132 Hdl 4yo Hcap good.............£21,921 |
| | 2/06 | Extr | 2m1f Cls4 Mdn Hdl soft ....£2,741 |

Highly tried in many of the season's top handicap hurdles last season; more than paid his keep by winning a valuable 4yo handicap at Chepstow last October, beating Ameeq by 1¹/₂l; failed to win again afterwards, but showed consistent form, his best effort coming when 21l fifth behind Detroit City in the Greatwood Hurdle at Cheltenham in November (2m1/₂f, good to soft, 9 ran) off a 9lb higher mark than his Chepstow win; back down to a mark he can probably win off (134) but appeals as a chaser in the making and should be effective in novice chases at around 2m4f, possibly further; has won on good ground and soft.

1272 Mansony (Fr)

8 b g Mansonnien - Hairly (Air De Cour)

A Moore (Ir)   Michael Mulholland

PLACINGS: 622/1713F6119F/1211-   **RPR 152c**

Starts		1st	2nd	3rd	4th	Win & Pl
29		9		4	1	2	£247,341
	4/07	Punc	2m Gd1 Ch good £83,959
	3/07	Naas	2m3f Ch heavy £13,196
137	12/06	Leop	2m1f 112-140 Ch Hcap sft-hvy £13,469
	3/06	Naas	2m Nov Ch heavy £8,101
	2/06	Navn	2m Nov Gd2 Ch sft-hvy...............................£23,517
	11/05	Naas	2m Ch heavy..£8,086
131	4/05	Punc	2m4f List 107-134 Hdl Hcap soft £34,628
	2/04	Thur	2m Hdl 5yo soft £6,803
	12/03	DRoy	2m Mdn Hdl soft £4,481

Smart chaser who looks a contender for Graded races over 2m-2m4f; didn't finish out of the first two last season, his finest hour coming when winning Punchestown's Grade 1 Champion Chase in April, benefiting from a strong gallop set by Newmill, Central House and Justified and staying on to beat the last-named by 1¼l; had earlier showed he stays further than the minimum when winning at Leopardstown and Naas, and when 5l second to Watson Lake in a Grade 2 contest at Gowran (2m4f, heavy); the Ryanair Chase could become his Festival target as an alternative to the Champion Chase.

1273 Mark The Book (Ire)

6 b g Mister Lord - Boardroom Belle (Executive Perk)

P Hobbs   D Allen

PLACINGS: 1/2113-   **RPR 132+h**

Starts		1st	2nd	3rd	4th	Win & Pl
4		2	1	1	-	£7,574
	3/07	Chep	3m Cls4 Nov Hdl heavy £2,602
	2/07	Extr	2m6¹/₂f Cls4 Mdn Hdl heavy £3,253

Dour stayer who won two novice hurdles in heavy ground last season, and looks a decent prospect for novice chases; beat Kofi by 10l at Exeter and Leading Authority by 11l at Chepstow, doing it very easily on the latter occasion and drawing plenty of plaudits; lined up 13 days later under a double penalty at Newbury, but was disappointing in finishing third at Master Eddy and Double Dizzy (3m¹/₂f, good to soft, 9 ran); ground was quicker than he had ever raced on, and it may have been that four runs in less than two months was one too many, so well worth considering for novice chases once he has been freshened up.

1274 Marleybow (Ire)

4 br g Presenting - Gaye Artiste (Commanche Run)

J H Johnson   Andrea & Graham Wylie

PLACINGS: 1-   **RPR 112+b**

Starts		1st	2nd	3rd	4th	Win & Pl
1		1	-	-	-	£1,370
	4/07	Hayd	2m Cls6 NHF 4-6yo good £1,370

Very promising unbeaten bumper performer; made

his racecourse debut at Haydock in April, and ran out a very impressive winner, leading 6f out, shaken up to assert and bounding clear for a 5l victory over Tropical Strait; could hardly have done it better, and will surely be placed to good effect in novice hurdles this season.

1275 Marodima (Fr)

4 b g Robin Des Pres - Balbeyssac (Beyssac)

P Nicholls   Million In Mind Partnership

PLACINGS: 2/21334215-   **RPR 114+h**

Starts		1st	2nd	3rd	4th	Win & Pl
9		2	3	2	1	£17,805
	2/07	Towc	2m Cls3 Nov Hdl heavy...................................£5,704
	11/06	Chep	2m¹/₂f Cls3 Nov Hdl 3yo gd-sft £5,205

Useful novice hurdler last season for Oliver Sherwood, and looks open to further improvement after moving to his current handler and for a switch to fences; won two of his eight starts last term, scoring at Chepstow and Towcester, the latter on heavy ground, hinting that staying will ultimately be what he does best; showed his best form in defeat when chasing home Laustra Bad at Chepstow, again on a testing surface; some way below his best on his final start in a Grade 2 at Kelso in March, but that run came at the end of a busy campaign, and he can leave that form well behind in novice chases at 2m4f-plus this term.

1276 Marshall Hall (Ire)

6 b g Saddlers' Hall - Nocturnal Pleasure (Supreme Leader)

F Murphy   Plantation Stud

PLACINGS: 05360/0535211120-   **RPR 140c**

Starts		1st	2nd	3rd	4th	Win & Pl
15		3	2	2	-	£29,904
111	3/07	Ayr	2m Cls4 100-112 Ch Hcap heavy £3,904
96	3/07	Ayr	2m Cls4 Nov 74-100 Ch Hcap soft £3,253
89	2/07	Catt	2m Cls4 89-115 Ch Hcap heavy £5,855

Progressive handicap chaser last season, starting on an official mark of 93 and ending on 134; racked up a hat-trick in the space of 11 days in February and March, showing tons of improvement on the final occasion to beat Brave Thought by 14l at Ayr; upped a whopping 19lb for that win, but still managed to finish second after a good round of jumping in the competitive Red Rum Handicap Chase at Aintree in April, beaten 1¹/₂l by Bambi De L'Orme (2m, good, 15 ran); probably over the top for the season when down the field at Punchestown on his final start (2m, good, 16 ran); has a tendency to jump left, so ideally suited by left-handed tracks; best over 2m on good ground or softer; only six and quite lightly raced, so further improvement looks likely.

1277 Martha's Kinsman (Ire)

8 b g Petoski - Martha's Daughter (Majestic Maharaj)

H Daly   Barlow, Hartley & Brereton

PLACINGS: 18/12/232132/473115-   RPR **132 + c**

Starts	1st	2nd	3rd	4th	Win & Pl
16	5	4	3	1	£45,225
119	3/07	Asct	3m6f Cls2 111-131 Ch Hcap good £15,658
114	1/07	Ludl	3m Cls4 89-115 Am Ch Hcap good..................£4,201
	2/06	Ludl	3m Cls4 Ch gd-fm...£4,697
	3/05	Tntn	2m3¹/₂f Cls3 Nov Hdl gd-sft £6,224
	12/03	Hntg	2m¹/₂f Cls6 NHF 4-6yo gd-sft £1,638

Progressive handicap chaser who is ideally suited by a test of stamina on good ground; won twice in the second half of last season, both times off a near two-month break; needed every inch of 3m to score at Ludlow in January, collaring Fill The Bunker by ³/₄l (good, 13 ran); raised 5lb, he tackled a marathon trip for the first time in a good 3m6f contest at Ascot at the end of March, and relished the test to beat Garryvoe by 1l, going clear three out and galloping on gamely; raised another 8lb, but closed out with another good effort to finish 4³/₄l fifth behind Alexanderthegreat at Cheltenham in April (3m2¹/₂f, but even that didn't look far enough); has gained all his wins going right-handed, and does need a sound surface to show his best.

1278 Massini's Maguire (Ire)

6 b g Dr Massini - Molly Maguire (Supreme Leader)

P Hobbs   Alan Peterson

PLACINGS: 4/1232/121U5314-   RPR **149 + h**

Starts	1st	2nd	3rd	4th	Win & Pl
13	4	3	2	2	£120,315
	3/07	Chel	2m5f Cls1 Nov Gd1 Hdl gd-sft £68,424
	11/06	Chel	2m5f Cls2 Nov Hdl gd-sft £12,526
	10/06	Chep	2m¹/₂f Cls4 Nov Hdl good £3,253
	5/05	Limk	2m2f NHF 4yo soft £4,901

High-class novice hurdler last season, and obvious potential to do well over fences; sprang a 20-1 surprise in the Ballymore Properties Novices' Hurdle at the Cheltenham Festival in March, where he was ridden from the front with more aggression than usual and responded by gamely holding off Tidal Bay by a neck (2m5f, good to soft, 15 ran); that marked a return to the form that saw him beat Wichita Lineman at the same venue in November, having been beaten three times in between; stepped up to 3m1/2f at Aintree, but appeared to not last out the trip in finishing a fading fourth behind Chief Dan George; chance he will go novice chasing this term, but likely to start off in Graded hurdles. *'I'm sure he'll be better over fences.' (Philip Hobbs, trainer)*

1279 Material World

9 b m Karinga Bay - Material Girl (Busted)

Miss S Smith   Southern Bloodstock

PLACINGS: 112243325/2/312/132-   RPR **149h**

Starts	1st	2nd	3rd	4th	Win & Pl
17	5	6	4	1	£90,547
136	12/06	Chel	3m Cls2 128-154 Hdl Hcap soft £12,526
121	2/06	Winc	2m6f Cls3 109-135 Hdl Hcap gd-sft £18,789
	11/03	Folk	2m6¹/₂f Cls4 Nov Hdl good £2,590
	5/03	Hrfd	2m1f Cls6 NHF 4-6yo good...........................£2,009
	4/03	MRas	2m1¹/₂f Cls6 NHF 4-6yo good £2,030

Talented, but fragile, mare who has only once finished outside the frame in 17 hurdles starts; had an eye removed a few seasons ago and at the start of last season her trainer had reservations about her going left-handed in a big field, but any fears were removed by her winning reappearance in a competitive handicap at Cheltenham as she came home strongly to score by a neck from Freetown; disappointing on her next start when third behind Labelthou at Haydock (heavy ground), but bounced back on her final start to finish ¹/₂l second to Oscar Park in the Pertemps Final at the Cheltenham Festival (3m, good to soft, 24 ran); loves Cheltenham and further improvement can't be ruled out, so the World Hurdle is a possible long-term aim; first main target is the Long Walk Hurdle at Ascot.

1280 Mckelvey (Ire)

8 b g Anshan - Chatty Actress (Le Bavard)

P Bowen   N Elliott

PLACINGS: 12/1221UP3U2/417612-   RPR **146 + c**

Starts	1st	2nd	3rd	4th	Win & Pl
20	6	5	2	1	£247,761
123	3/07	Bang	3m Cls2 115-130 Hdl Hcap good £9,108
130	7/06	Uttx	4m¹/₂f Cls1 List 120-146 Ch Hcap gd-fm.......£45,072
126	11/05	Weth	3m1f Cls3 116-126 Ch Hcap good £10,735
	5/05	Sedg	2m5f Cls3 Nov Ch good £5,473
	3/05	Ludl	3m Cls4 Nov Hdl heavy £4,087
	2/05	Newc	3m Cls4 Mdn Hdl heavy £2,632

Long-distance chaser whose biggest win came in the Summer National at Uttoxeter in July 2006; was laid out for the Grand National last season, and, after a pipe-opening win over hurdles, ran a screamer in the Aintree spectacular, working his way into contention on the final circuit and throwing down a challenge at the last, but failing by ³/₄l to catch the back-to-form winner Silver Birch (4m4f, good, 40 ran); finished lame there, and Peter Bowen is convinced he would have given Wales a famous win in the big race had he not broken down on the run-in; was reportedly making a good recovery during the summer, and the plan is to again give him a run over hurdles before another tilt at the National; looks one for the transfer window for those willing to keep the faith, and even then will need a sound surface to show his best form.

1281 Medicinal (Ire)

6 gr h Linamix - Pharmacist (Machiavellian)

E O'Grady (Ir)   S Mulryan

PLACINGS: 213750-114   **RPR 140+c**

Starts	1st	2nd	3rd	4th	Win & Pl
9	3	1	1	1	£22,071

7/07	Tipp	2m1f Ch heavy £7,003
5/07	Baln	2m1f Ch gd-fm..£6,536
5/06	Tour	2m1¹/₂f Hdl good £3,972

Listed winner on the Flat for Dermot Weld, a winner over hurdles in France, and proved himself a smart novice chaser during the summer who could well go on to better things; opened his account over fences on fast ground at Ballinrobe in May and then posted an even better performance on a testing surface at Tipperary in July, when he was held up before being produced late and going on to beat Smuggler's Song by 1l; below that form 12 days later in a decent-looking novice chase at Galway when managing only fourth place and beaten 14¹/₂l by Prairie Moonlight, with the horse he beat at Tipperary in second; clearly better than that effort and worth another chance.

1282 Mendo

7 b g Alderbrook - Ina's Farewell (Random Shot)

N Chance   Mrs M C Sweeney

PLACINGS: 13/245211-   **RPR 123+h**

Starts	1st	2nd	3rd	4th	Win & Pl
8	3	2	1	1	£23,312

3/07	Asct	2m Cls3 Nov Hdl good £6,263
3/07	MRas	2m3¹/₂f Cls4 Nov Cond Hdl soft £3,083
2/05	Sand	2m1¹/₂f Cls6 NHF 4-6yo soft £2,373

Smart bumper horse who is threatening to be better over hurdles and fences; quite highly tried in his early forays over timber last term, but benefited from a drop in grade to win his last two; easy winner of a moderate event at Market Rasen in March (2m4f, beat Brave Rebellion by 9l), and followed up with a more hard-earned success over 2m at Ascot, where he looked in trouble under pressure three out, but found plenty to get up on the run-in and beat Modicum by ¹/₂l (good ground); that looked an insufficient test of stamina, and he remains unexposed over further on an easy surface; handicaps (rated 125) and novice chases are his options this winter, and he will start off over the smaller obstacles.

1283 Mercuric

6 gr g Silver Patriarch - Seymourswift (Seymour Hicks)

Mrs J Harrington (Ir)   G C Hartigan

PLACINGS: 54137/5U02143-   **RPR 124c**

Starts	1st	2nd	3rd	4th	Win & Pl
12	2	1	2	2	£16,668

2/07	Thur	2m Ch yld-sft £6,536
2/06	DRoy	2m4f Mdn Hdl 5-6yo yield £3,812

Useful hurdler who went chasing halfway through

last season, winning once and posting improved form in Graded events; gained his victory over 2m at Thurles in February, but upped in trip afterwards, and that looked to serve him well; finished 4¹/₂l fourth behind Benefit Night at Naas (2m4f, heavy, 8 ran) before a further step up to 3m at Limerick in April, where he kept on at one pace in the straight to finish 7¹/₄l third behind subsequent Grade 1 winner Offshore Account (yielding, 8 ran); rated 115 over hurdles and 125 over fences, and both ratings offer hope that he can do well in handicaps this term. *'He's a decent horse, but he needs decent ground.' (Jessica Harrington, trainer)*

1284 Mick The Man (Ire)

6 b g Saddlers' Hall - Nuala's Pet (Buckskin)

N Meade (Ir)   James Grace

PLACINGS: 122221-   **RPR 134+b**

Starts	1st	2nd	3rd	4th	Win & Pl
6	2	4	-	-	£62,796

4/07	Punc	2m Gd1 NHF 4-7yo good £48,385
11/06	Navn	2m NHF 5-7yo yld-sft £4,766

Classy bumper performer last season, never finishing out of the first two in six starts, and bringing the curtain down with a Grade 1 success at the Punchestown festival; started 10-1 there, having been runner-up four times in a row (and been called some names as a result), but was an authoritative winner, leading 1f out and driven out to beat Woodbine Willie by 2l (2m, good, 19 ran); that rates right up with the best bumper form of last season, as does his earlier short-head second to subsequent Champion Bumper fourth Shirley Casper, to whom he was conceding lumps of weight, at Navan in December (2m, heavy, 8 ran); goes novice hurdling, and ought to make his mark in Graded company over 2m-2m4f.

1285 Mid Dancer (Fr)

6 b g Midyan - Dancer Lady (Pink)

A Chaille-Chaille (Fr)   S Mulryan

PLACINGS: 1/11111101/1112111-1   **RPR 167c**

Starts	1st	2nd	3rd	4th	Win & Pl
19	17	1	-	-	£822,003

5/07	Autl	3m5f Gd1 Ch v soft £243,243
4/07	Autl	2m3¹/₂f Gd2 Hdl v soft £53,209
3/07	Autl	2m6f Gd3 Ch heavy £45,608
12/06	Autl	2m6f Gd2 Ch heavy £74,483
6/06	Autl	3m1¹/₂f Gd1 Hdl v soft £99,310
5/06	Autl	2m5¹/₂f Gd2 Hdl v soft £54,310
5/06	Autl	2m2f Hdl 5yo v soft £14,566
4/06	Autl	2m6f Gd2 Ch heavy £74,483
12/05	Autl	2m2f Hdl 4yo holding...£20,426
11/05	Autl	2m4¹/₂f Gd3 Ch 4yo heavy £44,681
11/05	Autl	2m4¹/₂f List Ch 4yo heavy £23,830
10/05	Engh	2m1¹/₂f Ch 4yo v soft £15,660
9/05	Stra	2m3f Hdl 4yo soft...£12,255
9/05	Chol	2m1f Hdl 4yo good..£12,255
10/04	Engh	2m1¹/₂f Hdl 3yo v soft £13,521
10/04	Engh	2m1¹/₂f Hdl 3yo v soft £12,845
9/04	Comp	2m Hdl 3yo good £5,408

Outstanding French jumper who is unbeaten in 17

starts in France, and has some smart form in Britain, too; travelled over to Carlisle for an intermediate chase last October, and ran a smashing race behind Monet's Garden, chasing the grey hard up the straight and being beaten 2^1/2l at level weights (2m4f, heavy, 5 ran); was being considered for the King George, but connections ultimately decided he was a little too tender at the age of five, and instead concentrated on a campaign at home; went unbeaten in four further starts at Auteuil, culminating in a 15l victory in France's biggest chase, the Grand Steeple-Chase de Paris over 3m5f in May; was enjoying a nice summer break at the time of writing, but connections were not ruling out a crack at the King George this Christmas, with the Gold Cup an obvious option further down the line; races almost exclusively on heavy ground in France.

1286 Miko De Beauchene (Fr)

7 b g Nashamaa - Chipie D'Angron (Grand Tresor)

R Alner   Andrew Wiles

PLACINGS: 22224P/1823235/1P2U-   **RPR 140c**

Starts	1st	2nd	3rd	4th	Win & Pl
19	2	7	2	2	£30,805

	10/06	Chep	3m Cls4 Ch gd-sft	£5,332
109	11/05	Ling	2m7f Cls3 88-113 Hdl Hcap heavy	£4,782

Showed useful form in staying novice chases last season, and looks a strong candidate to pick up a good handicap this winter; won just once (slammed Teeton Babysham at Chepstow last October), but is especially interesting on the strength of his 3^1/2l second to Heltornic in Grade 2 company at Wetherby in February and a big run in the 4m1f National Hunt Chase at the Cheltenham Festival, where he was beginning to close alongside eventual winner Butler's Cabin when unseating his rider at the third-last (good to soft, 19 ran); that winner is now rated 149 after winning the Irish National, so this one's prospects are obvious off his official rating of 135; had disappointed on heavy ground, but could easily land a good staying handicap when conditions are not so testing. *'He needs to go left-handed.'* (Robert Alner, trainer)

1287 Milan Deux Mille (Fr)

5 b g Double Bed - Uberaba (Garde Royale)

D Pipe   F G & J E Wilson

PLACINGS: 21U35/671111385-   **RPR 144+c**

Starts	1st	2nd	3rd	4th	Win & Pl
14	5	1	2	-	£31,828

128	2/07	Kemp	2m4^1/2f Cls3 118-128 Ch Hcap gd-sft	£7,543
124	2/07	Catt	2m3f Cls3 94-124 Ch Hcap good	£5,855
109	1/07	Wwck	2m4^1/2f Cls4 77-109 Ch Hcap heavy	£3,253
102	1/07	Newb	2m2^1/2f Cls3 91-118 Ch Hcap heavy	£5,855
	12/05	Extr	1m5f Cls6 NHF 3yo soft	£2,977

Former bumper winner who failed to score over hurdles, but took to fences like a dream last season,

winning four on the bounce and shooting up the handicap by 3st; scored at Newbury, Warwick, Catterick and Kempton and also put up some fine efforts in defeat, notably when third behind Nozic at Chepstow (2m3^1/2f, heavy) and eighth behind L'Antartique in the Jewson Handicap at Cheltenham from a career-high mark of 144 (2m5f, good to soft); rounded off his campaign with a sound effort over the National fences to finish fifth in the Topham Chase at Aintree, a performance that was below his best over fences but nonetheless showed that he is a young chaser going places; set to start the season from a mark of 139 (started last term on 108), so won't find life easy, but his owner considered supplementing him for the Gold Cup at one point last season, so he is clearly highly regarded, and further improvement may not be out of the question. *'He's a big horse and was only a baby last season.' (Tom Malone, rider)*

1288 Militant (Fr)

7 b g Cyborg - Giuletta (Petit Montmorency)

J Dreaper (Ir)   Mrs P J Conway

PLACINGS: 27/92311-   **RPR 147+c**

Starts	1st	2nd	3rd	4th	Win & Pl
7	2	2	1	-	£18,381

	3/07	Navn	2m1f Nov Ch heavy	£10,997
	12/06	DRoy	2m Mdn Hdl soft	£3,812

Very promising chaser; showed progressive form in novice hurdles in the first half of last season, despite a back problem, and got off the mark in maiden company at Down Royal on Boxing Day; was given a break after that, and returned in March to post an impressive debut over fences in novice company at Navan, where he jumped with assurance, cruised up to dispute the lead three out and drew clear to beat Glen Harley by 12l (2m1f, heavy, 6 ran); lots to like about that debut, and there ought to be much more to come in handicap and possibly Graded company this term; likes soft ground - the softer the better - and yet to race beyond 2m2f.

1289 Millenium Royal (Fr)

7 ch g Mansonnien - Pink Champagne (Blue Courtier)

F Doumen (Fr)   J Vasicek

PLACINGS: 31/1116P2P/55010P-   **RPR 159+h**

Starts	1st	2nd	3rd	4th	Win & Pl
15	5	1	1	-	£190,809

152	2/07	Hayd	2m7^1/2f Cls2 133-159 Hdl Hcap heavy	£13,012
	11/05	Autl	3m Gd1 Hdl v soft	£95,745
	10/05	Autl	2m3^1/2f List Hdl Hcap v soft	£30,319
	9/05	Nanc	2m3f Hdl soft	£8,170
	11/03	Autl	1m7f Hdl 3yo v soft	£11,221

Hardly the most consistent staying hurdler, but talented at his best, as he showed on the second of three visits to Britain last season; that came in a Pertemps Handicap qualifier over 2m7^1/2f at

Haydock in February where, off a mark of 152, he sprang a 33-1 surprise by beating Hirvine by 1³/4l, leading two out and driven out for a hard-earned success in heavy ground; beat only Hirvine home when 20th in the final of the series at the Cheltenham Festival, and was pulled up in a Listed hurdle in France the following month; could be interesting over fences, as he probably needs something different to rekindle his enthusiasm.

1290 Miss Mitch (Ire)

6 b/br m King's Theatre - Party Woman (Sexton Blake)
R Alner   Clipper Logistics
PLACINGS: 140/16F12-P   **RPR 128h**

Starts	1st	2nd	3rd	4th	Win & Pl
8	2	1			£21,336
110	1/07	Hrfd	2m4f Cls3 94-120 Hdl Hcap soft		£6,506
	10/06	Towc	2m Cls4 Nov Hdl gd-sft		£3,904

Progressive mare over hurdles last season; won twice, relishing the stiff finish at Towcester last October, and showing herself to be suited by 2m4f at Hereford in January; ran her best race, though, in the valuable EBF Mares' Final at Newbury in March, putting in some strong late work to finish 3l second to Karello Bay (2m5f, good to soft, 18 ran); didn't really go on good ground when flopping on her final start at Uttoxeter in May; likely to be switched to fences this season, and connections will be hoping she can again advance to the mares' series final over the bigger obstacles.

1291 Mister Hight (Fr)

5 bl g Take Risks - Miss High (Concorde Jr)
W Mullins (Ir)   Peter Garvey
PLACINGS: 118F/941255-   **RPR 147h**

Starts	1st	2nd	3rd	4th	Win & Pl
10	3	2		1	£66,608
	12/06	Limk	2m Hdl 4yo yld-sft		£12,347
	2/06	Leop	2m Gd2 Hdl 4yo yield		£24,693
	12/05	Punc	2m Hdl 3yo soft		£5,881

Smart juvenile hurdler in 2005/06, put in some decent performances in top handicaps last season, and it is in that sphere that he is again likely to be seen to best effect; won a conditions hurdle at Limerick before finishing runner-up to Spring The Que under the welter weight of 11st 10lb in the Pierse Hurdle at Leopardstown (2m, heavy, 30 ran); also put in decent efforts when fifth in both the Totesport Trophy at Newbury (2m1f, soft, 20 ran) and when stepping up in trip for the Coral Cup at the Cheltenham Festival (2m5f, good to soft, 28 ran), where he was given lots to do and stayed on without reaching the leaders; goes very well on soft/heavy ground; starts the season on a fair mark and has scope for improvement over 2m5f-plus.

1292 Mobaasher (USA)

4 ch g Rahy - Balistroika (Nijinsky)
C Mann   Seasons Holidays
PLACINGS: 136-   **RPR 143+h**

Starts	1st	2nd	3rd	4th	Win & Pl
3	1		1		£17,196
	2/07	Font	2m2¹/₂f Cls4 Nov Hdl 4yo gd-sft		£2,602

Very smart juvenile hurdler last season, and connections have big plans for him this time around; lined up a 33-1 shot for the Triumph Hurdle after winning on his hurdling debut at Fontwell, and ran a cracker at the Festival to finish 11l third behind Katchit, belying his inexperience by jumping well in the main and keeping on up the hill (2m1f, good to soft, 23 ran); took on the winner again at Aintree, but the faster track was all against him, and he was beaten 23l into sixth this time; handicap mark of 147 looks pretty stiff, but trainer sees him as a Champion Hurdle horse, so there should be more to come; plan is to start him off in the valuable 4yo handicap hurdle at Chepstow in October.

1293 Modicum (USA)

5 b g Chester House - Wandesta (Nashwan)
N Richards   Mr & Mrs Duncan Davidson
PLACINGS: 232/62212-1   **RPR 132+h**

Starts	1st	2nd	3rd	4th	Win & Pl
9	2	5	1		£14,571
122	5/07	Sedg	2m1f Cls3 96-122 Hdl Hcap gd-fm		£5,010
	2/07	Muss	2m Cls4 Mdn Hdl good		£2,741

Made steady progress at around 2m over hurdles last season, and now set to go chasing; bumped into some smart rivals on his first forays over hurdles (second to Pevensey at Musselburgh), but got off the mark at the fourth time of asking when returning to Musselburgh and beating Make A Mark by 8l; looked all over the winner in a novice hurdle at Ascot on his next start when 3l clear 2 out, but was worn down on the run-in by Mendo (2m, good, 9 ran); bounced back, though, on his handicap debut at Sedgefield in May with a stylish success; seems to appreciate decent ground, so could be the type that his trainer brings south in search of better going, and should he take well to fences, the Arkle could be the long-term target.

1294 Mon Mome (Fr)

7 b g Passing Sale - Etoile Du Lion (New Target)
Miss V Williams   Mrs Vida Bingham
PLACINGS: 45/U2121121U/422434-   **RPR 150c**

Starts	1st	2nd	3rd	4th	Win & Pl
22	4	6	2	4	£111,802
130	4/06	Aint	2m4f Cls2 Nov 113-133 Am Ch Hcap gd-sft		£18,077
	1/06	Font	3m2¹/₂f Cls3 Nov Ch soft		£10,160
115	12/05	Plum	3m2f Cls3 89-115 Ch Hcap soft		£6,553
	11/05	Uttx	3m Cls4 Nov Ch heavy		£3,766

Admirably tough staying chaser who ran a string

of fine races in top handicaps last season; showed his aptitude for a slog in the mud when in the frame in the Welsh National (4l second behind Halcon Genelardais), Warwick Classic (4l second behind Ladalko), Sky Bet Chase (fourth behind Simon), Red Square Vodka Gold Cup (third behind Heltornic) and William Hill Handicap Chase at the Cheltenham Festival (8l fourth behind Joes Edge), all off marks in the high 130s or low 140s; starts the season on 141, and it will be a crying shame if a decent prize doesn't come his way when the mud is flying, as while he lacks a change of gear, there is nothing wrong with his resolve; possibly the type for the Grand National, but in the lap of the gods whether he gets his ground. *'He's a little star, not a big horse, and hopefully his turn will come.' (Venetia Williams, trainer)*

1295 Monet's Garden (Ire)

9 gr g Roselier - Royal Remainder (Remainder Man)

N Richards   David Wesley Yates

PLACINGS: 21/15521/1121/16141-   RPR **168**+c

Starts	1st	2nd	3rd	4th	Win & Pl
19	12	3		1	£380,552
	4/07	Aint	2m4f Cls1 Gd1 Ch good		£114,040
	2/07	Asct	2m3f Cls1 Gd1 Ch gd-sft		£84,675
	10/06	Carl	2m4f Cls3 Ch heavy		£6,506
	4/06	Ayr	2m4f Cls1 Nov Gd2 Ch good		£23,076
	2/06	Carl	2m Cls3 Nov Ch soft		£6,506
	11/05	Ayr	2m Cls3 Nov Ch soft		£7,603
	4/05	Aint	3m¹/₂f Cls1 Gd2 Hdl gd-sft		£34,800
	11/04	Wind	2m4f Cls1 Gd2 Hdl gd-sft		£23,200
	4/04	Prth	3m¹/₂f Cls3 Nov Hdl gd-sft		£7,586
	3/04	Carl	2m4f Cls4 Nov Hdl good		£4,046
	11/03	Kels	2m6¹/₂f Cls2 Nov Hdl good		£2,702
	2/03	Ayr	2m Cls6 NHF 4-6yo gd-sft		£2,016

Former Arkle runner-up who established himself as one of the top 2m4f chasers around with two Grade 1 successes in the second half of last season; was quietly campaigned in the build-up to the King George at Christmas, but ran a stinker in the Kempton showpiece; dropped back in trip afterwards, and showed just what he can do when held up in the 2m3¹/₂f Grade 1 Ascot Chase in February, in which he swiftly put his rivals to the sword from 3 out and galloped to an 8l victory over Thisthatandtother; could manage only a disappointing fourth in Cheltenham's Ryanair Chase, but the return to a flat track at Aintree the following month saw him in a much better light, and he comprehensively reversed form with Festival winner Taranis, scoring easily by 3¹/₂l; spectacular jumper who will go for the Old Roan Chase at Aintree and Huntingdon's Peterborough Chase before another crack at the King George, when his trainer will hope a different travel routine and more patient tactics will bring about a better outcome. *'We'll keep him to good ground this season, and with Cheltenham and Aintree closer together next year, he'll probably only run at one of them.' (Nicky Richards, trainer)*

1296 Money Trix (Ire)

7 gr g Old Vic - Deer Trix (Buckskin)

N Richards   Craig Bennett

PLACINGS: 2/1112/

Starts	1st	2nd	3rd	4th	Win & Pl
5	3	2	-		£30,324
	3/06	Kels	2m6¹/₂f Cls4 Nov Hdl gd-sft		£3,426
	2/06	Ayr	3m¹/₂f Cls4 Nov Hdl soft		£3,253
	1/06	Kels	2m2f Cls4 Nov Hdl 4-7yo gd-sft		£3,253

Progressive novice hurdler in 2005/06 who was due to go novice chasing last season, but missed the whole of the campaign after picking up a minor injury; won three times over timber, but much the pick of his form was a 5l second to Black Jack Ketchum in a Grade 1 contest at Aintree's Grand National meeting in 2006; plan is to give him a couple of runs in novice chases in the north to start with, but trainer believes he retains all his ability and that he can take high rank over fences; yet to race on ground that isn't on the easy side, but proven over 3m, and Grade 1 races like the Feltham Novices' Chase at Kempton and the Royal & SunAlliance Chase at Cheltenham are possible longer-term targets.

1297 Monkerhostin (Fr)

10 b g Shining Steel - Ladoun (Kaldoun)

P Hobbs   M G St Quinton

PLACINGS: 3213/12242643/344R5-   RPR **164**+c

Starts	1st	2nd	3rd	4th	Win & Pl
48	10	9	9	6	£439,531
145	11/05	Extr	2m1¹/₂f Cls1 Gd2 144-164 Ch Hcap gd-sft		£37,063
134	12/04	Chel	2m5f Cls1 Gd3 134-158 Ch Hcap good		£63,800
125	10/04	Strf	2m5¹/₂f Cls3 107-128 Ch Hcap soft		£15,022
147	3/04	Chel	2m5f Cls1 Gd3 139-165 Hdl Hcap good		£43,500
	2/04	Kemp	3m¹/₂f Cls1 Gd2 Hdl good		£23,200
130	11/03	Newb	2m3f Cls3 107-130 Hdl Hcap gd-fm		£7,085
	11/02	Wwck	2m¹/₂f Cls3 Nov Ch good		£4,693
120	4/02	Strf	2m1¹/₂f Cls3 95-120 Hdl Hcap good		£3,679
	2/02	Sedg	2m1f Cls4 Nov Hdl soft		£2,583
	5/01	Pari	2m1f Hdl 4yo gd-sft		£4,850

High-class chaser, but without a win since beating Kauto Star in the Haldon Gold Cup at Exeter in October 2005; lots of water has passed under the bridge since, notably a narrow second to Kicking King in the 2005 King George, but was never quite as good last term; made the frame on three occasions, finishing third behind Racing Demon in the Peterborough Chase at Huntingdon, and a never-threatening fourth behind Kauto Star in both the King George and the Cheltenham Gold Cup; started co-favourite for the Grand National, but refused at the seventh, before a below-par fifth behind Neptune Collonges at the Punchestown festival; hard to see him winning in handicaps (mark of 160 still looks tough), so connections will hope to pick up a Graded race or two.

1298 Moon Over Miami (Ger)

6 b g Dashing Blade - Miss Esther (Alkalde)

C Mann   Mrs A E Fulton & M T Lynch

PLACINGS: 48/112212-   RPR **133**h

Starts	1st	2nd	3rd	4th	Win & Pl
8	3	3	-	1	£39,843
11/06	Chel	2m¹/₂f Cls1 Nov Gd2 Hdl good			£19,957
5/06	Uttx	2m Cls4 Nov Hdl good			£2,928
5/06	Winc	2m Cls4 Nov Hdl good			£3,426

Proved himself a smart novice hurdler in the first half of last season, and expected to do well in an autumn/spring campaign over fences this term; posted his best form when coming from miles off the pace to beat War General by 1l in a Grade 2 contest at Cheltenham last November (2m¹/₂f, good, 9 ran), and showed that was no fluke when just pipped by Tagula Blue under a penalty in the same grade at Ascot the following month; missed the remainder of the campaign, however, as his blood was not right; reportedly blooming again at the time of writing, and set to make his return in a beginners' chase at Kempton in the autumn; looks a two-miler, and could make up into an Arkle contender; needs good ground.

1299 Mossbank (Ire)

7 b g Kadeed - Miromaid (Simply Great)

M Hourigan (Ir)   Gigginstown House Stud

PLACINGS: 17/11235F5/125F0P-   RPR **140**c

Starts	1st	2nd	3rd	4th	Win & Pl
14	3	2	1	-	£49,969
10/06	Clon	3m Nov Ch soft			£11,224
11/05	Fair	2m2f Nov Hdl 5yo heavy			£7,841
10/05	Limk	2m5f Nov List Hdl yield			£16,160

Looked a useful novice chaser in the first half of last season, before he rather fell apart after Christmas; won at Clonmel in October but showed his best form when around 14l fifth behind Cailin Alainn in the Grade 1 Drinmore Novice Chase at Fairyhouse at the beginning of December (2m4f, heavy, 10 ran); was given a break after a fall at Leopardstown over Christmas, but returned with a 13th behind Denman at the Cheltenham Festival before being pulled up at Punchestown in a novice handicap; bit of rebuilding to do, but a chase mark of 126 looks lenient on his best form, and he could do well in heavy-ground handicaps.

1300 Moulin Riche (Fr)

7 b g Video Rock - Gintonique (Royal Charter)

F Doumen (Fr)   J C Seroul

PLACINGS: 411F6216214/F2P/U35-   RPR **117**c

Starts	1st	2nd	3rd	4th	Win & Pl
21	4	5	1	2	£155,219
3/05	Chel	3m Cls1 Nov Gd2 Hdl good			£43,500
11/04	Autl	2m4¹/₂f Ch 4yo holding			£16,901
9/04	Autl	2m1¹/₂f Ch 4yo soft			£14,873
6/04	Autl	2m3¹/₂f List Hdl 4yo Hcap v soft			£25,352

Former Cheltenham Festival winner (in the 2005 Brit Insurance Hurdle) who missed most of last season through injury; last seen in Britain when a gambled-on favourite for the William Hill Handicap Chase at the 2006 Festival, but was let down by his jumping there and was pulled up; had prepped for that meeting by finishing 3¹/₂l second to King Bee in a handicap chase at Haydock, looking as though he would come on for the run; gives the impression he has a good staying handicap chase in him, but will probably need a good bit of dig in the ground to fulfil that promise.

1301 Mount Sandel (Ire)

6 b g Supreme Leader - Droichidin (Good Thyne)

O Sherwood   Trevor Hemmings

PLACINGS: 241/313P-   RPR **120+**h

Starts	1st	2nd	3rd	4th	Win & Pl
7	2	1	2	1	£7,713
11/06	Hrfd	2m3¹/₂f Cls4 Nov Hdl heavy			£3,578
4/06	Worc	2m Cls6 Mdn NHF 4-6yo good			£1,713

Useful bumper/hurdle performer whose best days surely lie ahead of him over fences; won a novice hurdle at Hereford last November before another good run at Newbury, where he finished 10¹/₂l third behind subsequent Grade 1 runner-up Sir Jimmy Shand (2m3f, soft, 15 ran); picked up a minor injury when stepped up to Grade 2 company on what turned out to be his final start of the season at Haydock in February; trainer holds him in high regard and will start him off over hurdles, where he doesn't look badly handicapped off a mark of 125, before possibly going down the novice-chase route later in the season.

1302 Mounthenry (Ire)

7 ch g Flemensfirth - Tudor Lady (Green Shoon)

C Byrnes (Ir)   Mrs Martha Reidy

PLACINGS: 3211122/F24355-1P345   RPR **139**h

Starts	1st	2nd	3rd	4th	Win & Pl
25	7	4	4	3	£138,197
5/07	Cork	2m Ch gd-fm			£7,003
3/06	Thur	2m4f Nov Gd2 Hdl soft			£33,672
2/06	Punc	2m Nov Gd2 Hdl yield			£24,693
1/06	Limk	2m Nov Hdl heavy			£11,673
11/05	Punc	2m Nov Hdl sft-hvy			£7,841
10/05	Punc	2m Mdn Hdl gd-yld			£5,881
3/05	Cork	2m NHF 5yo soft			£5,391

Former dual Grade 2 winner over hurdles, but struggled to match that level of form in novice chases last term; placed behind Gemini Lucy and Anothercoppercoast in the autumn before a return to hurdles in the middle of the campaign (best effort a third behind Celestial Wave at Navan); back over fences in the spring, and opened his account with an odds-on defeat of Feel Good Factor at Cork in May, but struggled again afterwards; will be given a pretty favourable rating over fences compared to his hurdles mark, and every chance he could make an impact in handicaps if he gets his act together; stays 2m4f and suited by plenty of cut in the ground.

1303 Mr Nosie (Ire)

6 b g Alphabatim - Cromogue Lady (Golden Love)

N Meade (Ir) Mrs P Sloan

PLACINGS: 1/11114/

Starts	1st	2nd	3rd	4th	Win & Pl
5	4	-	-	1	£83,054
	2/06	Leop	2m2f Nov Gd1 Hdl yield		£44,828
	12/05	Leop	2m Nov Gd2 Hdl yld-sft		£23,085
	10/05	Cork	2m Mdn Hdl 4yo gd-yld		£5,881
	5/05	DRoy	2m NHF good		£3,921

Very classy novice hurdler two seasons ago, winning twice in Graded company at Leopardstown, but missed the whole of last season with a leg problem; pick of his old form came in the Grade 1 Deloitte Novice Hurdle on Irish Gold Cup day, where he needed to be niggled along leaving the back straight for the last time but quickened up to lead off the home turn and shrugged off a mistake at the last to beat Royaldou by 3l; started 9-1 for the Royal & SunAlliance Hurdle at Cheltenham the following month, where he cut out much of the running and battled on gamely once headed turning in to finish 11l fourth behind stablemate Nicanor, his only defeat under Rules to date; obvious concern about him returning from leg injury, but he is reportedly on the way back, and will be an interesting candidate for Graded hurdles or novice chases if retaining his ability.

1304 Mr Pointment (Ire)

8 b g Old Vic - Bettyhill (Ardross)

P Nicholls Stockton Heath Racing

PLACINGS: 14/1415/122- RPR 136c

Starts	1st	2nd	3rd	4th	Win & Pl
9	4	2	-	2	£27,190
	11/06	Bang	2m4¹/₂f Cls4 Ch gd-sft		£5,400
	2/06	Fknm	2m4f Cls4 Nov Hdl 4-7yo soft		£5,205
	11/05	MRas	2m3¹/₂f Cls4 Nov Hdl gd-sft		£3,405
	12/04	Bang	2m1f Cls6 NHF 4-6yo good		£1,845

Smart novice chaser at around 2m5f last season for Charles Egerton, and is an interesting addition to the champion trainer's team; made a successful debut over fences last November at Bangor (beat Heez A Dreamer by 1¹/₄l) before chasing home leading staying novice Don't Push It at Cheltenham the following month, just running out of stamina up the hill and going down by 1³/₄l (2m5f, soft, 7 ran); the jury is out regarding whether he stays 3m, as he was beaten a distance by subsequent SunAlliance Chase winner Denman when trying the trip for the first time at Newbury in February, although the Racing Post Rating he earned there was only very slightly down on what he earned on his previous run; a handicap mark of 146 does not look particularly lenient, but his new handler is sure to get the best out of him, and further success is on the cards.

1305 Mr Strachan (Ire)

6 b g Zaffaran - Call Girl (Dromod Hill)

Mrs S Smith Mrs Susan Granger

PLACINGS: 6/F123109- RPR 139+h

Starts	1st	2nd	3rd	4th	Win & Pl
8	2	1	1	-	£14,531
	2/07	Uttx	2m4¹/₂f Cls3 Nov Hdl heavy		£5,205
	6/06	Weth	2m4¹/₂f Cls4 Nov Hdl gd-fm		£2,928

Smart novice hurdler last season, and expected to do even better over fences this winter; best effort over smaller obstacles came in testing ground at Uttoxeter in February, where he sluiced through the mud to win eased down by 32l from Aitch Doubleyou; that run convinced connections to run him in the Grade 2 Brit Insurance Novices' Hurdle at Cheltenham, but he showed signs of temperament going down to the start and was never travelling; also disappointing on his final outing at Haydock; should stay 3m, while his ability to handle soft ground will serve him well at the northern tracks, where he looks the type to run up a sequence in early-season novice chases before being aimed at bigger prizes further down the line. *'He's a very good jumper at home and has a lovely temperament.' (Sue Smith, trainer)*

1306 My Turn Now (Ire)

5 ch g In The Wings - Wishful (Irish River)

C Mann Mountgrange Stud

PLACINGS: 120/21111F161- RPR 142+h

Starts	1st	2nd	3rd	4th	Win & Pl
12	7	2	-	-	£51,095
	4/07	Chel	2m5¹/₂f Cls2 Nov Hdl good		£9,395
	2/07	Hntg	2m4¹/₂f Cls2 Nov Hdl soft		£13,012
	12/06	Tntn	2m1f Cls3 Nov Hdl soft		£5,855
	12/06	Sand	2m¹/₂f Cls3 Nov Hdl soft		£5,205
	11/06	Kemp	2m Cls4 Nov Hdl 4-6yo gd-sft		£4,554
	11/06	Ludl	2m Cls4 Nov Hdl 4-6yo good		£4,880
	3/06	Clon	2m NHF 4yo soft		£3,812

Prolific novice hurdler last season, and being aimed at the World Hurdle this time around; won six times, the pick of his successes being a comfortable 8l defeat of Lightning Strike in the Sidney Banks Memorial Novices' Hurdle at Huntingdon in February; met with his only defeats on the two occasions he tackled Graded company, and was not disgraced on either occasion; fell at the last in the Tolworth Hurdle at Sandown when gamely rallying to challenge Silverburn and Perce Rock, and again kept battling on when 10¹/₂l sixth behind Massini's Maguire in the Ballymore Properties Novices' Hurdle at the Cheltenham Festival (2m5f, good to soft, 15 ran); has the Grade 2 staying hurdle at Wetherby's Charlie Hall meeting as his starting point; suited by plenty of cut in the ground.

1307 My Way De Solzen (Fr)

7 b g Assessor - Agathe De Solzen (Chamberlin)

A King   B Winfield,A Longman,J Wright & C Fenton

PLACINGS: 115102/21112/212111-   **RPR 165+c**

Starts	1st	2nd	3rd	4th	Win & Pl
19	10	6	-	-	£408,753

3/07	Chel	2m Cls1 Gd1 Ch soft	£96,934
1/07	Hayd	2m4f Cls1 Nov Gd2 Ch heavy	£20,580
1/07	Chel	2m5f Cls1 Nov Gd2 Ch heavy	£19,957
11/06	Ling	2m Cls4 Ch soft	£3,904
3/06	Chel	3m Cls1 Gd1 Hdl good	£131,146
2/06	Font	2m4f Cls1 Gd1 Hdl heavy	£25,353
12/05	Chep	3m Cls1 Gd1 Hdl gd-sft	£28,510
2/05	Extr	2m1f Cls1 Nov List Hdl soft	£13,546
12/04	Bang	2m1f Cls4 Nov Hdl good	£3,546
11/04	Leic	2m Cls3 Nov Hdl gd-sft	£5,512

Former World Hurdle winner who proved he had pace to match his stamina in a brilliant novice chase campaign last season; jumped superbly from the start, posting wide-margin wins in testing conditions at Lingfield, Cheltenham and Haydock, and in between finding Fair Along 10l too good in the Grade 2 Henry VIII Novices' Chase at Sandown in December (2m, soft, 5 ran); soft ground at Cheltenham persuaded connections to stick to 2m for the Arkle Chase in March, and they were vindicated with a stunning success as he kicked for home off the home turn as others fell by the wayside, and powered up the hill to comprehensively floor old rival Fair Along by 5l in a very fast time (runner-up admittedly hampered by fallers 2 out, but wouldn't have won in any case); was almost flawless in the jumping department throughout his novice season, and that will stand him in good stead as he tackles open company this winter, with all roads leading to a Gold Cup clash with Kauto Star in March; could well meet him before then in the King George if the ground is soft.

1308 My Will (Fr)

7 b g Saint Preuil - Gleep Will (Laniste)

P Nicholls   The Stewart Family

PLACINGS: 21/2923234F3/132023-   **RPR 164+c**

Starts	1st	2nd	3rd	4th	Win & Pl
30	8	8	7	1	£317,775

11/06	Chel	3m3¹/₂f Cls1 Gd3 130-156 Ch Hcap gd-sft	£34,212
4/05	Prth	3m Cls2 Nov Ch soft	£10,394
1/05	Uttx	2m Cls1 Nov Gd2 Ch heavy	£20,300
1/05	Chel	2m5f Cls1 Nov Gd2 Ch good	£26,775
11/04	Wwck	2m¹/₂f Cls3 Nov Ch 4yo gd-sft	£9,104
10/04	MRas	2m1¹/₂f Cls3 Nov Ch soft	£10,121
11/03	Engh	2m¹/₂f Hdl 3yo v soft	£11,221
10/03	Fntb	2m Hdl 3yo soft	£4,675

High-class chaser who seems to have found improvement for the step up to 3m-plus and last season ran consistently well at just below the top level; showed that he goes particularly well fresh when scoring on his seasonal reappearance at Cheltenham in November by ¹/₂l from Idle Talk with 10l back to the previous season's Scottish National winner Run For Paddy; failed to score again, but other than when outclassed in the Gold

Cup, put up a series of solid efforts to finish either second or third, notably when runner-up to Little Brick in a Listed handicap at Wincanton, beaten only 3¹/₂l despite conceding 17lb (3m1¹/₂f, soft, 5 ran); starts the new campaign with a mark of 160 (10lb higher than last term), so unlikely to find things easy, but likely to be thereabouts in the big staying chases.

1309 Natal (Fr)

6 b g Funny Baby - Donitille (Italic)

P Nicholls   Mrs Monica Hackett

PLACINGS: 5/115114361/1214172-   **RPR 150+c**

Starts	1st	2nd	3rd	4th	Win & Pl
17	8	2	1	2	£125,247

2/07	Kemp	2m4¹/₂f Cls1 Nov Gd2 Ch soft	£17,408
12/06	Tntn	2m3f Cls3 Nov Ch gd-sft	£7,701
10/06	Extr	2m1¹/₂f Cls4 Ch good	£6,506
4/06	Aint	2m4f Cls1 Nov Gd2 Hdl good	£31,361
12/05	Tntn	2m1f Cls3 Nov Hdl good	£7,319
11/05	Newb	2m¹/₂f Cls3 Nov Hdl good	£7,202
5/05	Strf	2m1¹/₂f Cls3 Nov Hdl good	£6,067
5/05	Worc	2m Cls4 Nov Hdl 4yo gd-fm	£3,439

Very smart novice chaser last season with winning form between 2m2f and 2m4¹/₂f who might be one for the Paddy Power Gold Cup at Cheltenham in November; has won three times over fences so far, probably doing best of all in the Grade 2 Pendil Novices' Chase in February where he came from off the pace and stayed on well to beat stablemate Good Spirit by 3l; although he seems well suited by a flat track, he returned his joint-best Racing Post Rating at Cheltenham in November on only his second start over fences when chasing home a foot-perfect Fair Along, beaten 9l (sent off 8-11 favourite); not one of his stable's leading lights, but more than useful in his class and open to further improvement in handicaps from a mark of 144.

1310 Naunton Brook

8 b g Alderbrook - Give Me An Answer (True Song)

N Twiston-Davies   David Langdon

PLACINGS: /1P7P6130/8411530PP-   **RPR 144+c**

Starts	1st	2nd	3rd	4th	Win & Pl
25	6	1	3	2	£62,420

12/06	Extr	3m1¹/₂f Cls3 107-133 Ch Hcap soft	£7,807
11/06	Hexm	4m Cls3 109-135 Ch Hcap soft	£18,789
2/06	MRas	3m1f Cls3 92-118 Ch Hcap soft	£6,506
10/05	Towc	2m6f Cls3 96-120 Ch Hcap good	£5,512
10/04	Worc	2m7¹/₂f Cls3 Nov Ch good	£5,434
3/04	Wwck	3m1f Cls4 Nov Hdl good	£3,794

Thorough stayer over fences who relishes the mud; demonstrated his suitability for a gruelling test when successful over 4m on soft ground at Hexham and over 3m2f in a bog at Exeter, where he beat Kock De La Vesvre by 9l; acquitted himself very well in the Welsh National after having plenty of use made of him, finishing 16l fifth behind Halcon Genelardais (3m5¹/₂f, soft, 18 ran); forcing tactics again adopted when 5l third behind Ladalko off a career-high mark in a valuable Warwick contest (3m5f, heavy, 13 ran); perhaps showing effects of those exertions on last three starts, including when blinkered first time in the Grand National and blazing a trail again, pulled up after Becher's second time; tough, admirable type who may yet keep his nose in front in a big staying handicap.

1311 Negus De Beaumont (Fr)

6 b g *Blushing Flame - Givry (Bayolidaan)*

F Murphy   Warren Roberts

PLACINGS: 64/4063P/31111516-   **RPR 135+h**

Starts	1st	2nd	3rd	4th	Win & Pl
15	5	-	2	2	£25,043
120	2/07	Hrfd	3m2f Cls3 96-120 Hdl Hcap soft		£7,807
110	12/06	Uttx	3m Cls4 87-110 Hdl Hcap heavy		£5,205
100	11/06	Ayr	3m¹/₂f Cls4 84-110 Hdl Hcap soft		£3,253
93	11/06	Sedg	3m3¹/₂f Cls4 84-114 Hdl Hcap gd-sft		£3,904
88	11/06	Newc	3m Cls5 64-90 Hdl Hcap good		£2,928

Good staying novice hurdler last season, and appeals as the type to make his mark over fences; ran mainly in handicap company, racking up five wins that took his official handicap mark from 88 to 135; gained the last and most valuable win over 3m2f at Hereford in February, where he made all and galloped his rivals into the ground, beating Im A Witness by 13l; started 40-1 for the Brit Insurance Hurdle at the Cheltenham Festival the following month, and far from disgraced in finishing 24l sixth behind Wichita Lineman; likely to go chasing sooner rather than later, and has a profile that suggests he should do well. *'He stays well and will make a nice chaser.' (Niall Hannity, trainer's representative)*

1312 Nenuphar Collonges (Fr)

6 b g *Video Rock - Diane Collonges (El Badr)*

A King   Top Brass Partnership

PLACINGS: F/6111F21-   **RPR 138+c**

Starts	1st	2nd	3rd	4th	Win & Pl
8	4	1			£29,211
127	3/07	Uttx	3m Cls2 Nov 115-135 Ch Hcap soft		£12,676
110	11/06	Hrfd	2m3f Cls4 84-110 Ch Hcap soft		£5,778
102	11/06	Bang	2m1¹/₂f Cls4 Nov 84-102 Ch Hcap gd-sft		£3,904
	6/06	Diep	2m1¹/₂f Ch 4-5yo good		£4,634

Ex-French performer who progressed well in decent handicap chases at up to 3m last season; won three of his five starts for new connections, scoring at Bangor and Hereford in November, and ending his campaign in March off a 25lb higher mark with a ³/₄l defeat of Fast Forward in a novice handicap in the mud at Uttoxeter; in between suffered a fall at Exeter and a narrow defeat at Leicester, but put those efforts behind him with his Uttoxeter success; starts the season on a new mark of 134, and the best should still be yet to come; has raced only on ground with plenty of cut. *'We might have a crack at novice hurdles, because he's yet to try them and I think he'd do well.' (Alan King, trainer)*

1313 Neptune Collonges (Fr)

6 gr g *Dom Alco - Castille Collonges (El Badr)*

P Nicholls   J Hales

PLACINGS: 11U1/1412113/216F81-   **RPR 166+c**

Starts	1st	2nd	3rd	4th	Win & Pl
19	11	2	1	1	£325,199
	4/07	Punc	3m1f Gd1 Ch good		£101,351
152	11/06	Newc	3m Cls1 List 125-152 Ch Hcap gd-sft		£33,804
	2/06	Hayd	2m7¹/₂f Cls1 Nov Gd2 Hdl heavy		£17,106
	2/06	Weth	3m1f Cls1 Nov Gd2 Hdl soft		£16,663
	12/05	Sand	2m4¹/₂f Cls1 Nov Gd2 Hdl heavy		£16,464
	11/05	Chep	2m4f Cls4 Nov Hdl heavy		£3,507
	4/05	Autl	2m4¹/₂f Gd3 Ch 4yo heavy		£44,681
	2/05	Pau	2m3¹/₂f List Ch 4yo v soft		£18,723
	1/05	Pau	2m3¹/₂f Ch 4yo heavy		£11,574
	12/04	Pau	2m1f Ch 3yo heavy		£9,465
	12/04	Pau	2m1f Ch 3yo v soft		£10,141

Very smart staying hurdler who proved himself a tremendously progressive chaser over 3m-plus in his first season over fences last term; posted his most impressive performance on his final start in the Grade 1 Punchestown Guinness Gold Cup in April when resolutely beating a host of more experienced and classy chasers, with Kingscliff 3¹/₂l down in second and In Compliance a further 7l away, an effort that showed he is as capable on decent ground as he is on a testing surface; had earlier given away weight all round to win the Rehearsal Chase at Newcastle in November, beating Another Promise by 2l (who was receiving 23lb), and looked unlucky in the Cotswold Chase at Cheltenham when coming down at the second-last when seemingly holding every chance; finished eighth in the Gold Cup, but was beaten less than 13l and was the youngest in the line-up, so not difficult to see him getting closer next time with more experience on his side; has already achieved a great deal for one so inexperienced over fences, and sure to take plenty of beating in top staying contests during the winter before returning to Cheltenham in March. *'I can see him having a few trips to Ireland.' (Paul Nicholls, trainer)*

1314 New Alco (Fr)

6 b/br g *Dom Alco - Cabira Des Saccart (Quart De Vin)*

F Murphy   D McGowan & S Murphy

PLACINGS: 322/41221226/232267-   **RPR 147+c**

Starts	1st	2nd	3rd	4th	Win & Pl
17	2	9	2	1	£81,346
	12/05	Sedg	2m5f Cls4 Ch soft		£3,783
	10/05	Aint	2m¹/₂f Cls3 Mdn Hdl gd-sft		£7,007

Useful handicap chaser who had a winless campaign last season, but was only narrowly denied in some competitive events, and likely to be a fixture in the top handicaps once again; best efforts came at Cheltenham, when 3¹/₂l third behind Exotic Dancer in the Paddy Power Gold Cup last November (2m4¹/₂f, good to soft, 16 ran), a short-head second to D'Argent in a Listed handicap chase the following month (3m1¹/₂f, soft, 15 ran), and when ¹/₂l second to Whispered Secret in the

Grade 3 Ladbrokes Trophy in January (2m5f, heavy, 10 ran); not disgraced in sixth behind Joes Edge at the Festival, but below his best at Aintree; best on good to soft or softer; effective at 2m4f, but also stays very well; starts this season rated 12lb higher than last, which could be his biggest hurdle.

1315 New Little Bric (Fr)

6 ch g Bricassar - Doulina (Dastaan)

P Nicholls   Mrs Kathy Stuart

PLACINGS: 11/13117-   **RPR 152 + c**

Starts	1st	2nd	3rd	4th	Win & Pl
7	5		1		£63,323

2/07	Sand	2m4¹/₂f Cls1 Nov Gd1 Ch gd-sft		£28,510
12/06	Extr	2m3¹/₂f Cls3 Nov Ch gd-sft		£8,380
11/06	Plum	2m4f Cls4 Ch good		£5,226
1/06	Pau	2m1¹/₂f Hdl 5yo gd-sft		£8,607
12/05	Pau	2m1¹/₂f Hdl 4yo gd-sft		£8,851

Smart novice chaser after arriving from his native France last season, and likely to be aimed at decent handicaps between 2m4f and 3m this term; has won three of his five races so far, achieving most when winning the Grade 1 Scilly Isles Chase at Sandown in February, sealing the win with some fine leaps over the last two fences before coming home 8l clear of Aztec Warrior; may have finished only seventh behind L'Antartique in the Jewson Handicap at the Cheltenham Festival, but he was giving 15lb to the winner and was beaten less than 12l with some useful sorts in behind, an effort that earned him his best Racing Post Rating; surprising if he fails to win a valuable race or two.

1316 Newmill (Ire)

9 br g Norwich - Lady Kas (Pollerton)

J Murphy (Ir)   Mrs Mary T Hayes

PLACINGS: 5151P4/543111/4F145-   **RPR 161 + c**

Starts	1st	2nd	3rd	4th	Win & Pl
26	11	3	1	4	£500,118

2/07	Gowr	2m Gd2 Hdl heavy		£26,392
4/06	Punc	2m Gd1 Ch good		£85,972
3/06	Chel	2m Cls1 Gd1 Ch good		£165,358
1/06	Thur	2m4f Gd2 Ch yld-sft		£22,448
1/05	Leop	2m5f Nov Gd2 Ch heavy		£27,702
12/04	Clon	2m1f Ch soft		£5,839
2/04	Naas	2m4f Gd2 Hdl yield		£24,069
12/03	Navn	2m4f Nov Gd2 Hdl soft		£29,545
11/03	Fair	2m Nov Gd1 Hdl soft		£29,545
10/03	Wxfd	2m Nov Hdl 5yo good		£5,377
4/03	Fair	2m NHF 4-5yo good		£25,552

Had a storming 2005/06 season, establishing himself at the head of the 2m chase division when winning the Champion Chase at the Cheltenham Festival and then Punchestown's equivalent in imperious fashion; most disappointing in light of those heroics in a light campaign last season, and has a reputation to restore; his only success rather surprisingly came over hurdles, beating Macs Joy by 8l (receiving 8lb) in the Grade 2 Red Mills Trial Hurdle at Gowran Park in February; sent off 4-1 second-favourite behind Well Chief to retain his Cheltenham title, but was disappointing, leading/

disputing for much of the way, but folding tamely after the second-last to be beaten 8¹/₂l into fourth by Voy Por Ustedes (2m, good to soft, 10 ran); favourite for Punchestown's Champion Chase on his final outing, and despite jumping well from the front, his effort again petered out and he could finish only fifth behind Mansony; has won over 2m4f, but is better over the minimum.

1317 Nicanor (Fr)

6 b g Garde Royale - Uthane (Baly Rockette)

N Meade (Ir)   D P Sharkey

PLACINGS: 312/31F22111/

Starts	1st	2nd	3rd	4th	Win & Pl
11	5	3	2	-	£151,027

4/06	Punc	2m4f Nov Gd1 Hdl good		£42,759
3/06	Chel	2m5f Cls1 Nov Gd1 Hdl good		£57,020
1/06	Leop	2m4f Nov Gd3 Hdl yld-sft		£15,714
11/05	Navn	2m4f Hdl soft		£6,861
2/05	Thur	2m NHF 4yo yld-sft		£3,921

High-class novice hurdler in 2005/06, but missed the whole of last season after picking up a leg injury during his early training; very impressive in rattling up a hat-trick in the spring of 2006, most notably winning the Royal & SunAlliance Hurdle at Cheltenham, where he travelled easily throughout and had too much speed for Denman from the last, winning by 2¹/₂l and becoming the only horse so far to beat Paul Nicholls' ace; had prepped for that with a very impressive Grade 3 win in the mud at Leopardstown, and rounded off at the Punchestown festival with a workmanlike defeat of Mountenry; needs to prove he is over his problems, but Noel Meade insists it was a very minor injury that just needed time to heal; set to go novice chasing, and even his trainer is unsure what his best trip will be, but obviously has Cheltenham potential once again.

1318 Nickname (Fr)

8 b h Lost World - Newness (Simply Great)

M Brassil (Ir)   Mrs Claudia Jungo-Corpataux

PLACINGS: 11/24/11P22/1411111-   **RPR 170 + c**

Starts	1st	2nd	3rd	4th	Win & Pl
28	17	5	2	2	£632,068

3/07	Navn	2m4f Gd3 Ch heavy		£15,395
2/07	Naas	2m Gd2 Ch heavy		£26,392
2/07	Punc	2m Gd2 Ch soft		£23,313
1/07	Fair	2m1f Gd2 Ch heavy		£21,993
12/06	Leop	2m1f Gd1 Ch heavy		£31,379
11/06	Navn	2m4f Gd2 Ch yld-sft		£26,938
1/06	Leop	2m5f Nov Gd2 Ch heavy		£26,938
12/05	Leop	2m3f Ch soft		£8,331
4/04	Autl	2m4¹/₂f Gd2 Hdl holding		£47,535
3/04	Autl	2m3¹/₂f Gd3 Hdl holding		£38,028
11/03	Autl	2m4¹/₂f Gd1 Hdl 4yo v soft		£61,364
6/03	Autl	2m3¹/₂f Gd1 Hdl 4yo v soft		£51,136
4/03	Autl	2m3¹/₂f Gd2 Hdl 4yo v soft		£40,909
4/03	Autl	2m2f Gd3 Hdl 4yo v soft		£32,143
11/02	Engh	2m1¹/₂f Gd3 Hdl 3yo heavy		£30,368
5/02	Autl	2m1¹/₂f Hdl 3yo v soft		£19,141
5/02	Autl	1m7f Hdl 3yo soft		£13,546

Top-class 2m-2m4f chaser who swept all before him on his favoured soft/heavy ground in Ireland last season, and posted form on a par with British ace Voy Por Ustedes; thrived for being held up, winning six out of seven, most by wide margins; gained his sole Grade 1 success at Leopardstown's Christmas meeting, where he eased clear from the last to beat Central House by 14l; spent the remainder of the season defying his penalties in Grade 2/3 events with the minimum of fuss, beating Justified by 14l at Fairyhouse, Gemini Lucy by 12l at Naas, and old rival Central House by 7l and 13l at Punchestown and Navan; would have been a leading contender for the Champion Chase at Cheltenham, but connections always maintained he would not race there if the ground was not soft, and they were true to their word; one of the best around when conditions are testing, and connections will be hoping for a wetter run-up to the Cheltenham Festival in March, but likely to follow a similar programme in any case this winter.

1319 Nine De Sivola (Fr)

6 b g Video Rock - Quine De Chalamont (Do Do)

F Murphy   The Dprp Sivola Partnership

PLACINGS: 731P11150/523422F22-   **RPR 143+c**

Starts	1st	2nd	3rd	4th	Win & Pl
23	4	6	2	2	£114,372
127	1/06	Wwck	3m1f Cls2 127-153 Hdl Hcap soft		£13,012
	1/06	Catt	3m1¹/₂f Cls4 Nov Hdl good		£3,253
	12/05	Weth	2m7f Cls3 Nov Hdl heavy		£4,993
	11/05	Weth	2m4¹/₂f Cls4 Mdn Hdl good		£3,727

Staying chaser who is still a maiden over fences, but ended last season with gallant runs in both the Irish and Scottish Grand Nationals; went to Fairyhouse on the back of an unlucky fall in the National Hunt Chase at the Cheltenham Festival, and ran a cracker to finish 1l second to Festival winner Butler's Cabin (3m5f, good, 29 ran); started favourite at Ayr just 12 days later, and stayed on really well, but could not collar his well-handicapped stablemate Hot Weld, who fended him off by ¹/₂l (4m1f, good to firm, 23 ran); also finished second to the ill-fated Nil Desperandum in the Eider Chase at Newcastle earlier in the season; an obvious candidate for any contest where the emphasis is on stamina, but connections will be keen to find an easy opportunity for him to get his head in front before targeting more big handicaps.

1320 Ninetieth Minute (Ire)

4 b g Old Vic - Myown (Le Bavard)

T Taaffe (Ir)   D Cox

PLACINGS: 1-   **RPR 109+b**

Starts	1st	2nd	3rd	4th	Win & Pl
1	1	-	-	-	£3,968
	3/07	Clon	2m NHF 4yo sft-hvy		£3,969

Promising sort for novice hurdles; sent off 16-1 for his debut in an 18-runner bumper at Clonmel in March, and made the job look easy, taking it up 2f out and quickening away to win by 7l from hot

favourite Shuil Dara, who later ran well in a valuable bumper at Punchestown (sixth home has won since); evidently goes well with cut in the ground and from a staying family, so 2m4f and possibly eventually 3m should be within his compass; goes over hurdles and should have bright future.

1321 No Refuge (Ire)

7 ch g Hernando - Shamarra (Zayyani)

J H Johnson   Andrea & Graham Wylie

PLACINGS: 1211/1503/445-   **RPR 147h**

Starts	1st	2nd	3rd	4th	Win & Pl
11	4	1	1	2	£139,504
	11/05	Wind	2m4f Cls1 Gd2 Hdl good		£22,915
	3/05	Chel	2m5f Cls1 Nov Gd1 Hdl good		£58,000
	1/05	Wwck	2m5f Cls1 Nov Gd2 Hdl good		£23,200
	11/04	Aint	2m4f Cls2 Nov Hdl soft		£10,114

Former Royal & SunAlliance Hurdle winner (beat Racing Demon) who has not won since November 2005, and was seen out only three times last season; ran his best race in that brief campaign on the final start, when 4³/₄l fifth behind Mighty Man in the Grade 1 Long Walk Hurdle at Ascot in December (3m1f, good to soft, 9 ran); has looked a tricky customer on occasions, and has been tried in a visor, blinkers and cheekpieces; not the greatest jumper of hurdles, but may need to be tried over fences in a bid to revitalise him; suited by a bit of cut in the ground, and best at around 2m4f.

1322 Noble Request (Fr)

6 gr g Highest Honor - Restless Mixa (Linamix)

P Hobbs   Mrs Karola Vann

PLACINGS: 2131395/7712211/422-   **RPR 160h**

Starts	1st	2nd	3rd	4th	Win & Pl
19	5	6	2	1	£151,737
143	4/06	Sand	2m¹/₂f Cls2 Hdl good		£31,315
118	4/06	Ayr	2m Cls1 Gd2 138-158 Hdl Hcap good		£33,804
	2/06	Winc	2m Cls3 113-123 Hdl Hcap good		£6,506
	2/05	Tntn	2m1f Cls4 Nov Hdl good		£4,303
	1/05	Towc	2m Cls3 Nov Hdl gd-sft		£5,525

Classy 2m hurdler who gained his two biggest wins in the space of a week in April 2006, capturing the Scottish Champion Hurdle and Sandown's Betfred Million Hurdle, both at the expense of Faasel; set out on the Champion Hurdle trail last autumn, and looked to be going the right way when runner-up to Straw Bear in the Fighting Fifth at Newcastle and to Jazz Messenger in the Christmas Hurdle at Kempton; met with a setback, though, while being prepared for the Totesport Trophy and missed the remainder of the campaign; that was a great shame, as he tends to show his best form in the spring on good ground, and might well have run a big race in the Champion Hurdle; on the comeback trail, and connections will hope he shows the same degree of ability this autumn.

1323 Noir Et Vert (Fr)

6 b g Silver Rainbow - Danse Verte (Brezzo)

F Murphy   Plantation Stud

PLACINGS: 5/65611/5123112-   **RPR 136c**

Starts	1st	2nd	3rd	4th	Win & Pl
13	5	2	1	-	£40,500
	4/07	Carl	3m¹/₂f Cls3 Nov Ch good		£6,506
	4/07	Kels	3m1f Cls4 Ch good		£4,554
106	11/06	Muss	3m¹/₂f Cls4 80-106 Cond Hdl Hcap good		£3,904
98	4/06	Prth	3m3f Cls3 90-110 Cond Hdl Hcap gd-fm		£7,807
91	4/06	Prth	3m¹/₂f Cls4 Nov 84-110 Hdl Hcap good		£5,205

Fair hurdler who switched to fences last term, and was much improved over 3m-plus on good ground in the spring; won novice events at Kelso and Carlisle in the space of five days in April, and so nearly completed the hat-trick in a valuable handicap chase at the Punchestown festival, where he led six out, was joined at the last and battled on gamely, only to be nailed on the line by Irish National third American Jennie (3m1f, good, 14 ran); sound jumper who is young and very much on an upward curve; could well be contesting some very valuable events this season on fast ground.

1324 Noland

6 b g Exit To Nowhere - Molakai (Nureyev)

P Nicholls   J Hales

PLACINGS: 16/31111/

Starts	1st	2nd	3rd	4th	Win & Pl
7	5	-	1	-	£109,043
	3/06	Chel	2m¹/₂f Cls1 Nov Gd1 Hdl gd-sft		£57,020
	2/06	Extr	2m1f Cls1 Nov List Hdl gd-sft		£11,902
	1/06	Sand	2m¹/₂f Cls1 Gd1 Hdl soft		£28,510
	12/05	Chel	2m1f Cls3 Nov Hdl 4-6yo gd-sft		£8,417
	3/05	Winc	2m Cls6 Mdn NHF 4-6yo gd-sft		£2,009

High-class 2m hurdler who missed last season with a minor injury but is expected to make his return in novice chases this term; last seen when coming with a late run to get up in the dying strides to win the Supreme Novices' Hurdle at the Cheltenham Festival by a neck from Straw Bear, a fourth win on the bounce that confirmed him a highly progressive individual; had been at the head of the betting for last season's Arkle Trophy before even jumping a fence in public, likely to have that race as his main aim this time, and it will be no surprise should he run up a sequence as he bids to enhance his trainer's record at the Cheltenham Festival in March.

1325 Not Left Yet (Ire)

6 b/br g Old Vic - Dalus Dawn (Mandalus)

D Pipe   D A Johnson

PLACINGS: 040/120662/1F-   **RPR 128+c**

Starts	1st	2nd	3rd	4th	Win & Pl
11	2	2	-	1	£21,263
	10/06	Carl	2m4f Cls4 Ch gd-sft		£3,904
108	11/05	Chel	2m¹/₂f Cls3 Nov 96-110 Hdl Hcap gd-sft		£11,320

Very interesting staying handicap chase prospect;

saw a racecourse only twice last season and fell on the latter occasion as a 16-1 shot when travelling well in the 4m1f NH Chase at the Cheltenham Festival; had earlier made a successful seasonal reappearance and a winning debut over fences, eventually staying on strongly to win a beginners' chase at Carlisle by 6l from No Guarantees; won only once over hurdles (when landing a gamble at Cheltenham on Paddy Power Gold Cup day in 2005), but shapes as though he will be a better chaser, and connections are eyeing a crack at some decent prizes with him; worth noting that stablemate Celestial Gold ran well in the four-miler at the Festival before going on to do the Paddy Power/Hennessy Gold Cup double the following season. *'He'll go for all the top staying handicaps.' (David Pipe, trainer)*

1326 Numbersixvalverde (Ire)

11 b g Broken Hearted - Queens Tricks (Le Bavard)

M Brassil (Ir)   O B P Carroll

PLACINGS: 15131/584B4431/4946-   **RPR 139+c**

Starts	1st	2nd	3rd	4th	Win & Pl
36	5	8	5	6	£590,054
138	4/06	Aint	4m4f Cls1 Gd2 134-156 Ch Hcap gd-sft		£399,140
126	3/06	Fair	3m5f 125-153 Ch Hcap soft		£100,355
117	1/05	Gowr	3m 113-132 Ch Hcap sft-hvy		£34,628
106	12/04	Navn	3m 106-135 Ch Hcap soft		£13,754
	12/02	Punc	2m2f Mdn Hdl heavy		£5,503

Long-distance handicap chaser who won the Irish Grand National in 2005, and added to Ireland's recent rich heritage in the Aintree equivalent 12 months later, beating compatriot Hedgehunter by 6l under 10st 8lb; was brought along steadily for a repeat Aintree bid last season (two spins over hurdles and a staying-on fourth in a Grade 2 chase), but wilted a bit on a very hot afternoon in Liverpool in April, and, under 11st 3lb, could manage only a 43l sixth behind Silver Birch; approaching the veteran stage now, and the chances are his glory days are behind him, but will again be primed for Aintree, and could run another big race if the ground is a little easier than it was last time; sure to be lightly raced in the build-up.

1327 Nycteos (Fr)

6 ch g Chamberlin - Cynthia (Mont Basile)

P Nicholls   The Stewart Family

PLACINGS: 5613/5211F/601-   **RPR 145+c**

Starts	1st	2nd	3rd	4th	Win & Pl
12	4	1	1	-	£44,452
131	4/07	Chel	2m5f Cls1 Gd2 131-151 Ch Hcap good		£28,510
124	3/06	Chep	2m3¹/₂f Cls3 97-124 Ch Hcap heavy		£6,321
	2/06	Chep	2m3¹/₂f Cls4 Ch soft		£3,904
	3/05	Chep	2m¹/₂f Cls4 Mdn Hdl soft		£3,339

Winner of two of his three races over fences the season before last before falling in the Topham Chase at Aintree; that tumble clearly left its mark as he was off the track for nearly a year before returning over hurdles in March, and then failed to land a blow back over fences in the Racing Post Plate at the Cheltenham Festival; finally got his act together again in a Grade 2 limited handicap at Cheltenham in April when cutting out plenty of the running and coming home 3l ahead of Too Forward; raised 9lb for that success, but Racing Post Ratings indicate he is still ahead of the handicapper, so it will be no surprise if he is able to bag another decent handicap or two at around 2m5f. *'The Becher Chase might be the race for him this season.' (Paul Nicholls, trainer)*

1328 Oedipe (Fr)

5 ch g Chamberlin - Massada (Kashtan)

N Henderson   W J Brown

PLACINGS: 12221-   **RPR 135+c**

Starts	1st	2nd	3rd	4th	Win & Pl
5					£26,263
117	12/06	Kemp	2m4¹/₂f Cls3 Nov 111-130 Ch Hcap gd-sft	.........£12,526
	7/06	Diep	2m1¹/₂f Ch 4yo soft..£4,303

Ex-French chaser who made a stunning British debut in a novice handicap chase at Kempton on Boxing Day, where he led from halfway and simply jumped and galloped his rivals into submission, sealing victory with a giant leap at the last and coasting home 14l clear of Black Hills (in receipt of 11lb); was not seen out again, but the form could hardly have worked out better, with the second, third, fourth, fifth and one of the pulled-up horses all winning soon afterwards; starts the new season on a 20lb higher mark of 137, but with Black Hills having risen to a mark of 138 subsequently, it is clear he could still be well treated; exciting prospect if he returns in the same form, and could be aimed at something as a stepping stone to the Paddy Power Gold Cup.

1329 Ofarel D'Airy (Fr)

5 b g Cadoubel - Farali D'Airy (Marasali)

P Nicholls   The Stewart Family

PLACINGS: 2251321-   **RPR 143+c**

Starts	1st	2nd	3rd	4th	Win & Pl
7	2	3	1	-	£23,729
134	4/07	Chel	2m5f Cls3 Nov 113-134 Ch Hcap good.................£9,708
	1/07	Folk	2m Cls4 Mdn Ch gd-sft.......................................£3,904

Still a maiden over hurdles, but showed much better form when switched to fences last season and could do well in handicap company at around 2m5f; had no bother landing the odds in a maiden chase at Folkestone in January and ended his campaign by following two sound efforts in defeat (including at Cheltenham on heavy ground) with a 1l beating of Black Hills in a novice handicap back at Prestbury Park in April, showing a fine attitude to fight back and regain the lead when headed; had earlier been earmarked for the Jewson Handicap but missed the cut; starts the season on

a mark of 145 with a bright future; could be interesting in the Paddy Power Gold Cup. *'There's more improvement to come. He could start over hurdles as he's still a novice in that department.' (Paul Nicholls, trainer)*

1330 Offshore Account (Ire)

7 b g Oscar - Park Breeze (Strong Gale)

C Swan (Ir)   Brian Polly

PLACINGS: 3/63P72F/2701521111-   **RPR 150+c**

Starts	1st	2nd	3rd	4th	Win & Pl
19	5	4	2	-	£86,281
	4/07	Punc	3m1f Nov Gd1 Ch good £46,081
	4/07	Limk	3m Nov Gd3 Ch yield...£15,395
	3/07	Naas	2m4f Nov Ch heavy...£8,797
	2/07	Fair	2m5f Ch heavy...£5,836
	12/06	Gowr	2m2f Mdn Hdl heavy..£4,766

Half-brother to several classy chasers, notably The Listener and Distant Thunder, and has the potential to be as good as any of them; switch to chasing in January brought about dramatic improvement, and he rattled up a four-timer before the season was out; scored at Fairyhouse, Naas and Limerick before wrapping things up with a Grade 1 success over 3m1f at the Punchestown festival, where he was a length down when left clear by the last-fence fall of Aces Four and came home 11l to the good over Knight Legend; jumping is one of his strengths, while he stays 3m no problem and seems to handle all types of ground, so shouldn't be underestimated when taking on better opposition in this season's top chases; likely to start in a 2m6f Listed race at Punchestown, with the Grade 1 Champion Chase at Down Royal in November his first main target.

1331 Ollie Magern

9 b g Alderbrook - Outfield (Monksfield)

N Twiston-Davies   Roger Nicholls

PLACINGS: 11421U12/176405/U47-   **RPR 161c**

Starts	1st	2nd	3rd	4th	Win & Pl
34	11	5	-	5	£242,008
	10/05	Weth	3m1f Cls1 Gd2 Ch soft......................................£45,750
	2/05	Weth	3m1f Cls1 Nov Gd2 Ch gd-sft..........................£21,440
	12/04	Kemp	3m Cls1 Nov Gd1 Ch gd-sft.............................£41,650
	10/04	Chel	3m¹/₂f Cls2 Nov Ch good £11,121
	10/04	Fknm	2m5¹/₂f Cls3 Nov Ch good.................................£11,307
	9/04	Strf	3m Cls3 Nov Ch good £6,812
	10/03	Chel	3m1¹/₂f Cls3 Nov Hdl gd-fm £6,248
	10/03	Hntg	3m2f Cls4 Nov Hdl gd-fm......................................£2,870
	7/03	Strf	2m6¹/₂f Cls3 Nov Hdl good £5,356
	6/03	Hrfd	3m2f Cls4 Nov Cond Hdl gd-fm £3,493
	5/03	Strf	2m6¹/₂f Cls3 Nov Hdl good £5,538

Formerly high-class chaser who has steadily drifted into the doldrums; earned a peak RPR of 165 when winning the 2005 Charlie Hall Chase at Wetherby, but hasn't won since, and was seen out just three times before the turn of the year last season; unseated rider early at Ascot on reappearance, but turned in an encouraging effort when 19l fourth behind Kauto Star in the Betfair Chase at Haydock (3m, good to soft, 6 ran), bowling along in front until left for dead by brilliant winner; just a bit-part player behind the same horse in the King George the following month (3m, good to soft, 9 ran) and that was that for the season; is slowly dropping to a lenient mark and, over 3m on decent ground, may return to winning form in handicap grade, although the top echelon is pie in the sky now.

1332 Olmeto Collonges (Fr)

5 br g Brier Creek - Castille Collonges (El Badr)

Miss H Knight   T Cole & A Finney

PLACINGS: 6/25-1   **RPR 109+h**

Starts	1st	2nd	3rd	4th	Win & Pl
4	1	1	-	-	£10,872
	5/07	Uttx	2m Cls4 Nov Hdl gd-sft...................................£2,928		

Half-brother to high-class chaser Neptune Collonges; was placed over fences in France before arriving in Britain last season, and his trainer's intention was always to give him just a couple of runs over hurdles in his first campaign with her; probably needed the run on his debut, but went off on his summer holidays on the back of a 2m novice victory at Uttoxeter in May, where he pulled out all the stops to thwart 1-6 shot Shouldhavehadthat by 3/4l; like the runner-up, he is sure to want further in time, and the plan is to immediately return him to fences this term; could make up into a very decent staying novice. *'He's a fine, big horse who'll want soft ground and 3m. He could be very good in time.' (Henrietta Knight, trainer)*

1333 One Cool Cookie (Ire)

6 ch g Old Vic - Lady Bellingham (Montelimar)

C Swan (Ir)   Gigginstown House Stud

PLACINGS: 31/521339/131P313-   **RPR 154c**

Starts	1st	2nd	3rd	4th	Win & Pl
13	4	1	5	-	£104,056
	4/07	Fair	2m4f Gd1 Ch good...................................£44,219		
	12/06	Limk	2m3³/₄f Nov Gd2 Ch yld-sft...............£24,693		
	9/06	List	2m6f Ch heavy...................................£8,340		
	11/05	Limk	2m3f Mdn Hdl 4yo heavy...................£3,921		

Brother to In Compliance, and one of the leading novice chasers in Ireland at around 2m4f last season; highlight of his campaign was his all-the-way victory in an up-to-scratch Grade 1 Powers Gold Cup at Fairyhouse in April, where he beat dual Grade 1 novice chase winner Schindlers Hunt by 1¹/₂l (2m4f, good, 11 ran); tackled 3m-plus over fences for the first time in the Grade 1 Champion Novice Chase at the Punchestown festival, but possibly found the trip stretched his stamina in finishing third behind stablemate Offshore Account, and it could be that he will be most effective at around 2m4f; likely to start off in a Listed chase over 2m6f at Punchestown in October, and trainer has not ruled out a crack at the King George around Kempton's sharp 3m.

1334 Oneway (Ire)

10 b g Bob's Return - Rendezvous (Lorenzaccio)

M Rimell   Mark Rimell

PLACINGS: P/111114/33U/9320F6-   **RPR 161+c**

Starts	1st	2nd	3rd	4th	Win & Pl
24	6	2	4	2	£123,861
143	2/05	Sand	2m Cls2 138-156 Ch Hcap good...............£11,867		
135	1/05	Sand	2m Cls2 122-141 Ch Hcap gd-sft...........£12,070		
124	12/04	Hayd	2m Cls3 104-124 Ch Hcap gd-sft...........£16,705		
115	11/04	Weth	2m Cls3 99-125 Ch Hcap gd-sft.............£5,434		
107	10/04	Worc	2m4¹/₂f Cls3 107-125 Ch Hcap good........£6,744		
104	12/03	Ling	2m4¹/₂f Cls4 79-105 Am Ch Hcap soft.......£4,027		

Smart, if inconsistent, 2m chaser who is without a win since completing a five-timer in February 2005; showed his best form last season in December, finishing 14l third behind Kauto Star in the Grade 1 Tingle Creek Chase at Sandown (2m, soft, 6 ran), and again losing nothing in defeat when finding only subsequent Champion Chase hero Voy Por Ustedes too good in a Grade 2 at Kempton over Christmas (2m, good to soft, 5 ran); flopped next time in handicap company, but ran well in first-time blinkers as a 50-1 shot in the Champion Chase at Cheltenham, where he was still in contention when falling two out; last of six in Aintree's Melling Chase on his final start; best going right-handed on soft ground, and his early-season target is the Haldon Gold Cup at Exeter. *'We thought he may have finished second in the Champion Chase had he not come down and I believe he can find a bit more improvement this season.' (Mark Rimell, trainer)*

1335 Opera De Coeur (Fr)

5 b g East Of Heaven - Eden De Coeur (Lampon)

H Daly   The Hon Mrs A E Heber-Percy

PLACINGS: 1114/2P22P20-   **RPR 133h**

Starts	1st	2nd	3rd	4th	Win & Pl
11	3	4	-	1	£33,324
	3/06	Strf	2m¹/₂f Cls3 Nov Hdl 4yo gd-sft...............£7,516		
	2/06	Wwck	2m Cls3 Nov Hdl 4yo heavy...................£5,205		
	1/06	Wwck	2m Cls4 Nov Hdl 4yo soft...................£3,253		

Still a novice chaser, despite finishing second to three very smart performers over fences last season; attracted lots of attention when beaten 1³/₄l by Lennon on his chasing debut at Aintree last November, running on from an unpromising position but never challenging the eased-down winner (2m, good, 3 ran); blundered his way to a standstill in heavy ground next time, but returned to form when second to Trouble At Bay at Hereford in December and Aztec Warrior at Wincanton in January; reverted to hurdles afterwards, doing best when 1¹/₄l second to Michael Muck in a handicap at Uttoxeter in March (2m6¹/₂f, good to soft, 15 ran); will go back over fences this winter, and could just come into his own in 2m handicaps granted some cut in the ground.

1336 Opera Mundi (Fr)

5 b g Discover D'Auteuil - Gymnastique II (Aelan Hapi)

P Nicholls   Sir Robert Ogden

PLACINGS: 221U/1120-   RPR **145**+c

Starts	1st	2nd	3rd	4th	Win & Pl
8	3	3	-	-	£40,722

	1/07	Newb	2m1f Cls3 Nov Ch heavy	£5,855
121	11/06	Newb	2m2¹/₂f Cls3 Nov 103-123 Ch Hcap soft	£12,526
	2/06	Folk	2m4¹/₂f Cls4 Mdn Hdl soft	£3,253

Only moderate over hurdles, but was much improved when switched to fences last season and remains open to further progress at around 2m4f with give in the ground; won two novice contests at Newbury either side of the new year before just getting outspeeded by Ursis in a Grade 2 contest at Wincanton, a track that clearly didn't play to his strengths (2m, soft, 4 ran); disappointing on his final start when sent off favourite for the Racing Post Plate at the Cheltenham Festival, but worth forgiving him that defeat in a race that favours those with plenty of experience; has plenty of size, so could have plenty more to offer this term; could be one for the Vodafone Gold Cup at Newbury.

1337 Orbit O'Gold (USA)

5 ch g Kingmambo - Lily O'Gold (Slew O'Gold)

N Meade (Ir)   Mighty Macs Syndicate

PLACINGS: 26311010-   RPR **132**h

Starts	1st	2nd	3rd	4th	Win & Pl
8	3	1	1	-	£36,250

2/07	Punc	2m Nov Gd2 Hdl soft	£24,193
12/06	Navn	2m Hdl 4yo heavy	£6,672
11/06	Dpat	2m2¹/₂f Mdn Hdl 4yo soft	£3,812

Useful hurdler who won three of his eight starts in novice and handicap company last term; gained his final and biggest success at odds of 50-1 in a Grade 2 novice event at Punchestown in February, where he made all at his own pace, was ridden clear two out and held on by 2l from De Valira (2m, soft, 11 ran); started at less than half those odds in the Supreme Novices' Hurdle at the Cheltenham Festival the following month, and was still upside the leaders jumping two out before fading to finish 13th behind Ebaziyan (2m¹/₂f, soft, 22 ran); has winning form up to 2m2¹/₂f, and looks one for good 2m handicap hurdles, despite finishing well down the field in the Pierse Hurdle at Leopardstown in January.

1338 Ornais (Fr)

5 b g Michel Georges - Imperia II (Beyssac)

P Nicholls   The Stewart Family

PLACINGS: 42/120-   RPR **123**h

Starts	1st	2nd	3rd	4th	Win & Pl
5	1	2	-	1	£16,050

10/06	Extr	2m3f Cls3 Nov Hdl good	£5,205

Purchased to go chasing, and should be a useful recruit to the staying novice ranks this term; would

have gone straight over fences last season had he not won on his hurdling debut, but the manner of that 27l success persuaded connections to stay down that route; failed to go on from his debut win after arriving from France, however, getting beaten at odds-on at Taunton and then finishing down the field in the Brit Insurance Novices' Hurdle at Cheltenham; should find his calling over fences.

1339 Osana (Fr)

5 b g Video Rock - Voilette (Brezzo)

D Pipe   Thomas Barr

PLACINGS: 124102-   RPR **147**+h

Starts	1st	2nd	3rd	4th	Win & Pl
6	2	2	-	1	£24,873

2/07	Winc	2m Cls4 Nov Hdl soft	£3,904
11/06	Plum	2m Cls4 Nov Hdl soft	£3,904

Winner on the Flat in his native France last summer, proved himself a smart novice hurdler last season in Britain, and expected to do well when switched to chasing this term; made a lasting impression when bolting up at Wincanton in February by 6l from Song Of Songs, a performance that came on the back of a promising fourth behind Wichita Lineman in a Grade 2 at Cheltenham in January (2m4¹/₂f, heavy, 11 ran); did better than his finishing position suggests when beaten less than 8l by Pedrobob in the County Hurdle back at Cheltenham before appreciating the return to a flat track at Aintree and finding only Blythe Knight too good in the Grade 2 Top Novices' Hurdle (2m1¹/₂f, good, 8 ran); seems versatile regarding ground, and should stay 2m4f-plus over fences.

1340 Oscar Park (Ire)

8 b g Oscar - Parkavoureen (Deep Run)

D Arbuthnot   George Ward

PLACINGS: 11/112292/2F01-   RPR **147**+h

Starts	1st	2nd	3rd	4th	Win & Pl
12	5	4	-	-	£77,250

140	3/07	Chel	3m Cls1 List 131-157 Hdl Hcap gd-sft	£39,914
	11/05	Wind	2m4f Cls4 Nov Hdl good	£3,663
	10/05	Uttx	2m4¹/₂f Cls4 Nov Hdl gd-sft	£3,798
	1/05	Wwck	2m Cls1 List NHF 4-6yo soft	£10,218
	11/04	Wind	2m Cls6 NHF 4-6yo soft	£1,911

Talented staying hurdler; gave trainer David Arbuthnot his biggest win over jumps when landing the Pertemps Final at the Cheltenham Festival in March, where he led on the extended run to the final flight and kept on tenaciously to beat Material World by ¹/₂l; had endured a chequered campaign prior to that win, finishing second to Karanja at Newbury, falling at Haydock and getting stuck in the mud at Sandown; set to go novice chasing this winter, starting around November, and if he takes to fences, then a return to the Cheltenham Festival for the Royal & SunAlliance could well be on the cards; stays really well, and has won on all sorts of ground.

1341 Oscatello (USA)

7 b/br g Woodman - Galea Des Bois (Persian Bold)

P Hobbs   Rye Braune

PLACINGS: 2/2212111/7647-   **RPR 133+h**

Starts	1st	2nd	3rd	4th	Win & Pl
12	4	4	-	1	£26,032

4/06	Chel	2m5¹/₂f Cls2 Nov Hdl good	£9,395
3/06	MRas	2m3¹/₂f Cls4 Nov Cond Hdl heavy	£2,741
3/06	Hrfd	2m3¹/₂f Cls4 Nov Hdl good	£3,578
12/05	MRas	2m3¹/₂f Cls4 Mdn Hdl gd-sft	£2,220

Did well for Ian Williams, winning four novice hurdles, but transferred to current trainer halfway through last season; made his debut for the yard as a well-backed 8-1 shot in the Coral Cup at the Cheltenham Festival, and showed career-best form to finish 9¹/₂l fourth behind Burntoakboy (2m5f, good to soft, 28 ran); 2lb higher when stepping up to 3m¹/₂f for another valuable handicap hurdle at Aintree, but raced like a non-stayer, fading between the last two and finishing seventh behind Albertas Run; might go novice chasing now, and ought to win races if proving as adept over the bigger obstacles.

1342 Oslot (Fr)

5 b g Passing Sale - Une De Lann (Spoleto)

P Nicholls   The Stewart Family

PLACINGS: 12391-   **RPR 137+h**

Starts	1st	2nd	3rd	4th	Win & Pl
5	2	1	1	-	£19,997

128	4/07	Sand	2m4¹/₂f Cls2 111-137 Hdl Hcap gd-fm	£12,526
	12/06	Tntn	2m1f Cls4 Mdn Hdl gd-sft	£2,602

Multiple winner on the Flat in the provinces in France, and is a decent prospect for novice chases between 2m4f and 3m; landed a novice hurdle on his British debut at Taunton in December, but it was not until he was handed a stiffer test of stamina that he put up his best effort, driven out to win a competitive handicap hurdle at Sandown in April by 1³/₄l from Chilling Place; liked to uproot the odd hurdle last term, so will need to learn to respect his fences, but difficult to see him not winning races this term. *'He'll be part of a good novice chase team.' (Paul Nicholls, trainer)*

1343 Ossmoses (Ire)

10 gr g Roselier - Sugarstown (Sassafras)

D Forster   D M Forster

PLACINGS: 315/1212/761312/452-   **RPR 126h**

Starts	1st	2nd	3rd	4th	Win & Pl
17	5	4	2	2	£155,844

126	2/06	Hayd	3m4¹/₂f Cls1 Gd3 126-152 Ch Hcap heavy	£71,275
116	12/05	Kels	3m1f Cls2 116-142 Ch Hcap soft	£11,221
107	2/05	Uttx	3m2f Cls3 100-120 Ch Hcap soft	£9,152
101	12/04	Hayd	2m6f Cls3 92-115 Ch Hcap heavy	£17,063
	1/04	Weth	3m1f Cls4 Nov Ch soft	£5,400

Long-distance handicap chaser whose biggest win came in the 2006 Red Square Vodka Gold Cup at

Haydock (beat Model Son by 15l), and was second in the Midlands National the following month; had the Grand National as his target last season, and was brought along slowly with that in mind; fourth over hurdles and a one-paced fifth over fences at Wetherby on Boxing Day, but looked sharper at Ayr in March, where he finished a staying-on neck second to Amstecos in a 2m4f novice hurdle (soft, 9 ran, 41l break back to the third); all the more disappointing, then, that having had a perfect preparation, he was forced to miss the Grand National owing to an 11th hour setback; will have Aintree top of his agenda again, and unlikely to see too much action before the weights come out in February; loves a stiff test in the mud.

1344 Ostfanni (Ire)

7 b m Spectrum - Ostwahl (Waajib)

M Todhunter   Ian Hall Racing

PLACINGS: 320/11114P/1148205-6   **RPR 130h**

Starts	1st	2nd	3rd	4th	Win & Pl
19	6	2	1	2	£38,524

5/06	Kels	2m6¹/₂f Cls3 Hdl good	£5,205
5/06	Kels	2m6¹/₂f Cls3 Hdl gd-fm	£6,533
10/05	Chel	3m1¹/₂f Cls3 Nov Hdl good	£5,081
9/05	Hexm	2m4¹/₂f Cls4 Nov Hdl gd-fm	£3,479
8/05	Ctml	2m6f Cls4 Nov Hdl good	£4,076
8/05	Prth	2m4¹/₂f Cls4 Mdn Hdl good	£3,090

Useful handicap hurdler who is set to go novice chasing; regularly showed the best form of her life last season, notably finishing 1¹/₄l second to Accordello in a handicap at Aintree (2m4f, good, 16 ran), fifth behind Oscar Park in the Pertemps Final at the Cheltenham Festival (3m, good to soft, 24 ran) and 8l sixth behind Abragante in another decent contest at Haydock in May (3m, good, 19 ran); a winner on the Flat at Musselburgh in June, and clearly in good heart as she prepares to embark on her chase career; effective between 2m4f and 3m, best on good ground and should find opportunities against her own sex before and after the depths of winter.

1345 Otto Des Pictons (Fr)

5 b g Grand Tresor - Sarawak (Djarvis)

P Nicholls   The Stewart Family

PLACINGS: 522251-   **RPR 127+h**

Starts	1st	2nd	3rd	4th	Win & Pl
6	1	3	-	-	£15,429

114	4/07	Ayr	3m¹/₂f Cls2 Nov 104-123 Hdl Hcap gd-fm	£10,735

Interesting 3m novice chase prospect; it took him six attempts to get off the mark over hurdles in his first season last term, but he improved with each and every start; finished second three times but finally scored in a weak-looking race at Ayr in April when stepped up beyond 3m for the first time and cruising home by 17l from Ice Tea, who scored next time out; full of potential and should be winning plenty of races over fences.

1346 Oulart

8 ch g Sabrehill - Gaye Fame (Ardross)

D Hughes (Ir)   G T Pierse

PLACINGS: 47P6022823/6UFP0270-   **RPR 138h**

Starts	1st	2nd	3rd	4th	Win & Pl
29	3	6	1	3	£103,842
121	3/05	Chel	3m Cls1 List 119-140 Hdl Hcap good		£34,800
112	12/04	Leop	3m 99-125 Hdl Hcap soft		£9,857
	12/04	Clon	2m4f Mdn Hdl 4-6yo soft		£5,353

Smart stayer with top handicap form over both hurdles and fences, having won the Pertemps Final at the 2005 Cheltenham Festival and finished second to Point Barrow in the 2006 Irish Grand National (both on good ground); in dismal form over fences in the early part of last season, so switched to hurdles, and got back on track with a 1l second to Contessa Messina in a competitive handicap at Punchestown in February (3m, soft, 17 ran); started 16-1 for the Coral Cup at Cheltenham the following month, and ran with credit to finish 12l seventh behind Burntoakboy (2m5f, good to soft, 28 ran); still a maiden over fences, so could be found some soft novice races.

1347 Ouninpohja (Ire)

6 b g Imperial Ballet - Daziyra (Doyoun)

P Nicholls   Mrs M Findlay

PLACINGS: 132232-   **RPR 143+h**

Starts	1st	2nd	3rd	4th	Win & Pl
6	1	3	2	-	£43,462
	11/06	Tntn	2m1f Cls4 Mdn Hdl good		£4,880

Listed-placed middle-distance performer on the Flat, who showed himself to be a talented, if somewhat frustrating 2m hurdler last season; got off the mark first time out in a maiden race at Taunton last November before running very well in much better company, but without being able to get his head in front; looked the likely winner of the County Hurdle at Cheltenham two flights from home, but went down by 1l to Pedrobob (2m1f, good to soft, 28 ran); probably put up his best effort in the Scottish Champion Hurdle when tried from the front in blinkers, but still found one too good; not harshly treated on a mark of 141, but there is a question mark over his will to win.

1348 Our Ben

8 ch g Presenting - Forest Pride (Be My Native)

W Mullins (Ir)   Trevor Hemmings

PLACINGS: 1335/P213UP3/42F316-   **RPR 150c**

Starts	1st	2nd	3rd	4th	Win & Pl
22	5	2	6	1	£87,839
	4/07	Cork	3m List Ch gd-fm		£15,395
	1/06	Fair	2m1f Ch soft		£9,054
	12/04	Limk	2m6f Nov Gd3 Hdl heavy		£18,338
	11/04	Clon	2m Mdn Hdl 5yo yld-sft		£4,866
	2/04	Limk	2m NHF 5-7yo yld-sft		£4,866

Smart chaser, but some way short of top-class and

his best chance of a big prize is likely to be in a handicap, with the Grand National a realistic long-term target; best run last season came when runner-up to Mansony (who received 3lb) in a Leopardstown handicap chase on Boxing Day (2m1f, soft to heavy, 12 ran), and then showed his versatility regarding trip when landing the odds in a five-runner 3m Listed chase at Cork in April; also smart over hurdles (third in 2005 SunAlliance Hurdle) and finished third to Celestial Wave in a Grade 3 in January; by no means the most fluent of jumpers, often makes mistakes and fell at the last on his third start with the race won (2m2f, soft to heavy, sent off 4-7); unexposed over further than 3m (pulled up early in Irish National in 2006); seems to go on all types of ground.

1349 Our Bob (Ire)

5 gr g Bob Back - Mondeo Rose (Roselier)

W Mullins (Ir)   Trevor Hemmings

PLACINGS: 521-   **RPR 104b**

Starts	1st	2nd	3rd	4th	Win & Pl
3	1	1	-	-	£5,756
	4/07	Punc	2m2f NHF 5-7yo good		£4,669

Made steady progress in bumpers last season, and appeals as the type to continue the improvement in novice hurdles; unfancied when fifth behind stablemate Cooldine at Fairyhouse (2m, heavy, 13 ran) on his debut, then improved on his following start to finish second to Jack The Bus at the same track (2m, soft to heavy, 12 ran), keeping on at the same pace; appeared to benefit from the better ground and longer trip when getting off the mark in a 25-runner event at the Punchestown festival (third has won since), keeping on well inside the final furlong to beat Carrickmines by 1¹/₂l (2m2f, good, 25 ran); stoutly bred type, being by Bob Back out of a dam who was a winner over hurdles/fences up to 3m, so will probably do better at 2m4f-plus over hurdles.

1350 Our Vic (Ire)

9 b g Old Vic - Shabra Princess (Buckskin)

D Pipe   D A Johnson

PLACINGS: 2113/FPP/1P191/1223-   **RPR 173+c**

Starts	1st	2nd	3rd	4th	Win & Pl
19	9	3	2	-	£340,811
	10/06	Weth	3m1f Cls1 Gd2 Ch soft		£51,318
158	4/06	Chel	2m5f Cls1 Gd2 147-167 Ch Hcap good		£28,644
	2/06	Ling	2m4¹/₂f Cls1 Gd1 Ch heavy		£57,288
149	11/05	Chel	2m4¹/₂f Cls1 Gd3 130-154 Ch Hcap gd-sft		£62,722
	2/04	Asct	3m¹/₂f Cls1 Nov Gd2 Ch good		£20,825
	2/04	Extr	2m3¹/₂f Cls4 Nov Ch soft		£4,290
121	2/03	Winc	2m Cls3 99-123 Hdl Hcap gd-sft		£5,073
	1/03	Tntn	2m3¹/₂f Cls3 Nov Hdl 4-7yo soft		£5,428
	12/02	Extr	2m1f Cls4 Nov Hdl 4-6yo soft		£3,668

High-class if not altogether straightforward chaser between 2m5f and 3m1f, who remains lightly raced for his age and looks sure to play a major role in the big races just below the top level;

showed that he goes particularly well fresh when bolting up in the Charlie Hall Chase at Wetherby last October, putting himself in the Gold Cup picture by coming home 7l clear of subsequent Grade 1 winner Neptune Collonges; ultimately ran in the Ryanair Chase at the Cheltenham Festival after seemingly failing to stay 3m1¹/2f on heavy ground in the Cotswold Chase at Prestbury Park, and came tantalisingly close to scoring, running on late after seeming to lose interest at halfway and failing by only a neck to catch Taranis, to whom he was conceding 5lb (2m4f, good to soft, 9 ran); some way below par when upped to 3m1f again at Aintree, and remains a difficult one to gauge, although there is no doubting that he is a class act on his day who looks sure to win more races. *'He's a star. The Charlie Hall, where he could take on Denman, is the logical start for him, and he was pretty impressive when winning it last year.' (David Pipe, trainer)*

1351 Over The Creek

8 br g Over The River - Solo Girl (Le Bavard)

D Pipe   D A Johnson

PLACINGS: 5B2/11012/U50-   **RPR 125+c**

Starts	1st	2nd	3rd	4th	Win & Pl
11	3	2			£54,123
129	2/05	Newb	3m¹/₂f Cls3 103-129 Hdl Hcap gd-sft	...........£6,287
117	11/04	Aint	2m4f Cls3 109-125 Hdl Hcap soft	...........£15,393
105	11/04	Chel	2m¹/₂f Cls3 Nov 96-110 Hdl Hcap good	......£13,862

Three times a winner over hurdles who failed to spark when sent over fences last season following a two-year break, but is expected to do much better in staying novice chases this term; unshipped his rider on his return and was well beaten when tried in Grade 2 company behind Gungadu before a shot in the dark against Inglis Drever and co in the World Hurdle at Cheltenham; connections keen to draw a line under what happened last season and expect a brighter show in novice contests at around 3m. *'Things didn't quite go to plan last season.' (David Pipe, trainer)*

1352 Overstrand (Ire)

8 b g In The Wings - Vaison La Romaine (Arctic Tern)

R Newland   Dr R D P & Mrs L J Newland, C E Stedman

PLACINGS: 576461908/01103210F-   **RPR 145+h**

Starts	1st	2nd	3rd	4th	Win & Pl
35	2	2	3	3	£178,460
141	2/07	Asct	2m3¹/₂f Cls2 120-141 Hdl Hcap gd-sft	.........£50,104
126	12/06	Sand	2m¹/₂f Cls1 List 114-140 Hdl Hcap heavy	.......£28,510
120	11/06	Leic	2m Cls3 95-120 Hdl Hcap heavy	...............£6,263
115	2/06	MRas	2m1¹/₂f Cls4 95-115 Hdl Hcap gd-sft	...........£5,205
	8/05	Prth	2m¹/₂f Cls4 Claim Hdl 4-6yo gd-fm	.............£3,596
120	12/03	Sand	2m¹/₂f Cls1 List 114-140 Hdl Hcap gd-sft	.....£29,000
	11/03	Carl	2m1f Cls4 Nov Hdl heavy	.........................£2,759
	11/03	MRas	2m1¹/₂f Cls4 Nov Am Hdl good	...................£3,017
	5/03	Prth	2m4¹/₂f Cls4 Mdn Hdl good	.......................£4,261

Much-improved hurdler between 2m and 2m4f for his new trainer last season; was clearly well treated when scoring from a mark of 120 at Leicester in

November before following up in the William Hill Handicap Hurdle at Sandown the following week in good style by 7l from Whispered Promises; found out in top company in the World Hurdle at Cheltenham, but preceded that effort by defying a mark of 141 to win a competitive handicap at Ascot by 3/4l from Nation State, a fine effort that came on the back of placed runs in the Champion Hurdle Trial at Haydock and in the Totesport Trophy at Newbury; tremendous flag-bearer for his handler last season, but will find life much tougher this time and could find winning opportunities hard to come by. *'He's a fabulously tough horse.' (Richard Newland, trainer)*

1353 Pablo Du Charmil (Fr)

6 ch g Lyphard's Wish - Pacifie Du Charmil (Dom Pasquini)

D Pipe   Joe Moran

PLACINGS: 1122U0/1110-   **RPR 138+c**

Starts	1st	2nd	3rd	4th	Win & Pl
10	5	2			£55,285
	12/06	Wwck	2m Cls3 Nov Ch heavy	.......................£6,506
	11/06	Font	2m2f Cls3 Nov Ch gd-sft	....................£9,998
	11/06	Extr	2m1¹/₂f Cls4 Ch gd-fm	......................£6,506
	10/05	Autl	2m2f Hdl 4yo heavy	.........................£13,617
	10/05	Autl	2m2f Hdl v soft	..............................£15,660

Proved himself a smart novice chaser between 2m and 2m2f last season and should be able to bag a decent handicap or two this term; sent off favourite for his first three starts over fences and duly obliged, returning a Racing Post Rating of 138 each time but probably achieving most at Fontwell in November when making all and beating former Triumph Hurdle winner Penzance by 6l; failed to shine on his handicap debut in the Grand Annual Chase at the Cheltenham Festival, but was facing a field of battle-hardened performers and had a tough task on only his fourth start over fences; open to plenty of improvement and his best is probably yet to come. *'He'll be going for big handicap chases this season.' (David Pipe, trainer)*

1354 Pak Jack (Fr)

7 ch g Pitchounet - Miss Noir Et Or (Noir Et Or)

P Nicholls   Glencoe Inv

PLACINGS: 22/P15/2437343/82-22   **RPR 134c**

Starts	1st	2nd	3rd	4th	Win & Pl
19	1	8	3	2	£60,823
	1/05	Kemp	2m Cls2 Nov Ch good	.......................£10,514

Interesting handicap prospect between 2m4f and 3m; spent last year running in hunter chases for Richard Barber, finishing second three times from four starts; did particularly well over the National fences in the Fox Hunters' at Aintree in April, enjoying a battle royal with Scots Grey up the run-in and eventually going down by 1/2l to that in-form rival (2m5¹/2f, good, 27 ran); there was no disgrace in finishing runner-up to Iron Man at

Stratford in May, a rival who went on to win the Summer Plate at Market Rasen in August; starts the new campaign with a rating of 128, a mark that his new handler should have no trouble exploiting.

1355 Palarshan (Fr)

9 b/br g Darshaan - Palavera (Bikala)

H Daly   Sumner Wellesley

PLACINGS: 1/22311/920/5036P/2-   **RPR 141+c**

Starts	1st	2nd	3rd	4th	Win & Pl
17	4	4	3	-	£99,878
134	3/03	Chel	2m¹/₂f Cls1 Ch Hcap 129-153 Ch Hcap good		....£43,500
	2/03	Leic	2m Cls4 Nov Ch gd-sft		....£4,745
	4/02	Chel	2m1f Cls2 Nov Hdl 4yo gd-fm		....£8,541
	8/01	Pard	1m6f Hdl 3yo good		....£542

Talented chaser whose biggest (and most recent) win came in the 2003 Grand Annual Handicap Chase at the Cheltenham Festival; has been held back by injury problems since, and when he returned to Cheltenham for the Racing Post Plate in March, it was for his first start in precisely two years; served a reminder of both his and his trainer's ability to deliver on the big day, though, when running a blinder to finish 4l second to Idole First, staying on well up the hill in first-time cheekpieces (2m5f, good to soft, 23 ran); raised 4lb for that effort to a mark of 138, but remains well treated on the pick of his form, and trainer is sure to have some more big prizes in mind for him; effective from 2m-2m5f, but doesn't want the ground very soft, and probably won't run all that much.

1356 Pangbourne (Fr)

6 b g Double Bed - Valgrija (Big John)

A King   Trevor Hemmings

PLACINGS: 021191/4-   **RPR 104+h**

Starts	1st	2nd	3rd	4th	Win & Pl
7	3	1	-	1	£24,546
	4/06	Aint	2m1f Cls1 Gd2 NHF 4-6yo gd-sft		....£19,957
	2/06	Folk	2m1¹/₂f Cls6 NHF 4-6yo soft		....£1,713
	1/06	Hntg	2m¹/₂f Cls6 Mdn NHF 5-6yo gd-sft		....£1,713

Classy but quirky bumper performer two seasons ago, when his three wins included a late-rallying neck defeat of Tidal Bay in the Grade 2 contest at Aintree's Grand National meeting; only saw the track once last term, though, finishing 24l fourth behind Wichita Lineman in a 2m4f novice hurdle back at the Liverpool venue last October; obvious concern that he didn't race again, but would be one of the most talented bumper performers of the last couple of seasons, and could be worth another chance; races in an eyeshield, and best with a bit of cut in the ground.

1357 Papini (Ire)

6 ch g Lomitas - Pariana (Bering)

N Henderson   Newbury Racehorse Owners Group

PLACINGS: 12102/4093/71100-   **RPR 139+h**

Starts	1st	2nd	3rd	4th	Win & Pl
14	4	2	1	1	£54,841
130	1/07	Sand	2m¹/₂f Cls2 113-139 Hdl Hcap heavy		....£31,315
122	11/06	Hayd	2m Cls3 105-128 Hdl Hcap good		....£8,133
	1/05	Newb	2m¹/₂f Cls4 Nov Hdl 4yo gd-sft		....£3,689
	11/04	Newb	2m¹/₂f Cls4 Nov Hdl 3yo good		....£4,241

Useful 2m handicap hurdler, but one with a similarly inconsistent profile to stablemate Tarlac; won twice last season, following up a Haydock success with a front-running 5l defeat of Heathcote in a valuable heavy-ground contest at Sandown in January; went the same way as Tarlac thereafter, though, flopping as one of the fancied contenders in the Totesport Trophy at Newbury and as one of the outsiders in the County Hurdle at Cheltenham; is the right age to try his hand at chasing, and that could well be his game now.

1358 Paradi (Fr)

4 b/br g Video Rock - Gintonique (Royal Charter)

D Pipe   D A Johnson

PLACINGS: 151-   **RPR 112h**

Starts	1st	2nd	3rd	4th	Win & Pl
3	2	-	-	-	£11,749
	2/07	Sand	2m¹/₂f Cls3 Nov Hdl 4yo heavy		....£5,205
	11/06	Leic	2m Cls4 Nov Hdl 3yo soft		....£5,205

Promising hurdler at around 2m who won two of his three starts in Britain last season after arriving from France and now looks an exciting novice chase prospect; returned similar Racing Post Ratings when landing novice contests at both Leicester and Sandown, beating subsequent winner Lester Leaps In on the latter occasion; was below that form when sent off favourite for the Grade 1 Future Champion Finale Juvenile Hurdle at Chepstow on Welsh National day, managing only fifth place, some 20l behind Good Bye Simon, although he reportedly broke loose in the paddock before that outing; well regarded at home and sure to do well when switched to fences. *'He's a horse for the future and is a chaser in the making.' (David Pipe, trainer)*

1359 Parsons Legacy (Ire)

9 b g Leading Counsel - The Parson's Girl (The Parson)

P Hobbs   R A S Offer

PLACINGS: 1321635/7P292/15423-   **RPR 150+c**

Starts	1st	2nd	3rd	4th	Win & Pl
30	5	6	5	3	£120,703
124	11/06	Winc	3m1¹/₂f Cls1 List 123-145 Ch Hcap good		....£39,914
117	12/04	Leic	2m7¹/₂f Cls3 105-125 Ch Hcap good		....£7,046
	10/04	Ludl	2m4f Cls4 Ch gd-sft		....£4,716
	12/03	Leic	2m4¹/₂f Cls3 Nov Hdl gd-sft		....£3,552
	11/03	Newb	2m3f Cls3 Nov Hdl gd-fm		....£5,021

Long-distance handicap chaser who looks a

potential Grand National contender next spring; got his season off to the best possible start when winning the valuable Badger Ales Trophy at Wincanton last November, leading three out and galloping on to beat Preacher Boy by 2¹/₂l; fair fifth in the Hennessy next time (Preacher Boy third) and last of four at Cheltenham on New Year's Day, but was rested afterwards, and came back fresh and better than ever in the spring; strong-finishing second to Cloudy Lane in the Kim Muir at the Cheltenham Festival (3m¹/₂f, good to soft, 24 ran) and did even better when 1³/₄l third to Hot Weld in the Scottish National at Ayr (4m1f, good to firm, 23 ran); loves good ground, and will surely be campaigned with the big spring marathons in mind this term.

1360 Patriarch Express

10 b g Noble Patriarch - Jaydeeglen (Bay Express)

Mrs S Smith   A W Muir

PLACINGS: 1162635/121F14/4F85/

Starts	1st	2nd	3rd	4th	Win & Pl
22	7	3	1	2	£106,894

143	1/05	Chel	3m Cls1 Gd2 Hdl gd-sft	£34,800
130	12/04	Hayd	2m4f Cls2 126-144 Hdl Hcap gd-sft	£32,500
	10/04	Weth	2m4¹/₂f Cls3 104-130 Hdl Hcap gd-sft	£6,910
	11/03	Hayd	2m4f Cls3 Nov Hdl 4-6yo soft	£3,770
	11/03	Newc	2m4f Cls4 Nov Hdl good	£2,611
	10/02	Chel	2m¹/₂f Cls6 NHF 4-6yo good	£4,128
	9/02	Prth	2m¹/₂f Cls6 NHF 4-6yo gd-fm	£3,003

Classy staying hurdler who achieved a peak RPR of 159 in January 2005 (beat Korelo by a head in a Grade 2 at Cheltenham), but has been plagued by physical problems in recent seasons; the plan was to send him novice chasing last season, but he picked up an injury that forced him to miss the entire campaign; connections believe he has made a full recovery, and his schooling has left them optimistic about his chances of making a smooth transition to chasing; will start off in novice chases in the north, and if he can translate the ability he showed over hurdles to the larger obstacles, he should have few problems adding to his seven career wins.

1361 Patsy Hall (Ire)

7 b g Saddlers' Hall - Clahada Rose (Roselier)

A Martin (Ir)   C P Byrne

PLACINGS: /23121421/71F12U59P-   **RPR 151+c**

Starts	1st	2nd	3rd	4th	Win & Pl
22	5	7	1	2	£81,097

	12/06	Chel	3m1¹/₂f Cls2 Nov Ch soft	£12,642
	11/06	DRoy	2m4f Ch yld-sft	£6,672
	4/06	Fair	3m Hdl good	£13,469
120	1/06	Leop	3m 110-138 Hdl Hcap heavy	£15,265
	12/05	Gowr	3m Mdn Hdl yield	£4,901

Staying chaser with some smart form to his name for Michael Cunningham, and a classy addition to his shrewd new stable; begins the new campaign with an official chase rating of 136, but that looks lenient on the pick of his form, best of which was

an impressive 9l defeat of the classy Aces Four in a novice chase at Cheltenham in December (3m1¹/₂f, soft, 5 ran); followed that up with a Grade 1 second to Cailin Alainn at Leopardstown over Christmas (beaten 4¹/₂l), but form tailed off in the second half of the season, which included a 30l ninth behind Denman in the Royal & SunAlliance Chase; can be forgiven those disappointing efforts (had had some hard races) and looks the sort to be freshened up for a tilt at some big handicaps this season – possibly the Grand National; likes soft ground, and is very interesting indeed.

1362 Pauillac (Fr)

4 b g Useful - Jolie Mome (Art Francais)

D Pipe   D A Johnson

PLACINGS: 3113P-   **RPR 131h**

Starts	1st	2nd	3rd	4th	Win & Pl
5	2		2		£18,968

	1/07	Sand	2m¹/₂f Cls3 Nov Hdl 4yo heavy	£6,506
	12/06	Newb	2m¹/₂f Cls4 Nov Hdl 3yo soft	£4,229

Smart juvenile hurdler in the first part of last term who is highly regarded and expected to do well as a novice chaser this season; scored at Newbury and Sandown before an encouraging run in the Grade 2 Finesse Hurdle at Cheltenham in January when finishing 4¹/₂l third behind subsequent Triumph Hurdle winner Katchit (2m1f, heavy, 8 ran); failed to get in much of a blow on better ground at the Festival and was pulled up before two out; looks sure to make his mark over fences and will be at his best on a testing surface. *'He needs cut in the ground.' (David Pipe, trainer)*

1363 Pedrobob (Ire)

9 ch g Pierre - Jazzelle (Roi Guillaume)

A Mullins (Ir)   Barry Connell

PLACINGS: 5111123/171310-   **RPR 143+h**

Starts	1st	2nd	3rd	4th	Win & Pl
13	7	1	2	-	£100,305

135	3/07	Chel	2m1f Cls1 Gd3 135-161 Hdl Hcap gd-sft	£39,914
	12/06	Leop	2m Hdl heavy	£8,979
	10/06	Fair	2m Hdl sft-hvy	£6,672
	9/05	Gway	2m Mdn Hdl gd-fm	£6,861
	7/05	Gway	2m NHF gd-fm	£8,576
	6/05	Tipp	2m4f NHF good	£5,391
	5/05	Rosc	2m4f NHF 5-7yo firm	£4,411

Late-maturing sort who developed into a top-notch 2m handicap hurdler last season, third in the Totesport Trophy at Newbury (20 ran, soft, beaten just over 2l by Heathcote) before winning the County Hurdle at the Cheltenham Festival, where he stayed on really well up the hill to beat Ouninpohja by 1l; had earlier won hurdle events at Fairyhouse and Leopardstown; reportedly never travelled on good to firm ground at Fairyhouse on his final start before being well beaten on the Flat in June; is lightly raced for a nine-year-old (only 13 starts over hurdles) and may improve, while he could also make a smart novice chaser.

1364 Penny Pictures (Ire)

8 b g *Theatrical - Copper Creek (Habitat)*

D Pipe   Terry Neill

PLACINGS: 2782884B33/0745-5300   RPR **137**h

Starts	1st	2nd	3rd	4th	Win & Pl
35	4	3	6	3	£54,013

125	11/04	NAbb	2m6f Cls3 100-125 Hdl Hcap good.........................£6,516
110	4/04	Bang	2m1f Cls3 89-120 Hdl Hcap good.........................£5,077
	4/03	Ludl	2m Cls4 Nov Hdl 4yo good...................................£4,186
	3/03	Bang	2m1f Cls4 Mdn Hdl 4yo soft................................£3,494

Useful sort who can always be relied upon to run well in the big, competitive handicap hurdles at 2m4f-plus, but is without a win since November 2004; recorded Racing Post Ratings in excess of 130 on three of his five starts last term, probably doing best in the Long Distance Hurdle at Haydock in May when finishing around 4¹/₂l fifth behind stablemate Abragante after failing to quicken in the closing stages (2m7¹/₂f, good, 19 ran); tried over fences in July, but likely to be switched back to hurdles for a similar campaign to last year, although the handicapper probably needs to relent before he gets his head back in front.

1365 Penzance

6 ch g *Pennekamp - Kalinka (Soviet Star)*

A King   Elite Racing Club

PLACINGS: 111/347F83/1223271-0   RPR **142**+

Starts	1st	2nd	3rd	4th	Win & Pl
18	6	3	3	1	£134,772

4/07	Sand	2m¹/₂f Cls2 Hdl gd-fm...............................£20,283
5/06	Hrfd	2m3f Cls4 Ch good.....................................£4,880
3/05	Chel	2m1f Cls1 Gd1 Hdl 4yo good....................£58,000
2/05	Kemp	2m Cls1 Nov Gd2 Hdl 4yo soft....................£16,240
1/05	Hntg	2m¹/₂f Cls4 Nov Hdl good............................£3,542
1/05	Tntn	2m1f Cls4 Nov Hdl gd-sft.............................£4,407

Former Triumph Hurdle winner who has failed to make the top bracket, but showed decent form over hurdles and fences last season; placed behind some decent sorts in novice chases (Lennon, Denman and Fair Along) before missing the middle part of the season; returned in the spring, and after a disappointing run in the Scottish Champion Hurdle, got back on the winner sheet when dead-heating with Arcalis in a decent conditions hurdle at Sandown; closed out his campaign by finishing in mid-division in the Swinton Hurdle at Haydock in May; not easy to win with, but could get into handicap chases on a decent mark.

1366 Perce Rock

5 b g *Dansili - Twilight Secret (Vaigly Great)*

T Stack (Ir)   John P McManus

PLACINGS: 14/128-   RPR **142**h

Starts	1st	2nd	3rd	4th	Win & Pl
5	2	1	-	1	£25,506

12/06	Gowr	2m Mdn Hdl 4yo heavy.................................£4,766
1/06	Leop	2m NHF 4yo heavy.......................................£8,979

Former Champion Bumper fourth who looked set to develop into a leading novice hurdler last season, but proved a shade disappointing; won smoothly on his return to action in heavy ground at Gowran in December, and probably lost nothing in defeat when 4l second to Silverburn in the Grade 1 Tolworth Hurdle at Sandown the following month (heavy ground); blotted his copybook, though, when only eighth as the 11-8 favourite for a Grade 2 at Punchestown in February, and was found to be suffering from a respiratory tract infection; wasn't seen out again, but the plan is to go chasing with him this season, with the first main target a Grade 1 novice contest over 2m1f at Leopardstown on Boxing Day; connections are hopeful that he will develop into a contender for the Arkle.

1367 Percussionist (Ire)

6 b g *Sadler's Wells - Magnificient Style (Silver Hawk)*

J H Johnson   Andrea & Graham Wylie

PLACINGS: 1P13/122-   RPR **142**+c

Starts	1st	2nd	3rd	4th	Win & Pl
7	3	2	1	-	£19,186

10/06	Weth	2m Cls4 Ch soft..£3,904
12/05	Weth	2m Cls4 Nov Hdl soft....................................£3,810
11/05	Carl	2m1f Cls4 Nov Hdl soft.................................£2,912

Yorkshire Cup winner on the Flat, and while his jumps outings have been few and far between, he has shown some smart form; tried his hand at 2m novice chases last autumn, and got off to the perfect start when beating Altay by 19l at Wetherby, although he had to survive a very untidy jump at the last; beaten under a penalty on his two subsequent outings, although not disgraced in finishing 3l second to Harmony Brig at Ayr and ¹/₂l second to Regal Heights at Kelso, both in very testing conditions that aren't exactly up his street; no natural, and not in best of form on the Flat during the summer, but has a decent engine, and while he won't be given a hard campaign, he could pick up a handicap on ground just on the easy side of good.

1368 Pevensey (Ire)

5 b g *Danehill - Champaka (Caerleon)*

J Quinn   Dum Spiro Spero

PLACINGS: 211F-   RPR **130**+h

Starts	1st	2nd	3rd	4th	Win & Pl
4	2	1	-	-	£8,571

1/07	Muss	2m Cls3 Nov Hdl gd-sft...............................£5,205
12/06	Catt	2m Cls4 Mdn Hdl gd-sft................................£2,602

Improver on the Flat who landed a major gamble when winning the Duke of Edinburgh Handicap at Royal Ascot (1m4f, soft, 14 ran) in June, and having raced just four times over hurdles, he could make giant strides in that sphere this season; pick of his form over hurdles was a cheeky success in a competitive novice event at Musselburgh in January, where he made rapid headway on the bit to lead at the last before easing to a ³/₄l victory over Modicum; fell when still going well at the seventh at Ascot the following month, and wasn't seen out again over hurdles; has progressed to a mark of 98 on the Flat since then (from 90), and similar improvement over jumps would make him a candidate for a top handicap hurdle – possibly the Ladbroke at Ascot.

1369 Philson Run (Ire)

11 b g Un Desperado - Isis (Deep Run)

N Williams   Gale Force One

PLACINGS: 1/P117/8FP21P6/84-   **RPR 135+c**

Starts		1st	2nd	3rd	4th	Win & Pl
14		4	1	-	1	£154,335
131	2/06	Newc	4m1f Cls2 111-137 Ch Hcap heavy			£46,478
123	3/05	Uttx	4m1¹/₂f Cls1 List 121-147 Ch Hcap gd-sft			£58,000
112	2/05	Chep	3m2¹/₂f Cls3 104-118 Ch Hcap soft			£5,908
	2/04	Winc	3m1¹/₂f Cls6 Am Hunt Ch good			£1,561

Handicap chaser who is suited by an extreme test of stamina; was going well on his belated reappearance in the valuable Red Square Vodka Gold Cup at Haydock in February until a blunder at the second-last ended hopes, eventually finishing 34l eighth behind Heltornic (3m4¹/₂f, heavy, 16 ran); then, as 100-1 chance, ran the race of his life on unsuitably fast ground in Grand National, keeping tabs on the leaders until weakening from the home turn to be fourth, 17l behind Silver Birch (4m4f, good, 40 ran); expected to have two chase runs - in January and February - en route to Aintree and evidently doesn't need mud, but is rising 12 and time not on his side; one for the transfer window.

1370 Point Barrow (Ire)

9 b g Arctic Lord - Credit Transfer (Kemal)

P Hughes (Ir)   Mrs P Clune Hughes

PLACINGS: 50/690061/P04B133F2-   **RPR 149+c**

Starts		1st	2nd	3rd	4th	Win & Pl
28		7	3	2	2	£231,719
136	1/07	Leop	3m 108-136 Ch Hcap sft-hvy			£43,986
125	4/06	Fair	3m5f 117-143 Ch Hcap good			£97,586
	2/05	Navn	3m Nov Gd3 Ch heavy			£18,468
	1/05	Naas	3m Nov Gd2 Ch heavy			£25,394
	12/04	Fair	3m1f Ch yld-sft			£7,786
	2/04	Leop	2m4f Mdn Hdl good			£7,786
	12/03	Leop	2m NHF 5yo soft			£5,601

Irish Grand National winner in 2006, and seemingly even better in the second half of last season; put up a tremendous weight-carrying performance to win the valuable Pierse Leopardstown Handicap Chase in January under 11st 10lb, staying on gamely in the mud to collar the consistent A New Story in the closing stages; all roads pointed to Aintree after that, and after good runs in a Graded chase and a handicap hurdle, he started co-favourite for the Grand National, but got no further than the first; second in a handicap hurdle at the Punchestown festival

on his final outing; obviously talented and very game stayer, and his first big target will be the Hennessy Cognac Gold Cup at Newbury.

1371 Poquelin (Fr)

4 bl g Lahint - Babolna (Tropular)

P Nicholls   The Stewart Family

PLACINGS: 31361-   **RPR 131+h**

Starts		1st	2nd	3rd	4th	Win & Pl
5		2	-	2	-	£21,960
	4/07	Ayr	2m Cls2 Nov Hdl 4yo gd-fm			£9,395
	12/06	Kemp	2m Cls3 Nov Hdl 3yo gd-sft			£6,263

Promising youngster, who was Group-placed on the Flat in France and should make up into a decent 2m handicap hurdler this season; opened his account at Kempton's Christmas meeting by 1¹/₂l from Liberate, who had won his previous two starts, and rounded off his campaign with a win at Ayr, where he drew clear from three out to beat English City by 7l; probably showed his best form in the Triumph Hurdle at the Cheltenham Festival, however, when sent off at 50-1 but finishing sixth, beaten 23¹/₂l by Katchit after staying on well (2m1f, good to soft, 23 ran); starts the new campaign rated 134, and difficult to imagine his trainer not being able to exploit that mark.

1372 Portland Bill (Ire)

7 ch g Zaffaran - Donegal Moss (Le Moss)

R Alner   Alvin Trowbridge

PLACINGS: 753393/1F6132-   **RPR 121+h**

Starts		1st	2nd	3rd	4th	Win & Pl
12		2	1	4	-	£12,059
	1/07	Winc	2m6f Cls4 Nov Hdl soft			£3,426
105	11/06	Winc	2m6f Cls4 82-105 Hdl Hcap good			£3,083

Useful novice hurdler last season; won twice at Wincanton (better effort when short-heading Nougat De L'Isle in January) and was still progressing in defeat on his last two starts, culminating in a 14l second to Mac Federal at Kempton in February (2m5f, soft, 9 ran); tried fences on one occasion, but fell early on at Taunton in a race won by Abragante; is bred to be suited by chasing, though, and has an official rating of 113 over fences compared to 120 over hurdles, so could well be one to climb through the lower ranks before going on to something better; stays 2m6f and likes a bit of dig in the ground.

1373 Pouvoir (Fr)

4 gr g Verglas - Policia (Policeman)

A King   Mr & Mrs R Scott

PLACINGS: F22103-   **RPR 124+h**

Starts		1st	2nd	3rd	4th	Win & Pl
6		1	2	1	-	£9,684
	1/07	Kemp	2m Cls4 Nov Hdl 4yo soft			£3,904

Useful juvenile hurdler last season, although his

form tailed off at the end of the campaign; failed to score on his first three starts (fell once, and touched off by Degas Art on another occasion), but got off the mark in the style of an improving horse at Kempton in January, travelling sweetly and overcoming a stumble at the last to win by 14l from Prince Ary; was mentioned as a Triumph Hurdle possible, but stable had Katchit for that, so he instead went for the Fred Winter Juvenile Handicap Hurdle at the Festival; started favourite, but was a spent force from 3 out and trailed in a remote tenth behind Gaspara; weak in the market and only third of five at Ayr on his final outing; probably fairly handicapped on 121, and well regarded, so could progress in 2m handicap hurdles, especially on soft ground.

1374 Powerstation (Ire)

7 b g Anshan - Mariaetta (Mandalus)

M Phillips (Ir)   Fat Frog Syndicate

PLACINGS: 1/32221424P/4322232-   **RPR 150h**

Starts	1st	2nd	3rd	4th	Win & Pl
19	2	8	4	3	£104,469
	11/05	Navn	2m4f Nov Gd3 Hdl soft		£16,160
	2/05	Clon	2m2f NHF 5-7yo sft-hvy		£3,921

Classy and ultra-consistent hurdler between 2m4f and 3m who made the frame in all seven starts last season but has not won a race since November 2005; showed by far his best form on his final outing at Punchestown in April when keeping on for second behind Refinement in the Grade 1 Champion Stayers' Hurdle, albeit in a renewal that lacked the quality of previous years (3m, good, 9 ran); also did well when third to Burntoakboy in the Coral Cup at the Cheltenham Festival (from a mark of 139), but likely to find handicaps tough to win from his new official mark of 153; highly likely to do well in Graded contests in Ireland throughout the winter, however, but could still struggle to get his head in front.

1375 Preacher Boy

8 b g Classic Cliche - Gospel (Le Bavard)

R Hodges   Hunt & Co (Bournemouth) Ltd

PLACINGS: 6/1FP/225112F3/2323-   **RPR 142+c**

Starts	1st	2nd	3rd	4th	Win & Pl
9	2	3	3	-	£63,554
1ll	12/05	Winc	2m5f Cls3 89-114 Ch Hcap good		£5,608
	12/05	Winc	2m5f Cls3 Ch gd-sft		£5,709

Lightly raced staying chaser who did well in valuable handicaps last season; finished second to Parsons Legacy in the Badger Ales Trophy at Wincanton, before another cracking effort to finish 13l third behind State Of Play in the Hennessy Cognac Gold Cup at Newbury in November (3m2½f, soft, 16 ran); looked a potential Grand National horse that day, and that view was not weakened by his staying-on 3l second to Kerstino

Two in another valuable event at Sandown in January (3m½f, soft, 12 ran); picked up an injury there and needed a course of antibiotics, and wasn't right afterwards, including when a remote third of five behind Little Brick at Wincanton in February; has only had nine starts over fences, so could still do some damage off his handicap mark of 135, 2lb higher than in the Hennessy; stays well and acts on good and soft ground, and the Welsh National at Chepstow over Christmas is his first big target.

1376 Predateur (Fr)

4 b g Nikos - Fia Rosa (Royal Charter)

P Nicholls   T Kilduff, C Donlon & L Scott-Macdonald

PLACINGS: 3144-   **RPR 131+h**

Starts	1st	2nd	3rd	4th	Win & Pl
4	1	-	1	2	£15,349
	1/07	Tntn	2m1f Cls2 Nov Hdl soft		£13,012

Promising sort for novice chases; winner on the Flat in France last August before arriving in Britain and showing plenty of promise as a hurdler; got off the mark at Taunton in January, but achieved far more when filling fourth place behind subsequent Triumph Hurdle winner Katchit in the Grade 2 Finesse Hurdle at Cheltenham in January, where he was beaten 5¼l on testing ground (2m1f, heavy, 8 ran); below that form at Wincanton on his final start in February, but sure to have done well with a summer on his back and expected to improve for the switch to fences. *'He's strengthened up considerably during his break and could be an exciting prospect now he tackle fences.' (Paul Nicholls, trainer)*

1377 Premier Dane (Ire)

5 b g Indian Danehill - Crystal Blue (Bluebird)

N Richards   Jim Ennis

PLACINGS: 2152/1308033-0   **RPR 142h**

Starts	1st	2nd	3rd	4th	Win & Pl
12	2	2	3	-	£62,299
	5/06	Kels	2m2f Cls3 Hdl gd-fm		£6,263
	2/06	Muss	2m1f Cls2 Nov Hdl 4yo gd-fm		£12,572

Smart 2m handicap hurdler; ended a spell in the doldrums by finishing a close third behind Pedrobob off a mark of 135 as a 100-1 shot in the County Hurdle at the Cheltenham Festival, appreciating the end-to-end gallop and powering up the hill; followed up with a similar effort to finish 5¼l third behind Emmpat in the Grade 2 Scottish Champion Hurdle at Ayr (2m, good to firm, 9 ran), but was a little disappointing when only tenth in the Swinton Hurdle at Haydock on his final start; goes novice chasing, and has the potential to develop into a smart chaser at around 2m on good ground, although he will need to improve a lot to be an Arkle contender.

1378 Present Glory (Ire)

8 br g *Presenting - Prudent Rose (Strong Gale)*

D Arbuthnot   George Ward

PLACINGS: 9/263/214U/13-   **RPR 117h**

Starts	1st	2nd	3rd	4th	Win & Pl
10	2	2	2	1	£15,495
108	3/07	Asct	3m Cls3 106-130 Hdl Hcap good		£6,263
	11/05	Tntn	3m¹/₂f Cls3 Nov Hdl gd-fm		£5,465

Lightly raced staying hurdler; advertised his trainer's skills by returning from a 14-month absence to win a handicap hurdle at Ascot in March, leading at the third-last and asserting in a driving finish from the last to beat Mikado by 1³/4l; was put up 7lb for that success, but wouldn't have won even off his old mark at Cheltenham the following month, albeit he was not disgraced in finishing 15l third behind Abragante in a better handicap (3m, good, 10 ran); is certainly better than that, and even at the age of eight is still open to improvement after just ten hurdle runs; could go novice chasing, but trainer intends to also qualify for him for the Pertemps Final, which was won last season by stablemate Oscar Park.

1379 Princelet (Ire)

5 b g *Desert Prince - Soeur Ti (Kaldoun)*

N Henderson   John P McManus

PLACINGS: 1F/12P-   **RPR 126+h**

Starts	1st	2nd	3rd	4th	Win & Pl
5	2	1			£11,369
111	12/06	Kemp	2m Cls3 104-127 Hdl Hcap gd-sft		£6,263
	1/06	Tntn	2m1f Cls4 Nov Hdl gd-sft		£3,578

Lightly raced hurdler who lost an eye in a fall in February 2006, but showed courage to come back last season and post improved form in a light campaign; made his return in a 2m handicap hurdle at Kempton over Christmas, where he overcame some sketchy early jumping to lead 2 out and beat Orcadian by ³/4l; unlucky not to follow up at the same venue the following month (going well when sprawling on landing at the last, and only just pipped by Romany Prince), before a disappointing effort at Aintree; bounced back from that by running some excellent races on the Flat; open to further progress over hurdles, with Newbury's Totesport Trophy an obvious possibility.

1380 Private Be

8 b g *Gunner B - Foxgrove (Kinglet)*

P Hobbs   David And Daphne Walsh

PLACINGS: 22212/120131-   **RPR 146+c**

Starts	1st	2nd	3rd	4th	Win & Pl
11	4	5	1	-	£42,872
133	4/07	Aint	2m4f Cls2 Nov 117-142 Am Ch Hcap good		£18,789
	3/07	Bang	2m1¹/₂f Cls4 Ch heavy		£3,904
122	12/06	Extr	2m1f Cls3 99-125 Hdl Hcap soft		£5,205
	12/05	Tntn	2m3¹/₂f Cls4 Nov Hdl good		£3,891

Lightly raced gelding who progressed well in his first season over fences; impressive odds-on winner over 2m1¹/₂f at Bangor in March (made all, jumped well and beat Royal Paradise by 11l), but better was to come when he again made all in a novice handicap chase at Aintree's Grand National meeting, shrugging off a blunder at the last to beat Bob Hall by 3l (2m4f, good, 10 ran); has done all his racing over fences on left-handed tracks, and may need to go that way, as he hung left at Aintree; looks on a handy official mark (raised 6lb to 139) and no surprise if a better 2m4f handicap comes his way this winter, although front-running tactics may not be easily adopted in the most competitive events; looks one for Paddy Power Gold Cup calculations (won at undulating Exeter over hurdles).

1381 Procas De Thaix (Fr)

4 ch g *Ragmar - Isca De Thaix (Cimon)*

N Henderson   Richard Green Matthew Green Nj Henderson

PLACINGS: 120-   **RPR 108b**

Starts	1st	2nd	3rd	4th	Win & Pl
3	1	1	-	-	£13,718
	1/07	Newb	1m4¹/₂f Cls5 NHF 4yo heavy		£2,056

Useful bumper horse last season; won a junior event over 1m4¹/₂f on his debut in January, beating subsequent Grade 2 runner-up Just A Thought by ³/4l; returned to the same venue in March for a valuable sales-linked contest, and posted a similar level of form when ¹/2l second to Diamond Harry, who collared him in the last 100 yards (2m1¹/₂f, soft, 21 ran); below-par tenth on much quicker ground in one of the lesser bumpers at the Punchestown festival on his final start; no world-beater, but his trainer is sure to find some suitable novice hurdle openings for him on soft ground this winter.

1382 Punjabi

4 b g *Komaite - Competa (Hernando)*

N Henderson   Raymond Tooth

PLACINGS: 11421-   **RPR 150+h**

Starts	1st	2nd	3rd	4th	Win & Pl
5	3	1	-	1	£98,699
	4/07	Punc	2m Gd1 Hdl 4yo good		£46,081
	2/07	Kemp	2m Cls1 Nov Gd2 Hdl 4yo soft		£14,825
	1/07	Ludl	2m Cls4 Nov Hdl 4yo good		£3,578

Leading juvenile hurdler last season, and likely to take a similar route to Afsoun in his second campaign; won three of his five starts, notably running away with a Grade 2 at Kempton in February, and bringing down the curtain with a battling ³/4l defeat of Financial Reward in Grade 1 company at the Punchestown festival in April; in between suffered his two defeats at the hands of champion juvenile Katchit, finishing 17l adrift in the Triumph Hurdle at Cheltenham, but getting within 4l when second at Aintree; stamina might have been an issue at the Festival (was best at 1m on the Flat), and he has thus far looked most effective over a sharper 2m; travels well, and races like the Gerry Feilden, Christmas Hurdle and Kingwell Hurdle could be right up his street. *'He's much better dropped in – he did too much at Cheltenham.' (Nicky Henderson, trainer)*

1383 Puntal (Fr)

11 b g Bering - Saveur (Ardross)

D Pipe   Terry Neill

PLACINGS: 15UU1/68/60/5527P8-7   **RPR 142+c**

Starts	1st	2nd	3rd	4th	Win & Pl
45	11	8	1	2	£278,875
142	4/04	Sand	3m5¹/₂f Cls1 Gd3 121-147 Ch Hcap gd-fm		£87,000
	1/04	Asct	2m Cls3 Nov Ch soft		£8,093
	11/03	Newb	2m4f Cls1 Nov List Ch gd-sft		£16,286
	11/03	Chel	2m4¹/₂f Cls2 Nov Ch good		£16,614
	10/03	Chel	2m Cls3 Nov Ch gd-fm		£10,603
	2/03	Kemp	2m Cls1 Nov Gd2 Hdl good		£17,400
135	7/02	MRas	2m1¹/₂f Cls2 113-135 Hdl Hcap gd-sft		£23,200
	5/02	Strf	2m¹/₂f Cls3 Nov Hdl gd-fm		£4,323
	5/02	Worc	2m Cls4 Nov Hdl good		£2,709
	5/02	Hrfd	2m1f Cls4 Nov Hdl good		£3,189
	5/02	Sthl	2m Cls3 Nov Hdl good		£3,469

Former Betfred Gold Cup winner who has slipped down the ratings to a mark of 130, having failed to score since his big day in 2004; a little temperamental now, but showed signs last season that the ability is still there, most notably in a decent handicap at Wincanton in January when given a tremendous ride and failing by only ³/₄l to catch Maletton after being carried wide round the final bend (3m1¹/₂f, soft, 11 ran); was rated 149 at his peak, so is thrown in on his very best form, and it would be no surprise should he finally nick a race this term when everything falls into place.

1384 Quartano (Ger)

4 ch g Platini - Queen's Diamond (Konigsstuhl)

C Llewellyn   Malcolm C Denmark

PLACINGS: 114-   **RPR 116+b**

Starts	1st	2nd	3rd	4th	Win & Pl
3	2	-	-	1	£12,893
	1/07	Chel	1m4f Cls1 List Nov 4yo heavy		£9,819
	12/06	Extr	1m5f Cls5 NHF 3yo soft		£2,741

Interesting novice hurdle prospect; won junior bumpers at Exeter and Cheltenham last season, and posted a particularly meritorious performance at the latter track on New Year's Day, as he gave subsequent Champion Bumper runner-up Sophocles 4lb and a 7l beating (1m4f, heavy, 15 ran); might well have gone to the Cheltenham Festival himself had he not blotted his copybook at Ascot in February, where he possibly struggled to see out the 2m and finished 29l fourth behind Sir Harry Ormesher (good to soft, 11 ran); has strengthened up over the summer, and should see out the 2m better in novice hurdles.

1385 Quatre Heures (Fr)

5 b g Vertical Speed - Macyrienne (Saint Cyrien)

W Mullins (Ir)   John Mc's Winchester Syndicate

PLACINGS: 51101/8690-   **RPR 134h**

Starts	1st	2nd	3rd	4th	Win & Pl
9	3	-	-	-	£65,935
	4/06	Punc	2m Gd1 Hdl 4yo good		£47,034
	2/06	Fair	2m Hdl 4yo yield		£7,625
	1/06	Naas	2m Mdn Hdl 4-5yo soft		£5,242

Smart juvenile hurdler in 2005/06 (won Grade 1 Champion Four Year Old Hurdle at the Punchestown festival) who had a light campaign last season; down the field in a couple of Graded events at Auteuil in May/June 2006 before ninth in the Pierse Hurdle at Leopardstown (2m, soft to heavy, 30 ran), burdened with top weight but running well enough; again had a biggish weight when soundly beaten in the Totesport Trophy at Newbury (2m1f, soft, 20 ran) and not seen afterwards; best efforts around 2m on good/soft ground.

1386 Racing Demon (Ire)

7 b g Old Vic - All Set (Electric)

Miss H Knight   Mrs T P Radford

PLACINGS: 1/21312/1117/U13F54-   **RPR 169c**

Starts	1st	2nd	3rd	4th	Win & Pl
16	7	2	2	1	£146,299
	11/06	Hntg	2m4¹/₂f Cls1 Gd2 Ch good		£43,268
	2/06	Extr	2m3¹/₂f Cls3 Nov Ch gd-sft		£7,807
	12/05	Sand	2m Cls1 Nov Gd2 Ch soft		£18,332
	11/05	Extr	2m1¹/₂f Cls3 Nov Ch gd-sft		£9,525
	1/05	Extr	2m3f Cls4 Nov Hdl gd-sft		£3,926
	11/04	Extr	2m1f Cls3 Nov Hdl gd-sft		£5,746
	3/04	Hntg	2m¹/₂f Cls6 NHF 4-6yo good		£1,876

High-class chaser over 2m4f-plus; has shown a tendency to jump to his right throughout his career, and as a result shows his best form on right-handed tracks; unseated rider as a result of an alarming swerve on his Exeter reappearance last term, but bounced back with a career-best victory in the Grade 2 Peterborough Chase at Huntingdon, where he was better at his fences and showed a good turn of foot from the last to give Thisthatandtother 5lb and a 4l beating; tackled 3m for the first time the following month in the King George VI Chase at Kempton, and probably got the trip in finishing 9¹/₄l third behind Kauto Star (good to soft, 9 ran); not as good in the second half of the campaign, falling over hurdles at Kempton, finishing a below-par fifth behind Taranis at the Cheltenham Festival, and a well-held fourth behind Neptune Collonges at the Punchestown festival; the Peterborough Chase, King George and Ascot Chase are his likely targets this season, and he should remain a force in that sort of event if his jumping improves and becomes more economical; suited by a bit of ease in the ground.

1387 Rambling Minster

9 b g *Minster Son - Howcleuch (Buckskin)*

K Reveley   The Lingdale Optimists

PLACINGS: /111740/64551/4219P-   **RPR 137+c**

Starts	1st	2nd	3rd	4th	Win & Pl
22	6	3	1	3	£66,973

124	2/07	Sand	3m¹/₂f Cls2 122-145 Ch Hcap gd-sft £25,052
	1/06	Catt	3m1¹/₂f Cls4 Ch good £3,904
119	12/04	Newc	3m Cls2 99-119 Hdl Hcap good £13,468
112	11/04	Newc	3m Cls3 94-120 Hdl Hcap good £5,138
	5/04	Weth	2m4¹/₂f Cls3 Nov Hdl gd-sft £5,119
	11/03	Hexm	2m¹/₂f Cls6 NHF 4-6yo good £1,904

Unexposed chaser who has the ability to figure in this season's top staying handicaps if he can rediscover his best form from last term; won the Agfa Diamond Handicap Chase at Sandown in February on just his fourth start over fences, powering up the finishing hill to beat Kelami by ³/₄l; could manage only ninth next time when well backed for the William Hill Trophy at the Cheltenham Festival (3m1¹/₂f, good to soft, 23 ran), although a bad mistake at the first didn't help his cause, and he was stopped in his tracks when staying on two out; ran a stinker in the Scottish National on his final outing, but the ground there was far too quick; potentially well treated off a chase mark in the low 130s.

1388 Raslan

4 b g *Lomitas - Rosia (Mr Prospector)*

D Pipe   D J Reid

PLACINGS: 211202-18   **RPR 127+h**

Starts	1st	2nd	3rd	4th	Win & Pl
8	3	3			£15,263

125	5/07	Extr	3m¹/₂f Cls3 98-125 Hdl Hcap gd-fm £5,530
	1/07	Winc	2m Cls4 Nov Hdl 4yo soft £3,426
	12/06	Font	2m2¹/₂f Cls5 Mdn Hdl 3yo gd-sft £2,602

Dual winner on the Flat who took to hurdles well last season between 2m and 3m and is likely to shape into a decent handicapper; only twice finished out of the first two from eight starts (as a 25-1 shot in the Ballymore Properties Novices' Hurdle at Cheltenham and when tried over 3m3f on his final start) and showed his best form when scoring over 3m1/2f at Exeter in May by 4l from Sultan Fontenaille; has winning form on soft and quick ground, and his ability to also handle a variety of trips is sure to stand him in good stead.

1389 Raven's Run (Ire)

5 b g *Sea Raven - Sandy Run (Deep Run)*

M Cunningham (Ir)   Michael J Heaslip

PLACINGS: 51/1510-   **RPR 122+b**

Starts	1st	2nd	3rd	4th	Win & Pl
4	2	-	-	-	£11,768

	2/07	Naas	2m NHF 4-7yo sft-hvy £7,003
	12/06	Gowr	2m NHF 4yo heavy £4,766

Smart bumper performer who looks sure to do well in novice hurdles over 2m4f-3m; pick of his form

last term was an 8l defeat of subsequent Grade 1 winner Mick The Man in a bumper at Naas in February, making all and having his rivals in trouble turning for home, and in no danger from 2f out (2m, soft to heavy, 9 ran); took his chance in the Champion Bumper at the Cheltenham Festival the following month, but was never better than midfield on the quicker ground, and finished around 19l 14th behind Cork All Star; regarded as big and backward by his trainer, but said to have strengthened over the summer, and will be an exciting prospect for above-average novice hurdles given a trip. *'He won a point-to-point over 2m4f, and he'll need at least that over hurdles. He's a good horse with a bright future.' (Michael Cunningham, trainer)*

1390 Rebel Rhythm

8 b g *Robellino - Celt Song (Unfuwain)*

Mrs S Smith   The Fees R Us Syndicate

PLACINGS: 3/121713F/2F21341/6-

Starts	1st	2nd	3rd	4th	Win & Pl
18	6	3	4	1	£49,057

	4/06	MRas	2m4f Cls3 Nov Ch soft £6,506
	12/05	Weth	3m1f Cls4 Ch soft £4,279
	2/05	Bang	2m1f Cls4 Nov Hdl 4-7yo gd-sft £4,901
	12/04	Hayd	2m4f Cls3 Nov Hdl 4-7yo heavy £5,883
	11/04	Hayd	2m Cls3 Nov Hdl 4-7yo gd-sft...........................£5,502
	3/04	Weth	2m Cls6 NHF 4-6yo gd-sft.................................£2,037

Useful novice chaser in 2005/06, but picked up a leg injury that ruled him out of last season; pick of the form he showed two seasons ago suggests he could be well handicapped on a mark of 135, as in November 2005 he was beaten just 2¹/₂l by last season's Gold Cup third Turpin Green off level weights in a novice chase at Carlisle (2m4f, soft, 12 ran), while in April 2006 he beat Iron Man by 28l over the same trip at Market Rasen; seems to like soft ground and more effective in small fields, as he likes to dominate the opposition from the front; reportedly thriving at home and should have gone back into training in September, so should resume his career before Christmas; will be campaigned in handicap chases over 2m4f-plus.

1391 Redemption

12 b g *Sanglamore - Ypha (Lyphard)*

N Twiston-Davies   Michael Purtill

PLACINGS: 0/2F8648U07/1P488P0-   **RPR 149+h**

Starts	1st	2nd	3rd	4th	Win & Pl
60	9	4	4	4	£139,818

	10/06	Weth	3m1f Cls1 Gd2 Hdl soft £22,808
123	1/04	Chel	2m5¹/₂f Cls2 122-148 Hdl Hcap good £15,181
131	11/03	Newb	2m4f Cls2 122-145 Ch Hcap gd-sft...................£23,200
138	11/01	Asct	2m Cls2 125-138 Ch Hcap gd-fm £13,380
127	10/01	Weth	2m4¹/₂f Cls2 113-132 Ch Hcap good £9,064
	1/01	Weth	2m Cls4 Nov Ch heavy £3,003
	1/01	Plum	2m Cls4 Nov Ch gd-sft......................................£2,964
	2/00	Ludl	2m Cls4 Nov Hdl good £2,352
	12/99	Weth	2m Cls3 Nov Hdl gd-sft.....................................£3,461

Notorious hurdler/chaser who has never enjoyed the best of luck, crashing out of big races several times when holding a winning chance, and time is no longer on his side; ran an absolute blinder on his reappearance in a Grade 2 hurdle over 3m1f at Wetherby last October, defying a blunder at the last to beat My Way De Solzen by 6l when probably the fittest in the field; decent fourth behind Inglis Drever at Newbury a couple of starts later, but season fell apart thereafter as he switched unsuccessfully between hurdles and chases, albeit in very smart handicap and Graded company; extremely well handicapped over fences on his best form, but first time out is probably the time to catch him; one for optimists.

1392 Refinement (Ire)

8 b m Oscar - Maneree (Mandalus)

J O'Neill   Michael Tabor

PLACINGS: 1111131P/73413P2031-   **RPR 151h**

Starts		1st	2nd	3rd	4th	Win & Pl
25		12	2	4	3	£266,137
	4/07	Punc	3m Gd1 Hdl good			£83,784
145	12/06	Kemp	3m¹/₂f Cls2 119-145 Hdl Hcap gd-sft			£12,526
131	4/06	Aint	3m¹/₂f Cls1 List 125-145 Hdl Hcap gd-sft			£28,510
	2/06	Hntg	2m4¹/₂f Cls2 Nov Hdl sft			£13,012
123	1/06	Sand	2m4¹/₂f Cls3 114-124 Hdl Hcap soft			£9,395
	11/05	Winc	2m Cls3 Nov Hdl 4-6yo good			£6,916
	10/05	Towc	2m Cls3 Nov Hdl good			£4,459
	10/05	Uttx	2m Cls4 Nov Hdl 4-6yo gd-sft			£3,304
	4/05	Punc	2m Gd1 NHF yld-sft			£46,170
	11/04	Aint	2m1f Cls6 NHF 4-6yo soft			£6,754
	12/03	Asct	2m¹/₂f Cls6 NHF 4-6yo soft			£7,231
	10/03	Bang	2m1f Cls6 NHF 4-6yo soft			£1,673

Tough staying mare who was in and out of form last season but ended on a high note that has persuaded connections to put her broodmare career on hold; won Punchestown's Champion Bumper in 2005 and returned to the track in April to win the Grade 1 Champion Stayers' Hurdle, a victory that helped to erase the memory of some earlier baffling performances; had the likes of Essex, Brave Inca and Sky's The Limit behind that day, but the fact that the Racing Post Rating she earned was below what she had achieved in defeat in a Listed handicap at Aintree on her previous start suggests her rivals in Ireland were not at their best after a long campaign; now rated 152 and is one of those who will struggle with big weights in handicaps or have to play second fiddle to better horses in Pattern races.

1393 Regal Heights (Ire)

6 b g Grand Plaisir - Regal Hostess (King's Ride)

D McCain   Mrs Janet Heler

PLACINGS: 31/4511337/35212114-   **RPR 146+c**

Starts		1st	2nd	3rd	4th	Win & Pl
17		6	2	4	2	£60,172
	3/07	Kels	2m1f Cls2 Nov Ch heavy			£11,711
132	2/07	Hayd	2m Cls2 121-147 Ch Hcap heavy			£16,265
	1/07	Newc	2m¹/₂f Cls4 Ch soft			£4,754
	2/06	Carl	2m1f Cls4 Nov Hdl soft			£3,083
	1/06	Ayr	2m Cls4 Mdn Hdl heavy			£4,111
	4/05	Towc	2m Cls6 Mdn NHF 4-6yo gd-sft			£3,122

Three-time winner in his first season over fences,

and looks one for handicaps over 2m-2m4f; regularly crossed swords with some smart novices, including when winning in novice company at Newcastle (beat King Revo by 2¹/₂l) and Kelso (beat Percussionist by ¹/₂l); gained his third success in a handicap chase at Haydock in February, when he stayed on grimly in heavy conditions to beat Calatagan by 5l (2m, 5 ran); stepped up to Grade 1 company on his final outing at the Punchestown festival, and not disgraced in finishing fourth behind One Cool Cookie (2m4f, good, 11 ran); better in soft ground, and might have enough improvement to defy a mark of 142 this winter.

1394 Reveillez

8 gr g First Trump - Amalancher (Alleged)

J Fanshawe   John P McManus

PLACINGS: 116/2211/F8612-   **RPR 160+c**

Starts		1st	2nd	3rd	4th	Win & Pl
12		5	3	-	-	£136,046
145	4/07	Aint	3m1f Cls2 125-149 Ch Hcap good			£31,315
133	3/06	Chel	2m5f Cls1 Nov List 126-146 Ch Hcap good			£45,616
	2/06	Folk	2m5f Cls3 Ch gd-sft			£4,554
	1/05	Donc	2m3¹/₂f Cls4 Nov Hdl good			£3,757
	11/04	Wind	2m Cls2 Nov Hdl gd-sft			£10,374

High-class staying handicap chaser; didn't hit top form until the spring last season, finishing sixth in the Racing Post Plate at Cheltenham before improving for a step up to 3m1f at Aintree, where he came from off the pace to lead on the bit two out and galloped on well to beat Lankawi and Lacdoudal by 7l and 2¹/₂l (good, 18 ran); started favourite for the Betfred Gold Cup at Sandown just over a fortnight later, but didn't jump with any great fluency, and in the circumstances did well to finish 3l second to the front-running Hot Weld (3m5¹/₂f, good to firm, 10 ran); was 11lb well in there, so will find life tougher off his revised mark this term, but worth a crack at Graded chases now, and not inconceivable that he could make up into a King George/Gold Cup horse; likes good ground.

1395 Rindoon (Ire)

5 b g Beneficial - Upton Lodge (Clearly Bust)

E Sheehy (Ir)   Pearse Gately

PLACINGS: 6221102d-   **RPR 131h**

Starts		1st	2nd	3rd	4th	Win & Pl
7		2	2	1	-	£24,039
	2/07	Limk	2m Nov Hdl yld-sft			£8,871
	1/07	Thur	2m Mdn Hdl 4-5yo soft			£3,969

Explosive front-running novice hurdler last season; burned his way to victories at Thurles and Limerick, but found it impossible to dominate in the Supreme Novices' Hurdle, and finished a remote 20th; better than that, though, as he showed when running a remarkable race in a Grade 1 at the Punchestown festival (2m, good, 9 ran), where he set off at a frenetic pace and was worn down only on the run-in by Clopf, plugging on to finish just 1½l second (relegated to third); plan now is to go chasing, and if he is as bold over his fences as he was over hurdles, connections have a lot to look forward to. *'He's blessed with loads of natural speed and will handle any type of ground.' (Dusty Sheehy, trainer)*

1396 Ringaroses

6 b g Karinga Bay - Rose Ravine (Deep Run)

Miss H Knight   Mrs Nicholas Jones & Martin Broughton

PLACINGS: 16/11-   RPR **132**+h

Starts	1st	2nd	3rd	4th	Win & Pl
4	-	-	-	-	£13,331
	12/06	Asct	2m3¹/₂f Cls3 Nov Hdl gd-sft		£6,506
	11/06	Kemp	2m5f Cls4 Nov Hdl good		£3,904
	2/06	Ling	2m Cls6 NHF 4-6yo stand		£1,713
	12/05	Ludl	2m Cls6 NHF 4-6yo good		£2,453

Unbeaten hurdler from a high-class staying family (half-brother to Frosty Canyon and Red Cardinal, out of Stayers' Hurdle winner Rose Ravine); looked a contender for Cheltenham Festival novice hurdle honours when winning twice before the turn of the year, beating Nudge And Nurdle by 1½l at Kempton, and Breathing Fire by 3½l at Ascot; Ballymore Properties Hurdle appeared to be his intended target, but he was forced to miss a couple of intended prep races because of heavy ground, and in the end never made the Festival; won't be back in until December, so is one for the second half of the season, when he will be campaigned in Graded hurdle races.

1397 River City (Ire)

10 b g Norwich - Shuil Na Lee (Phardante)

N Chance   Mrs S Rowley-Williams

PLACINGS: 1111136/2UP1/343345-   RPR **162**+c

Starts	1st	2nd	3rd	4th	Win & Pl
27	10	2	4	3	£192,789
	4/06	Sand	2m Cls1 Gd2 Ch gd-fm		£57,020
	10/04	Aint	2m Cls1 Nov List Ch soft		£13,073
	8/04	NAbb	2m¹/₂f Cls3 Nov Ch gd-sft		£7,376
	8/04	NAbb	2m¹/₂f Cls3 Nov Ch gd-fm		£6,458
	7/04	Strf	2m1¹/₂f Cls3 Nov Ch good		£5,395
	7/04	Worc	2m Cls4 Nov Ch good		£4,105
116	4/04	Chep	2m¹/₂f Cls3 98-124 Hdl Hcap good		£5,639
	1/03	Donc	2m¹/₂f Cls4 Nov Hdl gd-sft		£3,582
	11/02	NAbb	2m1f Cls4 Nov Hdl soft		£3,613
	4/02	Asct	2m¹/₂f Cls6 NHF 4-6yo gd-fm		£2,709

Classy 2m chaser whose biggest win came in the Grade 2 Celebration Chase at Sandown in April 2006; didn't win last season, but gained plenty of prize-money in Grade 1 chases in Britain and Ireland; posted his best form when 6½l third behind Voy Por Ustedes in the Champion Chase at the Cheltenham Festival in March, battling on gamely up the hill (2m, good to soft, 10 ran); also in the frame behind Monet's Garden in the Ascot Chase, and when fourth behind Mansony at the Punchestown festival; firmly established now as just below the top level, but capable of picking up

a decent prize or two when the real stars of the division stay at home (official mark of 160 rules out handicaps); likes a sound surface. *'He travels and jumps so well, he'll always have a chance of picking up prize-money in something like the Champion Chase.' (Noel Chance, trainer)*

1398 Roll Along (Ire)

7 b g Carroll House - Callmartel (Montelimar)

C Llewellyn   Bryan & Philippa Burrough

PLACINGS: 1/11/1130-   RPR **132**+h

Starts	1st	2nd	3rd	4th	Win & Pl
7	5	-	1		£36,913
	11/06	Uttx	2m Cls2 Nov Hdl gd-sft		£12,700
	10/06	Chel	2m¹/₂f Cls3 Mdn Hdl gd-sft		£6,263
	1/06	Wwck	2m Cls1 List NHF 4-6yo soft		£8,927
	10/05	Fknm	2m Cls6 NHF 4-6yo good		£2,906
	10/04	Font	2m2¹/₂f Cls6 NHF 4-6yo gd-sft		£1,834

Useful hurdler who is set to try his hand at chasing this season; won his first five starts, adding to three bumper success with novice hurdle wins at Cheltenham (beat Ofarel D'Airy by 1½l) and Uttoxeter (in workmanlike fashion at odds of 1-4) last autumn; stepped up in class for the Grade 1 Challow Hurdle at Newbury in December, and while he lost his unbeaten tag, he was not far off his best in finishing 26l third behind top-notcher Wichita Lineman (2m5f, good to soft, 8 ran); was given a break until lining up in handicap company at Aintree's Grand National meeting, but trailed in a long last of 20 finishers behind Two Miles West (2m4f, good); likely to be given a try in another handicap hurdle in the autumn, but expected to switch to fences sooner rather than later. *'He wants decent ground.' (Carl Llewellyn, trainer)*

1399 Rosaker (USA)

10 b g Pleasant Tap - Rose Crescent (Nijinsky)

N Meade (Ir)   High Street Ceathar Syndicate

PLACINGS: 0/323P36/621/124524-   RPR **151**+h

Starts	1st	2nd	3rd	4th	Win & Pl
25	7	5	3	2	£182,698
	11/06	Navn	2m4f Gd2 Hdl yld-sft		£22,448
	12/05	Leop	3m Gd2 Hdl yld-sft		£23,085
	2/04	Navn	3m Gd2 Hdl soft		£22,923
	1/04	Gowr	3m Gd3 Hdl soft		£18,310
	11/03	Navn	2m4f Gd2 Hdl gd-fm		£21,104
	2/03	Naas	2m4f Nov Gd2 Hdl yield		£19,416
	12/02	Fair	2m Mdn Hdl 5-6yo soft		£5,503

Tough staying hurdler; looked as good as ever on his return from almost a year off at Navan last November, where he made most of the running in a Grade 2 contest and ran on gamely to beat Emotional Moment by 6l (2m4f, yielding to soft, 10 ran); ran a blinder in Grade 1 company next time when going down by just ³/₄l to Brave Inca in the Hatton's Grace Hurdle, before finishing in the money in a string of Irish Grade 2/3 hurdle races, behind the likes of Celestial Wave, Sweet Kiln and

Essex; grand old campaigner who should again make his presence felt in decent company when the ground is riding soft; stays 3m.

1400 Royal Auclair (Fr)

10 ch g Garde Royale - Carmonera (Carmont)

P Nicholls   Clive D Smith

PLACINGS: 42F/51529F00/65736F-   RPR **157+c**

Starts	1st	2nd	3rd	4th	Win & Pl
45	8	6	6	6	£477,706
155	12/05	Chel	3m1¹/₂f Cls1 List 129-155 Ch Hcap gd-sft		£28,510
145	11/04	Winc	3m1¹/₂f Cls1 List 127-145 Ch Hcap good		£46,400
	3/02	Chel	2m5f Cls1 Gd2 Ch good		£42,000
138	1/02	Chel	2m5f Cls2 Nov 111-138 Ch Hcap heavy		£12,721
	12/01	Extr	2m1¹/₂f Cls3 Nov Ch gd-sft		£8,515
	2/01	Sand	2m1¹/₂f Cls3 Nov Hdl 4yo heavy		£4,271
	12/00	Engh	2m1¹/₂f Hdl 3yo heavy		£10,567
	11/00	Engh	2m1¹/₂f Hdl 3yo heavy		£9,606

Talented and classy staying chaser who often runs well in top company but is difficult to win with and hasn't scored for nearly two years; generally below the peak of his powers in six starts last season, with the one stand-out run coming at Newbury in February when chasing home Kauto Star and L'Ami as a 40-1 shot in the Aon Chase (3m, soft, 6 ran); failed to sparkle elsewhere and ended the campaign with a fall in the Grand National, a race in which he finished second in 2005; back down to a mark of 147 having raced as high as 161, so well handicapped on the best of his form and might be interesting in a race like the Welsh National.

1401 Royal Rosa (Fr)

8 ch g Garde Royale - Crystalza (Crystal Palace)

J H Johnson   Andrea & Graham Wylie

PLACINGS: 61/112112/73/213P0P-   RPR **140+c**

Starts	1st	2nd	3rd	4th	Win & Pl
17	7	3	2	-	£84,008
	12/06	Weth	2m4¹/₂f Cls2 Nov Ch soft		£13,451
	2/04	Hayd	2m7¹/₂f Cls1 Nov Gd2 Hdl good		£17,850
	1/04	Ayr	2m4f Cls4 Nov Hdl 4-7yo heavy		£3,562
	12/03	Hexm	3m Cls4 Nov Hdl soft		£2,344
	4/03	Punc	2m Gd1 NHF good		£12,662
	3/03	Sand	2m1¹/₂f Cls6 NHF 4-6yo heavy		£2,384
	12/02	Newb	1m4¹/₂f Cls6 NHF 3-4yo good		£2,807

Talented but injury-prone jumper who was disappointing when making his long-awaited switch to fences last winter; started out brightly enough, finishing second to According To John at Carlisle (2m4f, heavy, 9 ran) before beating subsequent Cheltenham Festival winner L'Antartique by 9l at Wetherby (2m5f, soft, 3 ran); everything went pear-shaped afterwards, however, as he failed to complete twice and finished a remote 11th of 14 finishers behind Denman in the Royal & SunAlliance Chase; light at the end of the tunnel is his official chase mark of 130 (L'Antartique won at the Festival off 133), and no doubt he can win decent handicaps off that sort of rating if returning to his best; stays 3m and suited by soft ground.

1402 Royals Darling (Ger)

5 ch g Kallisto - Royal Rivalry (Sir Ivor)

N Henderson   Paul Green

PLACINGS: 1432201/2005-   RPR **140h**

Starts	1st	2nd	3rd	4th	Win & Pl
11	2	3	1	1	£32,381
	4/06	Ayr	2m Cls2 Nov Hdl 4yo good		£9,395
	7/05	Aabe	2m1f Hdl 3yo good		£1,844

Well-regarded hurdler who was twice runner-up to Detroit City as a juvenile in January/February 2006, but has been something of a disappointment since; started last season well, finishing 1l second to Verasi in the Lanzarote Hurdle at Kempton in January (2m5f, soft, 17 ran); found life a real struggle afterwards, though, finishing well down the field in a Grade 3 handicap at Sandown and the Coral Cup at Cheltenham, and trailing in a long last of five finishers when found an easier opportunity at Ayr in April; set to go chasing this season, and connections will be hoping that the new challenge brings out on the track what they have obviously seen at home; likes good ground.

1403 Rustarix (Fr)

6 b g Housamix - Star Of Russia (Soviet Star)

A King   Mrs R J Skan

PLACINGS: 2/73FP/44F84432/12-   RPR **127h**

Starts	1st	2nd	3rd	4th	Win & Pl
16	1	3	2	4	£30,788
	3/07	Tntn	2m3¹/₂f Cls3 Nov Hdl soft		£5,855

Ex-French hurdler who returned from 16 months off the track in the spring and hinted that he was still on the upgrade; won a 2m4f novice hurdle first time back at Taunton in March, where he led on the bit 2 out and had enough in hand to brush off a blunder at the last and beat Thirty Five Black by 3l (well backed beforehand); faced a stiffer test at Cheltenham in April, but posted improved form to finish 9l second to the classy My Turn Now at level weights (2m5¹/₂f, good, 9 ran); far from exposed, and the best should still be to come, whether it be over hurdles or fences; likely to want ease in the ground.

1404 Saintsaire (Fr)

8 b g Apeldoorn - Pro Wonder (The Wonder)

P Nicholls   The Stewart Family

PLACINGS: /33773/1P/214F4/165-   RPR **142+c**

Starts	1st	2nd	3rd	4th	Win & Pl
19	4	1	4	2	£69,605
127	11/06	Newb	2m1f Cls2 118-142 Ch Hcap soft		£21,991
117	12/05	Wind	2m4f Cls3 102-117 Ch Hcap gd-sft		£6,857
	3/05	Bang	2m1¹/₂f Cls3 Nov Ch good		£8,663
	12/02	Newb	2m1¹/₂f Cls3 Nov Hdl 3yo good		£4,095

Formerly a smart handicap chaser for Nicky Henderson, but found improvement for his current handler last season following a wind operation and is always likely to be dangerous in decent events between 2m and 2m4f; scored first time out in a decent little contest at Newbury last November, keeping on well once he had hit the front four out to beat Bambi De L'Orme by 1³/4l; raised 7lb for that success and failed to strike on either of his two subsequent outings (including when disappointing on quick ground over 2m4f on his final start), but still 6lb lower than he is rated over hurdles, and should be placed to win again.

1405 Schiehallion (Ire)

5 b g Pistolet Bleu - Lessons Lass (Doyoun)

N Henderson   Mr & Mrs Sandy Orr

PLACINGS: 14-   **RPR 112+b**

Starts	1st	2nd	3rd	4th	Win & Pl
2	1	-	-	1	£4,142
	11/06	Newb	2m¹/₂f Cls4 NHF 4yo heavy		£3,904

Useful novice hurdle prospect; made a winning debut last November in a heavy-ground bumper at Newbury, beating Jass by 5l, with next-time-out winners in third, fourth and sixth; started odds-on for a similar contest over the same course and distance the following month, but was up against it giving weight to the likes of Crocodiles Rock and Mendo, and could manage only a 26l fourth behind the former (soft, 22 ran); could be a force in decent novice hurdles when the mud is flying.

1406 Schindler's Gold (Ire)

5 ch g Oscar Schindler - Saraemma (Wolver Hollow)

T Taaffe (Ir)   D Cox

PLACINGS: 3-   **RPR 104b**

Starts	1st	2nd	3rd	4th	Win & Pl
1	-	-	1	-	£1,229

From the same family as The Illiad and evidently well regarded at home, as he made his debut in a hot Punchestown festival bumper alongside 12 previous winners; up with the leaders at halfway and stayed on gamely through the closing stages to be third, beaten 1l behind Meadow Vale and Arctic Tour, both previous scorers (2m, good, 24 ran); bumper win looks a formality and success over hurdles highly likely.

1407 Schindlers Hunt (Ire)

7 ch g Oscar Schindler - Snipe Hunt (Stalker)

D Hughes (Ir)   Slaneyville Syndicate

PLACINGS: 74212231/51211F25-   **RPR 152+c**

Starts	1st	2nd	3rd	4th	Win & Pl
16	5	5	1	1	£137,332
1/07	Leop	2m1f Nov Gd1 Ch soft			£35,135
12/06	Leop	2m1f Nov Gd1 Ch sft-hvy			£44,828
11/06	Punc	2m Ch soft			£5,957
3/06	Leop	2m Mdn Hdl yield			£8,578
11/05	Gowr	2m NHF 4-5yo yield			£4,901

Soft-ground performer who won two of Ireland's biggest novice chases last season; streaked home

in the Grade 1 Durkan New Homes Novice Chase at Leopardstown over Christmas, beating Hear The Echo by 10l (2m1f, soft to heavy, 9 ran) before following up over the same course and distance the following month in the Baileys Arkle Novice Chase, where he led two out and stayed on strongly to beat King Johns Castle by 2l (2m1f, soft, 7 ran); ran a disappointing race next time at Naas (eventually fell), but back to his best in the Powers Gold Cup at Fairyhouse in April, where he held every chance at the last but found One Cool Cookie 1¹/2l too strong (2m4f, good, 11 ran); would surely have gone close back over 2m at the Punchestown festival, but made a desperate hash of the second-last when holding every chance, and was an eased-down fifth behind Another Promise; clearly has stacks of ability, and will be an interesting contender for top handicaps and Graded chases.

1408 Scotsirish (Ire)

6 b g Zaffaran - Serjitak (Saher)

W Mullins (Ir)   Double R Stables Llp Syndicate

PLACINGS: 1/4/6181-   **RPR 134+h**

Starts	1st	2nd	3rd	4th	Win & Pl
5	2	-	-	1	£20,015
4/07	Fair	2m Hdl gd-fm			£13,196
1/07	Leop	2m Mdn Hdl soft			£6,536

Decent novice hurdler last season who wasn't far shy of the best, and should make his mark in the better novice chases; stepped up on hurdling debut to win comfortably in a maiden event at Leopardstown before being sent off 12-1 for the Ballymore Properties Novices' Hurdle at the Cheltenham Festival (2m5f, good to soft, 15 ran), and didn't run too badly considering he was taking a huge step up in class, finishing eighth (probably raced too keen early on); resumed winning ways when registering his best performance at Fairyhouse on good to firm ground in open company, clear last and eased close home to prevail by a snug 4l from Heavenly Blues; former point-to-point winner, so every chance he'll take to fences, and if he does, he'll be an exciting prospect.

1409 See You Sometime

12 b g Sharp Deal - Shepani (New Member)

J W Mullins   J A G Meaden

PLACINGS: 5532/45014864/22158-   **RPR 150+c**

Starts	1st	2nd	3rd	4th	Win & Pl
43	10	6	7	6	£258,145
138	10/06	Asct	3m Cls2 130-156 Ch Hcap gd-fm		£61,970
	2/06	Winc	3m1¹/₂f Cls1 Gd2 Ch good		£23,076
	12/04	Wind	2m4f Cls1 Nov Gd2 Ch soft		£21,175
	11/04	Font	2m2f Cls4 Ch good		£4,789
136	4/03	Chel	2m5¹/₂f Cls2 121-146 Hdl Hcap good		£11,194
131	2/03	Winc	2m6f Cls3 109-134 Hdl Hcap gd-sft		£16,008
	12/01	Newb	2m5f Cls2 Hdl gd-sft		£9,994
118	11/01	Chel	2m5f Cls3 107-131 Hdl Hcap good		£18,119
	6/01	Strf	2m6¹/₂f Cls3 Nov Hdl gd-fm		£3,796
97	5/01	Folk	2m4¹/₂f Cls4 Nov 73-97 Hdl Hcap gd-fm		£2,037

Old-timer who showed the best form of his life in

Silver Birch en route to a surprise victory in the Grand National

Twist Magic puts in another fine leap before winning at Aintree

A rare smile from Tony McCoy after Exotic Dancer's win in the Betfair Bowl

A fine leap from Monet's Garden during the Melling Chase at Aintree

Aces Four is about to win his third novice chase of the season

Al Eile lands his second Aintree Hurdle, and his third win in all at the track

valuable handicap chase company last autumn before his campaign was cut short by injury; runner-up at Kempton before a career-best effort to win the United House Gold Cup Handicap Chase at Ascot last October, leading his rivals a merry dance and coasting home 7l clear from Zabenz; loved the fast ground that day, but softer conditions were against him on his next two starts back at the Berkshire track, although there was no disgrace in finishing fifth to Demi Beau over an inadequate 2m1f; trainer insists he will be back again at the age of 13 later this season, but time may well be catching up with him, and he looks one for the transfer window for those tempted by his credentials. *'He won't race until next February/March.'* *(Seamus Mullins, trainer)*

1410 Self Respect (USA)

5 b g Lear Fan - Cap Of Dignity (Shirley Heights)

A King   Sir Robert Ogden

PLACINGS: 212P31-   **RPR 125+h**

Starts	1st	2nd	3rd	4th	Win & Pl
6	2	2	1	-	£23,285
4/07	MRas	2m3¹/₂f Cls4 Nov Hdl good			£2,928
10/06	Kemp	2m Cls1 Nov List Hdl good			£10,264

Useful novice hurdler last season, and looks open to improvement; boasted some smart form in the early part of the campaign, beating Moon Over Miami by 7l on good ground at Kempton, and finishing a very creditable 6l second to Kicks For Free in another Listed event at Haydock in November (2m, good to soft, 5 ran); flopped in heavy ground when fancied for a valuable Sandown handicap hurdle in December, and was given a mid-season break; returned four months later at Cheltenham (third of four, jumping out to his right throughout), but bounced back and ended on a high note his first try over 2m4f at Market Rasen, dotting up by 11l from Than Man Fox; at the right end of the weights to continue his progress in handicaps in his second season over hurdles; suited by good ground. *'He's got to go right-handed.'* *(Noel Williams, assistant trainer)*

1411 Seven Is My Number (Ire)

5 b g Pistolet Bleu - Waterloo Ball (Where To Dance)

D Pipe   D A Johnson

PLACINGS: 10-   **RPR 117+b**

Starts	1st	2nd	3rd	4th	Win & Pl
2	1	-	-	-	£11,404
12/06	Asct	2m Cls1 Gd2 NHF 4-6yo gd-sft			£11,404

Promising sort for 2m novice hurdles; made a deep and lasting impression on his debut in an Ascot bumper last December, where he was always going well and had no trouble in coming home 3¹/₂l in front of previous winner Earth Planet, a performance that saw him being discussed as a

likely type for the Champion Bumper; something was clearly awry next time, though, when he trailed home last of ten in a Grade 2 bumper at Newbury in which a repeat of his debut form would have seen him in the shake-up; has to bounce back from that disappointment, but expected to figure prominently in the 2m hurdling ranks. *'He has loads of potential and we have high expectations of him this season.'* *(David Pipe, trainer)*

1412 Shatabdi (Ire)

5 b/br m Mtoto - Violet Express (Cadoudal)

N Henderson   Robert Waley-Cohen

PLACINGS: 72421F138-   **RPR 136h**

Starts	1st	2nd	3rd	4th	Win & Pl
9	2	2	1	1	£102,731
2/07	Kemp	2m Cls1 Nov Gd2 Hdl soft			£14,999
2/07	Plum	2m Cls4 Nov Hdl heavy			£3,083

Ex-French mare who did well in novice hurdles for her new stable last season; raced three times in February, dotting up at Plumpton, falling at Ascot, but then enjoying her finest hour when winning the Grade 2 Dovecote Novices' Hurdle at Kempton, where she led at the 4th, drew clear from 2 out and beat subsequent winners Mendo and Oslot by 9l and 1¹/₄l (2m, soft, 5 ran); missed Cheltenham to be kept back for Aintree, and ran another cracker in a Listed handicap at the Merseyside venue, where she was left in the lead by the last-flight fall of Special Envoy, but was worn down in the shadow of the post by Two Miles West and Gods Token (2m4f, good, 22 ran); Scottish Champion Hurdle probably came too soon afterwards, and she finished last; could go on to better things over hurdles or fences.

1413 Sher Beau (Ire)

8 b g Beau Sher - Welsh Ana (Welsh Term)

P Fenton (Ir)   Noel Morrissey

PLACINGS: 2/1111/74172/33B66-F   **RPR 155c**

Starts	1st	2nd	3rd	4th	Win & Pl
14	4	1	2	1	£66,677
1/06	Gowr	2m4f Nov Ch gd-yld			£9,653
3/05	Fair	2m4f Nov Gd2 Hdl soft			£22,162
1/05	Naas	2m3f Hdl heavy			£11,543
11/04	Thur	2m2f Hdl yield			£5,839

Talented chaser whose trainer reported him to be more healthy during the summer than at any point in a winless campaign last term; posted his best RPR when 11¹/₂l third behind In Compliance and War Of Attrition in the Grade 1 John Durkan Memorial Chase at Punchestown in December, keeping on at the same pace after briefly leading four out (2m4f, heavy, 8 ran); wasn't the same afterwards (disappointing when a gambled-on favourite for the Paddy Power Chase over Christmas), but unlucky not to win his final start in a minor chase at Killarney in May, where he was in command and clear of Jim when falling at the last (2m4f, good, 8 ran); perfectly capable of challenging for Graded chases when on song; best at around 2m4f.

1414 Ship's Hill (Ire)

6 b g Oscar - Ballykea (Montelimar)

N Henderson   A Taylor

PLACINGS: 23/131-   RPR **119+h**

Starts	1st	2nd	3rd	4th	Win & Pl
5	2	1	2	-	£8,326

| 1/07 | Fknm | 2m Cls4 Nov Hdl gd-sft | £3,383 |
| 10/06 | Fknm | 2m Cls4 NHF 4-6yo good | £3,426 |

Promising young jumper who won twice over 2m at Fakenham in a light campaign last season; beat the classy My Turn Now by 2l in a bumper last October, and then, after a promising third on his hurdles debut at Haydock, returned to the Norfolk venue to hand out a 21l thrashing to Noble Ben; suited by good ground and a sharp track, and pedigree suggests there could be better to come when he tackles fences this term; clearly has ability and open to further progress, so could prove interesting at a decent level.

1415 Shirley Casper (Ire)

6 b m Presenting - Glen Empress (Lancastrian)

P Fenton (Ir)   J P Dunne

PLACINGS: F12/1143-   RPR **126+b**

Starts	1st	2nd	3rd	4th	Win & Pl
5	2	1	1	1	£34,470

| 12/06 | Navn | 2m Gd2 NHF 4-7yo heavy | £15,714 |
| 12/06 | Fair | 2m NHF 4-7yo soft | £8,101 |

Leading bumper performer last season, and an obvious candidate for Graded novice hurdles; won at Fairyhouse and Navan in December, but best form when in the frame in Grade 1 company at the Cheltenham and Punchestown festivals; finished 3l fourth behind Cork All Star at Prestbury Park in March (hampered inside final furlong) and similar level of form when 3¹/₄l third behind Mick The Man and stablemate Woodbine Willie at Punchestown; looks to be crying out for a step up in distance, and handles anything from good to heavy ground; has the option of going for easier mares' races, and should do well.

1416 Shouldhavehadthat (Ire)

5 b g Definite Article - Keep The Pace (Shardari)

F Murphy   Unchartered Waters

PLACINGS: 2/2341-2   RPR **121+h**

Starts	1st	2nd	3rd	4th	Win & Pl
6	1	3	1	1	£9,093

| 3/07 | Asct | 2m3¹/₂f Cls3 Mdn Hdl good | £6,263 |

Useful novice hurdler when trained by Nicky Henderson last season, and should do better over fences; showed obvious promise when getting

within 20l of the classy Tidal Bay on his debut at Cheltenham in December, and duly improved to get off the mark at Ascot three months later, where he relished the step up to 2m4f to easily beat Scotland Yard by 5l; started 1-6 to close out his campaign with a win at Uttoxeter in May, but heavy rain made conditions difficult, and while a mistake 2 out when going well in front did not help his cause, it was slightly disappointing that he was worn down close home by Olmeto Collonges (2m, good to soft, 14 ran); possibly unsuited by drop back to minimum trip, but at least the run gave him some extra experience, and he should leave that effort behind on better ground over fences. *'He's got unbelievable scope. From the first time we schooled him he was like a Grade A showjumper.' (Mick Fitzgerald, former rider)*

1417 Silent Oscar (Ire)

8 b g Oscar - Silent Shot (Random Shot)

H Rogers (Ir)   Patrick Convery

PLACINGS: 7/2/171361B/1443001-   RPR **159h**

Starts	1st	2nd	3rd	4th	Win & Pl
16	5	1	2	2	£118,231

4/07	Punc	2m Gd1 Hdl good	£81,081
5/06	Punc	2m Hdl soft	£7,863
3/06	Clon	2m Mdn Hdl yld-sft	£3,812
9/05	List	2m NHF gd-yld	£6,861
4/05	Punc	2m NHF soft	£8,821

Very smart 2m hurdler; sprang a 20-1 surprise in the Grade 1 Champion Hurdle at the Punchestown festival in April, leading 4 out and repelling the challenge of Macs Joy to score by a neck (2m, good, 8 ran); was actually confirming form with the runner-up there, as he had beaten Macs Joy by 2l in a 2m Flat race at the Curragh just 12 days earlier; Punchestown win represented a significant step up on anything he had achieved over timber before, but no reason to believe it was a fluke, and his trainer certainly sees him as a Champion Hurdle horse this season; effective on anything but extreme ground, and will be campaigned in Graded races over 2m-2m4f.

1418 Silver Birch (Ire)

10 b g Clearly Bust - All Gone (Giolla Mear)

G Elliott (Ir)   Brian Walsh (co Kildare)

PLACINGS: 24P/111/4PPF/382421-   RPR **150+c**

Starts	1st	2nd	3rd	4th	Win & Pl
21	7	3	2	4	£537,504

138	4/07	Aint	4m4f Cls1 Gd3 134-158 Ch Hcap good	£399,140
132	12/04	Chep	3m5¹/₂f Cls1 Gd3 126-153 Ch Hcap heavy	£58,000
123	11/04	Aint	3m3f Cls2 122-146 Ch Hcap soft	£43,500
119	11/04	NAbb	3m2¹/₂f Cls3 93-119 Ch Hcap soft	£6,895
	1/04	Chep	3m2¹/₂f Cls4 Ch soft	£3,907
	1/03	Plum	3m1¹/₂f Cls3 Nov Hdl heavy	£5,473
	11/02	Chep	2m4f Cls3 Nov Hdl soft	£4,232

Long-distance chaser who returned to his very best to give his small Irish stable a surprise win in the Grand National at Aintree in April; had built up to that toughest of tests with a string of good efforts in defeat in cross-country and hurdle races, most notably finishing 3¹/₂l second to Heads Onthe Ground at the Cheltenham Festival in March (3m7f, soft, 16 ran); started 33-1 at Aintree, but bounced right back to the pick of his old form for Paul Nicholls to jump well in the main and stay on strongly from the second-last to hold off Mckelvey's determined challenge by ³/₄l (4m4f, good, 40 ran), was winning off a mark only 4lb higher than his career-high); seems to be over his injury problems, and likely to take a similar route to Aintree, where he will face the age-old problem of defending National winners – a lot more weight on his back; handles very soft ground well.

1419 Silverburn (Ire)

6 b g Presenting - Polly Puttens (Pollerton)

P Nicholls   Paul Green

PLACINGS: 21/21146-   RPR **146+h**

Starts	1st	2nd	3rd	4th	Win & Pl
7	3	2	-	1	£44,977

1/07	Sand	2m¹/₂f Cls1 Gd1 Hdl heavy	£25,659
11/06	Newb	2m¹/₂f Cls3 Nov Hdl soft	£7,516
3/06	Winc	2m Cls6 Mdn NHF 4-6yo soft	£1,713

Brother to Gold Cup hope and stablemate Denman, and an interesting novice chase prospect in his own right; showed his best when winning the Grade 1 Tolworth Hurdle at Sandown last season on only his fifth start under Rules, where he seemed unhindered by the gruelling underfoot conditions and came home by 4l from Irish raider Perce Rock; had earlier beaten subsequent Grade 2 winner Tagula Blue and got within 7l of Wichita Lineman, and went on to finish a sound fourth behind Massini's Maguire in the Ballymore Properties Novices' Hurdle at the Cheltenham Festival; probably best to put a line through his dismal effort in the Grade 1 Sefton Hurdle at Aintree on his final start as something was clearly amiss; likely to come into his own over fences, and it would be no surprise to see him develop into a leading contender for the SunAlliance Chase back at Cheltenham. *'He'll make a cracking chaser.'* *(Paul Nicholls, trainer)*

1420 Simon

8 b g Overbury - Gaye Memory (Buckskin)

J Spearing   Mrs Mercy Rimell

PLACINGS: 4273/4341211/52611F-   RPR **155+c**

Starts	1st	2nd	3rd	4th	Win & Pl
20	6	5	2	3	£149,897

143	2/07	Kemp	3m Cls1 Gd3 124-150 Ch Hcap soft	£57,020
132	1/07	Sthl	3m¹/₂f Cls1 List 118-142 Ch Hcap soft	£34,212
121	4/06	Bang	3m¹/₂f Cls3 107-130 Ch Hcap soft	£10,410
114	3/06	Uttx	3m Cls2 Nov 110-136 Ch Hcap heavy	£12,610
	1/06	Winc	2m5f Cls4 Nov Ch gd-sft	£7,222
	11/04	Wxfd	2m Nov Hdl 4-5yo yld-sft	£5,839

Much-improved staying chaser last season; won two valuable handicaps in the mud, surviving a

bad mistake at the last to beat Ardaghey by 9l in Southwell's Sky Bet Chase before producing a similarly dominant display in the Racing Post Chase at Kempton, where he powered clear from 2 out to beat Cornish Sett by 10l; that earned him a crack at the Grand National at Aintree, and while many wrote him off as a mudlark who would be unsuited by the drying ground, he was still travelling supremely well when falling at Valentine's on the second circuit, and would surely have been involved in the shake-up; that race will be a long-term target for him again this term, but a new official mark of 152 means he will have to improve to continue on his upward curve; strong, powerful sort, though, who carries weight well, and may not yet have reached the peak of his powers.

1421 Sir Boreas Hawk

5 b g Overbury - Fringe Benefit (Executive Perk)

G A Swinbank   William A Powrie

PLACINGS: 31/211-   RPR **128+h**

Starts	1st	2nd	3rd	4th	Win & Pl
5	3	1	1	-	£6,776

2/07	Catt	2m3f Cls4 Nov Hdl 4-7yo good	£3,253
1/07	Muss	2m Cls6 NHF 4-6yo good	£1,627
4/06	Hexm	2m¹/₂f Cls6 Mdn NHF 4-6yo good	£1,028

Exciting and well regarded hurdling prospect; improved with each run in bumpers before making a successful debut over hurdles at Catterick in February, travelling strongly on the heels of the leaders before putting the race to bed when surging clear between the last two and beating Monsieur by 14l (2m3f, good, 16 ran); plan is to get him fit by giving him an outing in a maiden on the Flat before targeting a decent handicap hurdle and, hailing from such a shrewd yard, there is every reason to believe he can do well off his official rating of 128; unbeaten on three starts on good ground, and may prove to be most effective at around 2m4f.

1422 Sir Frederick (Ire)

7 b g Insan - Promotor Fidei (Prominer)

W J Burke (Ir)   Seven Heads Syndicate

PLACINGS: U1P1715/426215P41-1P   RPR **144c**

Starts	1st	2nd	3rd	4th	Win & Pl
22	6	3	-	4	£134,779

126	8/07	Gway	2m6f 123-151 Ch Hcap gd-yld	£90,541
	4/07	Clon	2m4f Ch gd-fm	£6,536
	12/06	Fair	2m5¹/₂f Ch soft	£8,101
121	4/06	Gowr	2m4f 96-121 Hdl Hcap yld-sft	£8,340
115	2/06	Gowr	2m4f 94-122 Hdl Hcap soft	£8,979
	11/05	Thur	2m2f Hdl yield	£5,881

Smart handicap chaser who could be aimed at the Irish Grand National or Aintree version in the future; won a couple of novice chases last term, but returned from a four-month break to run the race of his life off a feather weight in the Galway Plate in August, travelling throughout like a much-improved horse and striding clear in the home straight to beat Ballyagran by 3l; set to be stepped up to 3m-plus at the time of writing, with his programme likely to be shaped by how he performs in races like the Denny Gold Medal Chase at Tralee and the Kerry National at Listowel; looks just the sort of sound jumper from a small Irish yard who could make his mark at Aintree one day.

1423 Sir Jimmy Shand (Ire)

6 b/br g Accordion - Morganone (Supreme Leader)

N Henderson   W H Ponsonby

PLACINGS: 110/1120P-   **RPR 147+h**

Starts	1st	2nd	3rd	4th	Win & Pl
8	4	1	-		£20,678
	12/06	Newb	2m3f Cls4 Nov Hdl 4-6yo soft		£4,554
	11/06	Folk	2m1¹/₂f Cls4 Nov Hdl 4-6yo heavy		£3,253
	3/06	Hntg	2m¹/₂f Cls6 NHF 4-6yo good		£1,713
	1/06	Ludl	2m Cls5 NHF 4-6yo good		£2,602

Good prospect for staying novice chases; looked smart in novice hurdles in the first half of last season, bolting up at Folkestone and Newbury before returning to the Berkshire track to finish 8l second to Wichita Lineman in the Grade 1 Challow Novices' Hurdle in December (2m5f, good to soft, 8 ran, finished 18l clear of the third in testing conditions); finished tired there, and was given a long break before taking on Wichita Lineman again in the Brit Insurance Hurdle at Cheltenham, but trailed in a remote 17th, and was even more disappointing when pulled up at Perth the following month; has a reputation to restore now, but will have been freshened up by his summer break and will be found some suitable opportunities over fences; could prove best at around 2m4f on decent ground. *'He's always been looked upon as a chaser in the making.' (Nicky Henderson, trainer)*

1424 Sizing Africa (Ire)

5 b g Bob's Return - Brown Forest (Brave Invader)

H de Bromhead (Ir)   Alan Potts

PLACINGS: 131-   **RPR 132+b**

Starts	1st	2nd	3rd	4th	Win & Pl
3	2	-	1	-	£13,513
	4/07	Fair	2m NHF 4-7yo good		£7,937
	10/06	Gowr	2m NHF 4yo good		£5,004

Classy bumper horse last season, winning two out of three, and looks an exciting novice hurdle prospect; opened his account at Gowran Park last October (beat Rare Bob by 8l) before travelling to Newbury for a competitive affair at the Hennessy meeting, where he finished 12l third behind Schiehallion; connections were left disappointed when he was balloted out of the Champion Bumper at Cheltenham in March, but he atoned for that in some small part by winning at Fairyhouse in April, beating subsequent Punchestown festival Grade 1 winner Mick The Man by 1¹/₄l on good

ground; will start out around October, and could easily make it to Cheltenham this time for one of the novice hurdles; has plenty of speed, but family tends to do well over 2m4f-plus. *'He put Mick The Man away fairly easily at Fairyhouse, and looks a real good one.' (Henry de Bromhead, trainer)*

1425 Sizing Europe (Ire)

5 b g Pistolet Bleu - Jennie Dun (Mandalus)

H de Bromhead (Ir)   Alan Potts

PLACINGS: 2/511351-   **RPR 129h**

Starts	1st	2nd	3rd	4th	Win & Pl
7	3	1	1	-	£28,627
	4/07	Punc	2m Nov Hdl good		£13,196
	11/06	Newb	2m1¹/₂f Cls3 Mdn Hdl gd-sft		£6,506
	10/06	Naas	2m NHF 4yo soft		£4,289

Progressive hurdler last season, winning twice and running well in Graded company; best of his wins came on his final start at the Punchestown festival, where he raced prominently and was ridden clear from the second-last to beat Big Zeb by 3¹/₂l (2m, good, 24 ran); twice got within hailing distance of De Valira in Graded events, beaten 9¹/₄l into third at Leopardstown's Christmas meeting (2m, heavy, 8 ran) and returning from a mid-season break to finish 5l fifth on good to firm ground at Fairyhouse; set to stay over hurdles until at least Christmas, and if he makes his mark in the better hurdles over 2m-2m4f, he could be aimed at something at the Cheltenham Festival; if he doesn't make the grade, he will be switched to fences midway through the season; versatile as regards ground.

1426 Sky's The Limit (Fr)

6 gr g Medaaly - Highness Lady (Cagliostro)

E O'Grady (Ir)   Raymond J Rooney

PLACINGS: 125/50121130/33627-   **RPR 138h**

Starts	1st	2nd	3rd	4th	Win & Pl
16	4	3	3	-	£110,080
144	3/06	Chel	2m5f Cls1 Gd3 129-144 Hdl Hcap good		£42,765
	12/05	Fair	2m2f Hdl heavy		£12,466
	10/05	Limk	2m2f Hdl 4yo gd-sft		£12,697
	12/04	Leop	2m Hdl 3yo soft		£9,169

Winner of the Coral Cup at Cheltenham in 2006 who started last season as a bright novice chase prospect, but failed to sparkle over fences and was ultimately switched back to hurdles; twice finished third but probably put up his best effort in a Grade 1 at Leopardstown on Boxing Day when last of six finishers behind Schindlers Hunt (2m1f, soft to heavy, 9 ran); no excuses were offered as to those lacklustre efforts, and the fact he was put back over hurdles for his final two outings suggests he might just not be as good as expected; not badly treated over hurdles (just 1lb higher than when scoring at the Festival), but has his novice status in tact over fences and will reportedly start the season by going chasing.

1427 Slim Pickings (Ire)

8 b g Scribano - Adapan (Pitpan)

T Taaffe (Ir)   Doubtful Five Syndicate

PLACINGS: 1317/21F412/33P3F53-   RPR **150+c**

Starts	1st	2nd	3rd	4th	Win & Pl
19	4	3	5	1	£144,839
	4/06	Cork	3m List Ch yld-sft		£15,714
	11/05	Punc	2m6f Nov Gd3 Ch sft-hvy		£17,776
	3/05	Leop	2m4f Mdn Hdl heavy		£7,841
	1/05	Gowr	2m NHF sft-hvy		£5,391

Handicap chaser who blossomed last spring following a change of stable, and produced the two best performances of his life; showed signs of a revival when still in contention when coming down at the last in the Thyestes Chase at Gowran in January (3m, heavy, 16 ran); loomed up three out in the Racing Post Plate at the Cheltenham Festival before being unable to find a change of gear between the last two, eventually finishing fifth behind Idole First (2m5f, good to soft, 23 ran); well fancied at long odds for Grand National after that and rewarded each-way backers with a tremendous performance, looking the likely winner three out before surrendering the momentum with a mistake at the last, finishing 2l third behind Silver Birch (4m4f, good, 40 ran); expect him to have his handicap mark protected by a campaign over hurdles before a return to Aintree.

1428 Snakebite (Ire)

7 gr g Taipan - Bee In The Rose (Roselier)

C Llewellyn   Malcolm C Denmark

PLACINGS: 3220/2124/4215-   RPR **135+c**

Starts	1st	2nd	3rd	4th	Win & Pl
12	2	5	1	2	£25,380
	12/06	Folk	3m1f Cls4 Ch soft		£3,904
	1/06	Ling	2m3¹/₂f Cls4 Nov Hdl 4-7yo good		£3,253

Promising chaser who is set to return from injury this season; finished in the frame behind Denman on his first two novice chase starts last autumn (beaten 18¹/₂l and 12l), but made light work of easier opposition at Folkestone in December; went straight into handicap company next time off a mark of 127, and started favourite for the Grade 2 Peter Marsh Chase at Haydock, but was a bitter disappointment and trailed in 28l fifth behind The Outlier in heavy ground; missed the remainder of the season, but reportedly recovered, and remains interesting for handicaps on left-handed tracks.

1429 Snap Tie (Ire)

5 b g Pistolet Bleu - Aries Girl (Valiyar)

P Hobbs   Mrs D L Whateley

PLACINGS: 1262-   RPR **117b**

Starts	1st	2nd	3rd	4th	Win & Pl
4	1	2	-	-	£6,857
	5/06	Limk	2m NHF 4yo good		£5,007

Useful bumper horse last season, and expected to do well over hurdles; had already won in Ireland before making his debut for Philip Hobbs at Cheltenham last October, where he finished 8l second to Imperial Commander; despite that defeat, started favourite for a Listed bumper over the same course and distance at the Open meeting, but could manage only sixth, beaten 25l by subsequent Festival winner Cork All Star; wasn't seen out again until Newbury in March, where he lost little in defeat to Helens Vision, going down by 3¹/₂l but giving the winner 17lb; should win races over timber, and could be one for the Cheltenham Festival if all goes well.

1430 Snowy Morning (Ire)

7 b g Moscow Society - Miss Perky (Creative Plan)

W Mullins (Ir)   Quayside Syndicate

PLACINGS: 22/211F/121121124-   RPR **154+c**

Starts	1st	2nd	3rd	4th	Win & Pl
9	5	3		1	£93,539
	2/07	Navn	3m Nov Gd2 Ch heavy		£21,993
	1/07	Gowr	2m4f Nov Ch heavy		£11,436
	12/06	Navn	2m4f Ch heavy		£7,863
	6/06	Punc	3m Mdn Hdl good		£5,719
	5/06	Baln	2m NHF 5-7yo yld-sft		£4,051

One of the leading staying novice chasers last season, and appeals as the type to do well in the big staying handicaps; connections wasted no time in sending him over fences on only his fourth start under Rules in December (dual point-to-point winner), when he landed the odds at Navan; successes at Gowran and back at Navan (Grade 2, by 4l from Gazza's Girl) then followed, before he posted his best effort when runner-up to Denman in the Royal & SunAlliance Chase at Cheltenham (3m1f, good to soft, 17 ran), staying on after being hampered and outpaced at the ninth, and beaten 10l; uncharacteristically poor display when only fourth of five finishers in the Grade 1 Champion Chase at Punchestown on his final start (3m1f, good), but the run is worth forgiving as he may have been over the top following some gruelling races; acts very well in the mud, and an official rating of 143 looks to underestimate him; could be one for the Hennessy.

1431 Sophocles

4 gr g In The Wings - Actoris (Diesis)

J Leavy (Ir)   Mrs Ann M Donnelly

PLACINGS: 2129-   RPR **127+b**

Starts	1st	2nd	3rd	4th	Win & Pl
4	1	2	-	-	£18,339
	2/07	Thur	2m NHF 4yo sft-hvy		£3,969

Classy bumper performer who will go novice hurdling this season; gained his only success to date by 8l at Thurles in February, but the following month ran a stormer as a 40-1 shot in the Champion Bumper at Cheltenham, coming from well off the pace under his female amateur rider, hanging left under pressure in the straight but running on well to finish 1¹/₄l second to Cork All Star (2m¹/₂f, good to soft, 24 ran); not as good at the Punchestown festival, where he could muster only the one pace in the straight and finished ninth behind Mick The Man (2m, good, 19 ran); evidently prefers a little cut, and should make his mark in Graded novice hurdles on his best form.

1432 Southern Vic (Ire)

8 b/br g Old Vic - Hug In A Fog (Strong Gale)

T Walsh (Ir)   Mrs Brenda Graham

PLACINGS: /42115/121151/1525F-   **RPR 157+c**

Starts	1st	2nd	3rd	4th	Win & Pl
16	7	3	-	1	£125,569
	10/06	Naas	2m Gd3 Ch soft		£17,959
	3/06	Navn	2m1f Nov Ch sft-hvy		£10,102
	1/06	Naas	3m Nov Gd2 Ch soft		£24,693
	12/05	Leop	3m Nov Gd1 Ch yld-sft		£34,574
	10/05	Gway	2m6f Ch sft-hvy		£9,234
	1/05	Leop	2m4f Hdl sft-hvy		£8,576
	12/04	Leop	2m4f Mdn Hdl soft		£6,813

Promised a lot as a novice chaser two seasons ago, but a shade disappointing in open company last term; started well enough with a Grade 3 success over 2m at Naas, and in hindsight ran a cracker when fifth under top weight in a valuable handicap at Navan, beaten just over 11l when asked to concede 18lb to subsequent Gold Cup fifth Cane Brake (3m, soft, 16 ran); went backwards afterwards, though, finishing fifth behind The Listener in the Lexus Chase, and well held when falling in the Thyestes Chase at Gowran; stays 3m well and loves the mud, but lacks the vital spark required to succeed in the top handicaps. *'You couldn't get it soft enough for him, and he's crying out for a trip.' (Conor O'Dwyer, jockey)*

1433 Special Envoy (Fr)

5 gr g Linamix - Pawnee Dancer (Dancing Brave)

P Bowen   Walters Plant Hire Ltd

PLACINGS: 341671F-   **RPR 145+h**

Starts	1st	2nd	3rd	4th	Win & Pl
7	2	-	1	1	£8,549
	3/07	Newb	2m¹/₂f Cls4 Nov Hdl gd-sft		£3,904
	1/07	Font	2m6¹/₂f Cls4 Mdn Hdl soft		£3,643

Young hurdler who improved in leaps and bounds throughout his novice campaign; won little races at Fontwell (2m6¹/₂f) and Newbury, and in between finished 11l seventh behind Ebaziyan in the Supreme Novices' Hurdle at the Cheltenham Festival; proved a real revelation, though, in a Listed handicap hurdle over 2m4f at Aintree in April, where he was 7l clear and extending his advantage when crashing out at the final flight, leaving Two Miles West to prevail in a three-way photo; had salt rubbed into the wound by being raised 12lb into the bargain, but is progressive and unexposed, and could yet have the last laugh;

could well be contesting Graded hurdles this winter, although it looks like good ground serves him best.

1434 Sporazene (Ire)

8 gr g Cozzene - Sporades (Vaguely Noble)

P Nicholls   Ged Mason

PLACINGS: 810/1F/4F7F630/114F-   **RPR 160+c**

Starts	1st	2nd	3rd	4th	Win & Pl
22	6	1	4	2	£154,148
	12/06	Extr	2m1¹/₂f Cls2 Ch soft		£15,658
	11/06	Kemp	2m Cls3 Ch good		£15,658
	10/04	Extr	2m1¹/₂f Cls3 Ch good		£5,606
151	3/04	Chel	2m1f Cls1 Gd3 138-151 Hdl Hcap good		£37,700
	5/03	Punc	2m Gd1 Hdl 4yo qd-yld		£44,286
	4/03	Ayr	2m Cls3 Nov Hdl 4yo good		£7,404

Former County Hurdle winner who did well in the new graduation chases last year and will now be sent after decent prizes at around 2m; scored on his return at Kempton in November, but achieved much more at Exeter the following month when making all and jumping supremely well to beat Mariah Rollins by 21l; earned a Racing Post Rating of 160 for that impressive success, but failed to go on from there, finishing around 20l behind Well Chief in the Game Spirit Chase at Newbury and then falling at the fifth in the Grand Annual at Cheltenham; has bags of talent, but will need his confidence restoring again after that tumble and a rating of 158 might force connections down the Pattern-race route, which proved his undoing a few years back. *'He was injured three years ago after winning his only novice chase and was forced to run in all the top races after that and lost his confidence, but the new graduation chases last season did him the world of good.' (Paul Nicholls, trainer)*

1435 Spot Thedifference (Ire)

14 b g Lafontaine - Spotted Choice (Callernish)

E Bolger (Ir)   John P McManus

PLACINGS: 1410/91096200/01141-   **RPR 147+c**

Starts	1st	2nd	3rd	4th	Win & Pl
49	13	7	2	5	£222,860
	4/07	Punc	4m2f Ch gd-fm		£17,595
144	12/06	Chel	3m7f Cls2 118-144 Ch Hcap soft		£14,405
	11/06	Chel	3m7f Cls2 Ch good		£21,921
	11/05	Chel	3m7f Cls2 Ch good		£18,789
143	3/05	Chel	3m7f Cls2 117-143 Ch Hcap gd-sft		£23,200
134	12/04	Chel	3m7f Cls2 108-134 Ch Hcap good		£13,526
	11/04	Chel	3m7f Cls2 Ch good		£17,400
	4/04	Punc	4m2f Ch good		£11,461
111	6/01	Kbgn	3m1f 86-121 Ch Hcap good		£10,484
104	6/01	Rosc	3m1¹/₂f 79-114 Ch Hcap good		£5,565
	5/01	Kbgn	3m1f Hunt Ch good		£3,895
	2/01	Thur	3m Hunt Ch soft		£4,730
	2/99	Clon	3m Hunt Ch soft		£2,455

The grand-daddy of the cross-country scene, having won no fewer than six times round the twists and turns of Cheltenham's banks course; added two of those wins last season at the big November and December meetings, putting up a career-best effort to beat French raider Plum'Tee on the latter occasion; a gallant fourth behind stablemate Heads Onthe Ground (to whom he was conceding 24lb) at the Cheltenham Festival, but rounded off by winning the La Touche Cup at Punchestown for the second time in April, albeit in a race where many rivals fell by the wayside; still retains all his enthusiasm, and set to return to his old stamping ground at the Paddy Power meeting in November.

1436 Spring The Que (Ire)

8 b g Parthian Springs - Que Tranquila (Dominion)

R Tyner (Ir)   Gaelforce Racing

PLACINGS: 1/6007153/34/21-   **RPR 133h**

Starts	1st	2nd	3rd	4th	Win & Pl
11	2	1	2	1	£66,291
116	1/07	Leop	2m 109-130 Hdl Hcap sft-hvy		£53,142
	1/05	Cork	2m Mdn Hdl soft		£5,881

Lightly raced hurdler in recent years, with only two starts since May 2005, but better than ever last term; showed long absence hadn't diluted his talent when a game 2^1/2l runner-up to View Mount Prince at Punchestown on his comeback (2m4f, heavy, 18 ran); showed the benefit of that outing when landing the valuable Pierse Hurdle at Leopardstown in January, making the most of his light weight and staying on gamely on the long run-in (final flight omitted) to beat top-weight Mister Hight by 2^1/2l; starts this campaign a stone higher in the weights, but is likely to mix hurdling with a bit of novice chasing, and the degree of success he enjoys under each code will dictate his campaign; stays 2m4f and appears to relish testing ground, although has run well on good.

1437 Square Mile (Ire)

7 ch g Bob Back - Mother Imelda (Phardante)

J O'Neill   John P McManus

PLACINGS: 11/13F/PP1-11   **RPR 133+c**

Starts	1st	2nd	3rd	4th	Win & Pl
10	6		1	-	£23,235
117	7/07	MRas	2m6^1/2f Cls3 107-120 Ch Hcap good		£6,506
	5/07	Uttx	2m6^1/2f Cls4 Nov Ch soft		£5,205
	4/07	Worc	2m7^1/2f Cls4 Ch good		£3,578
	10/05	MRas	2m3^1/2f Cls4 Nov Hdl good		£3,311
	7/04	Prth	2m^1/2f Cls6 NHF 4-6yo good		£2,184
	6/04	Worc	2m Cls6 NHF 4-6yo good		£1,961

Useful hurdler who made hay over fences during the summer and looks one to keep on the right side of in staying novice chases and handicaps; left behind two bitterly disappointing efforts at the start of the year when scoring at Worcester in April before following up at Uttoxeter and Market Rasen; earned a Racing Post Rating of 133 when registering his third win, sealing the race with fine jumps over the last two fences and coming home 2^1/2l clear of Killard Point, who had won his previous two races; clearly going the right way and has already proved his ability to handle different ground, and looks open to further improvement.

1438 Star De Mohaison (Fr)

6 b g Beyssac - Belle De Mohaison (Suvero)

P Nicholls   Sir Robert Ogden

PLACINGS: F61133/123111/11-   **RPR 160+c**

Starts	1st	2nd	3rd	4th	Win & Pl
14	8	1	3	-	£215,547
127	12/06	Sand	3m^1/2f Cls2 Ch gd-sft		£15,658
	11/06	Chel	3m1^1/2f Cls1 List 121-147 Hdl Hcap gd-sft		£28,510
	4/06	Aint	3m1f Cls1 Nov Gd2 Ch good		£45,616
	3/06	Chel	3m^1/2f Cls1 Gd1 Ch good		£79,828
	1/06	Font	2m6f Cls3 Nov Ch gd-sft		£9,395
	10/05	Aint	2m4f Cls3 Nov Ch soft		£10,114
	1/05	Hrfd	2m3^1/2f Cls4 Nov Hdl 4-7yo soft		£3,439
	11/04	Autl	2m2f Hdl 3yo v soft		£13,521

Winner of the SunAlliance Chase at the Cheltenham Festival the season before last and will be one of at least three Gold Cup hopes for his trainer when returning from the injury that prevented him from having a crack at the big race last term; made light work of winning what had looked a competitive Listed handicap hurdle at Cheltenham last November before a successful return to fences in an intermediate contest at Sandown, which he won by 1^1/4l from The Listener, who followed that effort by winning the Grade 1 Lexus Chase at Leopardstown; quoted at 14-1 for the Gold Cup after that win, but sidelined shortly after with a tendon strain; reportedly back in good health now and likely to make his return in the second half of the season; has some way to go to develop into a live Gold Cup contender, but he has time on his side and is open to further improvement.

1439 State Of Play

7 b g Hernando - Kaprice (Windwurf)

E Williams   Mr & Mrs William Rucker

PLACINGS: 81/5742/411151/164-   **RPR 165+c**

Starts	1st	2nd	3rd	4th	Win & Pl
15	6	2	1	3	£152,690
145	11/06	Newb	3m2^1/2f Cls1 Gd3 127-153 Ch Hcap soft		£85,530
128	4/06	Aint	3m1f Cls2 128-152 Ch Hcap good		£31,315
	11/05	Plum	3m2f Cls3 Nov Ch gd-sft		£6,524
	10/05	Chep	3m Cls3 Nov Ch gd-sft		£5,681
	6/05	Hrfd	2m3^1/2f Cls3 Nov Hdl gd-fm		£3,751
	3/04	Ludl	2m Cls6 NHF 4-6yo gd-sft		£2,562

Classy staying chaser who made his name, but also made his life difficult, in the space of seven minutes on his reappearance at Newbury; great training feat to have him spot-on for the Hennessy Cognac Gold Cup, and he was very impressive in victory, scoring by 4l from Juveigneur; that was off 145 and he went up 13lb amid talk of the King George, but he goes much better after a long break and was not seen out again until the Cheltenham Gold Cup, in which he acquitted himself very well until wilting slightly when the heat was turned up, beaten 11^1/2l into sixth behind Kauto Star (3m2^1/2f, good to soft, 18 ran); bounced big time when blundering his way around Aintree for a remote fourth behind Exotic Dancer the following month; likely to struggle off current mark in handicaps and will have to take on the best in conditions races; stays well, but doesn't take too much racing. *'The Charlie Hall would be an early objective, and then perhaps the Welsh National.' (Evan Williams, trainer)*

1440 Steel Band

9 ch g Kris - Quaver (The Minstrel)

P Roche (Ir)   Irish World Partners Syndicate

PLACINGS: 425144/U3F352435033-   **RPR 147c**

Starts	1st	2nd	3rd	4th	Win & Pl
51	4	7	8	7	£93,861
107	4/06	Tram	2m 88-109 Hdl Hcap good		£5,957
	10/04	Clon	2m2f Nov Ch sft-hvy		£8,273
103	2/04	Punc	2m 73-103 Hdl Hcap soft		£4,866
	12/02	Limk	2m Mdn Hdl 4yo heavy		£6,350

Winner of just one of his 24 starts over fences, but is a talented sort who regularly runs above expectations in Graded company; placed five times last season, but reserved his best form for his last two starts, when 8l third behind Nickname at 100-1 in a Grade 2 at Punchestown in February, and 4³/4l third behind Mansony at 40-1 in a Grade 1 at the same track's festival in April (2m, good, 7 ran); further improvement can't be entirely ruled out, as he seems to be getting his act together now.

1441 Stewarts House (Ire)

5 b g Overbury - Osocool (Teenoso)

A Moore (Ir)   C Jones

PLACINGS: 2/22-   **RPR 125b**

Starts	1st	2nd	3rd	4th	Win & Pl
2	-	2	-	-	£2,610

Ex-pointer who looks the type to do well in novice hurdles this season; returned one of the best bumper ratings of last season when second on his debut at Leopardstown in February, beaten 5l by Tranquil Sea but finishing 24l clear of the remainder (2m, heavy, 10 ran, tried to make all); again made the running at Naas the following month, but had to give best once more, this time to 8l scorer Venalmar (2m, heavy, 14 ran); that was a slightly disappointing effort (would have scored easily had he repeated his debut RPR) but should not detract too much from his obvious promise.

1442 Straw Bear (USA)

6 ch g Diesis - Highland Ceilidh (Scottish Reel)

N Gifford   John P McManus

PLACINGS: 11212/1421P-   **RPR 161h**

Starts	1st	2nd	3rd	4th	Win & Pl
10	5	3	-	1	£170,595
	2/07	Winc	2m Cls1 Gd2 Hdl soft		£39,914
	11/06	Newc	2m Cls1 Gd1 Hdl gd-sft		£45,072
	4/06	Aint	2m¹/₂f Cls1 Nov Gd2 Hdl gd-sft		£31,361
	1/06	Folk	2m1¹/₂f Cls4 Nov Hdl soft		£2,928
	1/06	Leic	2m Cls3 Nov Hdl soft		£5,070

High-class 2m hurdler; looked a potential

Champion Hurdle contender when hacking up in the Fighting Fifth at Newcastle on his return last autumn, beating Noble Request by 5l (2m, good to soft, 9 ran); very disappointing in the Christmas Hurdle (fourth behind Jazz Messenger), but was reportedly not himself that day, and proved the point by returning to form afterwards; finished second to Detroit City in the Agfa Hurdle at Sandown, and tuned up for Cheltenham with an impressive success in the Kingwell Hurdle at Wincanton in February, where he led at the third, went clear two out and ran on well to beat Afsoun by 7l; started 7-1 for the Champion Hurdle at Cheltenham in March, but ran an absolute stinker and was beaten from just after halfway (pulled up with broken blood vessels); clearly prone to the odd bad run, but highly talented, and Afsoun's close third in the Champion Hurdle underlined that fact; likely to start off over hurdles, with novice chasing an option further down the line.

1443 Streetshavenoname (Ire)

6 b g Old Vic - Glore River (Broken Hearted)

T Taaffe (Ir)   Enda Hunston

PLACINGS: 10/12696B-2   **RPR 129h**

Starts	1st	2nd	3rd	4th	Win & Pl
9	2	2	-	-	£20,636
	11/06	Limk	2m Mdn Hdl 5yo soft		£6,910
	3/06	Dpat	2m2f NHF yld-sft		£3,812

Showed enough promise in handicaps over hurdles to suggest a bright future over fences; made a successful reappearance on hurdling debut at Limerick last November, but best efforts came in defeat in valuable handicaps; finished sixth behind Spring The Que on only his third run over obstacles in the Pierse Hurdle at Leopardstown in January (2m, soft to heavy, 30 ran), and ran almost to same level when filling the same position behind Emmpat at Fairyhouse in April, beaten 11l (2m, good to firm, 23 ran); better to come as he gains experience and his versatility regards ground conditions will stand him in good stead; likely to be found plenty of opportunities.

1444 Studmaster

7 ch g Snurge - Danlu (Danzig)

Mrs J Harrington (Ir)   Mothership Racing Club

PLACINGS: 1221/321100/F55122-   **RPR 146h**

Starts	1st	2nd	3rd	4th	Win & Pl
16	5	5	1	-	£124,460
	12/06	Punc	2m4f Hdl heavy		£12,122
124	2/06	Leop	2m 100-128 Hdl Hcap yield		£14,142
114	1/06	Leop	2m 107-135 Hdl Hcap heavy		£54,241
	10/04	Tipp	2m Nov Gd3 Hdl soft		£20,630
	7/04	Fair	2m Mdn Hdl firm		£5,839

Talented hurdler whose biggest win came in the Pierse Hurdle at Leopardstown in January 2006; started out last season in novice chases, but that experiment was abandoned after a fall and a disappointing fifth at Galway in October; reverted to hurdles afterwards, and got back on the scoresheet when beating Kadoun by a neck in a conditions race at Punchestown on New Year's Eve (2m4f, heavy, 7 ran); second to Sweet Kiln in a similar contest at Naas next time, before rounding off in January with a 5l second to Celestial Wave on his first try over 3m in Grade 3 company at Gowran Park (heavy, 8 ran); likely to have another crack at fences this term, but has a future in Graded hurdles over a wide range of distances.

1445 Sublimity (Fr)

7 b g Selkirk - Fig Tree Drive (Miswaki)

J Carr (Ir)   W Hennessy

PLACINGS: 1444/11-   **RPR 170+h**

Starts	1st	2nd	3rd	4th	Win & Pl
6	-	-	-	3	£228,188
	3/07	Chel	2m¹/₂f Cls1 Gd1 Hdl soft		£205,272
	1/07	Navn	2m Hdl heavy		£7,470
	12/05	Leop	2m Mdn Hdl yld-sft		£6,861

Top-class 2m hurdler who went from relative obscurity to the top of the tree in a light campaign last season; hacked up on his seasonal return at Navan in January, giving connections a Cheltenham Festival dilemma; might have gone for the County Hurdle, but instead took on the best in a small field for the Champion, and ran out an emphatic winner, travelling sweetly throughout, leading at the last and stretching 3l clear of defending champ Brave Inca (ground much better than the official soft); form of that win is not hard to pick holes in (beat some ageing heroes and one or two who didn't run their race), but it was a fine performance on just his sixth start over hurdles, and in the normal course of things, he should be open to further improvement; has reportedly come in 'very heavy' from his summer break, but the plan is to aim him at the Fighting Fifth at Newcastle or Boylesports (former Bula) Hurdle at Cheltenham, then one run at Christmas, and then go straight to Cheltenham for the Champion; a worthy ante-post favourite to defend his crown, but likely to face younger pretenders this time.

1446 Supreme Prince (Ire)

10 b g Supreme Leader - Strong Serenade (Strong Gale)

P Hobbs   Mrs Karola Vann

PLACINGS: 9F1751F/305061/9563-   **RPR 151+c**

Starts	1st	2nd	3rd	4th	Win & Pl
28	9	2	3	-	£184,831
	4/06	Ayr	2m4f Cls2 132-158 Ch Hcap gd-sft		£18,859
	3/05	Newb	2m4f Cls1 List 133-156 Ch Hcap gd-sft		£58,000
	11/04	Newb	2m4f Cls2 119-145 Ch Hcap good		£26,100
	12/03	Asct	2m3¹/₂f Cls1 Nov Gd2 Ch soft		£20,100
	12/03	Chep	2m3¹/₂f Cls3 Ch gd-sft		£4,124
	2/03	Winc	2m6f Cls2 Nov Hdl gd-sft		£9,257
	11/02	Chep	2m4f Cls1 Nov Gd2 Hdl soft		£13,685
	10/02	Chep	2m4f Cls4 Nov Hdl good		£3,630
	10/01	Extr	2m1f Cls6 NHF 4-6yo gd-sft		£1,810

Handicap chaser who needs 2m4f, a flat track and

good ground; had just a light campaign in the spring last term, and ran well when sixth at 66-1 behind Burntoakboy in the Coral Cup at the Cheltenham Festival (8lb lower mark over hurdles) and when 11l third behind the very progressive Three Mirrors in a decent handicap chase at Ayr in April (2m4f, good to firm, 5 ran); that last run earned him a Racing Post Rating just 4lb off his career-best, suggesting he can still be competitive under his ideal conditions off his official mark of 140 (gained his biggest win in a valuable contest at Newbury in March 2005 off 142).

1447 Swaythe (USA)

6 b m Swain - Caithness (Roberto)

P Webber   The Syndicators

PLACINGS: 21-   **RPR 116+b**

Starts	1st	2nd	3rd	4th	Win & Pl
2	1	1	-	-	£15,053
	3/07	Sand	2m¹/₂f Cls1 List NHF 4-7yo heavy		£14,255
	11/05	Ling	2m Cls6 NHF 4-6yo stand		£1,809

Returned from 16 months off and showed improved form in mares' bumpers last term; needed the run at Fakenham on reappearance, but stayed on well when getting second wind to be runner-up to previous winner Fiddling Again (2m, good to soft, 10 ran); improved considerably for the outing and was an impressive winner of a Listed bumper at Sandown in March, leading over 1f out and keeping on dourly up the hill in the mud to beat Theatre Girl by 3¹/₂l; half-sister to the talented Stromness and likely to make her own mark over hurdles, especially with cut in the ground and against her own sex.

1448 Sweet Wake (Ger)

6 ch g Waky Nao - Sweet Royale (Garde Royale)

N Meade (Ir)   High Street Ceathar Syndicate

PLACINGS: 1156/8787-1   **RPR 144h**

Starts	1st	2nd	3rd	4th	Win & Pl
9	3	-	-	-	£31,133
	6/07	Rosc	2m Hdl gd-fm		£8,797
	1/06	Naas	2m Nov Hdl soft		£12,796
	12/05	Leop	2m Mdn Hdl 4yo yld-sft		£6,861

Highly regarded 2m hurdler who has yet to live up to his reputation, but did sign off for the summer with a confidence-boosting win; reportedly took an age to come to hand last term, but turned the corner in time for the County Hurdle at the Cheltenham Festival, and was not disgraced in finishing 3¹/₄l seventh behind Pedrobob, having travelled ominously well to two out (2m1f, good to soft, 28 ran); not far off that form when eighth behind Emmpat in a more valuable contest at Fairyhouse next time, and also ran quite well to finish 15l seventh behind Silent Oscar in the Grade 1 Champion Hurdle at the Punchestown festival;

needed to get his head in front, and was found a very simple opportunity against inferior rivals in a conditions hurdle at Roscommon in June; has since had a wind operation, and if that improves him, he could yet win the big handicap hurdle connections believe he has in him.

1449 Tagula Blue (Ire)

7 b g Tagula - Palace Blue (Dara Monarch)

I Williams   Boston R S Ian Bennett

PLACINGS: 8/3/121-   RPR **133h**

Starts	1st	2nd	3rd	4th	Win & Pl
5	2	1	1	-	£25,859
12/06	Asct	2m Cls1 Nov Gd2 Hdl good			£19,957
6/06	Font	2m2¹/₂f Cls4 Nov Hdl gd-fm			£3,253

Shaped with promise in a curtailed novice hurdle campaign last season, showing enough to indicate a bright future; stepped up considerably on the form of his debut Fontwell success when beaten 2l by Silverburn at Newbury in November (2m¹/₂f, soft, 12 ran), conceding the talented winner 5lb; underlined that level of performance on more suitable good ground when staying on well to beat three-time winner Moon Over Miami by ¹/₂l in a Grade 2 contest at Ascot in December; not seen out thereafter, but is the type to forge a career in valuable handicaps or over fences at the minimum trip or slightly further (never run over further than 2m3f). *'He would appreciate a stiff two miles.' (Ian Williams, trainer)*

1450 Tailor's Hall (Ire)

6 b g Saddlers' Hall - Designer Lady (Buckskin)

Mrs J Harrington (Ir)   Mrs G Galvin

PLACINGS: 35211-   RPR **140h**

Starts	1st	2nd	3rd	4th	Win & Pl
5	2	1	1	-	£19,502
3/07	Navn	2m7f Nov Hdl heavy			£13,196
3/07	Thur	2m4f Mdn Hdl heavy			£4,669

Good novice chase prospect, having done well over hurdles when stepped up in trip in the spring; got off the mark in maiden company at Thurles in March (2m4f, heavy, beat Tawnies by 4l) and followed up a fortnight later at Navan over 2m7f, beating subsequent Grade 2 winner Aitmatov by 5l in stylish fashion; was kept well away from the top novice hurdles last season, avoiding any hard races, and should show the benefits of that over fences this winter; has yet to race on anything but heavy ground, and looks sure to stay 3m and beyond; potential to develop into a Royal & SunAlliance Chase contender. *'He's improved with every run, and is a soft-ground 3m chaser in the making.' (Jessica Harrington, trainer)*

1451 Tamarinbleu (Fr)

7 b g Epervier Bleu - Tamainia (Lashkari)

D Pipe   The Arthur White Partnership

PLACINGS: /182024/2519/61P6-31   RPR **154+c**

Starts	1st	2nd	3rd	4th	Win & Pl
21	5	4	2	1	£135,533
140	6/07	Prth	3m Cls2 114-140 Ch Hcap good	£19,518
	12/06	Asct	2m5¹/₂f Cls2 Ch gd-sft	£15,716
	1/06	Ludl	2m Cls4 Ch good	£4,384
130	1/05	Sand	2m¹/₂f Cls1 List 119-145 Hdl Hcap gd-sft	£58,000
	11/03	Asct	2m¹/₂f Cls3 Nov Hdl 3yo soft	£4,784

Versatile performer who is best known as a chaser but also runs well over hurdles, and should have the winning of a decent handicap; started last season with his best effort over fences, recording a Racing Post Rating of 152 in finishing around 10l sixth behind Exotic Dancer in the Paddy Power Gold Cup at Cheltenham (2m4¹/₂f, good to soft, 16 ran); proved that he stays that trip with a short-head defeat of Crozan in a graduation chase at Ascot in December, and confirmed that notion in no uncertain terms in June when following a sound run over hurdles with a win in the 3m Perth Gold Cup, where he raced prominently before beating Kock De La Vesvre by 5l; now has a career-high chase mark of 150 (147 over hurdles), so unlikely to find life particularly easy, although there will be more opportunities now he has proved his ability over a variety of distances.

1452 Tango Royal (Fr)

11 gr g Royal Charter - Nazia (Zino)

D Pipe   B A Kilpatrick

PLACINGS: 1697000/8483314P-334   RPR **136+c**

Starts	1st	2nd	3rd	4th	Win & Pl
64	10	8	8	9	£252,168
125	12/06	Newb	3m Cls3 112-125 Ch Hcap gd-sft	£11,711
133	7/05	MRas	2m6¹/₂f Cls1 List 122-148 Ch Hcap good	£37,700
132	4/04	Chel	2m7/₂f Cls3 108-134 Ch Hcap good	£11,159
119	7/03	NAbb	2m6f Cls3 95-119 Hdl Hcap gd-sft	£7,700
112	5/03	Strf	2m¹/₂f Hdl 4yo gd-sft	£13,553
	9/00	Comp	2m1¹/₂f Hdl 4yo gd-sft	£3,362
	3/00	Autl	2m4¹/₂f Gd3 Ch 4yo v soft	£28,818
	3/00	Autl	2m1¹/₂f Gd3 Ch 4yo heavy	£28,818
	11/99	Engh	2m1¹/₂f Hdl 3yo holding	£10,764
	10/99	Toul	2m1¹/₂f Ch 3yo soft	£4,844

Smart handicap chaser at trips up to 3m; earned his biggest payday when winning Market Rasen's Summer Plate in 2005, and finally returned to the winner's enclosure for the first time since that win when scoring at Newbury last December; came out on top by ¹/₂l that day after a tussle down the straight with Irish Raptor (pair 22l clear of Desailly in third), clearly showing the benefit of a drop down the handicap to a mark of 125 having been rated as high as 142; does not win very often, but is game and consistent, recording a Racing Post Rating of 136 on four successive starts between December and June, and is still well handicapped on his best form.

1453 Taranis (Fr)

6 ch g Mansonnien - Vikosa (Nikos)

P Nicholls   Mrs A B Yeoman & C R Whittaker

PLACINGS: 3313/1U111/1F3112-   **RPR 164c**

Starts	1st	2nd	3rd	4th	Win & Pl
15			-		£261,112

	3/07	Chel	2m5f Cls1 Gd2 Ch gd-sft £99,785
129	2/07	Sand	2m6f Cls1 Gd3 126-152 Hdl Hcap soft £28,510
122	10/06	Chep	2m4f Cls1 List 121-147 Hdl Hcap gd-sft £25,659
135	4/06	Chel	2m5f Cls3 Nov 111-135 Ch Hcap good.........£9,708
	3/06	Winc	2m5f Cls3 Nov Ch soft £6,506
	1/06	Ludl	2m4f Cls3 Nov Ch good £7,620
121	11/05	Newb	2m2¹/₂f Cls3 Nov 99-125 Ch Hcap good £11,223
	1/05	Winc	2m Cls4 Nov Hdl soft £3,658

Tremendously consistent chaser between 2m4f and 2m6f who improved around 10lb last season and is now likely to ply his trade in Graded company just below the top level; showed his liking for Cheltenham last March with a tremendously gutsy performance to win the Ryanair Chase at the Festival, sealing the win with a couple of mighty jumps in the closing stages to hold Our Vic by a neck; had earlier looked a little unlucky in the Paddy Power Gold Cup at Prestbury Park in November when still going well but falling two from home in a race won by subsequent King George and Gold Cup runner-up Exotic Dancer; showed his versatility when scoring over hurdles at Chepstow in October and Sandown in February, and also proved that a flat track holds no terrors when stepped up to Grade 1 company for the first time and chasing home Monet's Garden in the Melling Chase at Aintree; not inconceivable that he will be tried over 3m this term, which would open up more opportunities, but looks sure to take plenty of beating over shorter distances and will be a tough nut to crack back at his favourite track.

1454 Tarlac (Ger)

6 ch g Dashing Blade - Tintina (General Assembly)

N Henderson   John P McManus

PLACINGS: 31150/1200-   **RPR 139h**

Starts	1st	2nd	3rd	4th	Win & Pl
9	3	1	1	-	£60,196

124	11/06	Asct	2m Cls2 107-133 Hdl Hcap soft £12,526
115	2/06	Sand	2m1¹/₂f Cls3 105-125 Hdl Hcap heavy £9,395
	1/06	Folk	2m1¹/₂f Cls4 Nov Hdl soft £2,928

Rather hit-or-miss 2m handicap hurdler, but has talent and could make a decent chaser; got last season off to a good start with a 1l defeat of Fait Le Jojo at Ascot, and put up a career-best effort in the valuable Ladbroke Hurdle back there in December when 2l second to Acambo off a 6lb higher mark (2m, good to soft, 20 ran); very disappointing afterwards, though, finishing well down the field in the Totesport Trophy at Newbury (started favourite) and the County Hurdle at Cheltenham; still on a decent mark over hurdles (134), so connections have options with him; seems best with cut in the ground on a right-handed track.

1455 Temoin

7 b g Groom Dancer - Kowtow (Shadeed)

N Henderson   The Unemployables

PLACINGS: 1110/P320-   **RPR 149h**

Starts	1st	2nd	3rd	4th	Win & Pl
8	3	1	1		£29,143

125	3/06	Newb	2m5f Cls3 105-125 Hdl Hcap good...................£5,205
110	2/06	Sand	2m4¹/₂f Cls3 Nov 94-120 Hdl Hcap good £5,205
	1/06	Plum	2m Cls4 Nov Hdl soft £4,229

Talented but enigmatic staying hurdler; pulled up in a Pertemps qualifier on his return last season, but bounced back with a fine effort in the Grade 1 Long Walk Hurdle at Ascot in December, when he kept on from the rear under strong driving to finish 2¹/₄l third behind Mighty Man (3m1f, good to soft, 9 ran); ran an extraordinary race next time in a conditions hurdle at Cheltenham, where he dropped quickly into a detached last of four on the approach to the home turn, but picked up again in the straight and stayed on stoutly to finish a diminishing ³/₄l second to Flight Leader (2m5f, heavy); sported first-time blinkers on his final start in the World Hurdle at the Cheltenham Festival, but ran no sort of race and trailed in last of the 13 finishers; not the most straightforward, but open to a bit of improvement over hurdles after just eight starts; likes cut in the ground.

1456 The French Furze (Ire)

13 ch g Be My Guest - Exciting (Mill Reef)

N Richards   Jim Ennis

PLACINGS: /0155380/3159F/3324-   **RPR 153+h**

Starts	1st	2nd	3rd	4th	Win & Pl
63	11	12	7	3	£231,589

	1/06	Chel	2m4¹/₂f Cls2 Hdl gd-sft £13,152
140	11/04	Ayr	2m4f Cls2 114-140 Hdl Hcap soft.................£10,082
	11/03	Newc	2m Cls1 Gd2 Hdl good £26,100
132	11/03	Ayr	2m4f Cls2 114-136 Hdl Hcap good................£13,702
	3/03	Sedg	2m5f Cls4 Nov Ch soft £3,887
136	1/00	Chel	2m1f Cls2 112-136 Hdl Hcap gd-sft £10,140
132	1/00	Hayd	2m Cls2 107-132 Hdl Hcap soft £6,652
0	2/98	Hntg	2m¹/₂f Cls3 Nov Hdl 4yo good £4,203
0	11/97	Chel	2m¹/₂f Cls2 Nov Hdl 3yo good £5,121
0	11/97	Plum	2m1f Cls4 Nov Hdl 3yo gd-fm £2,385
	8/97	Tram	2m Mdn Hdl 3yo good £2,713

Evergreen hurdler who is no back number, despite reaching the ripe old age of 13; main target will be the Grade 1 Fighting Fifth Hurdle at Newcastle in November, in which he finished 6¹/₄l third behind Straw Bear at 66-1 last season (2m, good to soft, 9 ran), taking his career record in that race to 2221533; no mere Newcastle specialist, though, as he showed when ploughing through the mud and at Haydock in January to finish 9l second to Afsoun in the Grade 2 Champion Hurdle Trial (2m, heavy, 8 ran); showing no signs that age is catching up with him at home, handles all types of ground, and his last seven wins have come on left-handed tracks. *'He still thinks he is about four; he's like one of these old men who still goes down the disco to chase the young ladies on a Saturday night.' (Nicky Richards, trainer)*

1457 The Listener (Ire)

8 gr g Roselier - Park Breeze (Strong Gale)

R Alner

Old Moss Farm

PLACINGS: 504F121S/111FF/2120-

RPR 171c

Starts	1st	2nd	3rd	4th	Win & Pl
17	6	3	-	1	£161,505

12/06	Leop	3m Gd1 Ch heavy	£67,241
1/06	Chel	2m5f Cls1 Nov Gd2 Ch gd-sft	£19,957
12/05	Wind	2m4f Cls1 Nov Gd2 Ch gd-sft	£20,051
12/05	Extr	2m3¹/₂f Cls2 Nov Ch soft	£12,231
2/05	Wwck	3m1f Cls3 Nov Hdl heavy	£6,565
1/05	Plum	2m5f Cls3 Nov Hdl 4-7yo soft	£5,564

Mud-loving staying chaser who confirmed his elevation to the top echelon with big runs in Ireland's top two races last season; put up a stunning performance in the Lexus Chase at Leopardstown over Christmas, where he made almost every yard and galloped Ireland's best chasers into the ground, coming home 8l and 5l to the good over Beef Or Salmon and War Of Attrition (3m, heavy, 6 ran); returned to the same venue six weeks later for the Hennessy Cognac Gold Cup, and looked set to repeat the dose turning for home, only to tie up on the run-in and get collared in the closing stages by Beef Or Salmon; took his chance in the Gold Cup, but the good to soft ground was too fast for him, and he could manage only a one-paced 11th behind Kauto Star (trainer also felt the extended distance stretched him); clearly one of the best around in hock-deep mud, and sure to be aimed at the same two races in Ireland; could also be dropped in trip; generally sound jumper.

1458 The Outlier (Ire)

9 gr g Roselier - Shuil A Cuig (Quayside)

Miss V Williams

P J Murphy

PLACINGS: 433/U21183/41021PPU-

RPR 148+c

Starts	1st	2nd	3rd	4th	Win & Pl
20	4	3	3	3	£70,327

129	1/07	Hayd	3m Cls1 Gd2 127-147 Ch Hcap heavy	£42,765
114	11/06	Towc	2m6f Cls4 98-114 Ch Hcap heavy	£6,397
107	2/06	Towc	2m3¹/₂f Cls4 89-115 Ch Hcap soft	£6,338
	1/06	Folk	2m5f Cls4 Mdn Ch gd-sft	£3,904

Stout staying chaser who is at his best in the mud; was seen to best effect in his preferred conditions in the Grade 2 Peter Marsh Chase at Haydock in January, when he raced prominently until going on and away at the fourth-last, jumping well and keeping on all the way to the line to beat subsequent Gold Cup third Turpin Green by 12l (was getting 21lb from the runner-up); failed to complete on last three starts, including when pulled up in the Grand National after taking them along in the early stages; starts the new campaign off a higher mark than he has won off, but there will be opportunities for him given his conditions. *'He jumps really well, is tough and stays well, but it has to be soft ground for him.' (Paul O'Neill, jockey)*

1459 Theatre Girl

4 b f King's Theatre - Fortune's Girl (Ardross)

A King

Let's Live Racing

PLACINGS: 31322-

RPR 112b

Starts	1st	2nd	3rd	4th	Win & Pl
5	1	2	2	-	£13,834

1/07	Weth	1m6f Cls5 NHF 4yo heavy	£1,370

Consistent performer in mares' bumpers last season, and should do well in long-distance novice hurdles this term; won over 1m6f in heavy ground at Wetherby in January, but was crying out for a stiffer test, and duly improved with two good runs in Listed events in the spring; battled on up the finishing hill to be 3¹/₂l second to Swaythe at Sandown in March (2m1/₂f, heavy, 14 ran), and then handled quicker ground well in the mares' bumper at Aintree's Grand National meeting, finishing 1³/₄l second to Turbo Linn, with a long break back to the third (2m1f, good, 20 ran); trainer usually converts his good bumper mares into novice hurdle winners, and this one looks another likely candidate for races against her own sex.

1460 Thisthatandtother (Ire)

11 b g Bob Back - Baden (Furry Glen)

P Nicholls

C G Roach

PLACINGS: 1F22/22214/3F/2527P-

RPR 158+c

Starts	1st	2nd	3rd	4th	Win & Pl
31	9	12	1	2	£381,029

3/05	Chel	2m5f Cls1 Gd2 Ch good	£87,000
2/04	Winc	2m Cls3 Nov Ch good	£10,847
12/03	Sand	2m Cls1 Nov Gd2 Ch good	£17,400
11/03	Chel	2m Cls1 Nov Gd2 Ch good	£20,825
10/03	Bang	2m1¹/₂f Cls3 Ch good	£4,225
1/03	Winc	2m Cls1 Gd1 Hdl gd-sft	£23,800
11/02	Winc	2m Cls3 Nov Hdl 4-6yo good	£4,891
10/02	Winc	2m Cls3 Nov Hdl good	£3,916
2/02	Winc	2m Cls6 NHF 4-6yo soft	£1,736

Very smart chaser at around 2m5f who came out on top of a titanic tussle with Fondmort to win the Festival Trophy at Cheltenham in 2005, but has yet to win another race and will be sent hunter chasing this term; missed a year through injury, but returned to action looking as good as ever in the Peterborough Chase at Huntingdon last November, where he weakened only after the last and went down by 4l to Racing Demon (2m4¹/₂f, good, 5 ran); ran a decent race to finish fifth under top weight in the Boylesports.com Gold Cup at Cheltenham the following month before another decent effort when runner-up to Monet's Garden in the Grade 1 Ascot Chase in February; those promising efforts, however, failed to materialise into a win as he was below his best back at the Festival before being pulled up in the National; likely to head to Aintree again in April. *'He'll be back in the new year after a breathing operation.' (Paul Nicholls, trainer)*

1461 Three Mirrors

7 b g Cloudings - Aliuska (Fijar Tango)

F Murphy   Sean J Murphy

PLACINGS: 5/6124/868/22221131-   RPR **138+c**

Starts	1st	2nd	3rd	4th	Win & Pl
19	5	5	1	1	£54,382
120	4/07	Ayr	2m4f Cls2 117-142 Ch Hcap gd-fm £18,789
107	4/07	Weth	2m4¹/₂f Cls3 107-133 Ch Hcap gd-fm.................£6,506
	3/07	MRas	2m4f Cls4 Ch gd-sft £5,205
	5/04	Tipp	2m Hdl 4yo gd-fm £6,813
	1/04	Gowr	2m Mdn Hdl 4yo soft £6,317

Novice chaser who really got his act together in the second half of last season, and ended up with an official mark of 135, compared to one of 106 as recently as March; won three of his last four, culminating in a 9l defeat of Locksmith in a quite valuable 2m4f handicap chase at Ayr in April, where he was always going well and kept on strongly; better going left-handed (turned over at even money at right-handed Carlisle on his penultimate start, jumping left); stays 2m4f; goes well on good to firm ground, open to further progress, and has earned a step up in grade this term.

1462 Tidal Bay (Ire)

6 b g Flemensfirth - June's Bride (Le Moss)

J H Johnson   Andrea & Graham Wylie

PLACINGS: 22/111221-   RPR **149+h**

Starts	1st	2nd	3rd	4th	Win & Pl
8	4	4	-	-	£87,877
	4/07	Aint	2m4f Cls1 Nov Gd2 Hdl good £31,361
	12/06	Chel	2m1f Cls2 Nov Hdl 4-6yo soft........................£9,395
	11/06	Carl	2m4f Cls4 Nov Hdl heavy £3,426
	10/06	Weth	2m4¹/₂f Cls4 Nov Hdl soft £3,426

Classy novice hurdler last season, but everything points to him being even better over fences; beaten only twice in six starts, and lost no caste on either occasion, finding Wichita Lineman 6l too good at Cheltenham in January before a neck second to Massini's Maguire at the Festival (2m5f, good to soft, 15 ran); elsewhere it was comfortable wins all the way, accounting for decent but inferior opposition on three occasions in the autumn, and signing off with an 8l defeat of Wins Now in Grade 2 company at Aintree's Grand National meeting, although the margin would have been less had the runner-up not blundered at the last when seemingly just coming off worse (2m4f, good, 10 ran); looks a real chaser in the making, and will surely go on to better things over fences this winter; stays at least 2m5f and yet to race on ground faster than good. *'Of all the horses I've ever ridden, this horse has the most potential. Even when he walks around the parade ring, you can see he's class.' (Paddy Brennan, former rider)*

1463 Tidal Fury (Ire)

5 b g Night Shift - Tidal Reach (Kris S)

J Jay   Twelfth Night

PLACINGS: 1/2311153/88141194-   RPR **140+c**

Starts	1st	2nd	3rd	4th	Win & Pl
16	7	1	2	2	£230,353
	1/07	Sthl	2m Cls3 Nov Ch soft...£7,222
	12/06	Hayd	2m Cls3 Nov Ch heavy £9,626
	11/06	Carl	2m Cls4 Ch soft £5,205
	11/05	Autl	2m2f Gp1 Hdl 3yo v soft £79,787
	10/05	Autl	2m2f Gd2 Hdl 3yo v soft £51,064
	9/05	Autl	2m2f Hdl 3yo v soft £19,745
	4/05	Autl	1m7f Hdl 3yo heavy £16,340

Did wonders for his small Newmarket yard when winning a string of good juvenile hurdles in France in 2005, and made his mark in novice chases in Britain last winter; won three of his first four in bold, front-running style, beating Akilak by 9l at Carlisle, Flying Enterprise (a 132-rated chaser) by 7l at Haydock and the 118-rated Archie Babe by 52l at Southwell, all in very soft ground; started just 16-1 for the Arkle at the Cheltenham Festival, but found that a different kettle of fish altogether, and was struggling from four out, eventually trailing in 50l ninth behind My Way De Solzen; below par over hurdles back at Auteuil in April; rated 141 over fences, and on some bits of form, that gives him a chance to make his mark in handicap chases this term; clearly relishes testing ground.

1464 Too Forward (Ire)

11 ch g Toulon - One Back (Meneval)

C Llewellyn   T L Gibson & D Mathias

PLACINGS: 431275/7125U2/19182-   RPR **160+c**

Starts	1st	2nd	3rd	4th	Win & Pl
30	6	7	3	2	£113,285
144	1/07	Chel	2m5f Cls1 List 126-152 Ch Hcap heavy...........£22,808
138	10/06	Weth	2m4¹/₂f Cls1 List 120-145 Ch Hcap soft £14,255
127	11/05	Newb	2m6¹/₂f Cls3 114-130 Ch Hcap good £12,626
	1/05	Folk	3m1f Cls4 Ch gd-sft £4,342
	1/02	Donc	3m¹/₂f Cls1 Nov Gd2 Hdl soft £10,800
	12/01	Folk	2m1¹/₂f Cls4 Nov Hdl 4-6yo heavy....................£2,356

Veteran 2m4f handicap chaser who was better than ever last season; won twice, beating Kinburn by 3l in soft ground at Wetherby last October, and defying a 6lb rise to beat Nozic by 7l in a Listed handicap chase at Cheltenham on New Year's Day, this time in heavy ground; another 8lb rise forced him into Grade 2 company at the Cheltenham Festival (eighth behind Taranis), but he ended his campaign with a very creditable 3l second to Nycteos in a Grade 2 handicap back at Cheltenham in April (2m5f, good, 6 ran); starts the season on a career-high mark of 153, which is bound to make life tough, and will limit him to the very best handicaps this term; loves Cheltenham and suited by plenty of give in the ground.

1465 Tot O'Whiskey

6 b g Saddlers' Hall - Whatagale (Strong Gale)

J M Jefferson   Boundary Garage (Bury) Limited

PLACINGS: 11100-   **RPR 122b**

Starts	1st	2nd	3rd	4th	Win & Pl
5	-	-	-	-	£5,687
	2/07	Catt	2m Cls5 NHF 5-6yo good		£1,850
	12/06	Catt	2m Cls6 NHF 4-6yo gd-sft		£2,056
	11/06	Hexm	2m¹/₂f Cls6 NHF 4-6yo soft		£1,782

Leading bumper horse from the north last season, and ought to do well in novice hurdles; won his first three starts, all by wide margins, at Hexham and Catterick (twice), completing the sequence under a big penalty with a resounding 9l defeat of Dand Nee in a bad contest in February; needed to improve considerably to justify odds of 10-1 in the Champion Bumper at Cheltenham, and while he could manage only 11th behind Cork All Star, he ran on in a manner that suggested he was already crying out for 2m4f and beyond; got outpaced in another Grade 1 bumper at the Punchestown festival, but should be well placed in the north.

1466 Trabolgan (Ire)

9 b g King's Ride - Derrella (Derrylin)

N Henderson   Trevor Hemmings

PLACINGS: 222/F11P/1221/1/

Starts	1st	2nd	3rd	4th	Win & Pl
12	5	5	-	-	£200,599
	11/05	Newb	3m2¹/₂f Cls1 Gd3 126-151 Ch Hcap good		£71,275
	3/05	Chel	3m¹/₂f Cls1 Gd1 Ch good		£81,200
	11/04	Ling	2m4¹/₂f Cls3 Ch heavy		£5,876
	1/04	Newb	2m3f Cls4 Nov Hdl soft		£3,640
	12/03	Asct	2m4f Cls3 Mdn Hdl good		£7,475

One-time high-class staying chaser who is poised to return to action this season after almost two years off with tendon trouble; hit the big time in 2005, winning the Royal & SunAlliance Chase at the Cheltenham Festival (beat Comply Or Die by 3l) and returning the following November to land the Hennessy Cognac Gold Cup at Newbury under top weight, forging clear from the last to give L'Ami 7lb and a 2¹/₂l beating; was regarded as a King George and Gold Cup horse until it all went wrong soon after that win, and connections will be hoping that he can return to that sort of level, though whether he can make the necessary jump after so long off is open to doubt; sound jumper and strong stayer, and has had only five starts over fences.

1467 Tranquil Sea (Ire)

5 b g Sea Raven - Silver Valley (Henbit)

E O'Grady (Ir)   Nelius Hayes

PLACINGS: 1/210-   **RPR 132+b**

Starts	1st	2nd	3rd	4th	Win & Pl
3	1	1	-	-	£7,402
	2/07	Leop	2m NHF 4-6yo heavy		£6,070

Interesting recruit to the 2m novice hurdle ranks;

raced three times in bumpers last season and followed up a sound debut second with one of the best performances of the season in that sphere; sent off even-money favourite at Leopardstown in February where he had no trouble coming home 5l in front of Stewarts Lane, with a yawning 24l back to Jadanli, who won and finished second three times from his next four starts; that performance earned a Racing Post Rating of 132, which would have been good enough to figure in the first half-dozen in the Champion Bumper at Cheltenham; already has point-to-point form, so will make a chaser in the long term, but likely to do well over hurdles in the meantime.

1468 Treasury Counsel (Ire)

5 br g Leading Counsel - Dunacarney (Random Shot)

N Henderson   The Not Afraid Partnership

PLACINGS: 3/21313-   **RPR 123h**

Starts	1st	2nd	3rd	4th	Win & Pl
6	2	1	3	-	£11,436
	3/07	Kemp	2m5f Cls3 104-130 Hdl Hcap good		£5,205
	12/06	Hrfd	2m3¹/₂f Cls4 Mdn Hdl gd-sft		£3,253

Progressive 2m4f novice hurdler last season, and should continue to do well at a reasonable level; won twice, beating Sherwoods Folly by 1¹/₂l at Hereford in December and bouncing back from a disappointing effort on heavy ground to beat Corker by 3¹/₂l in a handicap at Kempton in March; raised 8lb for that success, and put up his best effort in defeat on his final outing, when a staying-on 2¹/₂l third behind Oslot and Chilling Place at Sandown in April (2m4¹/₂f, good to firm, 17 ran); that was much the best race he has contested to date, and hinted that the best may yet be to come; connections have the option of trying him over fences. *'He definitely wants good ground.' (Nicky Henderson, trainer)*

1469 Trigger The Light

6 ch g Double Trigger - Lamper's Light (Idiot's Delight)

A King   Mr & Mrs F C Welch & Mrs A A Shutes

PLACINGS: 384/12216-   **RPR 130h**

Starts	1st	2nd	3rd	4th	Win & Pl
8	2	2	1	1	£11,986
	2/07	Tntn	3m¹/₂f Cls4 Nov Hdl soft		£4,111
	12/06	Wwck	2m5f Cls4 Mdn Hdl soft		£3,253

Promising sort who won two novice hurdles last season, but is seen as a staying chaser in the making; gained his wins in soft ground at Warwick and Taunton, posting his best figures at the latter venue when staying on strongly to beat Ornais by 3¹/₂l over 3m¹/₂f; faced his toughest task yet on his final start when saddled with 11st 10lb in the EBF Final at Sandown in March, and was far from disgraced in finishing 12l sixth behind Albertas Run (2m4¹/₂f, heavy, 16 ran, was giving lumps of weight away to all those who beat him); would have gone for the Brit Insurance at the Cheltenham Festival had the ground been softer, but was instead put away with a novice chase campaign this winter in mind; looks the type who could show marked improvement, being from the family of Martin's Lamp and Hurricane Lamp.

1470 Tritonix (Ire)

4 gr c Linamix - La Panthere (Pine Bluff)

P Hobbs   John P McManus

PLACINGS: 1131P-   **RPR 123 + h**

Starts	1st	2nd	3rd	4th	Win & Pl
5	3	-	1	-	£21,140

3/07	Wwck	2m Cls4 Nov Hdl good	£3,253
11/06	Hntg	2m¹/₂f Cls2 Nov Hdl 3yo good	£13,012
11/06	Bang	2m1f Cls4 Mdn Hdl 3yo gd-sft	£3,025

Useful juvenile hurdler last season, winning three of his five starts and beaten only when taking on the very best; scored by wide margins at Bangor and Huntingdon in November before what proved subsequently to be a very decent effort when 14l third behind Katchit at Cheltenham in December (2m1f, soft, 12 ran, level weights); was given a long break, missing the Cheltenham Festival and returning with a decisive success against older novices at Warwick at the end of March; sent off at just 10-1 to exact his revenge on Katchit on good ground at Aintree in April, but quickly lost his pitch from three out and was pulled up before the last (Tony McCoy reported he had a breathing problem); highly regarded, and could do well in handicaps if his wind problems have been sorted out.

1471 Trompette (USA)

5 b m Bahri - Bold Bold (Sadler's Wells)

N Henderson   Elite Racing Club

PLACINGS: 31615/31F0-   **RPR 137 + h**

Starts	1st	2nd	3rd	4th	Win & Pl
9	3	-	2	-	£14,682

115	1/07	Ludl	2m Cls3 99-125 Hdl Hcap gd-sft	£6,263
	3/06	Plum	2m Cls4 Nov Hdl 4yo soft	£3,904
	2/06	Plum	2m Cls4 Nov Hdl gd-sft	£3,083

Half-sister to Ambobo, and a decent hurdler in her own right; looked well handicapped when absolutely lagging up off a mark of 115 over 2m at Ludlow in January, where she led on the bit 2 out and drew clear to beat Theatre Diva by 5l; went up 15lb for that win, but might have followed up next time but for a crashing fall 2 out in a better contest won by Clouding Over at Southwell; started 33-1 for the County Hurdle on her final outing, and was far from disgraced in finishing 9¹/₂l 11th of 28 behind Pedrobob; has had just nine starts over hurdles, and there could yet be a bit more to come from her; has gained all her wins over a sharp 2m on easy ground.

1472 Trouble At Bay (Ire)

7 b g Slip Anchor - Fight Right (Crystal Glitters)

A King   Nigel Bunter

PLACINGS: 4111110/2544/712430-   **RPR 143 + c**

Starts	1st	2nd	3rd	4th	Win & Pl
17	6	2	1	4	£74,121

12/06	Hrfd	2m Cls3 Nov Ch gd-sft	£7,606
2/04	Kemp	2m Cls1 Gd2 Hdl 4yo good	£17,400
1/04	Chel	2m1f Cls2 Nov Hdl 4yo good	£9,613
12/03	Chel	2m¹/₂f Cls2 Nov Hdl 3yo gd-sft	£11,087
12/03	Winc	2m Cls4 Nov Hdl 3yo good	£1,946
11/03	Hrfd	2m1f Cls4 Nov Hdl 3yo gd-fm	£2,443

Smart hurdler (peak rating of 143) who made a successful return from a two-year absence through injury last season; showed the benefit of a pipe-opener over hurdles by getting off the mark over fences at the first time of asking at Hereford in December, where he hardly put a foot wrong and drew clear from 3 out to beat Opera De Coeur and Ursis by 7l and 3¹/₂l (2m, good to soft, 7 ran); ran to a similar level next time when 10l second to Royal Shakespeare at Kempton, but rather disappointing on his last three outings, doing best when reverting to the smaller obstacles and finishing third behind Straw Bear and Afsoun in Wincanton's Kingwell Hurdle; official chase rating of 134 looks fair, and he could do well if putting his best foot forward in handicap chases; suited by 2m on good ground.

1473 Tumbling Dice (Ire)

8 b g King's Theatre - Eva Fay (Fayruz)

T Taaffe (Ir)   Mrs John Donegan

PLACINGS: 2F33/173P13P/201554-   **RPR 153 c**

Starts	1st	2nd	3rd	4th	Win & Pl
32	7	3	5	3	£123,863

	12/06	Cork	2m Gd2 Ch heavy	£26,938
	2/06	Clon	2m4f Ch yld-sft	£8,979
	10/05	Cork	2m4f Nov Ch gd-yld	£12,004
115	12/04	Punc	2m4f 101-123 Hdl Hcap soft	£9,246
110	11/04	Punc	2m4f 95-125 Hdl Hcap yld-sft	£8,516
104	3/04	Wxfd	2m4f 90-107 Hdl Hcap yld-sft	£6,569
100	1/04	Cork	2m4f 82-115 Hdl Hcap soft	£10,299

Smart chaser whose handicap mark forced him to compete in Graded chases last season, and did so with some degree of success; well beaten in the Paddy Power Gold Cup at Cheltenham, but much better next time in a Grade 2 over 2m at Cork, where he hacked up by 10l in heavy ground from Jim; below that form on three subsequent outings in small-field Grade 2 chases between 2m-2m4f, twice behind Nickname (btn 17¹/₂l into fifth at Punchestown on soft ground); loves the mud and effective between 2m and 2m4f, but likely to be confined to similar sorts of races unless the handicapper relents a little.

1474 Turko (Fr)

5 gr g Turgeon - Cambaria (Nice Havrais)

P Nicholls   The Stewart Family

PLACINGS: 411221652/11217P-   **RPR 148+c**

Starts	1st	2nd	3rd	4th	Win & Pl
15	6	4	-	1	£94,207
2/07	Font	2m4f Cls3 Nov Ch soft			£9,481
11/06	Winc	2m5f Cls1 Nov Gd2 Ch good			£20,893
10/06	Aint	2m4f Cls3 Nov Ch good			£9,759
2/06	Winc	2m Cls4 Nov Hdl gd-sft			£4,554
11/05	Newb	2m¹/₂f Cls3 Nov Hdl 3yo good			£7,157
8/05	Claf	2m2f Hdl 3yo v soft			£10,894

Smart novice chaser last season at around 2m4f, but will have to find some improvement if he is to overcome his current mark of 150 in handicaps; won three of his six races over fences, doing best at Fontwell in February when handing out an emphatic beating to stablemate Phar Bleu, coming home unchallenged; below that form when tried over 3m-plus in the SunAlliance Chase at Cheltenham, but not disgraced in finishing 20l behind stablemate Denman, while something was clearly amiss when he pulled up at Aintree on his final start; might be interesting in the Paddy Power Gold Cup at Cheltenham, having run well over the course and distance last season when runner-up to subsequent Arkle winner My Way De Solzen.

1475 Turpin Green (Ire)

8 b g Presenting - Coolshamrock (Buckskin)

N Richards   Trevor Hemmings

PLACINGS: 11331/13252/1P235-   **RPR 168+c**

Starts	1st	2nd	3rd	4th	Win & Pl
15	3	4	3	-	£164,888
11/06	Carl	2m4f Cls2 Ch soft			£15,658
11/05	Carl	2m4f Cls3 Nov Ch soft			£7,352
4/05	Aint	2m4f Cls1 Nov Gd2 Hdl gd-sft			£29,000
11/04	Aint	2m¹/₂f Cls3 Nov Hdl 4-6yo soft			£6,175
10/04	Uttx	2m Cls4 Nov Hdl heavy			£3,471

Progressive, but enigmatic, staying chaser; beat Exotic Dancer in a minor race at Carlisle on his reappearance last term, but was a bitter disappointment in the Hennessy at Newbury, where he was beaten with a circuit to run and pulled up; did better when second in the Peter Marsh Chase at Haydock (12l behind The Outlier), but the zenith of his campaign came when he was 5l third in the Cheltenham Gold Cup in first-time blinkers, as he travelled strongly, but just lacked the finishing kick of Kauto Star and Exotic Dancer (3m2¹/₂f, good to soft, 18 ran); looked well treated for the Grand National on that evidence, but missed that in favour of the Betfair Bowl, and showed the other side of his character again by spitting out the dummy at an early stage and trailing in last; has the Betfair Chase at Haydock and Gold Cup on the agenda this term, with connections also looking at the prospect of taking him over to Ireland. *'We'll probably campaign him a fair bit at Haydock.' (Nicky Richards, trainer)*

1476 Twist Magic (Fr)

5 b g Winged Love - Twist Scarlett (Lagunas)

P Nicholls   Barry Fulton Tony Hayward Michael Lynch

PLACINGS: 3/316153P/12F1-   **RPR 159+c**

Starts	1st	2nd	3rd	4th	Win & Pl
12	4	1	3	-	£117,235
4/07	Aint	2m Cls1 Nov Gd1 Ch good			£71,275
12/06	Fknm	2m¹/₂f Cls3 Nov Ch gd-sft			£7,858
12/05	Winc	2m Cls4 Nov Hdl 3yo gd-sft			£3,590
6/05	Autl	1m7f Hdl 3yo v soft			£14,298

High-class 2m novice chaser in his first season over fences last term, and now looks a principal contender for the Champion Chase; rounded off at Aintree in April with a fine win in the Grade 1 Maghull Chase, jumping slickly and speedily to hand out a 5l beating to Arkle Trophy runner-up Fair Along; would surely have had a hand in the finish of that contest at the Cheltenham Festival but for falling at the second-last when lying in third place having yet to make his challenge; had earlier opened his account over fences with a 24l demolition of Royal Shakespeare before coming off second-best in a Grade 2 at Kempton behind Jack The Giant after making a crucial error at the second-last (2m, good to soft, 6 ran); clearly reminds his trainer of former Champion Chase winner Azertyuiop, and will be trained with that one race in mind this season, for which he is already as short as 6-1. *'He has the world at his feet. He could head straight for the Haldon Gold Cup at Exeter on November 6. I suspect he could be best going left-handed.' (Paul Nicholls, trainer)*

1477 Ungaro (Fr)

8 b g Epervier Bleu - Harpyes (Quart De Vin)

K Reveley   Sir Robert Ogden

PLACINGS: 4F24/31124165/11166-   **RPR 155+c**

Starts	1st	2nd	3rd	4th	Win & Pl
20	7	3	1	3	£105,844
12/06	Kemp	3m Cls1 Nov Gd1 Ch gd-sft			£40,102
11/06	Hntg	2m4¹/₂f Cls3 Nov Ch good			£6,665
10/06	Kels	2m1f Cls4 Ch gd-sft			£5,205
2/06	Sand	2m6f Cls1 Gd3 120-146 Hdl Hcap good			£28,510
11/05	Sedg	2m5¹/₂f Cls3 92-117 Hdl Hcap soft			£4,808
11/05	Hntg	2m5¹/₂f Cls3 Nov Hdl good			£5,088
11/03	Ayr	2m Cls6 NHF 4-6yo soft			£1,988

(128 / 115 in left margin of table)

Showed very smart novice chase form in the first half of last season, following up wins at Kelso and Huntingdon by beating Boychuk by 10l in the Grade 1 Feltham Novices' Chase over 3m at Kempton on Boxing Day; returned from a three-month break in the Royal & SunAlliance Chase at Cheltenham, but could manage only a slightly disappointing sixth behind Denman (3m¹/₂f, good to soft, 17 ran), and was again below par behind Aces Four at Aintree; record away from Cheltenham and Aintree since the start of the 2005-06 season reads F24311241111, and the pick of his form has been on right-handed, flat tracks, so the King George could yet emerge as a viable target.

1478 United (Ger)

6 b m Desert King - Una Kasala (Law Society)

Mrs L Wadham   R B Holt

PLACINGS: 11/18P5/02511143-   **RPR 145h**

Starts	1st	2nd	3rd	4th	Win & Pl
14	6	1	1	1	£153,791

	2/07	Font	2m4f Cls1 Gd2 Hdl soft	£22,536
140	1/07	Sand	2m4¹/₂f Cls2 123-149 Hdl Hcap heavy	£18,789
134	12/06	Hayd	2m4f Cls2 133-159 Hdl Hcap heavy	£19,518
	4/05	Punc	2m Gd1 Hdl 4yo soft	£48,369
	3/05	Strf	2m¹/₂f Cls3 Nov Hdl 4yo gd-sft	£7,397
	2/05	Hntg	2m¹/₂f Cls4 Mdn Hdl soft	£3,458

Started off in handicap hurdles last season, but did well to graduate successfully to a higher level; won in heavy ground at Haydock and Sandown before completing the hat-trick in the Grade 2 National Spirit Hurdle at Fontwell in February, where she routed Refinement by 14l in the soft; even that run was surpassed, though, when she made the frame in the World Hurdle at the Cheltenham Festival, where despite the drying ground she led from three out until headed between the last two, eventually finishing 14l fourth behind Inglis Drever (3m, good to soft, 14 ran); slightly below that form in Grade 1 at Punchestown, when third behind Refinement, beaten 5¹/₂l (3m, good, 9 ran), but the ground excuses that to some extent; stays over hurdles and will reportedly follow the new mares' programme, with a 2m4f £100,000 contest at the Cheltenham Festival as the ultimate prize.

1479 Val Du Ciron (Fr)

4 b g True Brave - Dix Huit Brumaire (General Assembly)

Miss H Knight   The Hon Mrs Peter Tower

PLACINGS: 1-   **RPR 109+b**

Starts	1st	2nd	3rd	4th	Win & Pl
1	1	-	-	-	£2,602

	3/07	Ludl	2m Cls5 NHF 4-6yo good	£2,602

Half-brother to Dix Villez, a useful staying chaser who was placed in the Munster National and Cork National last season; started a well-backed odds-on shot for his debut in a good-ground bumper at Ludlow in March, and never gave his supporters a moment's worry, leading 3f out and bounding clear to beat subsequent winner Nakoma by 11l; could not have done much more on that first start, and looks an interesting prospect for decent novice hurdles, especially when he is stepped up in distance.

1480 Venalmar

5 b g Kayf Tara - Elaine Tully (Persian Bold)

M Morris (Ir)   Michael O'Flynn

PLACINGS: 421-   **RPR 119b**

Starts	1st	2nd	3rd	4th	Win & Pl
3	1	1	-	1	£6,664

	3/07	Naas	2m NHF 4-6yo heavy	£5,136

Progressive form in bumpers last season, and

should make up into a decent novice hurdler; made his debut in a maiden hurdle (finished fourth of 22 at Punchestown, beaten 13¹/₂l when unfancied), but then switched to bumpers; stepped up a lot on final start to win 14-runner event at Naas by 8l from the useful Stewarts House, travelling strongly in atrocious conditions and scoring comfortably; quite stoutly bred, and likely to stay at least 2m4f.

1481 Verasi

6 b g Kahyasi - Fair Verona (Alleged)

G L Moore   F Ledger J Bateman

PLACINGS: 0F/911035/065601300-   **RPR 138+h**

Starts	1st	2nd	3rd	4th	Win & Pl
20	4	2	2	-	£84,136

130	1/07	Kemp	2m5f Cls2 121-147 Hdl Hcap soft	£25,052
124	12/05	Sand	2m¹/₂f Cls1 List 111-137 Hdl Hcap heavy	£28,510
115	11/05	Sand	2m¹/₂f Cls3 110-125 Hdl Hcap heavy	£5,452
	12/04	Font	2m2¹/₂f Cls4 Nov Hdl 3yo good	£3,387

Tough handicap hurdler whose sights will no doubt once again be aimed at the top contests, and chances are he will pick up a race; below his best in first half of last season, but returned to form with a vengeance to take the valuable Lanzarote Hurdle (now run over 2m5f) at Kempton in January, beating Royals Darling by 11l in soft ground; matched that performance when third, beaten only 1l by Taranis, in the Grade 3 Sandown Handicap Hurdle the following month (2m6f, soft, 16 ran), keeping on well up the hill; very disappointing in the Coral Cup and a Listed handicap hurdle at Aintree final two starts; needs at least 2m4f nowadays, and acts well on soft ground; mark of 137 will not make life easy, but could come down a bit if he takes a few runs to come to hand.

1482 Vic Venturi (Ire)

7 ch g Old Vic - Carmen Lady (Torus)

P Fenton (Ir)   J P Dunne

PLACINGS: 12/131213/12625P-   **RPR 141c**

Starts	1st	2nd	3rd	4th	Win & Pl
13	4	4	2	-	£107,363

	10/06	Gway	2m1f Nov Gd3 Ch heavy	£17,959
	4/06	Fair	2m4f Nov Gd2 Hdl gd-yld	£21,550
	12/05	Limk	2m6f Nov Gd1 Hdl heavy	£18,468
	10/05	Gway	2m4f Nov Hdl soft	£9,234

Smart novice chaser last season, and looks one for good handicaps over 2m4f-plus; made the perfect start in the Grade 3 Ballybrit Novice Chase over 2m1f at Galway last October, jumping well on the whole out of the heavy ground and beating Conna Castle by 1l; was twice runner-up in Graded company afterwards (including when 7l adrift of Mister Top Notch in a Grade 1 at Leopardstown), but posted his best RPR when 9³/₄l fifth behind L'Antartique off a mark of 134 in the Jewson Novices' Handicap Chase at the Cheltenham Festival; didn't jump too well there, nor in Grade 1 novice company at the Punchestown festival (pulled up), but starts the season on a very fair mark of 132, and can win a decent handicap if getting his act together.

1483 Vodka Bleu (Fr)

8 b g Pistolet Bleu - Viva Vodka (Crystal Glitters)

D Pipe   D A Johnson

PLACINGS: P11612112311/2P0400-   **RPR 151 + c**

Starts	1st	2nd	3rd	4th	Win & Pl
27	9	4	3	1	£131,051

11/04	Newb	2m4f Cls1 Nov Gd2 Ch good	£20,300
11/04	Chel	2m4¹/₂f Cls2 Nov Ch good	£13,068
10/04	Chep	2m3¹/₂f Cls3 Nov Ch good	£8,044
9/04	MRas	2m6¹/₂f Cls2 Nov Ch gd-fm	£13,416
8/04	Hntg	2m4¹/₂f Cls4 Ch gd-fm	£4,116
6/04	NAbb	2m6f Cls3 Nov Hdl soft	£5,148
6/04	Worc	3m Cls4 Mdn Hdl gd-fm	£3,439
3/03	Hayd	2m Cls6 NHF 4-6yo good	£2,065
1/03	Leop	2m NHF 4yo soft	£5,601

Very smart chaser who won in Grade 2 company as a novice and showed last season that he retains all his ability when returning from two years on the sidelines with tendon trouble; ran a blinder on his return in the Paddy Power Gold Cup at Cheltenham in November, kicking clear after the second-last before getting caught by the hugely progressive Exotic Dancer and going down by 3l in the subsequent Gold Cup runner-up (2m4¹/₂f, good to soft, 16 ran); beaten only 14l by Monet's Garden in the Grade 1 Ascot Chase in February, but was way below his best on his remaining starts; seemingly trained to the minute for his reappearance last season and was unlucky to run into one so talented as the winner, but starts this time on a mark of 135, only 1lb higher than last term, and no surprise to see him back at Prestbury Park in November in a bid to go one better.

1484 Voy Por Ustedes (Fr)

6 b g Villez - Nuit D'Ecajeul (Matahawk)

A King   Sir Robert Ogden

PLACINGS: 31U1633/111112/21U1-   **RPR 170 + c**

Starts	1st	2nd	3rd	4th	Win & Pl
20	10	2	4	-	£423,020

3/07	Chel	2m Cls1 Gd1 Ch gd-sft	£176,762
12/06	Kemp	2m Cls1 Gd2 Ch gd-sft	£40,383
3/06	Chel	2m Cls1 Gd1 Ch gd-sft	£79,828
2/06	Winc	2m Cls1 Nov Gd2 Ch soft	£17,106
12/05	Wwck	2m Cls3 Nov Ch soft	£7,140
12/05	Plum	2m1f Cls3 Nov Ch soft	£7,858
11/05	Wwck	2m1¹/₂f Cls3 Nov Ch 4yo good	£6,994
1/05	Hntg	2m1¹/₂f Cls4 Nov Hdl good	£3,549
11/04	Engh	2m1¹/₂f Hdl 3yo holding	£13,521
10/04	Nanc	2m1f Hdl 3yo v soft	£5,070

Top-class 2m chaser who followed up his Arkle success in 2006 with victory in last season's Queen Mother Champion Chase at the Cheltenham Festival; was not the champion chaser in the 2m category – that honour fell to Kauto Star, who beat him by 7l in the Tingle Creek – but took full advantage of that superstar's step up to the staying division by beating Dempsey by 1¹/₂l in March, after odds-on favourite Well Chief departed in the

early stages; had previously opened his account for the season with victory over Oneway in a Grade 2 contest at Kempton over Christmas, before himself unseating early on in the Game Spirit at Newbury; tough and classy sort who has been beaten just twice in completed starts over fences, and will again be the one to beat in the 2m division when there is some dig in the ground; likely to take a similar route to last season, with the Tingle Creek and Champion Chase his main targets once again.

1485 War Of Attrition (Ire)

8 br g Presenting - Una Juna (Good Thyne)

M Morris (Ir)   Gigginstown House Stud

PLACINGS: 2/1172/1115211/1223-   **RPR 171 + c**

Starts	1st	2nd	3rd	4th	Win & Pl
21	10	6	1	-	£564,955

10/06	Punc	2m6f List Ch soft	£14,816
4/06	Punc	3m1f Gd1 Ch good	£99,310
3/06	Chel	3m2¹/₂f Cls1 Gd1 Ch good	£228,080
11/05	Clon	2m4f Gd2 Ch yld-sft	£27,702
10/05	Punc	2m6f List Ch good	£15,236
4/05	Punc	2m Nov Gd1 Ch soft	£43,972
2/05	Naas	2m Nov Ch sft-hvy	£8,576
11/04	Thur	2m6f Ch yield	£7,299
12/03	Navn	2m Hdl 4yo soft	£6,273
12/03	Punc	2m Mdn Hdl 4-5yo yield	£5,377

Cheltenham Gold Cup winner in 2006, but was ruled out of last season's contest after picking up an injury midway through the campaign; had looked as good as ever on his return last season, when beating Watson Lake by 11l at Punchestown; however, below his best on three subsequent starts (albeit in Grade 1 company on ground softer than ideal for him), finishing in the frame behind Beef Or Salmon at Down Royal (touched off by a neck in a thriller), In Compliance at Punchestown and The Listener at Leopardstown (beaten 13l); was quickly ruled out for the remainder of the season when heat was detected in a leg, and only rated 50-50 to return to action this season – and even then, it will be after Christmas for a light campaign geared towards Cheltenham; impossible to include in Ten to Follow lists from the outset, but a watching brief is advised before the transfer period.

1486 Watson Lake (Ire)

9 b g Be My Native - Magneeto (Brush Aside)

N Meade (Ir)   John Corr

PLACINGS: 3/2114614/236441P47-   **RPR 158 + c**

Starts	1st	2nd	3rd	4th	Win & Pl
31	10	5	2	7	£215,648

2/07	Gowr	2m4f Gd2 Ch heavy	£21,993
3/06	Navn	2m4f Gd3 Ch sft-hvy	£14,367
11/05	Naas	2m Gd3 Ch heavy	£16,160
10/05	Limk	2m1f Ch yld-sft	£12,466
2/05	Navn	2m Nov Gd2 Ch heavy	£20,777
11/04	Fair	2m4f Nov Gd1 Ch soft	£41,197
11/04	Navn	2m4f Nov Gd3 Hdl yield	£8,759
1/04	Leop	2m4f Nov Gd3 Hdl yield	£16,021
12/03	Navn	2m2f Mdn Hdl soft	£6,721
11/02	DRoy	2m NHF heavy	£4,868

Dyed-in-the-wool Grade 2/3 chaser who is effective

from 2m-2m4f and likes soft ground; hardy sort who always runs in just about every suitable event in Ireland, and can usually be relied upon to pick up a win or two; had to wait until a Grade 2 over 2m4f at Gowran in February to get his head in front last term, but claimed the notable scalp of subsequent Grade 1 winner Mansony, going clear on the run-in for a 5l success; well held on his last three starts, and on balance doesn't look as good as he was two or three years ago; still capable of picking up races below the top level, though.

1487 Wee Forbees (Ire)

5 b g Shernazar - Gender Gap (Shecky Greene)

J H Johnson   Matthew Green And J H Johnson

PLACINGS: 5311P-   RPR **125+h**

Starts	1st	2nd	3rd	4th	Win & Pl
5	2	-	1	-	£5,912
	3/07	Sedg	2m4f Cls4 Nov Hdl gd-fm		£2,277
	1/07	Catt	3m1¹/₂f Cls4 Nov Hdl soft		£3,253

Interesting novice chase prospect, having done well in novice hurdles over 2m4f-3m1¹/₂f last season; took a couple of runs to get the hang of things, but was then most impressive when making all at Catterick in January (beat In Dream's by 11l in ordinary contest) and Sedgefield in March (beat subsequent winner Escayola eased down by 7l, form worked out quite well); started 16-1 in Grade 1 company at Aintree on his final start, but was pulled up in a race won by Chief Dan George; likely to go over fences now, and should do well granted a test of stamina.

1488 Well Chief (Ger)

8 ch g Night Shift - Wellesiena (Scenic)

D Pipe   D A Johnson

PLACINGS: 3/15111/23F1221/1F3-   RPR **167+c**

Starts	1st	2nd	3rd	4th	Win & Pl
19	9	4	3	-	£485,421
	2/07	Newb	2m1f Cls1 Gd2 Ch soft		£34,373
	4/05	Sand	2m Cls1 Gd2 Ch good		£58,000
176	1/05	Chel	2m Cls1 Gd2 156-176 Ch Hcap gd-sft		£63,800
	4/04	Aint	2m Cls1 Nov Gd1 Ch good		£58,000
	3/04	Chel	2m Cls1 Gd1 Ch good		£81,200
	2/04	Tntn	2m¹/₂f Cls4 Nov Ch soft		£4,121
138	11/03	Winc	2m Cls1 Gd2 132-152 Hdl Hcap gd-fm		£18,600
	2/03	Kemp	2m Cls1 Nov Gd2 Hdl 4yo good		£17,400
	2/03	Tntn	2m1f Cls3 Mdn Hdl soft		£5,233

Top-class 2m chaser who returned to action last season after nearly two years on the sidelines with niggling leg trouble; shrugged off that lengthy absence with a tremendous reappearance in the Grade 2 Game Spirit Chase at Newbury in February, slamming Ashley Brook by 11l and leaping to the head of the betting for the Champion Chase, in which he finished runner-up to Moscow Flyer in 2005; seen by many as the banker of the meeting at Cheltenham and consequently sent off the even-money favourite, but jumped only one fence before falling, and

again left his connections tearing their hair out when failing to see out the 2m4f trip and finishing only third behind Monet's Garden in the Melling Chase at Aintree on his only other start; supremely talented individual who goes particularly well at Cheltenham (won the Arkle as a novice and carried top weight to victory in the Victor Chandler Chase at the track) and will be heading back to Prestbury Park in March to try to finally gain the recognition he deserves. *'Last season was a bit of an anticlimax, but he's ready to do battle once again in the autumn, when he could start off in the Tingle Creek at Sandown. Then we'd take it from there, with the Champion Chase his target again in the spring.' (David Pipe, trainer)*

1489 West End King (Ire)

5 b g Old Vic - Last Princess (Le Prince)

Miss H Knight   M F Broughton & Partners

PLACINGS: 1-   RPR **112+b**

Starts	1st	2nd	3rd	4th	Win & Pl
1	1	-	-	-	£2,055
	1/07	Hntg	2m¹/₂f Cls5 Mdn NHF 5-6yo soft		£2,056

Half-brother to classy staying chaser Strath Royal; made a good impression on his debut in a soft-ground bumper at Huntingdon in January, where, despite being easy to back and looking green beforehand, he swept into the lead with 2f to go and stormed clear to beat Atouchbetweenacara by 5l; that wasn't the greatest bumper ever staged, but a couple of those among the 17 beaten horses did come out and frank the form with a win later on; obviously has the potential to do well in novice hurdles, and ought to be suited by further than 2m.

1490 Whispered Secret (Ger)

8 b g Selkirk - Wells Whisper (Sadler's Wells)

D Pipe   David Manasseh

PLACINGS: 223112140U4/4574312-   RPR **136c**

Starts	1st	2nd	3rd	4th	Win & Pl
31	8	6	3	6	£95,055
127	1/07	Chel	2m5f Cls1 Gd3 124-150 Ch Hcap heavy		£31,361
134	10/05	Chel	2m4¹/₂f Cls3 112-134 Ch Hcap good		£9,526
	8/05	NAbb	2m¹/₂f Cls4 Nov Ch gd-fm		£3,684
	8/05	Sthl	2m5¹/₂f Ch good		£4,173
118	6/05	Hntg	2m5¹/₂f Cls3 95-118 Hdl Hcap gd-fm		£4,735
	7/04	Worc	2m4f Cls4 Nov Hdl gd-fm		£3,465
	5/04	Font	2m2¹/₂f Cls4 Nov Hdl gd-fm		£4,440
	5/04	Bang	2m1f Cls4 Nov Hdl good		£3,884

Smart handicapper who raced only three times in the main part of last season, but ran consistently and looks capable of picking up another decent contest at around 2m5f; finished in the frame each time, scoring over fences at Cheltenham in January when driven out to get the better of New Alco, with subsequent Festival winner Idole First back in third; showed his versatility when switched back to hurdles on his final start in the Sandown Handicap Hurdle in February when finding only

Taranis too good and going down by ¹/₂l (first start over hurdles in 19 months) with plenty of tough handicappers in behind (2m6f, soft, 16 ran); not a natural jumper of fences, but goes on most ground and likely to pop up with a win or two again this term. *'He's not over-big, but he's tough and genuine.'* *(David Pipe, trainer)*

1491 Wichita Lineman (Ire)

6 b g King's Theatre - Monumental Gesture (Head For Heights)

J O'Neill   John P McManus

PLACINGS: 1108/121112-   RPR **154+h**

Starts	1st	2nd	3rd	4th	Win & Pl
10	6	2	-	-	£121,973
	3/07	Chel	3m Cls1 Nov Gd2 Hdl gd-sft		£45,616
	1/07	Chel	2m4¹/₂f Cls1 Nov Gd2 Hdl heavy		£17,106
	12/06	Newb	2m5f Cls1 Nov Gd1 Hdl gd-sft		£22,808
	10/06	Aint	2m4f Cls3 Nov Hdl 4-6yo good		£6,506
	3/06	Newb	2m¹/₂f Cls6 NHF 4-6yo gd-fm		£2,193
	11/05	Newb	2m¹/₂f Cls6 NHF 4yo good		£3,725

Fine young hurdler who emulated stablemate Black Jack Ketchum by winning the Brit Insurance Novices' Hurdle at the Festival in March and now looks likely to develop into a smart novice chaser; ultimately made light work of winning his Cheltenham engagement, a success that came after three earlier wins, including the Grade 1 Challow Hurdle at Newbury in December, where he beat Sir Jimmy Shand by 8l; returned a Racing Post Rating of 154 on three occasions last term, including when beaten at odds of 4-6 on his final start in the Grade 1 Sefton Hurdle at Aintree, a race in which he went down by 4l to Chief Dan George; no surprise to see him back at Cheltenham in March bidding for glory over fences. *'He's a good horse and tough, but he's lazy.'* *(Jonjo O'Neill, trainer)*

1492 Wild Cane Ridge (Ire)

8 gr g Roselier - Shuil Na Lee (Phardante)

L Lungo   Ashleybank Investments Limited

PLACINGS: 1/21141/121F8/21264-   RPR **148+c**

Starts	1st	2nd	3rd	4th	Win & Pl
17	8	4	-	2	£67,339
134	11/06	Ayr	2m4f Cls2 134-154 Ch Hcap soft		£19,014
	2/06	Ayr	2m4f Cls3 Nov Ch soft		£6,506
	11/05	Newc	2m4f Cls4 Ch gd-sft		£3,988
	4/05	Kels	2m6¹/₂f Cls4 Nov Hdl soft		£3,965
	12/04	Hexm	3m Cls4 Nov Hdl heavy		£3,687
	11/04	Carl	2m4f Cls4 Nov Hdl 4-6yo heavy		£3,978
	4/04	Ayr	2m Cls6 NHF 4-6yo soft		£3,549
	3/04	Carl	2m1f Cls6 NHF 4-6yo heavy		£1,925

Mud-loving long-distance handicap chaser; gained his sole win last term at Ayr in November, but posted his best form off higher marks in two of Haydock's big races; finished a staying-on ¹/₂l second to Kandjar D'Allier in the Tommy Whittle Chase in December (3m, heavy, 14 ran), and after a disappointing effort in the Peter Marsh, returned to form in February in the Red Square Vodka Gold Cup, plugging on to finish 19l fourth behind

Heltornic (3m4f, heavy, 16 ran); starts the new season on a mark of 142 (2lb higher than in the Tommy Whittle), and will have all the same events on his agenda this term; needs very deep ground, and could be worth a crack at a National if conditions are in his favour.

1493 Wins Now

6 ch g Croco Rouge - Valdaia (Sadler's Wells)

N Madden (Ir)   John P McManus

PLACINGS: 260/2F11152-   RPR **145+h**

Starts	1st	2nd	3rd	4th	Win & Pl
10	3	3	-	-	£44,824
	2/07	Punc	2m Nov Hdl heavy		£8,892
	1/07	Cork	2m2f Hdl sft-hvy		£7,937
	12/06	Navn	2m Mdn Hdl sft-hvy		£4,766

Much-improved novice hurdler in the second half of last season, and crying out for a switch to fences; won at Navan and Cork before completing the hat-trick in quite impressive style at Punchestown in February, making his attack approaching the last and quickening clear to beat Montana Bay by 2¹/₂l (2m, heavy, 8 ran); jumping had not always been fluent, and again proved his undoing in the Supreme Novices' Hurdle at the Cheltenham Festival, where he nevertheless stayed on up the hill to finish 4³/₄l fifth behind Ebaziyan (2m¹/₂f, soft, 22 ran); stepped up to 2m4f at Aintree, and ran a cracker, throwing down the only meaningful challenge to Tidal Bay but badly blundering at the last and coming home 8l adrift (good, 10 ran); has the size and scope to improve over fences, and looks just the type to give the bigger obstacles more respect; a potential Arkle contender. *'He'll make a better chaser in time.'* *(Niall Madden, trainer)*

1494 Wise Owl

5 b g Danehill - Mistle Thrush (Storm Bird)

D Pipe   The Wise Partners

PLACINGS: 2121-8   RPR **122h**

Starts	1st	2nd	3rd	4th	Win & Pl
5	2	2	-	-	£10,081
114	4/07	Chep	2m¹/₂f Cls3 105-130 Hdl Hcap good		£4,880
	2/07	Tntn	2m4f Mdn Hdl gd-sft		£3,578

Three-time winner on the Flat who took well to hurdles last season and could do well in handicaps between 2m and 2m4f; scored at Taunton and Chepstow before shaping with plenty of promise when upped in grade for the Swinton Hurdle at Haydock on his final start, boxing on at one pace to finish eighth, around 7l behind Leslingtaylor (2m, good, 23 ran); unexposed after only five starts over hurdles, and not difficult to see his current mark of 123 looking lenient in a few months.

1495 Woodbine Willie (Ire)

6 b g Zaffaran - Good Foundation (Buckskin)

P Fenton (Ir)   James J Gleeson

PLACINGS: F412/22-   RPR **131**b

Starts	1st	2nd	3rd	4th	Win & Pl
5		1		1	£21,471
	3/06	Clon	2m2f NHF 5yo soft	-	......................£3,812

Classy bumper performer for the last couple of seasons, and now poised to go novice hurdling; has finished runner-up on his last three outings, including by $1/2$l to Clopf at Limerick in March 2006, and by 2l to Mick The Man in Grade 1 company at the Punchestown festival in April; will surely have no problem returning to winning ways in novice hurdles, and will surely be contesting Graded events unless things go horribly wrong; acts on good and heavy ground.

1496 Yes Sir (Ire)

8 b g Needle Gun - Miss Pushover (Push On)

P Bowen   Ms Y M Hill And T J Healy

PLACINGS: 5F/1111111554417-157   RPR **155+c**

Starts		1st	2nd	3rd	4th	Win & Pl
39		16	4	2	2	£196,238
	5/07	Kels	3m1f Cls3 Ch gd-fm			......................£5,855
	4/07	Ayr	2m4f Cls1 Nov Gd2 Ch gd-fm			..............£25,780
	8/06	NAbb	3m2^1/$_2$f Cls3 Nov Ch gd-sft			.............£10,372
130	7/06	MRas	2m6^1/$_2$f Cls1 List 120-146 Ch Hcap good			........£37,063
	7/06	Strf	2m1^1/$_2$f Cls3 Nov Ch good			..........£7,620
	6/06	Hexm	2m4^1/$_2$f Cls3 Nov Ch gd-sft			...............£6,338
	6/06	Strf	2m4f Cls3 Nov Ch gd-fm			...................£6,338
	5/06	Bang	2m4^1/$_2$f Cls4 Nov Ch heavy			...............£5,530
	5/06	Kels	2m1f Cls3 Nov Ch gd-fm			...................£6,953
144	8/05	Bang	2m1f Cls2 118-144 Hdl Hcap gd-sft			........£19,500
	5/05	Kels	2m2f Cls3 Hdl gd-fm			.....................£7,465
	5/05	Kels	2m6^1/$_2$f Cls2 Hdl gd-fm			..................£12,087
135	4/05	Sand	2m2f Cls2 120-141 Hdl Hcap good			..........£15,857
125	3/05	Chep	2m1^1/$_2$f Cls3 99-125 Hdl Hcap heavy			........£4,726
	2/05	Chep	2m1^1/$_2$f Cls4 Nov Hdl soft			.................£3,423
	12/04	Chep	2m4f Cls4 Nov Hdl soft			..................£3,413

Very smart chaser, straight off the Peter Bowen production line of tough, versatile performers who can take plenty of racing; won seven on the trot in the summer of 2006, and after a mid-season lull, returned to his best back on good ground in the spring; finished fourth behind Aces Four in a Grade 2 novice chase at Aintree (probably didn't last out 3m1f in that company), and just eight days later ran away with another Grade 2 over 2m4f at Ayr, where he made all and ran his rivals ragged, beating Natal by 11l; couldn't live with the top two-milers in Sandown's Celebration Chase, but picked up another win in a minor race at Kelso before fair efforts on ground too slow in the Summer Hurdle at Market Rasen and the Galway Plate; best at around 2m4f, and sure to be ambitiously campaigned in handicap and Graded company. *'At the top level, he needs fast ground to be at his best.' (Peter Bowen, trainer)*

1497 You're Special (USA)

10 b g Northern Flagship - Pillow Mint (Stage Door Johnny)

F Murphy   Mrs Diane O'Rourke

PLACINGS: 125222/315/P3621P1F/   RPR **131**b

Starts		1st	2nd	3rd	4th	Win & Pl
125	3/06	Chel	3m^1/$_2$f Cls2 118-139 Am Ch Hcap good			.............£30,010
119	12/05	Donc	3m2f Cls2 117-131 Ch Hcap gd-sft			...............£13,949
118	12/04	Chel	2m5f Cls4 99-125 Cond Ch Hcap good			.............£9,918
	6/03	Hexm	2m4^1/$_2$f Cls4 Nov Ch gd-fm			..................£3,861
	5/03	Ctml	3m2f Cls4 Nov Ch good			..................£4,485
	5/03	Aint	2m4f Cls3 Nov Ch gd-sft			.................£5,828
	4/02	Weth	2m4^1/$_2$f Cls4 Nov Hdl good			.................£3,143
	11/01	Newc	2m4f Cls4 Nov Hdl good			..................£2,625

Smart staying chaser who missed last season, but is reportedly back in training and could make up into a Grand National prospect; highlight of his 2005/06 season was when springing a 33-1 shock in the Kim Muir Handicap Chase at the Cheltenham Festival (3m^1/2f, good, 21 ran), keeping on well from two out to beat Mon Mome by 3^1/2l (benefiting from wind surgery); subsequently made favourite for the Betfred Gold Cup at Sandown (3m5^1/2f, good to firm, 18 ran), but fell at the 16th when well in touch; normally a safe jumper; usually tongue-tied; seems to act on any ground.

1498 Zabenz (NZ)

10 b g Zabeel - In The Country (In The Purple)

P Hobbs   Michael H Watt

PLACINGS: 0053/34122549/232P5-   RPR **147+c**

Starts		1st	2nd	3rd	4th	Win & Pl
24		5	4	4	3	£183,709
	11/05	Hrfd	3m1^1/$_2$f Cls4 Ch good			..................£4,561
	8/02	Sara	2m3f Gd1 Hdl Hcap soft			..................£45,041
	6/02	Flem	2m4f Hdl Hcap soft			..................£40,757
	6/02	Moon	2m Hdl Hcap soft			.....................£9,331
	6/02	Flem	2m3f Hdl good			..................£9,155

Long-distance chaser who looks handicapped to win a decent prize; raced off a mark of 140 on all five starts last term, and was twice runner-up in valuable handicaps at Ascot, beaten 7l by See You Sometime in October (3m, good to firm, 11 ran) and 12l by Billyvoddan in the Silver Cup in December (3m, good to soft, 18 ran); pulled up when a leather broke early on in the Grand National, but underlined his liking for a right-handed track and sound surface in the Betfred Gold Cup at Sandown, where he threw down the last challenge to Hot Weld approaching the final fence, but blundered away his chance, eventually allowed to come home in his own time in fifth; still on 140 for the start of the new campaign, so his chance of winning a similar contest is obvious, although a return of one win from 18 starts in Britain is not encouraging.

1499 Zilcash

4 b g Mujahid - Empty Purse (Pennine Walk)

A King   David Bellamy & Stephen Williams

PLACINGS: 2222F4-11   **RPR 136h**

Starts	1st	2nd	3rd	4th	Win & Pl
8	2	4	-	1	£23,385

5/07	Aint	2m¹/₂f Cls4 Nov Hdl good	£3,904
4/07	Towc	2m Cls4 Nov Hdl gd-fm	£3,253

Useful 2m-2m4f hurdler; finished second in his first four novice events last season, notably beaten 1³/4l by Labelthou in a Grade 2 contest at Warwick in January (2m5f, heavy, 7 ran); fell at Cheltenham next time, but returned there for the Fred Winter Juvenile Handicap Hurdle at the Festival and ran a cracker under 11st 7lb, battling on gamely from 2 out to finish 8¹/4l fourth behind subsequent Grade 1 runner-up Gaspara (2m¹/₂f, good to soft, 24 ran, was conceding 10lb to the winner); needed to get his head in front for the sake of his confidence, and was duly found simple opportunities at Towcester and Aintree in the spring, winning with any amount in hand at odds of 1-6 and 2-5; starts the season rated 144 (4lb higher than at the Cheltenham Festival), and likely to contest some of the better handicap hurdles in the autumn.

£1million*

totetentofollow

totesport & *RACING POST*

*Guaranteed minimum pool before deduction

Big-money dividends for the overall top ten scoring entries – plus winners of the monthly prizes

You may enter as many lists as you wish – each list of ten selections costs £10 or €16 to enter

Remember entries must be received no later than 8pm on Thursday, November 15, 2007

THREE WAYS TO ENTER

▶▶Enter online and you can monitor your entry by going to: **totetentofollow.co.uk**

▶▶Enter by phone and you can monitor your entry by calling: **0871 200 2030**

▶▶Complete the entry form on page 33 and post with your cheque/postal order to: **PO Box 116, Wigan, WN3 4WW**

Horses listed by trainer

R Alner
1233 Kingscliff (Ire)
1257 Lindop
1286 Miko De Beauchene (Fr)
1290 Miss Mitch (Ire)
1372 Portland Bill (Ire)
1457 The Listener (Ire)
D Arbuthnot
1340 Oscar Park (Ire)
1378 Present Glory (Ire)
K Bailey
1260 Longshanks
A Balding
1062 Briareus
K Bishop
1032 Ashley Brook (Ire)
E Bolger (Ir)
1177 Heads Onthe Ground (Ire)
1435 Spot Thedifference (Ire)
P Bowen
1017 Always Waining (Ire)
1036 Ballycassidy (Ire)
1053 Blue Splash (Fr)
1123 Dunbrody Millar (Ire)
1128 Ellerslie Tom
1199 Irish Wolf (Fr)
1200 Iron Man (Fr)
1242 Lankawi
1280 Mckelvey (Ire)
1433 Special Envoy (Fr)
1496 Yes Sir (Ire)
M Brassil (Ir)
1019 Ambobo (USA)
1318 Nickname (Fr)
1326 Numbersixvalverde (Ire)
W J Burke (Ir)
1422 Sir Frederick (Ire)
C Byrnes (Ir)
1068 Cailin Alainn (Ire)
1073 Carthalawn (Ire)
1302 Mounthenry (Ire)
J Carr (Ir)
1445 Sublimity (Fr)
A Chaille-Chaille (Fr)
1285 Mid Dancer (Fr)
N Chance
1282 Mendo
1397 River City (Ire)
G A Charlton
1067 Bywell Beau (Ire)
J Crowley (Ir)
1170 Hairy Molly (Ire)
M Cunningham (Ir)
1389 Raven's Run (Ire)
H Daly
1012 Alderburn
1048 Billyvoddan (Ire)
1063 Briery Fox (Ire)
1207 Jaunty Times
1277 Martha's Kinsman (Ire)
1335 Opera De Coeur (Fr)

1355 Palarshan (Fr)
H de Bromhead (Ir)
1424 Sizing Africa (Ire)
1425 Sizing Europe (Ire)
F Doumen (Fr)
1164 Grand Bleu (Ire)
1219 Kasbah Bliss (Fr)
1224 Kelami (Fr)
1236 L'Ami (Fr)
1289 Millenium Royal (Fr)
1300 Moulin Riche (Fr)
T Doumen (Fr)
1149 Foreman (Ger)
J Dreaper (Ir)
1288 Militant (Fr)
G Elliott (Ir)
1418 Silver Birch (Ire)
J Fanshawe
1394 Reveillez
P Fenton (Ir)
1413 Sher Beau (Ire)
1415 Shirley Casper (Ire)
1482 Vic Venturi (Ire)
1495 Woodbine Willie (Ire)
D Forster
1343 Ossmoses (Ire)
N Gifford
1442 Straw Bear (USA)
E Griffin (Ir)
1223 Kazal (Fr)
1264 Lounaos (Fr)
B Hamilton (Ir)
1020 Amstecos (Ire)
Mrs J Harrington (Ir)
1097 Cork All Star (Ire)
1147 Foligold (Fr)
1156 Gazza's Girl (Ire)
1158 Gemini Lucy (Ire)
1184 Hide The Evidence (Ire)
1234 Knight Legend (Ire)
1267 Macs Joy (Ire)
1283 Mercuric
1444 Studmaster
1450 Tailor's Hall (Ire)
N Henderson
1006 Afrad (Fr)
1007 Afsoun (Fr)
1015 All Star (Ger)
1018 Amaretto Rose
1038 Barbers Shop
1052 Blue Shark (Fr)
1071 Caracciola (Ger)
1088 Classic Fiddle
1096 Copsale Lad
1103 Crozan (Fr)
1106 Dancing Bay
1121 Duc De Regniere (Fr)
1144 Fleet Street
1151 French Opera
1168 Greenhope (Ire)
1205 Jack The Giant (Ire)

1216 Juveigneur (Fr)
1225 Kenzo III (Fr)
1239 La Dame Brune (Fr)
1270 Maharbal (Fr)
1328 Oedipe (Fr)
1357 Papini (Ire)
1379 Princelet (Ire)
1381 Procas De Thaix (Fr)
1382 Punjabi
1402 Royals Darling (Ger)
1405 Schiehallion (Ire)
1412 Shatabdi (Ire)
1414 Ship's Hill (Ire)
1423 Sir Jimmy Shand (Ire)
1454 Tarlac (Ger)
1455 Temoin
1466 Trabolgan (Ire)
1468 Treasury Counsel (Ire)
1471 Trompette (USA)
M Hickey (Ir)
1034 Ballistraw (Ire)
P Hobbs
1061 Boychuk (Ire)
1084 Chilling Place (Ire)
1115 Detroit City (USA)
1120 Dream Alliance
1138 Fair Along (Ger)
1152 French Saulaie (Fr)
1217 Kalca Mome (Fr)
1241 Lacdoudal (Fr)
1247 Lead On (Ire)
1253 Liberate
1261 Lord Henry (Ire)
1273 Mark The Book (Ire)
1278 Massini's Maguire (Ire)
1297 Monkerhostin (Fr)
1322 Noble Request (Fr)
1341 Oscatello (USA)
1359 Parsons Legacy (Ire)
1380 Private Be
1429 Snap Tie (Ire)
1446 Supreme Prince (Ire)
1470 Tritonix (Ire)
1498 Zabenz (NZ)
R Hodges
1375 Preacher Boy
M Hourigan (Ir)
1000 A New Story (Ire)
1031 Arteea (Ire)
1043 Beef Or Salmon (Ire)
1086 Church Island (Ire)
1140 Field Commander (Ire)
1183 Hi Cloy (Ire)
1299 Mossbank (Ire)

A Maguire (Ir)
1226 Kerryhead Windfarm (Ire)
D Hughes (Ir)
1079 Central House
1165 Grangeclare Lark (Ire)
1174 Hardy Eustace (Ire)
1215 Justpourit (Ire)
1346 Oulart
1407 Schindlers Hunt (Ire)
P Hughes (Ir)
1370 Point Barrow (Ire)
J Jay
1463 Tidal Fury (Ire)
J M Jefferson
1465 Tot O'Whiskey
J H Johnson
1027 Arcalis
1046 Bewleys Berry (Ire)
1109 Degas Art (Ire)
1173 Hard Act To Follow (Ire)
1197 Inglis Drever
1227 Key Time (Ire)
1251 Lennon (Ire)
1259 Locksmith
1274 Marleybow (Ire)
1321 No Refuge (Ire)
1367 Percussionist (Ire)
1401 Royal Rosa (Fr)
1462 Tidal Bay (Ire)
1487 Wee Forbees (Ire)
A King
1051 Blazing Bailey
1105 D'Argent (Ire)
1134 Evelith Echo
1171 Halcon Genelardais (Fr)
1185 Hills Of Home (Ire)
1190 Howle Hill (Ire)
1194 Il Duce (Ire)
1202 Itsa Legend
1218 Kandjar D'Allier (Fr)
1220 Katchit (Ire)
1307 My Way De Solzen (Fr)
1312 Nenuphar Collonges (Fr)
1356 Pangbourne (Fr)
1365 Penzance
1373 Pouvoir (Fr)
1403 Rustarix (Fr)
1410 Self Respect (USA)
1459 Theatre Girl
1469 Trigger The Light
1472 Trouble At Bay (Ire)
1484 Voy Por Ustedes (Fr)
1499 Zilcash
Miss H Knight
1033 Aztec Warrior (Ire)
1076 Cave Hill (Ire)
1139 Faucon Bleu (Fr)
1160 Glasker Mill (Ire)
1175 Harris Bay
1332 Olmeto Collonges (Fr)
1386 Racing Demon (Ire)

1396 Ringaroses
1479 Val Du Ciron (Fr)
1489 West End King (Ire)
E Lavelle
1240 Labelthou (Fr)
J Leavy (Ir)
1431 Sophocles
C Llewellyn
1111 Dempsey (Ire)
1256 Limited Edition (Ire)
1384 Quartano (Ger)
1398 Roll Along (Ire)
1428 Snakebite (Ire)
1464 Too Forward (Ire)
L Lungo
1045 Berwick Law (Ire)
1492 Wild Cane Ridge (Ire)
N Madden (Ir)
1493 Wins Now
C Mann
1008 Air Force One (Ger)
1292 Mobaasher (USA)
1298 Moon Over Miami (Ger)
1306 My Turn Now (Ire)
A Martin (Ir)
1122 Dun Doire (Ire)
1361 Patsy Hall (Ire)
D McCain
1092 Cloudy Lane
1119 Double Eagle
1191 Idle Talk (Ire)
1393 Regal Heights (Ire)
N Meade (Ir)
1009 Aitmatov (Ger)
1025 Aran Concerto (Ire)
1035 Ballyagran (Ire)
1074 Casey Jones (Ire)
1087 Clarnazar (Ire)
1090 Cleni Boy (Fr)
1157 Gem Daly (Fr)
1172 Harchibald (Fr)
1182 Heron's Flight (Ire)
1193 Iktitaf (Ire)
1209 Jazz Messenger (Fr)
1210 Jered (Ire)
1250 Leading Run (Ire)
1284 Mick The Man (Ire)
1303 Mr Nosie (Ire)
1317 Nicanor (Fr)
1337 Orbit O'Gold (USA)
1399 Rosaker (USA)
1448 Sweet Wake (Ger)
1486 Watson Lake (Ire)
J Moffatt
1083 Chief Dan George (Ire)
A Moore (Ir)
1230 King Johns Castle (Ire)
1272 Mansony (Fr)
1441 Stewarts House (Ire)
G L Moore
1016 Altilhar (USA)

Horses listed by trainer

1178 Heathcote
1481 Verasi
M Morris (Ir)
1480 Venalmar
1485 War Of Attrition (Ire)
A Mullins (Ir)
1026 Aranleigh (Ire)
1363 Pedrobob (Ire)
J W Mullins
1222 Kawagino (Ire)
1409 See You Sometime
T Mullins (Ir)
1082 Chelsea Harbour (Ire)
W Mullins (Ir)
1005 Adamant Approach (Ire)
1013 Alexander Taipan (Ire)
1049 Black Harry (Ire)
1060 Bothar Na (Ire)
1095 Cooldine (Ire)
1104 Cuchulains Son (Ire)
1126 Ebaziyan (Ire)
1133 Force Leader (Ire)
1141 Financial Reward (Ire)
1143 Fiveforthree (Ire)
1161 Glencove Marina (Ire)
1179 Hedgehunter (Ire)
1187 Homer Wells (Ire)
1203 J'y Vole (Fr)
1258 Livingstonebramble (Ire)
1268 Mad Fish (Ire)
1291 Mister Hight (Fr)
1348 Our Ben
1349 Our Bob (Ire)
1385 Quatre Heures (Fr)
1408 Scotsirish (Ire)
1430 Snowy Morning (Ire)
F Murphy
1004 Aces Four (Ire)
1023 Another Promise (Ire)
1189 Hot Weld
1212 Joes Edge (Ire)
1237 L'Antartique (Fr)
1249 Leading Man (Ire)
1276 Marshall Hall (Ire)
1311 Negus De Beaumont (Fr)
1314 New Alco (Fr)
1319 Nine De Sivola (Fr)
1323 Noir Et Vert (Fr)
1416 Shouldhavehadthat (Ire)
1461 Three Mirrors
1497 You're Special (USA)
J Murphy (Ir)
1094 Convincing
1316 Newmill (Ire)
R Newland
1065 Burntoakboy
1352 Overstrand (Ire)
P Nicholls
1022 Andreas (Fr)
1030 Armaturk (Fr)
1041 Beau Michel (Fr)

1080 Cerium (Fr)
1098 Cornish Sett (Ire)
1112 Denman (Ire)
1114 Desert Quest (Ire)
1125 Earth Planet (Ire)
1166 Granit Jack (Fr)
1169 Gungadu
1188 Hoo La Baloo (Fr)
1221 Kauto Star (Fr)
1229 Kicks For Free (Ire)
1238 L'Aventure (Fr)
1245 Le Duc (Fr)
1246 Le Volfoni (Fr)
1262 Lou Du Moulin Mas (Fr)
1275 Marodima (Fr)
1304 Mr Pointment (Ire)
1308 My Will (Fr)
1309 Natal (Fr)
1313 Neptune Collonges (Fr)
1315 New Little Bric (Fr)
1324 Noland
1327 Nycteos (Fr)
1329 Ofarel D'Airy (Fr)
1336 Opera Mundi (Fr)
1338 Ornais (Fr)
1342 Oslot (Fr)
1345 Otto Des Pictons (Fr)
1347 Ouninpohja (Ire)
1354 Pak Jack (Fr)
1371 Poquelin (Fr)
1376 Predateur (Fr)
1400 Royal Auclair (Fr)
1404 Saintsaire (Fr)
1419 Silverburn (Ire)
1434 Sporazene (Ire)
1438 Star De Mohaison (Fr)
1453 Taranis (Fr)
1460 Thisthatandtother (Ire)
1474 Turko (Fr)
1476 Twist Magic (Fr)
K O'Brien (Ir)
1124 Duty (Ire)
M O'Brien (Ir)
1108 De Valira (Ire)
1132 Essex (Ire)
1150 Forget The Past
1196 In Compliance (Ire)
E O'Grady (Ir)
1075 Catch Me (Ger)
1091 Clopf (Ire)
1281 Medicinal (Ire)
1426 Sky's The Limit (Fr)
1467 Tranquil Sea (Ire)
J O'Neill
1011 Albertas Run (Ire)
1044 Berings Express (Fr)
1050 Black Jack Ketchum (Ire)
1057 Bob Hall (Ire)
1066 Butler's Cabin (Fr)
1100 Crocodiles Rock (Ire)
1107 De Soto

1117 Don't Push It (Ire)
1136 Exotic Dancer (Fr)
1176 Hasty Prince
1392 Refinement (Ire)
1437 Square Mile (Ire)
1491 Wichita Lineman (Ire)
M Phillips (Ir)
1374 Powerstation (Ire)
D Pipe
1001 Abragante (Ire)
1002 Acambo (Ger)
1021 An Accordion (Ire)
1064 Buena Vista (Ire)
1077 Celestial Gold (Ire)
1078 Celtic Son (Fr)
1085 Christdalo (Ire)
1089 Classified (Ire)
1113 Desert Air (Jpn)
1116 Dom D'Orgeval (Fr)
1155 Gaspara (Fr)
1201 It Takes Time (Ire)
1211 Joaaci (Ire)
1244 Laustra Bad (Fr)
1263 Lough Derg (Fr)
1265 Lucifer Bleu (Fr)
1269 Madison Du Berlais (Fr)
1287 Milan Deux Mille (Fr)
1325 Not Left Yet (Ire)
1339 Osana (Fr)
1350 Our Vic (Ire)
1351 Over The Creek
1353 Pablo Du Charmil (Fr)
1358 Paradi (Fr)
1362 Pauillac (Fr)
1364 Penny Pictures (Ire)
1383 Puntal (Fr)
1388 Raslan
1411 Seven Is My Number (Ire)
1451 Tamarinbleu (Fr)
1452 Tango Royal (Fr)
1483 Vodka Bleu (Fr)
1488 Well Chief (Ger)
1490 Whispered Secret (Ger)
1494 Wise Owl
1093 Comply Or Die (Ire)
1159 Getoutwhenyoucan (Ire)
1213 Just Classic
B Pollock
1243 Launde (Ire)
J Queally (Ir)
1010 Al Eile (Ire)
J Quinn
1055 Blythe Knight (Ire)
1081 Character Building (Ire)
1102 Crow Wood
1232 Kings Quay
1252 Leslingtaylor (Ire)
1368 Pevensey (Ire)
K Reveley
1387 Rambling Minster
1477 Ungaro (Fr)

N Richards
1003 According To John (Ire)
1042 Bedlam Boy (Ire)
1118 Double Default (Ire)
1127 Echo Point (Ire)
1135 Ever Present (Ire)
1137 Faasel (Ire)
1208 Jazz D'Estruval (Fr)
1293 Modicum (USA)
1295 Monet's Garden (Ire)
1296 Money Trix (Ire)
1377 Premier Dane (Ire)
1456 The French Furze (Ire)
1475 Turpin Green (Ire)
M Rimell
1101 Crossbow Creek
1334 Oneway (Ire)
P Roche (Ir)
1024 Anothercoppercoast (Ire)
1440 Steel Band
H Rogers (Ir)
1417 Silent Oscar (Ire)
M Scudamore
1181 Heltornic (Ire)
E Sheehy (Ir)
1186 Holly Tree (Ire)
1214 Justified (Ire)
1395 Rindoon (Ire)
O Sherwood
1072 Caribou (Fr)
1131 Eric's Charm (Fr)
1266 Lyes Green
1301 Mount Sandel (Ire)
Miss S Smith
1279 Material World
Mrs S Smith
1305 Mr Strachan (Ire)
1360 Patriarch Express
1390 Rebel Rhythm
J Spearing
1206 Jacks Craic (Fr)
1420 Simon
T Stack (Ir)
1366 Perce Rock
P Stafford (Ir)
1054 Blueberry Boy (Ire)
C Swan (Ir)
1129 Emmpat (Ire)
1330 Offshore Account (Ire)
1333 One Cool Cookie (Ire)
G A Swinbank
1014 Alfie Flits
1028 Arctic Echo
1421 Sir Boreas Hawk
T Taaffe (Ir)
1070 Cane Brake (Ire)
1130 Emotional Moment (Ire)
1142 Finger Onthe Pulse (Ire)
1162 Glenfinn Captain (Ire)
1228 Kicking King (Ire)
1231 Kings Advocate (Ire)

1320 Ninetieth Minute (Ire)
1406 Schindler's Gold (Ire)
1427 Slim Pickings (Ire)
1443 Streetshavenoname (Ire)
1473 Tumbling Dice (Ire)
C Tizzard
1056 Bob Bob Bobbin
1145 Flight Leader (Ire)
1248 Leading Authority (Ire)
M Todhunter
1344 Ostfanni (Ire)
A Turnell
1047 Bible Lord (Ire)
N Twiston-Davies
1029 Ardaghey (Ire)
1039 Baron Windrush
1040 Battle Cry
1154 Fundamentalist (Ire)
1163 Golden Child (Ire)
1195 Imperial Commander (Ire)
1198 Irish Raptor (Ire)
1235 Knowhere (Ire)
1271 Mahogany Blaze (Fr)
1310 Naunton Brook
1331 Ollie Magern
1391 Redemption
R Tyner (Ir)
1069 Callherwhatulike (Ire)
1148 Footy Facts (Ire)
1436 Spring The Que (Ire)
Mrs L Wadham
1478 United (Ger)
T Walsh (Ir)
1204 Jack High (Ire)
1432 Southern Vic (Ire)
P Webber
1153 Full House (Ire)
1447 Swaythe (USA)
D Weld (Ir)
1058 Bobs Pride (Ire)
E Williams
1110 Demi Beau
1439 State Of Play
I Williams
1037 Bambi De L'Orme (Fr)
1449 Tagula Blue (Ire)
Miss V Williams
1059 Border Castle
1099 Cracking Cliche
1146 Flintoff (USA)
1167 Green Belt Flyer (Ire)
1180 Heez A Dreamer (Ire)
1192 Idole First (Ire)
1254 Lightning Strike (Ger)
1255 Limerick Boy (Ger)
1294 Mon Mome (Fr)
1458 The Outlier (Ire)
N Williams
1369 Philson Run (Ire)

Last season's Racing Post Ratings

Horse	Rating	Horse	Rating	Horse	Rating	Horse	Rating	Horse	Rating
Kauto Star	184	Noble Request	160	Tumbling Dice	153	Tidal Bay	149	Bambi De L'Orme	145
Exotic Dancer	177	Reveillez	160	Alexander Taipan	152	Amaretto Rose	148	Bothar Na	145
Our Vic	173	Sporazene	160	Ballycassidy	152	Baron Windrush	148	Butler's Cabin	145
Beef Or Salmon	172	Star De Mohaison	160	Bob Bob Bobbin	152	Black Harry	148	Copsale Lad	145
The Listener	171	Too Forward	160	Kawagino	152	Bob Hall	148	D'Argent	145
War Of Attrition	171	Don't Push It	159	Le Volfoni	152	Catch Me	148	Dream Alliance	145
Nickname	170	Millenium Royal	159	Mansony	152	Crow Wood	148	Ever Present	145
Sublimity	170	Silent Oscar	159	New Little Bric	152	Full House	148	Field Commander	145
Voy Por Ustedes	170	Twist Magic	159	Schindlers Hunt	152	Kazal	148	Heads Onthe Ground	145
Inglis Drever	169	Fair Along	158	According To John	151	The Outlier	148	Hot Weld	145
Racing Demon	169	Forget The Past	158	Blythe Knight	151	Turko	148	Il Duce	145
Dempsey	168	Hi Cloy	158	Demi Beau	151	Wild Cane Ridge	148	Liberate	145
Monet's Garden	168	Thisthatandtother	158	Fundamentalist	151	Abragante	147	Nycteos	145
Turpin Green	168	Watson Lake	158	Gungadu	151	Ardaghey	147	Opera Mundi	145
In Compliance	167	Arcalis	157	Joaaci	151	Ballistraw	147	Overstrand	145
Mid Dancer	167	Crossbow Creek	157	Patsy Hall	151	Boychuk	147	Special Envoy	145
Well Chief	167	Faasel	157	Refinement	151	Bywell Beau	147	United	145
Detroit City	166	Justified	157	Rosaker	151	Carthalawn	147	Wins Now	145
Hardy Eustace	166	Madison Du Berlais	157	Supreme Prince	151	Euro Leader	147	An Accordion	144
Neptune Collonges	166	Royal Auclair	157	Vodka Bleu	151	Finger Onthe Pulse	147	Briareus	144
Afsoun	165	Southern Vic	157	Acambo	150	Hasty Prince	147	De Soto	144
Denman	165	Central House	156	Cornish Sett	150	Kalca Mome	147	Dun Doire	144
Halcon Genelardais	165	Chief Dan George	156	Ebaziyan	150	Militant	147	Emotional Moment	144
Iktitaf	165	Crozan	156	Essex	150	Mister Hight	147	Glencove Marina	144
My Way De Solzen	165	Juveigneur	156	Irish Wolf	150	New Alco	147	Green Belt Flyer	144
State Of Play	165	Limerick Boy	156	Lennon	150	No Refuge	147	Greenhope	144
Ashley Brook	164	Idle Talk	155	Lough Derg	150	Osana	147	Homer Wells	144
Black Jack Ketchum	164	L'Antartique	155	Mon Mome	150	Oscar Park	147	Jazz D'Estruval	144
Desert Quest	164	Lacdoudal	155	Natal	150	Sir Jimmy Shand	147	L'Aventure	144
Jazz Messenger	164	Sher Beau	155	Offshore Account	150	Spot Thedifference	147	Launde	144
Monkerhostin	164	Simon	155	Our Ben	150	Steel Band	147	Milan Deux Mille	144
My Will	164	Ungaro	155	Parsons Legacy	150	Zabenz	147	Naunton Brook	144
Taranis	164	Yes Sir	155	Powerstation	150	Aran Concerto	146	Sir Frederick	144
Blazing Bailey	163	Another Promise	154	Punjabi	150	Bewleys Berry	146	Sweet Wake	144
Foreman	163	Cerium	154	See You Sometime	150	Flintoff	146	Gazza's Girl	143
L'Ami	163	Flight Leader	154	Silver Birch	150	Gaspara	146	Heez A Dreamer	143
Aces Four	162	Hoo La Baloo	154	Slim Pickings	150	Granit Jack	146	Kerryhead Windfarm	143
Kingscliff	162	Iron Man	154	Buena Vista	149	Harchibald	146	Mobaasher	143
River City	162	Jack The Giant	154	Cailin Alainn	149	Heltornic	146	Nine De Sivola	143
Al Eile	161	Kasbah Bliss	154	Chilling Place	149	Hide The Evidence	146	Ofarel D'Airy	143
Armaturk	161	Katchit	154	Dom D'Orgeval	149	Irish Raptor	146	Ouninpohja	143
Cane Brake	161	One Cool Cookie	154	Idole First	149	Labelthou	146	Pedrobob	143
Newmill	161	Snowy Morning	154	Kelami	149	Livingstonebramble	146	Trouble At Bay	143
Ollie Magern	161	Tamarinbleu	154	Lucifer Bleu	149	Mckelvey	146	Afrad	142
Oneway	161	Wichita Lineman	154	Massini's Maguire	149	Private Be	146	Anothercoppercoast	142
Straw Bear	161	Adamant Approach	153	Material World	149	Regal Heights	146	Caracciola	142
Andreas	160	Alderburn	153	Point Barrow	149	Silverburn	146	Gemini Lucy	142
Billyvoddan	160	Knowhere	153	Redemption	149	Studmaster	146	It Takes Time	142
Macs Joy	160	The French Furze	153	Temoin	149	Always Waining	145	Jack High	142

Last season's Racing Post Ratings

Kandjar D'Allier 142	Mr Strachan 139	Itsa Legend 135	Woodbine Willie 131	Tot O'Whiskey 122
Limited Edition 142	Numbersixvalverde 139	Kenzo III 135	Altilhar 130	Wise Owl 122
Locksmith 142	Papini 139	Kicks For Free 135	Barbers Shop 130	Leading Authority 121
Lord Henry 142	Tarlac 139	Lyes Green 135	Cooldine 130	Portland Bill 121
My Turn Now 142	A New Story 138	Negus De Beaumont 135	Leslingtaylor 130	Shouldhavehadthat 121
Penzance 142	Bedlam Boy 138	Oedipe 135	Mad Fish 130	Hills Of Home 120
Perce Rock 142	Burntoakboy 138	Philson Run 135	Maharbal 130	Mount Sandel 120
Percussionist 142	Cork All Star 138	Snakebite 135	Ostfanni 130	Ship's Hill 119
Preacher Boy 142	Desert Air 138	Cleni Boy 134	Pevensey 130	Venalmar 119
Premier Dane 142	Echo Point 138	Fiveforthree 134	Trigger The Light 130	Faucon Bleu 118
Puntal 142	Jaunty Times 138	Fleet Street 134	Christdalo 129	Moulin Riche 117
Saintsaire 142	Leading Man 138	Foligold 134	Dancing Bay 129	Present Glory 117
Blue Splash 141	Lou Du Moulin Mas 138	Holly Tree 134	Lindop 129	Seven Is My Number 117
Character Building 141	Nenuphar Collonges 138	Mick The Man 134	Sizing Europe 129	Snap Tie 117
Degas Art 141	Ossmoses 138	Pak Jack 134	Streetshavenoname 129	Berwick Law 116
Ellerslie Tom 141	Oulart 138	Quatre Heures 134	Convincing 128	Quartano 116
Emmpat 141	Pablo Du Charmil 138	Scotsirish 134	Cuchulains Son 128	Swaythe 116
Harris Bay 141	Sky's The Limit 138	All Star 133	Hairy Molly 128	Earth Planet 115
Jacks Craic 141	Three Mirrors 138	Arteea 133	Leading Run 128	Marodima 114
Palarshan 141	Verasi 138	Border Castle 133	Miss Mitch 128	Cave Hill 113
Vic Venturi 141	Aztec Warrior 137	Dunbrody Millar 133	Not Left Yet 128	Jered 112
Blueberry Boy 140	Callherwhatulike 137	Heathcote 133	Sir Boreas Hawk 128	Marleybow 112
Church Island 140	Duc De Regniere 137	Moon Over Miami 133	J'y Vole 127	Paradi 112
Classified 140	Financial Reward 137	Opera De Coeur 133	Laustra Bad 127	Schiehallion 112
Glasker Mill 140	Oslot 137	Oscatello 133	Otto Des Pictons 127	Theatre Girl 112
Grangeclare Lark 140	Penny Pictures 137	Spring The Que 133	Raslan 127	West End King 112
Hard Act To Follow 140	Rambling Minster 137	Square Mile 133	Rustarix 127	Evelith Echo 111
Joes Edge 140	Trompette 137	Tagula Blue 133	Sophocles 127	Clarnazar 110
Kings Advocate 140	Chelsea Harbour 136	Arctic Echo 132	Battle Cry 126	Golden Child 109
Longshanks 140	De Valira 136	Casey Jones 132	Heron's Flight 126	Hedgehunter 109
Marshall Hall 140	Justpourit 136	Crocodiles Rock 132	Princelet 126	Ninetieth Minute 109
Medicinal 140	Le Duc 136	Duty 132	Shirley Casper 126	Olmeto Collonges 109
Miko De Beauchene 140	Mahogany Blaze 136	Mark The Book 132	Double Eagle 125	Val Du Ciron 109
Mossbank 140	Mr Pointment 136	Martha's Kinsman 132	La Dame Brune 125	Ambobo 108
Royal Rosa 140	Noir Et Vert 136	Modicum 132	Lead On 125	Procas De Thaix 108
Royals Darling 140	Shatabdi 136	Orbit O'Gold 132	Over The Creek 125	Berings Express 106
Tailor's Hall 140	Tango Royal 136	Ringaroses 132	Self Respect 125	Gem Daly 106
Tidal Fury 140	Whispered Secret 136	Roll Along 132	Stewarts House 125	Our Bob 104
Air Force One 139	Zilcash 136	Sizing Africa 132	Wee Forbees 125	Pangbourne 104
Aitmatov 139	Albertas Run 135	Tranquil Sea 132	Beau Michel 124	Schindler's Gold 104
Ballyagran 139	Amstecos 135	Caribou 131	Key Time 124	Cracking Cliche 103
Bobs Pride 139	Aranleigh 135	Double Default 131	Mercuric 124	Rebel Rhythm 101
Briery Fox 139	Bible Lord 135	Kings Quay 131	Pouvoir 124	French Opera 97
Clopf 139	Cloudy Lane 135	Lankawi 131	Mendo 123	
Grand Bleu 139	Footy Facts 135	Lightning Strike 131	Ornais 123	
King Johns Castle 139	French Saulaie 135	Pauillac 131	Treasury Counsel 123	
Knight Legend 139	Glenfinn Captain 135	Poquelin 131	Tritonix 123	
Lounaos 139	Howle Hill 135	Predateur 131	Classic Fiddle 122	
Mounthenry 139	Imperial Commander 135	Rindoon 131	Raven's Run 122	

Last season's Topspeed Ratings

Kauto Star	169
Well Chief	169
Nickname	168
In Compliance	167
Dempsey	166
My Way De Solzen	166
Iktitaf	165
Halcon Genelardais	164
War Of Attrition	164
Desert Quest	163
Detroit City	163
Exotic Dancer	162
Straw Bear	161
Racing Demon	160
State Of Play	160
Voy Por Ustedes	160
Faasel	158
Noble Request	158
Our Vic	158
The Listener	158
Ashley Brook	157
Crossbow Creek	157
Denman	157
Arcalis	156
Newmill	156
Fair Along	155
Juveigneur	155
Millenium Royal	155
Monet's Garden	155
Sporazene	155
Turpin Green	155
Andreas	154
Don't Push It	154
Jack The Giant	154
Katchit	154
Sher Beau	154
Star De Mohaison	154
Taranis	154
Thisthatandtother	154
Armaturk	153
Billyvoddan	153
Macs Joy	153
One Cool Cookie	153
Ballycassidy	152
Central House	152
New Little Bric	152
Acambo	151
Afsoun	151
Another Promise	151
Demi Beau	151
Oneway	151
River City	151
Schindlers Hunt	151
The French Furze	151
Beef Or Salmon	150
Blythe Knight	150
Essex	150
Hoo La Baloo	150
L'Antartique	150
Madison Du Berlais	150
Mon Mome	150
Wichita Lineman	150
Cailin Alainn	149
Kasbah Bliss	149
Patsy Hall	149
Snowy Morning	149
Watson Lake	149
Caracciola	148
D'Argent	148
Iron Man	148
Knowhere	148
Neptune Collonges	148
The Outlier	148
Turko	148
Crow Wood	147
Hi Cloy	147
Jazz Messenger	147
Le Volfoni	147
Osana	147
Twist Magic	147
According To John	146
Aces Four	146
Bambi De L'Orme	146
Baron Windrush	146
Bob Hall	146
Kingscliff	146
Labelthou	146
Reveillez	146
See You Sometime	146
Southern Vic	146
Too Forward	146
Ungaro	146
United	146
Yes Sir	146
Hasty Prince	145
Il Duce	145
Kalca Mome	145
Kawagino	145
Limerick Boy	145
Opera Mundi	145
Slim Pickings	145
Sublimity	145
Gemini Lucy	144
Kazal	144
Natal	144
Silver Birch	144
Steel Band	144
Foreman	143
Gazza's Girl	143
Greenhope	143
Heez A Dreamer	143
Idole First	143
Liberate	143
Mister Hight	143
Monkerhostin	143
Pedrobob	143
Tarlac	143
Afrad	142
Chilling Place	142
L'Ami	142
Massini's Maguire	142
Mckelvey	142
Ouninpohja	142
Private Be	142
Sir Jimmy Shand	142
Tidal Bay	142
Vic Venturi	142
Wild Cane Ridge	142
Blazing Bailey	141
Bothar Na	141
Catch Me	141
Cerium	141
Hardy Eustace	141
Inglis Drever	141
Kings Advocate	141
Milan Deux Mille	141
Mobaasher	141
Offshore Account	141
Ollie Magern	141
Premier Dane	141
Sweet Wake	141
Buena Vista	140
Bywell Beau	140
Ebaziyan	140
Irish Raptor	140
Launde	140
Marshall Hall	140
Overstrand	140
Punjabi	140
Sir Frederick	140
Wins Now	140
Aitmatov	139
Bobs Pride	139
Copsale Lad	139
Financial Reward	139
L'Aventure	139
Mounthenry	139
Boychuk	138
Cane Brake	138
Duty	138
Grangeclare Lark	138
Jacks Craic	138
Silverburn	138
Tumbling Dice	138
Al Eile	137
Aran Concerto	137
Border Castle	137
De Soto	137
Ellerslie Tom	137
Granit Jack	137
Palarshan	137
Penny Pictures	137
Percussionist	137
Preacher Boy	137
Refinement	137
Tidal Fury	137
Bewleys Berry	136
Briareus	136
Cork All Star	136
Desert Air	136
Gungadu	136
Heltornic	136
Irish Wolf	136
Lennon	136
Moon Over Miami	136
Oscar Park	136
Puntal	136
Adamant Approach	135
Ballyagran	135
Footy Facts	135
New Alco	135
Oslot	135
Pablo Du Charmil	135
Papini	135
Clopf	134
Foligold	134
Harchibald	134
Idle Talk	134
Justpourit	134
Lacdoudal	134
Locksmith	134
Naunton Brook	134
Penzance	134
Saintsaire	134
Tagula Blue	134
Trouble At Bay	134
Verasi	134
Anothercoppercoast	133
Aranleigh	133
Blueberry Boy	133
Bob Bob Bobbin	133
French Saulaie	133
Holly Tree	133
Knight Legend	133
Leading Man	133
My Turn Now	133
Oedipe	133
Pak Jack	133
Perce Rock	133
Philson Run	133
Alexander Taipan	132
Echo Point	132
Field Commander	132
Fiveforthree	132
Justified	132
Kerryhead Windfarm	132
Regal Heights	132
Simon	132
Spot Thedifference	132
Spring The Que	132
Trompette	132
Vodka Bleu	132
Butler's Cabin	131
Crocodiles Rock	131
Dunbrody Millar	131
Forget The Past	131
Kings Quay	131
Lord Henry	131
Mahogany Blaze	131
Mossbank	131

Last season's Topspeed Ratings

Nenuphar Collonges ...131	Classified ...126	Mr Strachan ...122	Glasker Mill ...114	Ornais ...102
Numbersixvalverde ...131	Flintoff ...126	Rosaker ...122	Lounaos ...114	Rebel Rhythm ...102
Opera De Coeur ...131	Gaspara ...126	Supreme Prince ...122	Always Waining ...113	Caribou ...101
Quatre Heures ...131	Heads Onthe Ground ...126	Ardaghey ...121	Berwick Law ...113	West End King ...101
Rindoon ...131	Howle Hill ...126	Carthalawn ...121	Ossmoses ...113	Heron's Flight ...100
Altilhar ...130	Shirley Casper ...126	Fleet Street ...121	Tritonix ...113	Hot Weld ...100
Character Building ...130	Zilcash ...126	Heathcote ...121	A New Story ...112	Lead On ...100
Cooldine ...130	Abragante ...125	Joaaci ...121	Cloudy Lane ...112	Lucifer Bleu ...100
Degas Art ...130	Crozan ...125	Mercuric ...121	Dream Alliance ...112	Callherwhatulike ...99
Dom D'Orgeval ...130	Hard Act To Follow ...125	Nine De Sivola ...121	Marodima ...112	Theatre Girl ...99
Hedgehunter ...130	Hide The Evidence ...125	Square Mile ...121	Orbit O'Gold ...112	Arctic Echo ...98
Imperial Commander ...130	Kicks For Free ...125	Tot O'Whiskey ...121	Ostfanni ...112	Dun Doire ...98
It Takes Time ...130	Lou Du Moulin Mas ...125	Wise Owl ...121	Schiehallion ...112	Mick The Man ...98
Lankawi ...130	Pouvoir ...125	Zabenz ...121	Sizing Europe ...112	La Dame Brune ...96
Mansony ...130	Powerstation ...125	Aztec Warrior ...120	Church Island ...111	Temoin ...96
Material World ...130	Roll Along ...125	Longshanks ...120	Cuchulains Son ...111	Woodbine Willie ...96
Modicum ...130	Scotsirish ...125	Martha's Kinsman ...120	Jack High ...111	Kandjar D'Allier ...95
Our Ben ...130	Sky's The Limit ...125	Snakebite ...120	Quartano ...111	Faucon Bleu ...93
Pauillac ...130	Tamarinbleu ...125	Black Harry ...119	Shouldhavehadthat ...111	Wee Forbees ...93
Trigger The Light ...130	Tango Royal ...125	Finger Onthe Pulse ...119	Ballistraw ...110	Maharbal ...92
Whispered Secret ...130	Double Eagle ...124	Grand Bleu ...119	Dancing Bay ...110	Ringaroses ...92
Amaretto Rose ...129	Full House ...124	Kelami ...119	Tranquil Sea ...110	Rustarix ...92
An Accordion ...129	Homer Wells ...124	Mendo ...119	Briery Fox ...109	Golden Child ...91
Chief Dan George ...129	Key Time ...124	Tailor's Hall ...119	Itsa Legend ...109	Marleybow ...91
J'y Vole ...129	Le Duc ...124	Amstecos ...118	Mid Dancer ...109	Evelith Echo ...90
Leslingtaylor ...129	Mr Pointment ...124	Christdalo ...118	Militant ...109	French Opera ...90
Livingstonebramble ...129	Nycteos ...124	Lindop ...118	Pevensey ...109	Gem Daly ...88
Mad Fish ...129	Oulart ...124	Not Left Yet ...118	Bible Lord ...107	Mark The Book ...88
Medicinal ...129	Shatabdi ...124	Portland Bill ...118	Duc De Regniere ...107	Ever Present ...87
Point Barrow ...129	Streetshavenoname ...124	Bedlam Boy ...117	Joes Edge ...107	Leading Run ...87
Predateur ...129	Burntoakboy ...123	Convincing ...117	Leading Authority ...107	Seven Is My Number ...87
Glenfinn Captain ...128	De Valira ...123	Mount Sandel ...117	Self Respect ...107	Double Default ...84
Noir Et Vert ...128	Emotional Moment ...123	Oscatello ...117	Lough Derg ...106	Sir Boreas Hawk ...82
Royals Darling ...128	Lightning Strike ...123	Otto Des Pictons ...117	Olmeto Collonges ...106	Redemption ...77
Silent Oscar ...128	Lyes Green ...123	Cleni Boy ...116	Over The Creek ...106	Our Bob ...76
Special Envoy ...128	My Will ...123	Hairy Molly ...116	Ship's Hill ...106	Procas De Thaix ...74
Albertas Run ...127	Ofarel D'Airy ...123	Jazz D'Estruval ...116	Snap Tie ...106	Swaythe ...74
Alderburn ...127	Parsons Legacy ...123	Princelet ...116	Beau Michel ...105	Arteea ...73
All Star ...127	Studmaster ...123	Raslan ...116	Earth Planet ...105	Cave Hill ...71
Emmpat ...127	Treasury Counsel ...123	Raven's Run ...116	Fundamentalist ...105	Present Glory ...70
Euro Leader ...127	Battle Cry ...122	Flight Leader ...115	Glencove Marina ...105	Clarnazar ...68
Laustra Bad ...127	Black Jack Ketchum ...122	Green Belt Flyer ...115	Negus De Beaumont ...105	Harris Bay ...60
Miss Mitch ...127	Blue Splash ...122	Limited Edition ...115	Rambling Minster ...105	Hills Of Home ...59
Poquelin ...127	Chelsea Harbour ...122	Paradi ...115	Sizing Africa ...104	Cracking Cliche ...58
Royal Auclair ...127	Jaunty Times ...122	Three Mirrors ...115	Stewarts House ...104	Jered ...57
Royal Rosa ...127	Kenzo III ...122	Air Force One ...114	Berings Express ...103	Pangbourne ...57
Sophocles ...127	King Johns Castle ...122	Barbers Shop ...114	Classic Fiddle ...103	Schindler's Gold ...53
Casey Jones ...126	Miko De Beauchene ...122	Cornish Sett ...114	No Refuge ...102	Venalmar ...43
				Val Du Ciron ...10

Last season's horses with points

No.	Horse	Pts	No.	Horse	Pts	No.	Horse	Pts	No.	Horse	Pts
1002	Acambo	32	1112	Dom D'Orgeval	20	1241	L'Antartique	57	1384	Roman Ark	24
1003	According To John	20	1113	Dream Alliance	10	1244	Ladalko	29	1385	Rosaker	15
1005	Aces Four	45	1115	Dun Doire	10	1245	Launde	12	1387	Ross River	16
1007	Afrad	10	1116	Dunbrody Millar	62	1247	Le Passing	20	1391	Royal Shakespeare	12
1008	Afsoun	35	1119	Ebony Light	17	1249	Leading Contender	10	1394	Rubberdubber	15
1010	Al Eile	36	1120	Echo Point	10	1250	Leading Man	31	1398	Saintsaire	15
1012	Alderburn	30	1121	Elvis Returns	22	1252	Lennon	22	1400	Scots Grey	29
1014	All Star	12	1125	Essex	15	1253	Limerick Boy	22	1404	Senorita Rumbalita	10
1017	Amstecos	20	1127	Eurotrek	62	1254	Livingonaknifedge	17	1409	Silverburn	34
1018	Andreas	41	1128	Exotic Dancer	171	1256	Lord Henry	10	1410	Sir Jimmy Shand	20
1019	Apollo Lady	10	1129	Faasel	10	1261	Lord Sam	28	1411	Sir Oj	20
1026	Ashley Brook	19	1130	Fair Along	49	1264	Madison Du Berlais	58	1417	Some Touch	24
1028	Astarador	10	1131	Fair Question	20	1267	Mansony	28	1418	Sonevafushi	10
1031	Aux Le Bahnn	10	1132	Far From Trouble	14	1268	Marcel	34	1421	Sporazene	15
1032	Aztec Warrior	34	1138	First Row	28	1270	Martha's Kinsman	33	1422	St Matthew	12
1034	Back In Front	10	1142	Flying Enterprise	35	1272	Massini's Maguire	66	1423	Standin Obligation	12
1035	Back To Bid	14	1146	Forget The Past	25	1273	Material World	23	1424	Star De Mohaison	35
1038	Ballytrim	10	1152	Gallant Approach	29	1274	McKelvey	29	1426	State Of Play	61
1039	Bambi De L'Orme	32	1155	Geeveem	10	1277	Merdeka	10	1429	Straw Bear	50
1041	Barbers Shop	10	1157	Glasker Mill	14	1279	Mighty Man	62	1431	Studmaster	12
1042	Baron Windrush	50	1162	Good Spirit	10	1282	Mister Hight	12	1432	Sublimity	76
1045	Beef Or Salmon	60	1164	Granit Jack	10	1284	Mister Quasimodo	10	1433	Supreme Builder	10
1046	Benetwood	20	1166	Grecian Groom	47	1286	Monet's Garden	54	1439	Tamarinbleu	15
1048	Billyvoddan	62	1167	Green Belt Flyer	34	1293	Mossy Green	10	1440	Taranis	49
1049	Black Harry	22	1171	Gungadu	27	1301	My Way De Solzen	69	1441	Tarlac	12
1050	Black Jack Ketchum	15	1172	Hairy Molly	10	1302	My Will	29	1449	The Listener	44
1051	Blazing Bailey	60	1174	Halcon Genelardais	61	1304	Natal	25	1451	The Pious Prince	10
1054	Blu Teen	10	1176	Handy Money	21	1306	Neptune Collonges	25	1452	The Railway Man	14
1059	Boychuk	15	1179	Hardy Eustace	82	1308	Newmill	24	1455	Tidal Bay	45
1061	Brave Inca	78	1180	Harmony Brig	10	1310	Nickname	114	1459	Too Forward	19
1064	Briareus	19	1182	Harris Bay	32	1312	Nil Desperandum	32	1460	Toofarback	10
1067	Buena Vista	22	1188	Hoo La Baloo	10	1314	Nippy Des Mottes	10	1464	Trouble At Bay	14
1068	Bureaucrat	10	1193	Iktitaf	25	1326	O'Muircheartaigh	10	1465	Tumbling Dice	27
1075	Cerium	36	1194	Il Duce	10	1330	Only Vintage	10	1466	Turko	10
1078	Chief Yeoman	20	1198	In Compliance	29	1333	Oscar Park	41	1467	Turnstile	14
1084	Clopf	15	1199	Inglis Drever	69	1337	Our Ben	15	1469	Two Miles West	57
1086	Cloudy Lane	42	1208	Jack The Giant	32	1341	Patman Du Charmil	14	1471	Umbrella Man	17
1087	Coat Of Honour	10	1210	Jaunty Times	36	1344	Patsy Hall	16	1472	Undeniable	21
1093	Copsale Lad	26	1212	Jazz Messenger	47	1346	Pepporoni Pete	10	1473	Ungaro	51
1094	Cornish Rebel	15	1214	Joaaci	20	1349	Phar Bleu	20	1474	Verasi	42
1095	Cornish Sett	27	1215	Joes Edge	62	1353	Point Barrow	36	1477	Vodka Bleu	12
1096	Craven	10	1217	Justpourit	10	1361	Princelet	10	1478	Voy Por Ustedes	79
1099	D'Argent	36	1218	Juveigneur	22	1363	Private Be	55	1481	Watson Lake	15
1101	Dancing Bay	10	1220	Kandjar D'Allier	22	1366	Racing Demon	25	1482	Well Chief	25
1104	De Soto	27	1221	Karanja	19	1369	Rasharrow	10	1484	Wichita Lineman	55
1105	Demi Beau	32	1222	Karello Bay	37	1374	Refinement	16	1485	Wild Cane Ridge	15
1106	Dempsey	39	1226	Kauto Star	170	1375	Regal Heights	37	1492	Wyldello	10
1107	Denman	64	1230	Kerry Lads	10	1377	Reveillez	29	1493	Yaboya	10
1108	Desert Air	10	1233	Kicks For Free	15	1379	Ringaroses	10	1496	You Sir	10
1110	Detroit City	65	1235	Killaghy Castle	24	1383	Roll Along	12			

Last season's top-ten winning lists

Maple Leaf (731)
Voy Por Ustedes 79
Brave Inca 78
Monet`s Garden............54
Neptune Collonges 25
Exotic Dancer 171
Kauto Star..................170
Black Jack Ketchum 15
Nickname 114
Iktitaf (S).........................0
In Compliance (S) 0
Substituted out 25

Caeden (707)
My Way De Solzen 69
Mighty Man 62
Wichita Lineman 55
Voy Por Ustedes (S)........54
Ungaro 51
Iktitaf 25
Exotic Dancer 171
Kauto Star..................170
Detroit City (S)................15
The Market Man 0
Substituted out 35

Broken Cashier (703)
Brave Inca 78
State Of Play 61
Beef Or Salmon.............60
Voy Por Ustedes (S)........54
In Compliance...............29
Forget The Past 25
Exotic Dancer 171
Kauto Star..................170
Black Jack Ketchum 15
Detroit City (S)...............15
Substituted out 25

A Luckhurst (701)
Brave Inca 78
Detroit City 65
State Of Play 61
Beef Or Salmon.............60
Voy Por Ustedes (S) 54
Taranis 49
Kauto Star..................170
Black Jack Ketchum 15
Nickname 114
In Compliance (S) 0
Substituted out 35

A Luckhurst (701)
Brave Inca 78
Detroit City 65
State Of Play 61
Beef Or Salmon.............60
Voy Por Ustedes (S) 54
Taranis 49
Kauto Star..................170
Black Jack Ketchum 15
Nickname 114
In Compliance (S) 0
Substituted out 35

J Woods (698)
Brave Inca 78
Inglis Drever 69
My Way De Solzen 69
Detroit City 65
Denman 64
Monet`s Garden............54
Voy Por Ustedes (S) 54
Racing Demon 25
Kauto Star..................170
Black Jack Ketchum 15
Substituted out 35

I Harvey (697)
Voy Por Ustedes 79
Brave Inca 78
Detroit City 65
Denman 64
Beef Or Salmon.............60
Taranis 49
My Way De Solzen (S) 44
Kauto Star..................170
Black Jack Ketchum 15
The Listener (S) 12
Substituted out 61

Maple Leaf (695)
Brave Inca 78
Mighty Man 62
Beef Or Salmon.............60
Monet`s Garden............54
Forget The Past (S) 25
Well Chief (S) 25
Exotic Dancer 171
Kauto Star..................170
Black Jack Ketchum 15
L`Ami 0
Substituted out 35

Maple Leaf (694)
Voy Por Ustedes 79
Brave Inca 78
Detroit City 65
Monet`s Garden............54
Exotic Dancer 171
Kauto Star..................170
Black Jack Ketchum 15
Our Ben 15
The Listener (S) 12
Iktitaf (S).........................0
Substituted out 35

J Bennett (692)
Brave Inca 78
My Way De Solzen 69
Detroit City 65
Denman 64
Straw Bear 50
Well Chief......................25
Exotic Dancer 171
Kauto Star..................170
Black Jack Ketchum (S) 0
War Of Attrition (S) 0
Substituted out 0

G Seal Gwent 689
Conor's A Clown London 688
Fpf Fantasy 10 Dublin 688
Maple Leaf Hemel Hempstead 687
Maple Leaf Hemel Hempstead 682
D White Coventry 678
Heavygang Brookvale 677
M White Taunton 676
S Cochrane West Yorkshire 674
Robert Winchcole Glasgow 673
I Faucitt Lancaster 671
Maple Leaf Hemel Hempstead 670
Maple Leaf Hemel Hempstead 670
Brownladtherealchamp Epsom 669
D Browne Ashford 669
Sallybrook King Bury 669
M Bingham Widnes 668
J Rush Filey 667
S Harris Bradford 667
J Woods Atherton 666
D Court Slough..665
Maple Leaf Hemel Hempstead 665
Sonofspider Sri Lanka 665
A Luckhurst Maidstone 664
Learjet3 County Armagh..................................663
A Newman Cheltenham 662
Maple Leaf Hemel Hempstead 662
G Price Bridlington 661
One Big Mac County Dublin 661
The Broken Cashier London 661
A Rowsell Hampton 660
Maple Leaf Hemel Hempstead 660
S Blackford Crowborough 659
S Jadhav Blackburn 659
Three Legged Donkeys Brough 659

Maple Leaf Hemel Hempstead 658
Thebuzzword Warrington 658
Unbeaten Wicklow..658
Bootle Jockey Club Bootle 657
Jdarms Leicester 657
The Fat Dancers Nottingham...........................657
A Luckhurst Maidstone 655
Thebuzzword Warrington 655
I Harvey Bedlington 654
Maple Leaf Hemel Hempstead 654
S Loynds Waltham St. Lawrence 654
T Wallis Harlow 654
The Two Puddings Warrington 654
Robert Winchcole Glasgow.............................653
Thebuzzword Warrington 653
A Luckhurst Maidstone 651
A Peppiatt Reading 651
N Bungay Warminster 651
The Ritual London 651
Thebuzzword Warrington 651
Pj Deakin Littleborough 650
Rejects 2 Newark 650
Aahgowangowan Co Waterford 649
D Jehan Rochford 649
Laugh A Lot Melton Mowbray 649
S Morris Gwent 649
A Luckhurst Maidstone 648
Edwardseva Bromley 648
M White Taunton 648
Maple Leaf Hemel Hempstead 648
Maple Leaf Hemel Hempstead 648
D Murray Smith Oakham 646
F Barker Witney 646
Goatfinger Ruislip 646
M Goodall Moreton-In-Marsh..........................646

Last season's top-scoring entries

S Perkins Sale	646	W Compton Grays	634
K Smith Rayleigh	645	Boxmoor Racing Hemel	633
Mary Sinclair Newbury	645	K Smith Rayleigh	633
R Wheeler Yeovil	645	Ms A Smith Sunderland	633
17 Sutton	644	Robert Winchcole Glasgow	633
A McGuire Tamworth	644	The Postulator County Dublin	633
Arkle`s Mate Bath	644	A A, N, S & T Wigan	632
B Mastin Brigg	644	P Ferrie Ely	632
Dr M Gibbons Hay-On-Wye	644	J Hankinson High Wycombe	631
Chase Stable Chipping Norton	643	M Ross Carlisle	631
G Poole Acton	643	Maple Leaf Hemel Hempstead	631
Glens Jems Northampton	643	T O'Reilly Ireland	631
Maple Leaf Hemel Hempstead	643	I Anderson Huntly	630
Miosdream Galway	643	J Kay Bury	630
Blackbranmunster Sheffield	642	J Patel London	630
Maple Leaf Hemel Hempstead	642	Asiandonkeys County Kildare	629
Monsterhorses1 Haverhill	642	Dr C Smyth County Meath	629
B Foreman Ascot	641	John The Printer Wigan	629
Ten Good Things Galway	641	K&A Racing Leicester	629
A Doak London	640	Mabel Henry & Buster Blandford Forum	629
D Murray Smith Oakham	640	Maple Leaf Hemel Hempstead	629
I Godfrey London	640	P Allen March	629
K Rimmer Oldham	640	P Walker Rickmansworth	629
Ms A Smith Sunderland	640	S McCarthy Killarney	629
Thebuzzword Warrington	640	This Time Bathgate	629
Wizards Dublin	640	Wilkinsons Wonders Dewsbury	629
All Star Racing Stourbridge	639	B Foreman Ascot	628
Bevan House Banditos Liverpool	639	Jakobsladder Preston	628
D Sinclair Milton Keynes	639	Kauto Is A Star Melksham	628
Maple Leaf Hemel Hempstead	639	Maple Leaf Hemel Hempstead	628
Nakis Cyprus	639	Miosdream Galway	628
Robert Winchcole Glasgow	639	Newc_Scum Galway	628
A Kitcher Chesterfield	638	P Lucas Esher	628
D Snowden Scarborough	638	A Scamardella Hailsham	627
M McCartan County Down	638	Arazis Army Horsham	627
Mrs J Wilcock Worthing	638	Nelsonpk Shipley	627
R Huntley Wallington	638	P Towler Littlehampton	627
D Gough Gloucester	637	Bbs Dublin	626
F Barker Witney	637	Colin Thecab Pimlico London	626
Frank`s Impekables Morden	637	D Barraclough London	626
Give Me The Money Belfast	637	D Jehan Rochford	626
M Bingham Widnes	637	Diggermen County Down	626
Organ Clan Broadway	637	Goatfinger Ruislip	626
Steady Eddie Cardiff	637	S McLoughlin Wigan	626
B Hurt Shakespeare Street	636	Sachmo Buckie	626
Butt The Nelson Spilsby	636	The Two Yozzers Hull	626
K Aubrey Gerrards Cross	636	Arazis Army Horsham	625
K Smith Rayleigh	636	Community Boys London	625
K Smith Rayleigh	636	M Wolfe London	625
Kates 40 Moreton-In-Marsh	636	Manubest Newmarket	625
Lewis Brothers Willenhall	636	Moneyspiders Broadstone	625
The Broken Cashier London	636	N Connolly Banbury	625
W Armstrong Croydon	636	Nakis Cyprus	625
A Kenny Dublin	635	P Andrews Newmarket	625
Brightside Lichfield	635	B Hurt Shakespeare Street	624
D Heffernan County Laois	635	Houghton Circle Leicester	624
N Durant Halstead	635	Maple Leaf Hemel Hempstead	624
A Reduscoe Gillingham	634	Muddy Marvellous Hull	624
D Cooper Gillingham	634	P Moran County Dublin	624
D Murray Smith Oakham	634	R Paget Tonbridge	624
K Smith Rayleigh	634	S Mulkeen Leeds	624
Miss C Bettinson Stamford	634	Starman Stafford	624
P Avery Enfield	634	Cockpit Crew Brentwood	623
The Polecats Northampton	634	D Turner Hyde	623